Communicating in Small Groups:

Principles and Practices

SEVENTH EDITION

Steven A. Beebe
Southwest Texas State University

John T. Masterson
Texas Lutheran University

Boston · New York · San Francisco
Mexico City · Montreal · Toronto · London
Madrid · Munich · Paris
Hong Kong · Singapore · Tokyo
Cape Town · Sydney

Series Editor: Karon Bowers
Editor-in-Chief: Karen Hanson
Associate Development Editor: Alyssa Pratt
Series editorial assistant: Jennifer Trebby
Marketing Manager: Mandee Eckersley
Composition and Prepress Buyer: Linda Cox
Manufacturing Manager: Megan Cochran
Editorial-Production Coordinator: Mary Beth Finch
Editorial-Production Service: Thomas E. Dorsaneo
Text Design and Electronic Composition: Andrea Miles, Menagerie

For related titles and support materials, visit our online catalog at www.ablongman.com

Between the time Website information is gathered and then published, it is not unusual for some sites to have closed. Also, the transcription of URLs can result in unintended typographical errors. The publisher would appreciate notification where these errors occur so that they may be corrected in subsequent editions.

Cataloging in Publication information not available at press time.
ISBN: 0-205-35956-6

Printed in the United States of America
10 9 8 7 6 5 4 3 2 1 RRD-VA 07 06 05 04 03 02

Dedicated to Sue and Nancy

Brief Contents

Detailed Contents

Chapter 4 ▶ Relating to Others in Small Groups   70

Chapter 5 ▶ Improving Group Climate 104

Chapter 6 ▶ Understanding Nonverbal Dynamics 131

Chapter 12 ▶ Improving Productivity in Groups and Teams 318

Preface

I n the preface to the first edition of *Communicating in Small Groups: Principles and Practices* we wrote, "The underlying premise of this textbook is that effective group communication requires a knowledge of the basic principles and complex dynamics that characterize small group interaction, together with practice in applying those principles." Providing a balance between principles and practice, theory and skills, knowledge and application has been our goal in each edition of the book as we have revised it over the past twenty years.

Although our goal has remained the same, the past two decades have resulted in much new information about group and team communication. With the seventh edition of this best-selling book, we have continued to tell students what they need to know about groups and teams, while also providing appropriate context and background to help them apply their new knowledge.

A Balance of Principles and Practices

When we present research conclusions, we hear our students' voices echoing in our heads, asking, "So what?" As a result, we have tried to offer news about the latest thinking about small group research while also helping students understand how these principles relate to their lives: "How does this research help enhance the quality of meetings?" "What research can help groups and teams make better decisions?" "What are the most important principles and applications of research about groups and teams that will enhance collaboration?" These and other questions guide our digest of small group and team principles and are the focus of the "Putting Principles into Practice" section at the end of each chapter. We always strive to be mindful that principles and research conclusions without application to real-life situations are just a list of information. We seek to present principles and practices of small group communication that make a difference in the lives of our students, who will spend much of their lives collaborating with others.

members thoughtfully use techniques and strategies to help them make progress toward their goal depending on what is (or is not) happening in the group. Use techniques wisely.

Putting Principles into Practice

In this chapter we discussed several prescriptive approaches that a group or team can use to solve a problem. Groups often need some plan or structure to help their members define, analyze, and solve a problem. We described four kinds of problem-solving formats: (1) reflective thinking, (2) brainstorming, (3) ideal solution, and (4) single question. Review the following suggestions for applying these problem-solving approaches to the groups in which you participate.

Reflective Thinking: Traditional Problem Solving

▶ To help your group or team define and limit a problem, phrase it as a question.
▶ Do not start suggesting solutions until your group has thoroughly analyzed a problem.
▶ Consider using tools such as *is/is not* analysis, force-field analysis, Pareto charts, and cause-and-effect (fishbone) diagrams to help your group analyze the problem.
▶ Formulate criteria for a good solution before you begin suggesting solutions.
▶ Use brainstorming to help your group generate possible solutions.
▶ If the other group members agree, you may need to change the criteria you have selected during the analysis phase of reflective thinking.
▶ Make sure that reflective thinking is the best method for your group; another problem-solving approach may work better.
▶ To help make sure that everyone knows and follows through on his or her assignment, consider using an action chart or a flowchart.

Brainstorming

▶ Make sure all team members understand the ground rules for brainstorming. Do not evaluate solutions until you have finished brainstorming.
▶ If group members do not follow the brainstorming rules, you may have to (1) restate the rules, (2) ask them to keep quiet, (3) ask them to record the ideas of others, or (4) ask them to leave the group.
▶ If oral brainstorming does not work, consider having each member of the group work individually; consider using other brainstorming formats such as Delphi, nominal-group, affinity, and electronic brainstorming.
▶ Try to draw less-talkative group members into the discussion; compliment members when they come up with good ideas.
▶ Set aside a definite amount of time for brainstorming.

246 ◁ *Chapter Nine: Using Problem-Solving Techniques*

www.ablongman.com/beebe

Theoretical principles are useful and inherently valuable, but describing theories without helping students apply principles can result in informed yet unskilled group members. Although students typically clamor for skills and techniques that will offer shortcuts to success, an overemphasis on technique does not give students the scaffolding of principles on which to hang their skills. Skills do not give students inventive options to help them manage the many obstacles and opportunities that arise when collaborating with others. Effective group and team communication occurs when theoretical principles that help explain and predict group and team communication are balanced with skills, competencies, and practices that foster application. That's why we continue to offer "Practice" activities in a section at the back of each chapter and now also on the accompanying Website, www.ablongman.com/beebe.

Popular Features We've Retained

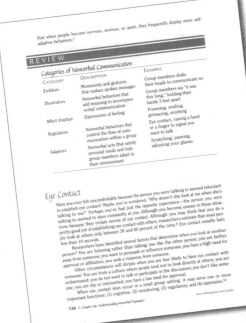

What students and instructors liked best about previous editions is our get-to-the-point writing style coupled with our comprehensive distillation of group communication principles and research. We have also received praise for the clear applications of the research we describe. We've done our best to keep the features instructors and students like best about our book: a lively, engaging writing style, references to the most recent, relevant research we can find, an emphasis on presenting not too much and not too little information about groups and teams, and a comprehensive, accurate digest of small group principles and practices.

We've revised and updated our pedagogical features, including chapter objectives, discussion questions, end-of-chapter activities, references, and exercises. We continue to distill the key principles and skills of small group communication in review boxes to help students remember key ideas.

What's New in This Edition?

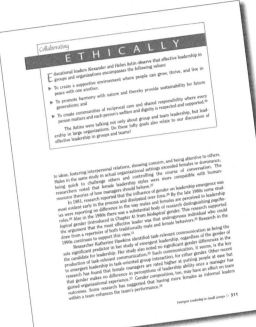

The seventh edition contains a number of new features, changes, and additions. Here's a summary of the changes we have made:

Expanded Teams Coverage

We've continued to expand our coverage of teams and teamwork in every chapter with new sections in Chapter 1 that feature the latest research findings about team member characteristics. New material in Chapter 4 discusses how to establish team ground rules, and Chapter 12 includes new material about how to facilitate team meetings.

"Collaborating Ethically" Feature

Each chapter includes a new feature, titled "Collaborating Ethically," that presents ideas, questions, or mini case studies to help students think through ethical issues when communicating in groups and teams.

"Collaborating via Technology" Feature

New to this edition is a boxed feature, called "Collaborating via Technology," that includes tips for using technological tools to collaborate in groups and teams. Also new are references to Websites that offer a wealth of information about groups and teams.

Expanded Technology Coverage

New research conclusions about using e-mail, electronic brainstorming, and other technology are included in Chapters 9 and 12. There is also updated coverage in every chapter on how to use the Internet and electronic databases to conduct research for small group discussions.

Revised "Practice" Activities

There are many new chapter-end activities, including references to an abundance of exercises and activities that are now available on the Web.

And Much, Much More

This edition also includes new material on the role of diversity in groups and teams, updated discussion of research-based strategies to enhance group decision making and problem solving, new and practical strategies for dealing with group and team members who do not collaborate well, new discussion of how to manage group and team conflict, revised discussion of small group problem-solving competencies, and an updated discussion of leadership in groups and teams.

Supplemental Resources for Instructors

Instructor's Manual and Test Bank with Transparency Masters
by Valerie Manno Giroux, University of Miami

For each chapter in the text, the Instructor's Manual and Test Bank provides a chapter summary, learning objectives, transparency masters, and discussion activities and exercises for group and team work. The Test Bank portion offers hundreds of test questions in multiple-choice, true/false, short-answer, and essay formats.

Computerized Test Bank

This computerized version of the test bank is available in Tamarack's easy-to-use TestGen software, which lets you prepare tests for printing as well as for network and online testing. Full editing capability is available for Windows and Macintosh.

PowerPoint Presentation Package
by Valerie Manno Giroux, University of Miami

A PowerPoint presentation provides lecture slides based on key concepts in the text. The presentation is available to download, free of charge, on the Web at www.ablongman.com/ppt.

About the Website for This Edition

Students who visit the Companion Website that accompanies the seventh edition (www.ablongman.com/beebe) will find an online study guide that has practice tests, learning objectives, and useful links to communication sites on the Internet. There are also easy-to-print chapter-specific questionnaires and checklists to help in preparing for and analyzing group work activities. The Companion Website is authored by Sue Stewart at Southwest Texas State University.

In addition to the book-specific website, students and instructors can also access the Allyn and Bacon Communication Studies Website at www.ablongman.com/commstudies for more resources to help them in their studies.

Acknowledgments

We've worked together as co-authors for a quarter of a century, and we believe our close collaboration and friendship help make this a better book. However, this book is a collaborative project not only between us as authors, but also with a support team of communication scholars, editors, colleagues, reviewers, students, and supportive family members.

Specifically, we appreciate the helpful and constructive reviews of the sixth edition by Robert D. Harrison, Gallaudet University; Valerie Manno Giroux, University of Miami; Karen M. Coffey, Monroe Community College; Thomas G. Endres, University of St. Thomas; David E. Walker, Middle Tennessee State University; and M. Scott Poole, Texas A&M University.

From the preceding list, we also wish to thank Thomas G. Endres, David E. Walker, and Valerie Manno Giroux for reviewing an initial draft of the seventh edition.

In our more than two decades of collaborating on this book, we have worked with a variety of publishers and editors as publishing houses have merged. The editorial staff at Allyn and Bacon has been among the best we've worked with. Tom Jefferies offered brilliant ideas and helpful tips to refine and polish our ideas and words. Karon Bowers, Senior Editor, was a constant source of both structure and support through the entire process of preparing the seventh edition of this book.

Steve thanks his colleagues and students at Southwest Texas State University (SWT) for their encouragement and support. Russ Wittrup, a gifted teacher who formerly taught at SWT, was a fount of information and ideas for this edition. Dan Love, a good friend and outstanding group-communication teacher at SWT, offered many useful suggestions and constant support. Sue Stewart, also a friend and SWT colleague, provided many ideas and suggestions and was especially helpful in developing ideas for "Collaborating via Technology." Kosta Tovstiadi, a friend and graduate student at SWT from Pyatigorsk, Russia, offered skilled research support, assisted in confirming Web addresses, and helped in numerous other ways. We also want to acknowledge the expertise of Dennis and Laurie Romig of Performance Resources in Austin, Texas, for their rich knowledge and practical insight about groups and teams. Jim Bell, who teaches in SWT's College of Business Administration, is a valued friend and gifted teacher who offered a wealth of suggestions and ideas about teamwork.

John thanks his friends, colleagues, and students at Texas Lutheran University, who continue to challenge and inspire him daily. Janet Hill, in particular, keeps him on track and, most of the time, out of trouble.

Finally, as in our previous editions, we offer our appreciation and thanks to our families, who continue to teach us about the value of teamwork and collaboration. Much has changed since we began this project together almost 25 years ago. John's sons, John III and Noah, were then in elementary school. Today, though grown and living far from their dad, they continue to make him smile with pride at their successes. Nancy Masterson continues, as always, as John's greatest love, best friend, and most respected critic.

Steve's son Mark was a newborn when the first edition was published. Son Matt was born when the second edition was published. As they are now taking their places in the worlds of work and college, they continue to teach their dad about communication, collaboration, and teamwork. Susan Beebe has been an integral part of the author team in this and every previous edition. She is again lovingly acknowledged for her unparalleled talent of working with words and her unfailing gift of love and support.

Steven A. Beebe
San Marcos, Texas

John T. Masterson
Seguin, Texas

Chapter Outline:

Objectives:

After studying this chapter, you will be able to:

▶ Define small group communication.

▶ Discuss the characteristics of a team.

▶ List and describe the advantages and disadvantages of working with others in groups and teams.

▶ Compare and contrast primary and secondary groups.

▶ Describe differences between individualistic and collectivistic cultures.

▶ Identify the four elements of becoming a competent small group communicator.

▶ Identify nine group communication competencies.

Introducing Group and Team Principles and Practices

"We are all dependent on one another, every soul of us on Earth."
—George Bernard Shaw

Human beings have always been creatures who collaborate. Our social nature results in our participation in groups and teams of all kinds. Today's globe-shrinking technology makes it possible for us to be linked together in groups and teams even when there may be no other person physically present. We are connected to others.

Using a variety of research methods, scholars from many disciplines have reached a similar conclusion about humankind: We are social beings. We need to establish meaningful relationships with others. We are raised in family groups, educated and entertained in groups, and we work and worship in groups. When an important problem arises, we seek the advice of others. Even when physically isolated, we may seek a virtual group experience through e-mail, computer chat rooms, or other cyberspace experiences that link us together. Whatever the method of collaborating (and most of our collaborating still happens face-to-face), we consistently rely on groups and teams to help find answers to important issues.

This book is about groups. More specifically, it is about communication in groups and teams.

Our goal is to provide you with a broad understanding of communication processes and practical advice to help you become a more-effective group and team participant. The book will primarily deal with task-oriented small groups—groups with a specific objective to achieve, information to share, problem to solve, or decision to make. We will also apply research findings to teams—coordinated, more-structured groups of people who work together to achieve common goals.

Most of the theory and strategies we offer are about participation in live, real-time, noncyberspace groups and teams. Although technology makes virtual group meetings possible, most of your meetings and team collaborations will still be live and in person. An overwhelming majority of the research conclusions that we draw on are based on face-to-face group experience. We will, however, also draw on a fast-growing body of research examining collaboration on the Internet and in other technologically mediated group settings.

The *communication* that occurs in groups will be this book's focus. One scholar, discussing the importance of communication to an organization, describes communication as

the lifeblood . . .

the glue that binds . . .

the oil that smooths . . .

the thread that ties . . .

the force that pervades . . .

the binding agent that cements all relationships.[1]

These metaphors apply to communication in groups and teams as well as to large corporations. Communication makes it possible for groups and teams to exist and function.

What Is Small Group Communication?

Consider these situations:

As the nation is challenged with multiple terrorist attacks, the president of the United States calls for the formation of a Task Force Against Terrorism.

Tech.com is considering making a takeover bid for Digital.com. The chief executive officer calls company executives together to examine the virtues and pitfalls of the possible merger.

To prepare for the final exam in your algebra class, you and several class members meet three nights each week to study.

Each of these three examples involves a group of people meeting for a specific purpose. And as group members communicate with one another, they are communicating transactively; they are simultaneously responding to one another as they express ideas, information, and opinions. Although the groups' purposes are quite different in these three scenarios, these groups have something in common—something that distinguishes them from a cluster of people waiting for a bus or riding in an elevator, for example. Just what is that "something"? What are the characteristics that make a group a group? We define **small group communication** as *communication among a small group of people who share a common purpose or goal, who feel a sense of belonging to the group, and who exert influence on one another.* Next, we will examine this definition more closely.

Reduced to its essence, **communication** is the process of acting on information.[2] Someone does or says something, and there is a response in action, word, or thought. Information merely presented to others does not mean there is communication: Information is not communication. "But I told you what I wanted!" "I put it in the memo. Why didn't you do what I asked?" "It's in the syllabus." Such expressions of exasperation assume that if you send a message, someone will receive it. However, communication does not operate in a linear, input–output process. What you send is rarely what others understand. Simple models of communication that show a source, message, noise, channel, receiver, and communication context can help us understand the elements of human communication, but they don't really capture the process nature of communication.

Human communication is a **transactive process**—messages are sent and received simultaneously—by which we make sense out of the world and share that sense with others. As you talk to someone, you respond to that person's verbal and nonverbal messages, even while you may be in mid-sentence.[3] In the context of a small group, even if you remain silent or nod off to sleep, your nonverbal message provides information to others about your emotions and interest. The transactive nature of communication suggests that you cannot *not* communicate.

Do groups need to communicate face-to-face to be considered a group? Even though most small group interaction involves live and in-person discussion, more and more small group meetings occur in a **mediated setting**—a setting in which the channel of communication is a phone line, fiber-optic cable, TV signal, or other means of sending messages to others; the interaction is not face-to-face. In the twenty-first century, it has become increasingly easy and efficient to collaborate using the Internet, telephone conference calls, video teleconferences, and other technological means of communicating. So, yes, a group can be a group without meeting face-to-face. In the past fifteen years we have learned more about how mediated communication can enhance group communication. For example, there is evidence that groups linked together only by e-mail or a computer network can generate more and better ideas than groups that meet face-to-face.[4] Such communication may, nonetheless, be hindered by sluggish feedback or delayed replies, which are not problems when we meet in person. And although more ideas may be generated in a mediated meeting, complex problems and relationship issues are better handled in person than on the Internet or another mediated network.[5] In most cases, in-person communication affords the best opportunity to clarify meaning and resolve uncertainty and misunderstanding. We will discuss the use of technology in groups and teams throughout the book in a special feature called "Collaborating Via Technology." In Chapter 12, we will give special emphasis to using technology to enhance group productivity.

Does the quality of communication really affect what a group accomplishes? Because this is a book about group communication, you won't be surprised that our answer is yes. Researchers have debated, however, the precise role of communication in groups in contributing to a group's success. Success depends on a variety of factors besides communication, such as the personality of the group members, how motivated the members are to contribute, how much information members have, and the innate talent group members have for collaboration. Several researchers have found that the way group members communicate with each other is crucial in determining what happens when people collaborate.[6]

A Small Group of People

A group includes at least three people; two people are usually referred to as a **dyad**. The addition of a third person immediately adds an element of increased complexity and uncertainty to the transactive communication process. The probability increases that two will form a coalition against one. And although the dynamics of group roles, norms, power, status, and leadership are also present in two-person transactions, they become increasingly important in affecting the outcome of the transaction when three or more people are communicating.

Collaborating via

T E C H N O L O G Y

Just a few years ago, if you wanted to collaborate with others in a group online you needed to purchase special, expensive software. Today a variety of tools and software are available free online to help you set up an e-group conference or chat group. Check out the following Website for information about establishing an electronic group:

www.groups.yahoo.com/local/news.html

With this site you can set up an e-group account.

If at least three people are required for a **small group**, what is the maximum number it may have and still be considered small? Scholars do not agree on a specific number. However, having more than 12 people (some say 13, others say 20) in a group significantly decreases individual members' interaction. The larger the group, the less influence each individual has on the group and the more likely that subgroups will develop. With 20 or more people, the communication more closely resembles a public-speaking situation, when one person addresses an audience, providing less opportunity for all members to participate freely. The larger the group, the more likely that group members will become passive rather than actively involved in the discussion.

Meeting with a Common Purpose

The president's Terrorism Task Force, the Tech.com Company, and your algebra study group have one thing in common—their members have a specific purpose for meeting. They share a concern for the objectives of the group. Although a group of people waiting for a bus or riding in an elevator may share the goal of transportation, they do not have the same collective goal. Their individual destinations are different. Their primary concerns are for themselves, not for others. As soon as their individual goals are realized, they leave the bus or elevator. On the other hand, a goal keeps a committee or discussion group together until that goal is realized. Many groups fail to remain together because they never identify their common purpose. While participants in small groups may have somewhat different motives for their membership, a common purpose cements the group together.

Feeling a Sense of Belonging

Not only do group members need a mutual concern to unite them, but they also need to feel they belong to the group. Commuters waiting for a bus probably do not feel part of a collective effort. Members of a small group, however, need to have a sense of *identity* with the group; they should be able to feel it is their group. Members of a small group are perceptually aware that a group exists and that they are members of the group.

Exerting Influence

Each member of a small group, in one way or another, potentially influences others. Even if a group member sits in stone silence while other group members actively verbalize opinions and ideas, the silence of that one member may be interpreted as agreement by another. As we will discuss in Chapter 6, nonverbal messages have a powerful influence on a group's climate.

At its essence, the process of influencing others defines leadership. To some degree, each group member exerts some leadership in the group because of his or her potential to influence others. Although some groups have an elected or appointed leader, most group members have some opportunity to share in how the work gets done and how group members relate to each other. Thus, if we define the role of leader rather broadly, each group member has an opportunity to help lead the group through contributions and suggestions. Regardless of its size, a group achieves optimal success when each person accepts some responsibility for influencing and leading others.

To repeat our definition: *Small group communication is defined as communication among a small group of people who share a common purpose or goal, who feel a sense of belonging to the group, and who exert influence on one another.*

The Importance of Teams

"Go, team!" You can hear this chant at most group sports events. Whether playing a touch-football game or the Super Bowl, members of sports teams are rewarded for working together. Corporate America has also learned that working in teams can enhance productivity, efficiency, worker satisfaction, and corporate profits. Regardless of whether its members play football or design and build integrated circuits, a **team** is a coordinated group of individuals organized to work together to achieve a specific, common goal. Teamwork is increasingly emphasized as a way to accomplish tasks and projects because teamwork works. An effectively functioning team gets results.[7] Research clearly documents the increased use of teams in corporate America during the past two decades, especially in larger, more-complex organizations.[8]

Because we have clearly defined small group communication, you may be wondering, "What's the difference between a group and a team?" Often people use the terms "group" and "team" interchangeably. But are they different concepts, or is there merely a semantic difference between a group and a team? Our view is that teams are often more highly structured than typical small groups. All teams are small groups, but not all groups operate as a team.

Our definition of small group communication clearly fits the definition of team: Teams are typically a small group of people with a common purpose and a sense of belonging, who exert influence on one another. But highly effective teams usually have at least four additional attributes that give the term "team" distinct meaning: Let's take a closer look at how distinctions are sometimes made between teams and groups.

1. Teams usually have clearly defined team-member responsibilities, such as positions on a sports team (first base, shortstop, and so on).
2. The rules and expectations of how the team operates are clearly spelled out; sports team competitions usually have a referee to enforce the rules of the game.
3. Team goals are explicitly clear and specific (win the game, or win the championship).
4. Teams usually develop a clear way of coordinating their efforts; sports teams discuss and practice how to work together.

Teams develop clearly defined roles, duties, and responsibilities for team members. People who belong to a team usually have a clear sense of their particular role or function on the team. As on a sports team, each team member has an understanding of how his or her job or responsibility helps the team achieve the goal. The roles and responsibilities of team members are explicitly discussed. If one team member is absent, other team members know what needs to be done to make the team function effectively. Sometimes team members may be trained to take on several roles just in case a team member is absent; this kind of training is called **cross-functional team-role training.** Understanding other team members' responsibilities helps the team to work more effectively.[9] In a group, the participants may perform specific roles and duties, but on a team greater care must be devoted to explicitly ensuring that the individual roles and responsibilities are clear and are linked to a common goal or outcome. In fact, the key challenge in team development is to teach individuals who are used to performing individual tasks how to work together.

Teams have clearly defined rules and expectations for team operation. A second difference between groups and teams is that teams develop specific operating systems to help them function well. A **rule** is a prescription for acceptable behavior. For example, a team may establish as a rule that all meetings will start and end on time. Or if a team member is absent from a meeting, the absent member will contact the meeting leader. Although expectations develop in groups, in a team those expectations, rules, and procedures are often overtly stated or written down. Team members know what the rules are and how those rules benefit the entire team.

Teams develop clear, well-defined goals. A third way to contrast groups and teams is the clarity and importance of the team goal. Team goals are usually very specific and measurable. They are also larger and more significant than could be achieved by any individuals on the team. A sports team knows that the goal is to win the game. An advertising team's goal is to sell the most product. Yes, all groups, too, have a goal, but the goal may be less measurable or clear. A team develops a goal so that the members know when they've achieved the goal.

Teams have coordinated and collaborative methods for accomplishing the work. A fourth difference between groups and teams involves the methods team members use to accomplish their goals. Team members discuss how to collaborate and work together. Sports teams spend many hours practicing how to anticipate the skills of other team members so that, like an intricate dance, all team members are moving to the same beat. Team members develop interdependent relationships; what happens to one impacts everyone on the team. Of course, team members may be given individual assignments; but those assignments are clearly coordinated with other team members' duties so that all members are working together. Coordination and collaboration are the hallmark methods of a team. Although groups work together, they may accomplish their goal with less collaboration and coordination.

Even though we've made distinctions between groups and teams, we are not saying they are dramatically different entities. Think of these two concepts as existing on a continuum; some gatherings will have more elements of a group, whereas others will be closer to our description of a team. Keep in mind also that all teams are small groups, which means that throughout the book when we refer to a team we will also be referring to a small group. And the principles and practices of effective small group communication will thus also apply to teams.

Characteristics of an Effective Team

Business and nonprofit organizations tend to use the term *team* rather than *group* to identify individuals who work together to achieve a common task. Corporate training departments often spend much time and money to train their employees to be better team members. What skills do such training programs focus on? Most of them include the communication principles and practices that we will emphasize in this book: Problem solving, decision making, listening, and conflict management. In addition to communication skills, team members also set goals, evaluate the quality of their work, and establish team operating procedures.[10]

Several researchers have been interested in studying how to make teams function better. One study found that team members need work schedules compatible with those of their colleagues, adequate resources to obtain the information needed to do the work, leadership skills, and help from the organization to get the job done.[11] Using studies of several real-life teams (such as NASA, McDonald's, and sports teams), Carl Larson and Frank LaFasto identified eight hallmarks of an effective team. The more of these characteristics a team has, the more likely it is that the team will be effective.[12]

REVIEW

Comparing Groups and Teams

	GROUPS	TEAMS
Roles and responsibilities	Roles and responsibilities may be discussed but not always explicitly defined or developed.	Roles and responsibilities are clearly developed and discussed.
Rules	Rules and expectations are often not formally developed and evolve according to the group's needs.	Rules and operating procedures are clearly discussed and developed to help the team work together.
Goals	Goals may be discussed in general terms.	Clear, elevating goals drive all aspects of team accomplishment.
Methods	Group members interact, and work may be divided among group members.	Team members collaborate and explicitly discuss how to coordinate their efforts and work together. Teams work together interdependently.

A Clear, Elevating Goal Having a common, well-defined goal is the single most important attribute of an effective team. But having a goal is not enough; the goal should be elevating and important—it should excite team members and motivate them to make sacrifices for the good of the team. Sports teams use the elevating goal of winning the game or the championship. Corporate teams also need an exciting goal that all team members believe is important.

A Results-Driven Structure Teams need an efficient system or method of organizing how they work together. Team structure is the way in which a team is organized; who reports to whom and who does what are key elements in developing a team structure. It is useful, therefore, for teams to develop a clear sense of the roles and responsibilities of each team member. A team needs individuals who perform both task roles (getting the job done) and maintenance roles (managing the team process) to be high performing. A structure that is not results-driven, one that tolerates ineffective meetings, busywork, and "administrivia," always detracts from team effectiveness.

Competent Team Members Team members need to know not only *what* their assignment is but also *how* to perform their job. Team members need to be trained and educated so they know what to do and when to do it. Without adequate training in both teamwork skills and job skills, the team will likely flounder.[13]

Unified Commitment The motto of the Three Musketeers—"all for one and one for all"—serves as an accurate statement of the attitude team members should have when working together to achieve a clear, elevating goal. Team members need to feel united by their commitment and dedication to achieve the task.

A Collaborative Climate Effective teams foster a positive group climate and the skills and principles needed to achieve their potential. Effective teams operate in a climate of support rather than defensiveness. Team members should confirm one another, support one another, and listen to one another as they perform their work. In Chapter 5 we will identify strategies for enhancing team climate.

Standards of Excellence A team is more likely to achieve its potential if it establishes high standards. Goals that cause the team to stretch a bit can serve to galvanize a team into action. Unobtainable or unrealistic goals, however, can result in team frustration. If the entire team is involved in setting goals, the team is more likely to feel a sense of ownership toward the standards it has established.

External Support and Recognition Teams in any organization do not operate in isolation. They need support from outside the team to help acquire the information and materials needed to do the job. Team members also need to be recognized and rewarded for their efforts by others outside the team. Most coaches acknowledge the "home-field advantage" that flows from the enthusiastic support and accolades of team followers. Corporate teams, too, need external support and recognition to help them function at maximum effectiveness.

Principled Leadership Teams need effective leaders. This is not to say that a team requires an authoritarian leader to dictate who should do what. On the contrary, teams usually function more effectively when they adopt contingency approaches to leadership. In most effective teams, leadership responsibilities are spread throughout the team. We will discuss leadership principles in more detail in Chapter 11.

Characteristics of Effective Team Members

In their most recent research about teams, Frank LaFasto and Carl Larson found that not only does an effective team possess certain positive characteristics, but that individual team members have special attributes that contribute to team success.[14] After surveying 6,000 team members and leaders, they found that the following six team-member characteristics are likely to enhance team success.

Experience Effective team members have practical experience in managing the problems and issues they face; they've "been there and done that" before. Less-experienced team members tend not to see the big picture and lack the technical background needed to accomplish the task.

Problem-Solving Ability Analyzing information and issues while staying focused on the problem and possible solutions are characteristics of effective team members. Lack of focus on the team problem and indecisiveness have a negative impact on team success.

Having clear individual roles is important for team success. What roles do the people in this picture have?

Openness LaFasto and Larson call this characteristic the basic ingredient for team success; having team members who are open, straightforward, and willing to appropriately discuss delicate issues is a predictor of team success. Team members who are not open to new ideas and who participate less are perceived as less valuable to the team.

Supportiveness Supportive team members listen to others, are willing to pitch in and accomplish the job, and have an optimistic outlook about team success. Nonsupportive members try to control team members and focus on their individual interests rather than team interests.

Action Oriented Team members who focus on "strategic doing" rather than only on "strategic pondering" are vital for team success. Effective team members respond when action needs to be taken. Procrastinating and being slow to take action reduce team effectiveness.

Positive Personal Style Effective team members are motivated, patient, enthusiastic, friendly, and well liked. In contrast, being competitive within the team, and being argumentative and impatient, are perceived as hindrances to team success.

Enhancing Team Effectiveness

Once you understand the characteristics of an effective team, the challenge—either as team facilitator or team participant—is to ensure that the team achieves its potential. The following strategies may prove useful in helping you develop team strengths.[15]

1. *Learn the strengths of each team member.* Before making team assignments, a coach usually takes some time to learn about the players. Team members have different strengths and talents. Learning about team members' abilities helps establish individual roles and responsibilities. Research by a team of scholars found that one of the most important fac-

tors in team success was ensuring that each team member knew what he or she was supposed to do. These same researchers found that this was a skill that could be taught to team members with positive results; teams who had training in how to clarify their individual roles were more successful than teams that did not have such training.[16] Effective teams do not operate on the star system, where only a few members are hailed for their effectiveness.[17]

2. *Clarify group expectations and set team ground rules.* Teams function better if team members explicitly discuss how the team should operate. Most team-building sessions include an opportunity for team members to develop a common vision of how the team will function. Discussing such issues as the value of being on time for meetings, reaching consensus, and having everyone's input on all ideas helps participants learn how to work together.

3. *Identify barriers that may keep the team from achieving its goal.* Gathering information, reviewing the issues under consideration, and analyzing the current situation are useful steps that help teams identify and overcome difficulties as they proceed.

4. *Develop a plan to accomplish the goal.* Just as most sports teams have a playbook, any team needs a plan to accomplish a goal. A plan should be designed to help the group overcome obstacles that are keeping it from achieving its goal.

5. *Put the plan into action.* Planning and plotting strategy will not get the job done. Teams need a systematic effort to implement the ideas and suggestions offered. Often the most efficient way is to divide the plan into small, manageable tasks. Frequent communication about progress on completing assignments will reassure team members that they are working together to achieve a goal.

6. *Evaluate the plan and team procedures.* As the team works together, it needs to evaluate how things are going, stopping to assess whether the group's approach is achieving the desired results. Just like football coaches who look at films of last week's game, the team needs to replay its procedures and examine whether they are appropriate.

Advantages and Disadvantages of Working in Groups and Teams

There is no question about it: You will work in groups and teams. Collaborative projects are becoming the mainstay method of accomplishing work in all organizations. From kindergarten through graduate school students are frequently called on to work on group projects.

Why are groups and teams such an often-used method of getting results? Because, most of the time, groups do achieve higher quality results than individuals working in isolation.[18] Knowing how groups and teams operate can help manage any uncertainty and anxiety about working with others. Yet why do many people still find working in groups and teams frustrating and unproductive? One company estimated that it lost $71 million a year because of inept management of meetings. Another study reported that one-third of the chief executive officers of the companies studied thought meetings were of "marginal value or not worth the time."[19]

What are your feelings about working in groups and teams? Maybe you dread attending group meetings. Perhaps you agree with the observation that a committee is a group that keeps minutes but wastes hours. You may believe that groups bumble and stumble along until they reach some sort of compromise—a compromise with which no one is pleased. "To be effective," said one observer, "a committee should be made up of three people. But to get anything done, one member should be sick and another absent."

Some people absolutely hate working in groups. Have you ever experienced grouphate? Susan Sorensen described **grouphate** as the dread and repulsion many people feel about working in groups, teams, or meetings. But here's some good news: Grouphate appears to diminish among group members who receive training and instruction about working in groups.[20] By understanding both the advantages and potential pitfalls of working collaboratively, you will form more realistic expectations while capitalizing on the virtues of group work and minimizing the obstacles to success.[21]

Advantages

1. *Groups and teams have more information than individuals do.* Because of the variety of backgrounds and experiences that individuals bring to a group, the group as a whole has more information and ideas from which to seek solutions to a problem than one person would have alone. Research clearly documents that a group with diverse backgrounds, including ethnic diversity, results in better-quality ideas. With more information available, the group is more likely to discuss all sides of an issue and is also more likely to arrive at a better solution.[22] Although group and team members tend to first share what they and other group members already know, groups still hold an advantage in having greater potential information to share with other group members.[23]

2. *Groups and teams stimulate creativity.* Research on groups generally supports the maxim that "two heads are better than one" when it comes to solving problems.[24] Groups usually make better decisions than individuals working alone, because groups have more approaches to or methods of solving a specific problem. A group of people with various backgrounds, experiences, and resources can more creatively consider ways to solve a problem than one person can.

3. *You remember what you discuss.* Working in groups and teams fosters improved learning and comprehension. Imagine that your history professor announces that the final exam next week is going to be comprehensive. History is not your best subject. You realize you need help. What do you do? You may form a study group with other classmates. Your decision to study with a group of people is wise; education theorists claim that when you take an active role in the learning process, your comprehension of information is improved. If you studied for the exam by yourself, you would not have the benefit of asking and answering questions posed by other study group members. By discussing a subject with a group, you learn more and improve your comprehension of the subject.

4. *You are more likely to be satisfied with a decision you help make.* Group problem solving provides an opportunity for group members to participate in making decisions and achieving the group goal. Several research studies suggest that individuals who help solve problems in a group are more committed to the solution and better satisfied with their participation in the group than if they weren't involved in the discussion.

5. *You gain a better understanding of yourself.* Working in groups helps you gain a more accurate picture of how others see you. The feedback you receive makes you aware of personal characteristics that are not known to you but that are known to others. Whether the interaction is advantageous or disadvantageous depends largely on how you respond to the feedback others provide. If someone tells you that you are obnoxious and difficult to work with, you may respond by ignoring the comment, disagreeing with the observation, or examining your behavior to see if the criticism is justified. By becoming sensitive to feedback, you can understand yourself better (or at least better understand how others perceive you) than you would if you worked alone. Group interaction and feedback can be useful in helping you examine your interpersonal behavior and in deciding whether you want to change your communication style.

Why do these advantages occur? One explanation is called **social facilitation.** Social facilitation describes the tendency for people to work harder simply because there are other people present.[25] Why do some people do this? It is suggested that the increased effort may occur because people need and expect positive evaluations from others; some people want to be liked and they work harder when others are around to gain more positive strokes. Social facilitation seems to occur with greater consistency if the group task is simple rather than complex.

Disadvantages

Although working in small groups and teams can produce positive results, problems sometimes occur when people congregate. Perhaps you have heard the sentiment that committees are groups of the uninformed assigned by the unwilling to do the unnecessary. Consider some of the disadvantages of working in groups. Identifying these potential problems can help you avoid them.

1. *Group members may pressure others to conform to the majority opinion.* Most people do not like conflict; they generally try to avoid it. Some people believe that in an effective group, members readily reach agreement. But this tendency to avoid controversy in relationships can affect the quality of a group decision. What is wrong with group members reaching agreement? Nothing, unless they are agreeing to conform to the majority opinion or even to the leader's opinion. Group members may agree on a bad solution just to avoid conflict. Social psychologist Irving Janis calls this phenomenon **groupthink**—when groups agree primarily in order to avoid conflict.[26] Chapter 10 discusses conflict in small groups, talks about groupthink in more detail, and suggests how to avoid it.

2. *An individual group or team member may dominate the discussion.* In some groups it seems as if one person must run the show. That member wants to make the decisions and,, when all is said and done, insists that his or her position on the issue is the best one. "Well," you might say, "if this person wants to do all the work, that's fine with me. I won't complain. It sure will be a lot easier for me." Yes, if you permit a member or two to dominate the group, you may do less work yourself, but then you forfeit the greater availability of knowledge and more creative approaches that come with full participation. Other members may not feel satisfied because they too feel alienated from the decision making. If they do not enjoy working on the project, the group will suffer from their reduced input.

Try to use the domineering member's enthusiasm to the group's advantage. If an individual tries to monopolize the discussion, other group members should channel that interest more constructively. The talkative member, for example, could be given a special research assignment. Of course, if the domineering member continues to monopolize the discussion, other group members may have to confront that person and suggest that others be given an opportunity to present their views.

3. *Some group members may rely too much on others to get the job done.*

"Charlie is a hard worker. He'll see that the job is done right."

"Ayako seems to really like taking charge. She is doing such a good job.
The group really doesn't need me."

"No one will miss me if I don't show up for the meeting this afternoon. There will be enough people to do the work."

Such statements are made when group members are not aware of each individual's importance in the group. A danger of working in groups is that individuals may be tempted to rely too much on others rather than pitch in and help. The name for this problem is **social loafing**. Some group members hold back on their contributions (loaf), assuming others will do the work. Another reason why this sometimes occurs is because when working in a group or team no one will be able to pin the lack of work on a single group member. There is less accountability for who does what.[27] Working together distributes the responsibility of accomplishing a task. Spreading the responsibility among all group members should be an advantage of group work. However, when some group members allow others to carry the workload, problems can develop. Just because you are part of a group does not mean that you can get lost in the crowd. Your input is needed. Do not abdicate your responsibility to another group member.[28]

To avoid this problem, try to encourage less-talkative group members to contribute to the discussion. Also, make sure each person knows the goals and objectives of the group. Encouraging each member to attend every meeting helps, too. Poor attendance at group meetings is a sure sign that members are falling into the "Let Charlie do it" syndrome. Finally, see that each person knows and fulfills his or her specific responsibilities to the group.

Reprinted with special permission of King Features Syndicate

4. *Working with others in a group or team takes longer than working alone.* For many people, one of the major frustrations about group work is the time it takes to accomplish tasks. Not only does a group have to find a time and place where everyone can meet (sometimes a serious problem in itself), but a group simply requires more time to define, analyze, research, and solve problems than do individuals working alone. It takes time for people to talk and listen to others. Still, such input usually results in a better solution. You have to remind yourself and the group, "If we want a better solution, it is going to take time, patience, and understanding." And, as you've heard, time is money! One researcher estimates that one 2-hour meeting attended by 20 executives would cost the equivalent of a week's salary for one of them.[29]

REVIEW

Advantages and Disadvantages of Working in Groups and Teams

ADVANTAGES

Groups have more information.

Groups are often more creative.

Working in groups improves learning.

Group members are more satisfied if they participate in the process.

Group members learn about themselves.

DISADVANTAGES

Group members may pressure others to conform.

One person may dominate the discussion.

Members may rely too much on others and not do their part.

Group work takes more time than working individually.

When Not to Collaborate

Although we've noted significant advantages to working in groups and teams, our discussion of the disadvantages of groups and teams suggests there may be situations when it's best *not* to collaborate in groups and teams. What situations call for individual work? Read on.

When the Group or Team Has Limited Time. If a decision must be made quickly, it may sometimes be better to delegate the decision to an expert. In the heat of battle, commanders usually do not call for a committee meeting of all their troops to decide when to strike. True, the troops may be better satisfied with a decision that they have participated in making, but the obvious need for a quick decision overrides any advantages that may be gained from meeting as a group.

When an Expert Already Has the Answer. If you want to know what it's like to be president of a university, you don't need to form a committee to answer that question; go ask one or more university presidents what they do. Or, if you want to know mathematical formulas, scientific theories, or other information that an expert could readily tell you, go ask the expert rather than forming a fact-finding committee. Creating a group to identify what an expert already knows, wastes time.

When the Information Is Readily Available from Research Sources. In this Internet information age, a wealth of information is available to us at the click of a mouse. It may not be necessary to form a committee to chase after information that already exists. A group or team may be helpful if the information needed is extensive and help is needed to conduct an exhaustive search. But if names, facts, dates, or other pieces of information can be quickly found in an almanac, encyclopedia, or Internet search engine, use those methods rather than spinning your wheels making a simple task more complex by forming a group to get the information. Don't reinvent the wheel with a group or team.

When Unmanageable Conflict and Contention Are Present. Although both of your authors are optimists, sometimes bringing people together for discussion and dialogue is premature. When conflict clearly may be combustible, it may be best to first try other communication formats before putting warring parties in a group to discuss. What may be needed instead of group discussion is a more-structured communication such as mediation or negotiation with a leader or facilitator to guide the discussion. Or, if group members have discussed an issue and just can't reach a decision, they may decide to let someone else make the decision for them. The judicial system is used when people can't or won't work things out in a rational, logical discussion. A judge provides strong leadership structure and the opposing attorneys argue the case in the search for truth. Don't avoid groups just because of conflict. As you will learn in Chapter 10, conflict is virtually always present in groups; disagreements can challenge a group to develop a better solution. But if the conflict is intractable, another method of making the decision may be best.

Types of Small Groups

So far you have read about the key characteristics of groups and teams, the importance of studying small group communication, and several advantages and disadvantages of working in groups. Besides understanding what a small group is, how a group and a team are similar and different, and why you should study groups and teams, you need to keep in mind that small group communication can range from a relatively unstructured, spontaneous discussion of an issue to a more formal, planned presentation.

Groups are formed for several reasons.[30] As you will find in Chapter 3, some groups originate to fulfill basic needs for association and community. Others are formed to solve a specific problem, to make a decision, or to gather information.

To give you an idea of the variety and purposes of our association with others in groups, we will discuss the role of both primary and secondary groups.

Primary Groups

A **primary group** is a group whose main purpose is to fulfill the basic need to associate with others. Your family provides one of the best illustrations of a primary group. In "The Death of the Hired Man," poet Robert Frost mused, "Home is the place where, when you have to go there / They have to take you in." Family communication usually does not follow a structured agenda; family conversation is informal. Conversation is also informal within other primary groups, such as informal cliques of friends or workers who interact over an extended period of time. Primary-group members associate with one another for the joy of community—to fulfill the basic human need to be social.

The main task of the primary group is to perpetuate the group so that members can continue to enjoy one another's companionship. Because people want to maintain these ties, they may be eager to conform to the behavior of the group. Teenagers who embrace the latest style in clothing or music often do so not only because they genuinely enjoy what is in vogue but also because they need to fit in with their peers. Primary groups do not meet regularly to make decisions unless a meeting is necessary to perpetuate the social patterns of the group. As with any group, some members may assert more influence than others. The key reward of belonging to a primary group, however, is simply the satisfaction of being a member.

Secondary Groups

Secondary groups exist to accomplish a task or achieve a goal. Most of the groups you belong to at work or school are secondary groups. You are not involved in a committee or a class group assignment just for fun or to meet your social need for belonging (even though you may enjoy the group and make friends with other group members). The main reason you join secondary groups is to get something done. Next we will identify several kinds of secondary groups to which you may belong at some point in your life.

Problem-Solving Groups A **problem-solving group** exists to overcome some unsatisfactory situation or obstacles to achieving a goal. Many, if not most, groups in business and industry are problem-solving groups. The most common problem that for-profit organizations face is finding a way to make more money. Chapters 8 and 9 will review principles and suggestions for improving your group problem-solving ability.

Decision-Making Groups The task of a **decision-making group** is to make a choice among several alternatives. The group must identify what the possible choices are, discuss the consequences of the choices, and then select the alternative that best meets a need or achieves the goal of the group or parent organization.[31] A committee that screens applicants for a job has the task of making a decision. The group must select one person from among the many alternatives available. A city council that must decide where to build a new airport looks at the alternatives recommended by a consulting firm. The council's job is to choose one site from the several that are recommended.

As we will discuss in Chapter 8, decision making is usually a part of the problem-solving process. Groups that have a problem to solve usually must identify several possible solutions and decide on the one that best solves the problem. Although all group problem solving involves making decisions, not all group decision making solves a problem. In Chapter 12 we will apply principles and strategies to enhance both decision making and problem solving in organizational settings.

Study Groups As a student, you are no doubt familiar with **study groups**. The main goal of these groups is to gather information and learn new ideas. We have already noted that one advantage of participating in a group is that you learn by being involved in a discussion. A study group also has the advantage of having access to more information and a wider variety of ideas through the contribution of different individuals.

In small groups individuals have access to more information and resources to help them in solving a problem than they would have working alone. What types of small groups would be helpful for teachers?

Therapy Groups A **therapy group**, also called an *encounter group, support group,* or *T-group,* strives to provide treatment for group members' personal problems or provides encouragement and support to help manage stress. Such groups should be led by professionals who are trained to help members overcome, or at least manage, individual problems in a group setting. Group therapy takes advantage of the self-understanding that members gain as they communicate with one another. Members also learn how they are perceived by others. By participating in a therapy group, people with similar problems can benefit from how others have learned to cope. Groups such as Weight Watchers and Alcoholics Anonymous also provide positive reinforcement when members have achieved their goals. By experiencing therapy with others, members take advantage of the greater knowledge and information available to the group.

Committees A **committee** is a group of people who are elected or appointed by a larger group for a specific task. Some committees are formed to solve problems. Others are appointed to make a decision or simply to gather information so that another group, team, or committee can make a decision. Some committee members are appointed to a **standing committee** (one that remains active for an extended time period); others serve on an **ad hoc committee** (one that disbands when its special task has been completed). Like many other people, you may react negatively to serving on a committee. Committee work is often regarded as time-consuming, tedious, and ineffective—except in increasing the sale of aspirin! Perhaps you have heard these sentiments about committees:

A committee is a way of postponing a decision.

A committee is a group of people who individually can do nothing and who collectively decide nothing can be done.

Although frustration with committees is commonplace, you are not doomed to have a negative experience when working with others in a committee. Throughout this text we review principles and skills of group communication that can help you enhance the quality of committee meetings. In Chapter 12 we will provide specific tips for chairing and participating in meetings.

REVIEW

Types of Small Groups

GROUP TYPE	GROUP PURPOSE	EXAMPLES
Primary group	To fill the basic need to associate with others	Family Close friends
Secondary group	To accomplish a task or achieve a goal	Problem-solving group Decision-making group Study group Therapy group Committee

Me Versus We: An Obstacle to Collaboration in Groups and Teams

The personal pronouns *I, me,* and *my* represent a primary stumbling block to our collaboration with others in small groups. Most North Americans champion individual achievement over collective group or team accomplishment. Researchers describe our tendency to focus on individual accomplishment as **individualism**. According to Geert Hofstede, individualism is the "emotional independence from groups, organizations, or other collectivities."[32] Individualistic cultures value individual recognition more than group or team recognition. They encourage self-actualization, being all that you can be *as an individual.* The United States, Britain, and Australia usually top the list of countries in which individual rights and accomplishment are valued over collective achievement.

By contrast, **collectivistic cultures** value group or team achievement more than individual achievement. People from Asian countries such as Japan, China, and Taiwan typically value collaboration and collective achievement more than those from individualistic cultures. Venezuela, Colombia, and Pakistan are other countries in which people score high on a collective approach to work methods.[33] In collective cultures, *we* is more important than *me.* Although collectivistic cultures usually think of a group as the primary unit in society, individualistic cultures think about the individual.[34]

As you might guess, people from individualistic cultures tend to find it more challenging to collaborate in group projects than do people from collectivistic cultures. Table 1.1 contrasts individualistic and collectivistic approaches to working in small groups.

If you and members of your group or team operate from an individualistic cultural perspective, it will be more challenging to develop collaborative approaches to solve problems, make decisions, and accomplish the work of the group. We are not suggesting that you total-

Table 1.1   Individualism and Collectivism in Small Groups

INDIVIDUALISTIC ASSUMPTIONS	COLLECTIVISTIC ASSUMPTIONS
The most effective decisions are made by individuals.	The most effective decisions are made by teams.
Planning should be centralized by the leaders.	Planning is best done by all concerned.
Individuals should be rewarded.	Groups or teams should be rewarded.
Individuals work primarily for themselves.	Individuals work primarily for the team.
Healthy competition between colleagues is more important than teamwork.	Teamwork is more important than competition.
Meetings are mainly for sharing information with individuals.	Meetings are mainly for making group or team decisions.
To get something accomplished, you should work with individuals.	To get something accomplished, you should work with the whole group or team.
A key objective in group meetings is to advance your own ideas.	A key objective in group meetings is to reach consensus or agreement.
Team meetings should be controlled by the leader or chair.	Team meetings should allow all team members to bring up what they want.
Group or team meetings are often a waste of time.	Group or team meetings are the best way to achieve a quality goal.

Source: Adapted from John Mole, *Mind Your Manners: Managing Business Cultures in Europe* (London: Nicholas Brealey, 1995).

ly abandon your cultural value of individualism. But being aware of individualistic group-member tendencies explains why working in groups can be frustrating and time consuming.

When rewarding team members, should you reward them as individuals or collectively as an entire team? Rewarding team members collectively seems to work best if team members enjoyed working in the team, were highly committed to the team and its goals, and team members liked working together more than they prefer working individually.[35] One of the most important strategies for overcoming a focus on individual concerns is for a group or team to develop what Larson and LaFasto call a "clear and elevating goal" that the entire group can support.[36] Without an overarching group goal, individual agendas are likely to be more important than the group agenda.

Becoming a Competent Small Group Communicator

In the chapters ahead, we offer principles and skills designed to enhance your competence as a member of a small group. A **competent group communicator** is a person who is able to interact appropriately and effectively with others in small groups and teams. Michael Mayer found that the two most important behaviors of group members were (1) fully participating in the discussion especially when analyzing the problem, and (2) offering encouraging, supportive comments to others.[37] Stated succinctly, participate and be nice. One model suggests that there are four levels of attaining competence at any skill or set of skills. This model can be applied to becoming a competent group communicator.

First, many communicators in small groups exhibit *unconscious incompetence;* they are unaware that they are ineffective or that they behave in inappropriate ways. Group members who talk too much or try to bully others to get their way may not be aware of behaving inappropriately. Or those who offer little encouragement and seek only to criticize others may think that they are being helpful; in reality such insensitive behavior is destructive. These interpersonally inept individuals may be oblivious to the needs of others.

The second level of competence is called *conscious incompetence*—a situation in which individuals are aware that they lack the abilities to function effectively, but they simply do not know how to behave appropriately. After reading a chapter or two of this book, you may become aware of some skills you need to polish in order to improve your effectiveness.

The third level of competence, *conscious competence,* occurs when the communicator understands the effective or appropriate behavior but is not yet completely comfortable with adopting it. The individual has to work mindfully and with some deliberate effort at being competent.

The fourth level of competence, *unconscious competence,* is reached when you no longer need to consciously tick off each step of the skill-performance process; you know you have become more comfortable and the skill is now part of your "natural" behavior.

We are not suggesting that the ultimate goal is mindlessly to apply principles of group communication skills. We are suggesting, however, that as you develop practice in using these skills, you will become more comfortable and develop a greater ease in adapting skills and practices to your own style and personality.

Researchers who have studied how to enhance communication competence suggest that three elements are involved in becoming a truly competent communicator: (1) you must be motivated, (2) you must have appropriate knowledge, and (3) you must have the skill to act appropriately.[38]

Motivation is an internal drive to achieve a goal. To be motivated means you have a strong desire to do your best, even during inevitable periods of fatigue and frustration. If you are motivated to become a competent small group communicator, you probably have an understanding of the benefits or advantages of working with others in groups.

To work together effectively, individuals will need to develop common goals and a collective focus rather than pursue only individual goals. Why might some cultures find this easier to achieve than others?

The second element, **knowledge**, means you have the information to competently do what needs to be done. One key purpose of this book is to give you knowledge that can help you become a more competent communicator in groups, on teams, and during the many meetings you will undoubtedly attend in the future.

The final element in being a competent communicator is **skill**. Just having the desire to be effective (motivation) or being able to rattle off lists of principles and theories (knowledge) doesn't ensure that you will be competent unless you have the skill to put the principles into practice. The subtitle of this book—*Principles and Practices*—emphasizes the importance of being able to translate into action what you know and think.

Research supports the common sense conclusion that practicing group communication skills, especially when you practice the skills in a group or team setting, enhances your group performance.[39]

An Introduction to Group Problem-Solving Competencies

Although we've described the elements of being a competent group or team member, you may still be wondering, "What specifically do effective group members do?" Katherine Hawkins and Bryant Fillion surveyed personnel managers to find out what the managers considered the most important skills necessary for success in groups and teams. Their results are included in Table 1.2, listed in priority order.[40] To provide a comprehensive overview of some of the essential competencies that we will present, we offer the following nine competencies as an introduction to the essential skills for members of problem-solving

Table 1.2 Important Skills for Group and Team Members

1. Listen effectively
2. Understand roles and responsibilities
3. Actively contribute to the group
4. Ask clear questions
5. Establish and maintain rapport with others
6. Be sensitive to people with different cultural backgrounds
7. Use clear, concise, accurate, and professional language
8. Communicate well with people who have different professional backgrounds
9. Give clear and accurate instructions
10. Nonverbally have a positive professional image (appropriate grooming and attire)
11. Help resolve conflicts
12. Accurately summarize information to the group
13. Give brief, clear, and well-organized, informative presentations to the group when appropriate

Source: K. W. Hawkins and B. P Fillion, "Perceived Communication Skill Needs for Work Groups," *Communication Research Reports* 16 (1999): 167–74.

groups. It's important to emphasize that this introduction targets *problem-solving* discussion, not other group goals such as sharing information or socializing in groups. As we noted earlier, to solve a problem or to achieve a goal you must seek to overcome an obstacle. There is more communication research about how to solve problems and make effective decisions in small groups and teams than on any other topic. The overview presented here sketches some of the core competencies that can result in more-effective group outcomes that we will amplify in the chapters ahead.

The nine competencies are grouped into four categories. **Problem-oriented** competencies focus on defining and analyzing the problem. **Solution-oriented** competencies concern identifying solution criteria, generating solutions, and evaluating solutions. **Discussion-management competencies** deal with communication that helps the group stay focused on the task and manages the interaction. Finally, **relational competencies** are concerned with managing conflict and maintaining a positive group climate. These competencies were identified after examining several bodies of research and consulting with several instructors of small group communication.[41] What follows is a preview of these competencies. We will discuss the principles and practices of each of the competencies throughout the book.

Problem-Oriented Competencies

1. *Define the problem.* Effective group members clearly and appropriately define or describe the problem to be solved. Ineffective group members either inaccurately define the problem or make little or no attempt to clarify the problem or issues confronting the group.

2. *Analyze the problem.* Effective group members offer statements that clearly and appropriately examine the causes, obstacles, history, symptoms, and significance of the problem to be solved. Ineffective members either don't do this or inaccurately or inappropriately analyze the problem.

Solution-Oriented Competencies

3. *Identify criteria.* Effective group members offer clear and appropriate comments that identify the goal the group is attempting to achieve or identify specific criteria (or standards for an acceptable solution or outcome) for the problem facing the group. Ineffective group members don't clarify the goal or establish criteria for solving the problem. Ineffective groups aren't sure what they are looking for in a solution or outcome.

4. *Generate solutions.* Effective group members offer several possible solutions or strategies to overcome the obstacles or decide on the issues confronting the group. Ineffective group members offer fewer solutions, or they rush to make a decision without considering other options or before defining and analyzing the problem.

5. *Evaluate solutions.* Effective group members systematically evaluate the pros and the cons of the solutions that are proposed. Ineffective group members don't examine the positive and negative consequences as well as both the benefits and potential costs of a solution or decision.

Discussion-Management Competencies

6. *Maintain task focus.* Effective group members stay on track and keep their focus on the task at hand. Although almost every group wanders off track from time to time, the most effective groups are mindful of their goal and sensitive to completing the work before them. Effective group members also summarize what the group is discussing to keep the group oriented. Ineffective group members have difficulty staying on track and frequently digress from the issues at hand, and they also seldom summarize what the group has done, which means that group members aren't quite sure what they are accomplishing.

7. *Manage interaction.* Effective group members don't monopolize the conversation and actively look for ways to draw quieter members into the discussion. Neither are they too quiet; they contribute their fair share of information and look for ways to keep the discussion from becoming a series of monologues; they encourage on-task, supportive dialogue. Ineffective group members either rarely contribute to the discussion or monopolize the discussion by talking too much. They also make little effort to draw others into the conversation and are not sensitive to the need for balanced interaction among group members.

Relational Competencies

8. *Manage conflict.* Conflict occurs in the best of groups. Effective group members are sensitive to differences of opinion and personal conflict, and they actively seek to manage the conflict by focusing on issues, information, and evidence rather than personalities. Ineffective group members deal with conflict by making it personal; they are insensitive to the feelings of others and generally focus on personalities at the expense of issues.

9. *Maintain climate.* Effective group members look for opportunities to support and encourage other group members. Although they may not agree with all comments made, they actively seek ways to improve the climate and maintain positive relationships with other group members through both verbal and nonverbal expressions of support. Ineffective group members do just the opposite; they are critical of others and with their frowning faces and strident voices nonverbally cast a gloomy pall over the group. Ineffective members rarely use appropriate humor to lessen any tension between members.

Communicating effectively in small groups and teams involves a variety of competencies. Even as we present these nine competencies, we are not suggesting that these are the

E T H I C A L L Y

*U*nderlying each of the nine group communication competencies is the importance of being an ethical communicator. **Ethics** are the beliefs, values, and moral principles by which we determine right or wrong. Ethical principles are the basis for many of the decisions we make in our personal and professional lives. We conclude the first chapter in the book by spotlighting the importance of being an ethical group communicator.

For most people, being ethical means being sensitive to others' needs, giving people choices rather than forcing them to do what you want, keeping private information that other people share with you in confidence, not intentionally decreasing others' feeling of self-esteem, and being honest in presenting information. Unethical communication does just the opposite: It forces views on others and demeans their integrity.

When communicating in groups and teams, it is important to give people choices rather than to insist that your ideas or solutions are always superior. Ethical principles influence both the methods of decision making and the final decision outcome. For example, if you believe all people should be treated fairly and with respect, you will reject the idea that only people of a certain race, ethnic background, or religion should belong to a particular group or organization. Or, if you believe you have an ethical responsibility to support your group, you will make an extra effort to find the time to complete the task you were assigned to do. Although group members may not spend much time explicitly talking about ethics, virtually every action that group members make is influenced by ethical principles.

only things you need to learn; instead, we do so to offer a practical beginning to the essentials of communicating in small group problem solving and decision making.

A competent communicator has not only knowledge and skill but also the motivation to work well with others. Several years ago, Robert Fulghum, author of *All I Really Need to Know I Learned in Kindergarten,* suggested that while he was in kindergarten he mastered the basics of getting along with others and accomplishing tasks effectively. This book is designed to add to what you learned in both kindergarten and your later life to help you become a valued member of the groups to which you belong.

Putting Principles into Practice

Groups and teams are an integral part of society. This chapter has explained the importance of studying small group communication. To apply some of the principles of groups, consider these suggestions:

- ▶ Work in small groups to benefit from the knowledge and information that others have but that you lack.
- ▶ Work in small groups to take advantage of other members' creative approaches to problem solving and decision making.
- ▶ Learn to recognize the key elements that make a team effective:

  A clear, elevating goal

  A results-driven structure

  Competent team members

  Unified commitment

  A collaborative climate

  Standards of excellence

  External support and recognition

  Principled leadership
- ▶ Cultivate individual team-member characteristics that enhance team effectiveness:

  Experience

  Problem-solving ability

  Openness

  Supportiveness

  Action-oriented approach

  Positive personal style
- ▶ When you want to improve your understanding and comprehension of a subject or issue, form a discussion group and talk about the topic with others.
- ▶ Work in small groups so that you can participate in making decisions that affect you. You will be more likely to support a decision if you have contributed to the discussion.
- ▶ Try to learn something new about yourself when you work with others in small groups.
- ▶ Do not let others pressure you to conform to the group's majority opinion just for the sake of agreement.
- ▶ Do not let one or two members of a small group dominate the discussion. If they do, you lose many of the advantages of working in groups.
- ▶ Avoid the trap of relying too much on other group members. Assume your fair share of the responsibility for getting things done.
- ▶ Avoid frustration by accepting the fact that groups take more time to accomplish tasks than do individuals.
- ▶ Focus on the specific competencies needed to participate effectively in a small group so that you can employ them more efficiently.
- ▶ Try to be motivated, knowledgeable, and skilled whenever you are a member of a small group.
- ▶ Help your group get a task accomplished by defining and analyzing the problem, identifying criteria, generating solutions, evaluating solutions, and maintaining task focus.

PRACTICE

Agree–Disagree Statements

Read each statement once. Mark whether you agree (A) or disagree (D) with each statement. Take five or six minutes to do this.[42]

_____ 1. A primary concern of all group members should be to establish an atmosphere in which all feel free to express their opinions.

_____ 2. In a group with a strong leader, an individual is able to achieve greater personal security than in a leaderless group.

_____ 3. Often individuals who are part of working groups should do what they think is right regardless of what the groups decide to do.

_____ 4. It is sometimes necessary to use autocratic methods to obtain democratic objectives.

_____ 5. Sometimes it is necessary to push people in the direction you think is right, even if they object.

_____ 6. It is sometimes necessary to ignore the feelings of others in order to reach a group decision.

_____ 7. When leaders are doing their best, one should not openly criticize or find fault with their conduct.

_____ 8. Democracy has no place in a military organization, an air task force, or an infantry squad when actually in battle.

_____ 9. Much time is wasted talking when everybody in the group has to be considered before making a decision.

_____ 10. Almost any job that can be done by a committee can be done better by having one individual responsible for the job.

_____ 11. By the time most people reach maturity, it is almost impossible for them to increase their skills in group participation.

After you have marked the preceding statements, form small groups and try to agree or disagree unanimously with each statement. Try especially to find reasons for differences of opinion. If your group cannot reach agreement or disagreement, you may change the wording in any statement to promote unanimity.

Get–Acquainted Scavenger Hunt

Your instructor will ask you to find people in your class or your group who match as many of the following questions as possible. Use this as a way of getting better acquainted with people with whom you will be working or learning.

1. Someone with the same eye color. _____

2. Someone born in the same state. _____

3. Someone who has the same astrological sign. _____

4. Someone who likes the same sport. _____

5. Someone who likes your favorite food. _____

6. Someone who has the same number of letters in his or her name. _____

7. Someone who feels it is okay to cry in public. _____

8. Someone who is the youngest in the family. _____

9. Someone who would like to write a book. _____

10. Someone who has seen the same movie at least three times. _____

11. Someone who has traveled outside the United States. _____

12. Someone who likes to ski. _____

13. Someone who is an only child. _____

14. Someone who can speak two languages. _____

15. Someone who likes to cook. _____

Group Communication Journal

Keep a journal in which you describe, analyze, and evaluate your interactions with others in small groups during the semester. After each group activity, assignment, or case study, record your analysis of the group interaction. Consider organizing your journal entries this way:

1. *Describe what happened.* Make brief notes identifying what occurred during your group meeting.

2. *Analyze what happened.* Cite principles and research from your text to help you interpret why your group behaved as it did.

3. *Evaluate what happened.* What did the group do well? What could your group have done to improve its performance? What could you have done to improve the group?

Keep your entries in a notebook. Your instructor may collect your journal from time to time to assess your ability to describe, analyze, and evaluate your group experiences.

 Your companion Website has more practice activities, questionnaires, and checklists!
www.ablongman.com/beebe

Notes

1. Gerald M. Goldhaber, *Organizational Communication,* 6th ed. (Dubuque, IA: Brown, 1993) 5.

2. Frank E. X. Dance and Carl Larson, *Speech Communication: Concepts and Behavior* (New York: Holt, Rinehart & Winston, 1972).

3. Our definition of human communication is based on a discussion in Steven A. Beebe, Susan J. Beebe, and Mark V. Redmond. *Interpersonal Communication: Relating to Others* (Boston: Allyn and Bacon, 2002).

4. A. K. Offner, T. J. Kramer, and J. P. Winter, "The Effects of Facilitation, Recording, and Pauses on Group Brainstorming," *Small Group Research* 27 (1996): 283–98; V. Brown and P. B. Paulus, "A Simple Dynamic Model of Social Factors in Group Brainstorming," *Small Group Research* 27 (1996): 91–114; M. W. Kramer, C. L. Kuo, and J. C. Dailey, "The Impact of Brainstorming Techniques on Subsequent Group Processes," *Small Group Research* 28 (1997): 218–42; V. Brown, M. Tumeo, T. S. Larey, and P. B. Paulus, "Modeling Cognitive Interactions During Group Brainstorming," *Small Group Research* 29 (1997): 495–526.

5. See Susan G. Straus, "Getting a Clue: The Effects of Communication Media and Information Distribution on Participation and Performance in Computer-Mediated and Face-to-Face Groups," *Small Group Research* 27 (February 1996): 115–42; Susan G. Straus, "Technology, Group Process, and Group Outcomes: Testing the Connections in Computer-Mediated and Face-to-Face Groups," *Human-Computer Interaction* 12 (1997): 227–66; Suzanne P. Weisband, "Group Discussion and First Advocacy Effects in Computer-Mediated and Face-to-Face Decision Making Groups," *Organizational Behavior and Human Decision Processes* 53 (1992): 352–80.

6 A. J. Salazar, "Ambiguity and Communication Effects on Small Group Decision-Making Performance," *Human Communication Research* 23 (1996): 155–192; R. Y. Hirokawa, D. DeGooyer, and K. Valde, "Using Narratives to Study Task Group Effectiveness," *Small Group Research* 31 (2000): 573–591; S. Jarboe, "Procedures for Enhancing Group Decision Making," in R. Y. Hirokawa and M. S. Poole, eds., *Communication and Group Decision Making* (Thousand Oaks, CA: Sage, 1996).

7. For an excellent review of teamwork principles and strategies, see Dennis A. Romig, *Breakthrough Teamwork: Outstanding Results Using Structured Teamwork* (New York: Irwin, 1996).

8. J. R. Katzenback and D. K. Smith, *The Wisdom of Teams: Creating the High-Performance Organization.* (New York: HarperBusiness, 1993); M. Schrage, *No More Teams! Mastering the Dynamics of Creative Collaboration* (New York: Currency Doubleday, 1995); Romig, *Breakthrough Teamwork*; D. D. Chrislip and C. E. Larson, *Collaborative Leadership* (San Francisco: Jossey-Bass, 1994).

9. D. J. Devine, L. D. Clayton, J. L. Philips, B. B. Dunford, S. B. Melner, "Teams in Organizations: Prevalence, Characteristics, and Effectiveness, *Small Group Research*, 30 (1999): 678–711.

10. See P. R. Scholtes, Brian L. Joiner, and Barbara J. Streibel, *The Team Handbook*, 2nd ed. (Madison, WI: Joiner Associates, 1996); Romig, *Breakthrough Teamwork*, Schrage, *No More Teams!*

11. R. Y. Hirokawa and J. Keyton, "Perceived Facilitators and Inhibitors of Effectiveness in Organizational Work Teams," *Management Communication Quarterly* 8 (1995): 424–46.

12. Carl E. Larson and Frank M. J. LaFasto, *Teamwork: What Must Go Right/What Can Go Wrong* (Beverly Hills, CA: Sage, 1989).

13. Devine, Clayton, Philips, Dunford, and Melner, "Teams in Organizations."

14. Frank LaFasto and Carl Larson, *When Teams Work Best* (Thousand Oaks, CA: Sage, 2001). Our discussion of the six characteristics of effective team members is based on information presented in Chapter 1, pages 4–25.

15. Adapted from David W. Johnson and Frank P. Johnson, *Joining Together: Group Theory and Group Skills* (Englewood Cliffs, NJ: Prentice Hall, 1975), 304.

16. E. Salas, D. Rozell, J. E. Dirskell, and B. Mullen, "The Effect of Team Building on Performance: An Integration," *Small Group Research* 39 (1999): 309–329.

17. Devine, Clayton, Philips, Dunford, and Melner, "Teams in Organizations;" Salas, Rozell, Driskell, and Mullen, "The Effect of Team Building on Performance."

18. R. Forrester and A. B. Drexler, "A Model for Team-Based Organization Performance," *Academy of Management Executives* 13 (1999): 36–49.

19. Roger K. Mosvick and Robert B. Nelson, *We've Got to Start Meeting Like This!* (Glenview, IL: Scott, Foresman, 1987).

20. S. Sorensen, "Grouphate," paper presented at the International Communication Association, Minneapolis, Minnesota, May 1981.

21. The discussion of the advantages and disadvantages of working in small groups is based in part on Norman R. F. Maier, "Assets and Liabilities in Group Problem Solving: The Need for an Integrative Function," *Psychological Review* 74 (1967): 239–49. See also Michael Argyle, *Cooperation: The Basis of Sociability* (London: Routledge, 1991).

22. Robert A. Cooke and John A. Kernaghan, "Estimating the Difference Between Group Versus Individual Performance on Problem-Solving Tasks," *Group & Organizational Studies* 12, no. 3 (Sept. 1987): 319–42.

23. Cooke and Kernaghan. "Estimating the Difference Between Group Versus Individual Performance on Problem-Solving Tasks."

24. D. D. Stewart, "Stereotypes, Negativity Bias, and the Discussion of Unshared Information in Decision-Making Groups," *Small Group Research* 29 (1998): 643–668; J. R. Larson, "Modeling the Entry of Shared and Unshared Information into Group Discussion: A Review and BASIC Language Computer Program," *Small Group Research* 28 (1997): 454–479.

25. R. Zajonc, "Social Facilitation," *Science* 149 (1965): 269–274; M. Gagne and M. Zuckerman, "Performance and Learning Goal Orientations as Moderators of Social Loafing and Social Facilitation," *Small Group Research* 30 (1999): 524–541; R. G. Geen, "Social Motivation," *Annual Review of Psychology* 42 (1991): 377–399.

26. Irving L. Janis, "Groupthink," *Psychology Today* 5 (Nov. 1971): 43–46, 74–76.

27. Gagne and Zuckerman, "Performance and Learning Goal Orientations."

28. A. BarNir, "Can Group- and Issue-Related Factors Predict Choice Shift? A Meta-Analysis of Group Decisions on Life Dilemmas," *Small Group Research* 29 (1998): 308–38.

29. Donaleson R. Forsyth, *An Introduction to Group Dynamics* (Monterey, CA: Brooks/Cole, 1983) 424.

30. For an excellent discussion of small group communication in naturalistic settings, see L. R. Frey, "The Naturalistic Paradigm: Studying Small Groups in the Postmodern Era," *Small Group Research* 25 (1994): 551–77; L. R. Frey, "Applied Communication Research on Group Facilitation in Natural Settings," in L. R. Frey, ed., *Innovations in Group Facilitation: Applications in Natural Settings* (Cresskill, NJ: Hampton 1995) 1–23.

31. For a comprehensive review of the history of group decision-making research, see L. R. Frey, "Remember and 'Remembering': A History of Theory and Research on Communication and Group Decision-Making," in R. Y. Hirokawa and S. M. Poole, eds., *Communication and Group Decision Making*, 2nd ed. (Thousand Oaks, CA: Sage, 1996) 19–51.

32. Geert Hofstede, *Culture's Consequences: International Differences in Work-Related Values* (Beverly Hills, CA: Sage, 1980) 221.

33. Hofstede, *Culture's Consequences*.

34. In addition to the work of Hofstede, see also John A. Wagner III and Michael K. Moch, "Individualism-Collectivism: Concept and Measure," *Group and Organizational Studies* 11 (September 1986): 280–304; Harry C. Triandis, Christopher McCusker, and C. Harry Hui, "Multimethod Probes of Individualism and Collectivism," *Journal of Personality and Social Psychology* 59 (1990): 1006–20; C. Harry Hui, "Measurement of Individualism-Collectivism," *Journal of Research in Personality* 22 (1988): 17–36; Charles R. Bantz, "Cultural Diversity and Group Cross-Cultural Team Research," *Journal of Applied Communication Research* (Feb. 1993): 1–20; Mitchell R. Hammer and Judith N. Martin, "The Effects of Cross-Cultural Training on American Managers in a Japanese-American Joint Venture," *Journal of Applied Communication Research* (May 1992): 161–82.

35. B. L. Kirkman and D. L. Shapiro, "Understanding Why Team Members Won't Share: An Examination of Factors Related to Employee Receptivity to Team-Based Rewards," *Small Group Research* 31 (2000): 175–209.

36. C. Larson and F. LaFasto, *Teamwork: What Must Go Right/What Can Go Wrong* (Beverly Hills, CA: Sage, 1989).

37. M. E. Mayer, "Behaviors Leading to More Effective Decisions in Small Groups Embedded in Organizations," *Communication Reports* 11 (1998): 123–32.

38. B. H. Spitzberg, "Communication Competence as Knowledge, Skill, and Impression," *Communication Education* 32 (1983): 323–29.

39. A. B. Hollingshead, "Group and Individual Training: The Impact of Practice on Performance," *Small Group Research* 29 (1998): 254–80.

40. K. W. Hawkins and B. P Fillion, "Perceived Communication Skill Needs for Work Groups," *Communication Research Reports* 16 (1999): 167–74.

41. Steven A. Beebe and J. Kevin Barge, "Assessing Small Group Problem Solving Communication Competencies," in Robert Cathcart and Larry Samovar (eds.), *A Reader in Small Group Communication* (New York: Roxbury, in press). Steven A. Beebe, J. Kevin Barge, and Colleen McCormick, The Competent Group Communicator, presented at the National Communication Association annual conference, New York, New York (November 1998).

42. Developed by Alvin Goldberg; University of Denver.

43. D. W. Johnson, *Reaching Out: Interpersonal Effectiveness and Self-Actualization* (Boston: Allyn and Bacon, 2000).

Chapter Outline:

Objectives:

After studying this chapter,
you will be able to:

▶ Discuss the nature and functions of
theory and theory construction.

▶ Explain the relevance of theory to the
study of small group communication.

▶ Discuss five general theories that
apply to small group communication.

▶ Explain the model of small group
communication presented in this
chapter.

▶ Identify some of the components of
small group communication.

Small Group
Communication
Theory

"To despise theory is to have the excessively vain pretension to do without knowing what one does, and to speak without knowing what one says."
—Fontenelle

Theory. It is a word people encounter almost daily in their casual conversations, in classrooms, and on news broadcasts. They discuss and evaluate theories of evolution, the theory of relativity, and quantum theory. Fictitious criminal investigators on television develop theories about what took place at a crime scene. Psychologists and parents create theories of personality development and theories of childrearing (in fact, there are practically as many theories of childrearing as there are parents). In short, theories abound—some are simple, some complex; some are formal, some informal; some are scientific, some unscientific. Yet few people take the time to think about what theories are. Where do they come from? How are they built? What do people do with them after they've got them?

Many people are intimidated by the word *theory*. To them, studying theory is an esoteric activity that has no relevance except for the scientist or the academician. Today's students are interested in relevant, practical kinds of knowledge, and sometimes they seem to assume that theory is neither relevant nor practical. Dance and Larson disagree, claiming that "theorizing is a very basic form of human activity."[1] Theory is *very* practical. Theorizing helps to explain or predict the events in people's lives. On a rudimentary level people theorize when they reflect on their past experiences and make decisions based on these experiences. Theory, then, has two basic functions: to explain and to predict. These functions are discussed more fully later in the chapter.

This chapter examines some of the central issues of group communication theory. First, we will discuss the nature of theory and the theory-building process. Second, we will turn our attention to the relevance and practicality of theory in the study of small group communication. Third, we will discuss five theoretical perspectives for the study of small groups. Finally, we will present a theoretical model of small group communication.

The Nature of Theory and the Theory-Building Process

Theories are very practical. Suppose, for example, that you do your weekly grocery shopping every Thursday after your late afternoon class. When you arrive at the store, you are pleased to see that several checkout lanes are open with no waiting at any of them. "Ah," you say, "I'll be out of here in short order." With your cart before you, you proceed up one aisle and down the next. To your dismay, you notice that each time you pass the checkout lanes, the lines have grown. By the time you have filled your cart, at least six people are waiting in each lane. You now have a twenty-minute wait at the checkout.

If the situation just described were to occur once, you would probably curse your luck or chalk it up to fate. If you find, however, that the same events occur each time you visit the market, you begin to see a consistency in your observations that goes beyond luck or fate. In noticing this consistency, you take the first step in building a theory. You have observed a *phenomenon*. You have witnessed a *repeated pattern* of events for which you feel there must be some *explanation*. So you ponder the situation. In your mind you organize all the facts available to you: the time of your arrival, the condition of the checkout lanes when you entered the store each time, and the length of the lines when you completed your shopping. Lo and behold, you discover that you have been arriving at the store at approximately 4:45 each afternoon and reaching the checkout lanes about twenty-five minutes later. You conclude that between the time you arrive and the time you depart, thousands of workers head for home, some of them stopping off at the store on the way. *Voilà*—you have a theory. You have organized your information to explain the phenomenon.

Assuming that your theory is accurate, it is now very useful for you. Having *explained* the phenomenon, you may now reasonably *predict* that under the same set of circumstances, events within the phenomenon will recur. In other words, if you continue to do your weekly shopping after your late class on Thursday, you will repeatedly be faced with long checkout lines. Given this knowledge, you can adapt your behavior accordingly, perhaps by doing your shopping earlier or later in the day.

On a more personal level, your theory about yourself—your **self-concept**—influences the choices you make throughout the day. You tend to do things that you see as being consistent (predictable) with your self-concept. In essence, this self-concept or "self-theory" serves to explain you to yourself, thereby allowing you to predict your behavior and to successfully select realistic goals. This is theory at its most personal and pervasive.

Theory building is a common, natural process of human communication. You notice consistencies in your experience and examine relationships among the consistencies. You then build an explanation of the phenomenon that allows you to predict future events and, in some cases, to exercise some control over situations. Some theories, of course, are very elaborate and formal, but even in these the fundamental features of explanation and prediction can be seen. In George Kelly's definition of theory we find reference to these features:

> A theory may be considered as a way of binding together a multitude of facts so that one may comprehend them all at once. When the theory enables us to make reasonably precise predictions, one may call it scientific.[2]

Theory is crucial to the study of group and team communication. The explanatory power of good theory helps make sense of the processes involved when people interact with others in a group. The predictive precision of theory allows people to anticipate probable outcomes of various types of communicative behavior in the group. Armed with this type of knowledge, people can adjust their own communicative behavior to help make group work more effective and rewarding.

Theory: A Practical Approach to Group Communication

Theory, both formal and informal, helps people make intelligent decisions about how to conduct themselves. Working in small groups is no exception. Everyone brings a set of theories to small group meetings—theories about oneself, about other group members, and about groups in general. Once in the group, people regulate their behavior according to these theories. They behave in ways consistent with their self-concepts. They deal with others in the group according to their previous impressions (theories) of them. If they believe (theorize) that groups are essentially ineffectual, that "a camel is a horse designed by a committee" or that "if you really want something done, do it yourself," then they probably

ETHICALLY

We noted in Chapter 1 that ethical principles help people decide what's right or wrong. It's not always easy. Consider the following:

You and your two roommates find an advertisement for a $3,500 big-screen color television. You have no TV in your apartment and were wondering how you could afford one. The advertisement says you may try out the TV in your home for six months with no obligation to buy. If not completely satisfied, you can return the set with no questions asked. If you decide to keep the set, you begin making monthly payments at that time. What will you do? Will you "purchase" the TV knowing that there is no way you can keep it past six months? Or not?

You may think there is a clear right answer but may be surprised to find that others hold the opposite view and see it just as clearly. Our theories of ourselves (self-concepts) include ethical beliefs and principles. Can you identify the ethical principle that explains your decision in this case?

will act accordingly and their prophecy will be fulfilled. If, in contrast, they come to the group convinced that groups are capable of working effectively, and if they know how to make the group work, they will behave very differently and contribute much more to the group's effectiveness.

Explanatory Function

To be practical, theories of small group communication must suggest ways in which participants can make group discussion more efficient and rewarding. The explanatory function of theory is important in this regard. If people understand why some groups are effective while others are not, or why certain styles of leadership are appropriate in some situations but not in others, then they are better prepared to diagnose the needs of their own groups. Studying theories of group interaction can help people understand that process and the ways in which different facets of it are related.

Predictive Function

People derive satisfaction from understanding a process, but the predictive function of theory is even more useful for them. Let's consider a hypothetical situation.

A CASE STUDY

The dean of student affairs at your college has become sensitive about reports from students that the activities scheduled for orientation week each year are silly. Specifically, students have been reacting to two of the dean's favorite activities at the first orientation mixer—a pass-the-orange-under-your-chin race and a find-your-own-shoes-in-the-middle-of-the-room relay race. Students claim to feel undignified during these activities. They feel they are being treated more as children than as adults. Bewildered, the dean remembers how much the class of 1981 enjoyed these activities and is at a loss about what to do. Therefore, the dean has appointed a group of students to investigate the matter. You are one of those students.

The committee is composed mostly of juniors and seniors. The dean thinks they have been around long enough to know the ropes. As president-elect of next year's sophomore class, you are the youngest of the six committee members. The chairperson is a graduating senior.

You arrive at the first meeting ready to work. The committee is to plan activities that are "more closely aligned with the needs of today's college men and women." You are excited about being a part of a decision-making process that will have a real effect. To your dismay, the other members of the group seem to disregard their task and spend the meeting discussing the prospects for the basketball team, hardly mentioning orientation-week activities for next fall. You leave the meeting confused but hopeful that the next meeting will be more fruitful. You resolve to take a more active role and to try to steer the meeting more toward the committee's task.

At the second meeting, you suggest that the committee really should discuss orientation week. Members concur, then make jokes about past orientation-week activities. When the chairperson makes no effort to keep the group on the track, you feel overwhelmed and bewildered.

Many theories, if you were familiar with them, might help you understand what is going on in this group—leadership theories, theories of group growth and development, problem-solving theories, various theories of interpersonal interaction, and so on. Basing your observations on theory, you might say, for example, that your inferior status as the youngest committee member reduces your ability to influence the group process. You might also say that the chairperson's leadership style is inappropriate to the task and situation. You might say that every group goes through an orientation period and that the time spent on trivia is a necessary part of the group process.

All these theories might be correct to a degree. At least you have a way of describing your group experience systematically. However, you have not met the test of practicality. While understanding that a process is satisfying, the more important question is what do you *do* with your understanding? Once you know something about group communication, how do you use what you know to help the group function more effectively?

In medicine a diagnosis is useless unless it suggests some course of treatment. Nevertheless, diagnosis—explanation—is a necessary first step. *Understanding* the process leads toward ways of *improving* the process, and herein lies the usefulness of the predictive quality of theory. By understanding a specific group and group communication in general, and by being aware of the alternative behaviors that are possible, you can use theory to select behaviors that will help you achieve the goal of your group. In other words, if you can reasonably predict that certain outcomes will follow certain types of communication, you can regulate your behavior to achieve the most desirable results. If, in the example of the dean's advisory committee, participants know that a necessary interpersonal orientation period is coming to a close and that some task-oriented statements will help the group achieve its goal, they can choose to make such statements. In this way, theory *informs* communicative behavior in small groups. Group members no longer behave randomly; they behave with understanding and purpose.

Some theories presented in this book explain group and team phenomena. These descriptive theories are referred to as **process theories**. Other theories, called **method theories**, take a prescriptive approach to small group communication. These how-to theories are particularly useful in establishing formats for solving problems and resolving conflicts in a group. Both types of theories add to the knowledge and skills that can make you a more effective communicator. Central to your effectiveness as a communicator is the ability to use words, which is the subject of the next section.

The Purpose of Communication in Small Groups: Reducing Uncertainty

A group cannot function without words; communication is the vehicle that allows a group to move toward its goals. Words call into being the realities, or potential realities, that they represent. Thus, a verbal description of an idea for a new product at a manufacturing company's board meeting creates a vision of that product for board members. Presented effectively, the description may result in new or changed attitudes and behaviors; the idea may be adopted. Words, then, have the power to create new realities and change attitudes; they are immensely powerful tools. Although this may seem obvious, it is a truth that often goes unnoticed. We spend so much of each day speaking, listening, reading, and writing that language seems commonplace to us. It is not. Through language we unravel the immense complexity that is our world. With language, we build the theories that reduce our uncertainty about ourselves and others.

Uncertainty

Dean Barnlund and others have proposed that the aim of speech communication is to reduce uncertainty.[3] According to this principle, communication organizes and makes sense out of all the sights, sounds, odors, tastes, and sensations in the environment. As Barnlund states, "Communication occurs any time meaning is assigned to an internal or external stimulus."[4] Thus, when people arrive at a meeting room and begin to shiver, the sensation brings to their minds the word *cold*. Within themselves, or on an *intrapersonal level,* they have reduced uncertainty about the nature of an experience. The room is too cold. Giving verbal expression to an experience organizes and clarifies that experience.

At the *interpersonal level* of communication, the reduction-of-uncertainty principle is even more clearly evident. As you get to know someone, you progressively discover what makes that person unique. You reduce uncertainty about him or her. By developing an explanation of that person's behavior, you can predict how he or she is likely to respond to future communication and events. You base your predictions on what you know about the person's beliefs, attitudes, values, and personality. In essence, you build a theory that allows you to explain another person's behavior, to predict that person's future responses, and to control your own communicative behavior accordingly. In other words, theories help reduce people's uncertainty about others.

Complexity

Getting to know someone is a process of progressively reducing uncertainty—and a lot of uncertainty exists, especially at the outset of working with others in groups and teams. Think back to your first day at college or to your first day in group communication class. You were probably surrounded by many unfamiliar faces. At times such as these, you feel tentative and think "What am I doing here?" and "Who are all of these other people?" Your feelings of uncertainty soar. In the cafeteria line you encounter a person you find attractive. You say, "Hi! Are you new? What do you think of school so far?" This takes a bit of courage because you do not know what kind of response you will get. So you are hesitant. You make small talk and look for signs in the other person's behavior that might indicate whether that person desires further communication. You communicate, observe the response, and base further communication on your interpretation of that response. This is a complex process, particularly because both you and another person must communicate, observe, respond, and interpret simultaneously!

The complexity of the process creates uncertainty—a sense of not being able to predict what will happen in the future. The presence of other people creates uncertainty because you don't know what they will do or say. Many communication theorists have noted that whenever an individual communicates with another person at least six people are involved: (1) who you think you are, (2) who you think the other person is, (3) who you think the other person thinks you are, (4) who the other person thinks he or she is, (5) who the other person thinks you are, and (6) who the other person thinks you think he or she is. All six of these people influence and are influenced by the communication—a very complex matter indeed, and one that contributes to people's uncertainty about interpersonal relationships. Nevertheless, people persist in communicating and find that, on the interpersonal level, communication reduces their uncertainty about others.

Small Groups: More Complexity and More Uncertainty

Table 2.1 shows dramatically how complexity increases with group size even when one relationship equals two, not six, people. When eight people interact, literally thousands of factors influence communication and are influenced by it—factors such as "who I think Ted thinks Rosa thinks Amit is" or "who I think Lourdes thinks Tom thinks I am."

Fortunately, people don't think consciously about all these factors all the time. They would be horribly debilitated if they did so. Nevertheless, these dynamics subtly influence people whenever they interact. The number of factors influencing people interacting in groups is staggering.

"Where are you going with this, Wingate?"

©The New Yorker Collection 2000 Nick Downes from cartoonbank.com

Table 2.1 Increase in Potential Relationships with an Increase in Group Size

SIZE OF GROUP	NUMBER OF RELATIONSHIPS
2	1
3	6
4	25
5	90
6	301
7	966

Source: From William M. Kephart, "A Quantitative Analysis of Intragroup Relationships," *American Journal of Sociology* 60 (1950). Reprinted by permission of the University of Chicago Press.

Theoretical Perspectives for the Study of Group and Team Communication

Thus far this chapter has discussed the nature of theory and its relationship to effective small group communication. It has pointed out that uncertainty and complexity are pervasive characteristics of small groups, while communication is the driving force that moves groups toward their goals.

Small group communication theory attempts to explain and predict group and team phenomena. Given the complexity of the process and the number of variables that affect small group communication, no single theory can account for all the variables involved, nor can one theory systematically relate the variables to one another. Therefore, a number of approaches to group communication theory have emerged in recent years. Each seeks to explain and predict group behavior while focusing on different facets of the group process. Five of these theoretical perspectives are described briefly here: (1) **social exchange theory**, (2) **systems theory**, (3) **symbolic convergence theory**, (4) **structuration theory**, and (5) **functional theory**.

Social Exchange Theory

Social exchange theory is a simple but powerful attempt to explain human behavior in terms that sound like a blend of behavioral psychology and economic theory. According to this theory, relationships can be described in terms of their rewards and costs, profits and losses. Rewards are pleasurable outcomes associated with particular behaviors; costs include such things as mental effort, anxiety, or even embarrassment.[5] Profit equals rewards minus costs; as long as rewards exceed costs, a relationship remains attractive.

Rewards and costs can take many forms in a group. As we will see more clearly in Chapter 3, fellowship, job satisfaction, achievement, status, and meeting personal needs and goals are all rewards that groups provide. However, group work takes time and effort and may be frustrating—all forms of cost. Social exchange theory predicts that as long as rewards exceed

Theories reduce uncertainty and guide our behavior in groups. How can theory help you in your group activities?

costs—that is, as long as group membership is profitable—group membership will continue to be attractive.

Small group variables such as cohesiveness and productivity are directly related to how rewarding the group experience is to its members. The basics of social exchange theory are useful in their descriptiveness. Keep them in mind as you read the remaining chapters and as you observe working groups.

Systems Theory

Perhaps the most prevalent approach to small group communication is that of systems theory. In many respects, **systems theory** represents the most promising perspective on small group communication because it is flexible enough to encompass the vast array of variables that influence group and team interaction.

One way to approach the concept of **system** is to think of your own body. The various organs make up systems (digestive, nervous, circulatory) that, in turn, make up the larger system: your body. Each organ depends on the proper functioning of other organs: a change in one part of the system causes changes in the rest of the system. Furthermore, the physiological system cannot be isolated from the environment that surrounds it; to maintain the proper functioning of your physiological systems, you must adjust to changes outside your body. A decrease in oxygen at a higher elevation will cause you to breathe more rapidly, a rise in temperature will make you perspire, and so forth. In other words, your body is an *open* system composed of interdependent elements. It receives *input* from the environment (food, air, water), *processes* that input (digestion and oxygenation), and yields an *output* (writing poetry, building cathedrals, cooking a fabulous dinner). Like the human body, a small group is an open system—composed of interdependent variables—that receives input, processes the input, and yields an output. The system also exhibits the properties of synergy, entropy, and equifinality.

Openness to Environment   A group does not operate in isolation; it is continually affected by interactions with its environment. New members may join, and former members may leave; demands from other organizations may alter the group's goals. Even the climate may affect the group's ability to work.

Interdependence   The various components of the group process are inter-related in such a way that a change in one component will alter the relationships among all other components. A shift in cohesiveness can change the group's productivity level. The loss of a group member or the addition of a new member effects a change felt throughout the system. **Interdependence** in the small group makes the study of small group communication fascinating and difficult: none of the variables involved may be understood properly in isolation.

Input Variables   By viewing them as parts of subsystems, the variables of small group communication can be categorized according to the systems-theory concept of input, process, and output. Input variables in the small group system include such things as group members and group resources, among them funds, tools, knowledge, purposes, relationships to other groups or organizations, and the physical environment.[6]

Process Variables   These variables relate to the procedures that the group follows to reach its goals. Many of these variables are represented in the Figure 2.1 in the next section.

Output Variables   Output variables—the outcomes of the group process—range from solutions and decisions to personal growth and satisfaction.

Synergy   Just as you are more than a composite of your various parts (you are *you,* after all) groups must be seen as more than the sum of their elements. **Synergy** is present when the whole is greater than the sum of its parts. When individuals form groups, something is created—the group—that didn't exist before; the group is more than the individuals who compose it.

Entropy   The measure of randomness or chaos in a system is called **entropy.** Systems tend to decay (entropy) if not balanced by some countervailing force. For example, interpersonal relationships separated by distance tend to cool rapidly, unless maintained actively through visits, letters, phone calls and emails. So, too, groups and teams experience entropy when they don't meet together regularly.

Equifinality   The principle of equifinality states that a system's final state may be reached by multiple paths and from different initial states; there is more than one way to reach the goal. This is an inherent characteristic of open systems. Conversely, systems (or groups and teams) that share the same initial conditions can reach very different end states.

Although systems theory does not explain small group phenomena, it serves as a useful organizational strategy. It also reminds us that a full understanding of group communication involves the broader contexts or environments in which groups operate. All the theories identified in this section are incomplete pictures of human behavior. Each does, however, provide insight into the maze of forces that affect small group communication.

Small groups can be viewed as open systems comprising different interdependent variables. What input and output variables might there be for the group in this photograph?

Symbolic Convergence Theory

If you consider your closest interpersonal relationships, you can probably remember a point at which the relationship took on a life of its own. You might describe it as when two acquaintances became friends: the relationship took on an identity based on your experiences together and your shared stories and visions of those experiences. Perhaps you develop "inside" or private jokes that have meaning only for the two of you.

Communication scholar Ernest Bormann has noted that groups take on this kind of shared personality as well. The symbolic convergence theory of communication explains how certain types of communication shape a group's identity and culture, which in turn influence other dynamics such as norms, roles, and decision making. Over time groups develop a collective consciousness with shared emotions, motives, and meanings.[7]

This group consciousness, Bormann says, evolves as group members share group fantasies or stories. Within this theory, fantasy does not mean something not grounded in reality. Rather, it has a technical meaning: the creative and imaginative shared interpretation of events that fulfills a group psychological or rhetorical need.[8] A psychological or rhetorical need can include such things as a need to take a break from work, to release tension, or to metaphorically deal with an issue facing the group. A fantasy is usually introduced as a story that captures the imagination of the group and momentarily takes the group away from the specific issue under discussion.

In groups, as in almost all forms of human endeavor, we can discern two levels of reality: (1) what actually happens and (2) our interpretations and beliefs about what happens. What remains in our memories and what guides our subsequent behavior is the latter.

If, for example, you are in a group discussing how to reduce cheating and other forms of academic dishonesty and a group member says "Hey, did anyone see the *Tonight Show* last

fantasy?
~moves g8 to a personal level?

Yʌou can find more information about group communication theories on the Web. For example, to learn more about fantasy themes and symbolic convergence theory, go to the excellent site at

http://oak.cats.ohiou.edu/~kr323396/fantasy.htm

For more on social exchange theory, go to:

http://oak.cats.ohiou.edu/~al891396/exchange.htm

night? They had a guy who won the national lying championship. He was so funny. He has been able to talk his way into getting photographed with the president of the United States." Another group member chimes in and says, "Yeah, I saw that. I had an uncle who used to tell whoppers. He once convinced my Aunt that he had won a million dollars in the lottery." Yet another group member says, "My brother is always playing practical jokes on my mom." Before you know it, the pace of conversation has quickened and other group members are telling stories about people who love to play practical jokes. A **fantasy theme** consists of the common or related content of the stories the group tells. In addition, the fantasy of one group member leads to a **fantasy chain**—a string of connected stories that revolve around a common theme. These fantasy chains help the group develop a shared sense of identity just as the unique stories and experiences you have with a close friend help give your relationship a unique identity. Usually a fantasy chain includes all the elements you would find in any well-told story. There are often elements of conflict, heroes, villains, and a plot that gives shape to the story.

By being mindful of the fantasies or stories that develop in a group, you can gain insight into what the group values. What may seem like "off task" behavior, such as talking about TV programs, movies, or events seemingly unrelated to the group's agenda, can be beneficial in giving the group a sense of identity. Noting the common themes of the group's fantasy (such as who the villains are in the stories or who wins or loses in the story) can also give you insight about a group's values and culture. And fantasies may be a way for groups to deal with sensitive issues in an indirect way.

By describing how people in groups come to share a common social reality, symbolic convergence theory explains how groups make decisions and make sense of the decision-making process.[9] It points out that groups, like individuals, have unique "personalities," cultures, or an identity built on shared symbolic representations related to the group and that these cultures evolve through the adoption of fantasy themes or group stories. A group's identity converges through these shared fantasies. Just as we try to understand an individual's behavior by taking into account "what sort of person she is," we must do the same for groups. Reflecting on the stories a group tells, which may at first seem off the topic, can give you insight into a group's personality, culture, values, and identity.

Structuration Theory

Another contemporary theoretical approach to help us understand how people behave in small groups is offered by Anthony Giddens[10] and further advanced by communication researcher Marshall Scott Poole and his colleagues.[11] **Structuration theory** provides a general framework that explains how people use rules and resources to interact in a social system. According to Poole, structuration explains how groups produce and reproduce social systems through group members' use of rules and resources in interaction. At first glance, this concept may seem complicated because of abstract terms;[12] however, we have already talked about two important terms in the definition—rules and systems.

A system, as you recall, is composed of many interdependent elements. Rules are explicit or implied prescriptions that affect how people behave in a group (system). "Don't talk while others are talking" and "Don't leave the meeting until the boss says everyone is dismissed" are examples of rules. These rules determine how the group structures itself and performs tasks, and how group members talk to one another. Structuration theory suggests that when we join a new group we use rules we learned in other groups to structure our behavior. For example, when you walked into your first college class, you probably drew on your experiences as a high-school student to know how to act. But groups also create their own rules and resources to determine what is appropriate and inappropriate. You learned that a college class is similar to but not exactly like high school. You also know that different classes have different rules or structure; some classes have informal rules, whereas others have more formal ones. One teacher may deduct points for lack of attendance, whereas another teacher may not take roll at all. How communication rules are organized is based on factors both internal and external to the group. Structuration theory helps explain why and how groups develop the rules and behavior patterns they adopt. It can be especially useful for understanding group communication within broader organizational cultures.[13]

For example, a group of jurors in a trial draws on rules each juror has observed from other juries and from dramatic depictions of jury deliberations. These rules guide individual behaviors in the group, which in turn *structure* further group communication. Structuration theory explains how such institutional antecedents are produced and reproduced through group interactions.[14]

Functional Theory

Much of this book aims to help you identify and enact behaviors that will help your groups reach intended goals. The term **function** refers to the effect or consequence of a given behavior within a group system. For example, communication can function to help a group make decisions or manage conflict. Communication has an effect on the group; it has a function. The notion of function is a useful idea that helps us conceptualize connections among behaviors and outcomes. Theories that concern themselves with group functions, then, are those that seek to identify and explain behaviors that help or allow a group to achieve its goals. Functional relationships exist within a group when an outcome occurs as a consequence of a specific behavior, which in turn was intended to produce the consequence.[15]

In Chapter 1 we identified group task competencies and group relationship competencies; in Chapter 4 we will discuss task roles and maintenance roles; Chapters 8 and 11 will introduce a *functional approach* to group problem solving and leadership. All these discussions are grounded in functional theories that explain how communication in groups functions to promote appropriate consequences—sound reasoning and critical thinking, preventing errors, and building productive relationships among group members.[16]

REVIEW

Theoretical Perspectives for the Study of Small Group Communication

1. Social exchange theory: Groups remain attractive to their members so long as the rewards of group membership exceed the costs.

2. Systems theory: The small group is an open system of interdependent elements, employing input variables and process variables to yield output.

3. Symbolic convergence theory: Group members develop a group consciousness and identity through the sharing of fantasies or stories which are often chained together and have a common theme.

4. Structuration theory: People use rules and resources in interaction to structure social systems.

5. Functional theory: Communication in groups functions to promote sound reasoning, preventing errors and building productive relationships among members.

New Technologies and Small Group Communication Theory

Like movable type, the telegraph, and the telephone, new information technologies are changing the way we live by restructuring how we communicate. Many group decisions in businesses and organizations are already computer assisted. Electronic messaging, the Internet, teleconferencing, and store-and-forward facilities smooth the flow of communication, even among participants who are often not face-to-face. The term **group decision support system (GDSS)** refers to any "computer-based information system used to support intellectual collaborative work."[17] GDSSs include technological support for agenda setting, rules for discussion such as parliamentary procedure, and communication technologies that allow multiple users to interact simultaneously.

We have only begun to imagine how these new technologies will affect group decision making over time. For now, though, we can consider them in light of some of the theories just discussed. For example, the use of technology can heighten or diminish the rewards and costs associated with group communication as viewed through social exchange theory. From a rules perspective, technologies impose their own sets of prescriptions for behavior that must be followed in order for successful communication to occur. As input and process variables within a system, GDSSs reshape group interaction as well as the resulting output variables. Depending on group members' reactions to technology, GDSSs can serve as the referents for group fantasy themes and become part of the group's shared reality.

Structuration theory is perhaps best suited to understanding the impact of technologies on groups. This theory shows that communication technologies such as GDSSs can be understood as structures—rules and resources.[18] Thus, theory can and should inform the development of such technologies insofar as they are *social* technologies.[19] Technology does not necessarily result in any particular group outcome; it is how the group works technology into its interaction that has the impact.

New technologies will increasingly reshape how groups make decisions and solve problems. Indeed, they are already a regular part of campus life for most students. The use of technology in both personal and organizational communication can provide greater structure and thus keep a group on task. We will discuss the impact of technology on groups and teams throughout the book and focus on organizational group and team settings in Chapter 12.

Describing Elements of Group and Team Communication

A model that takes into account all the possible sender, receiver, and message variables in a small group would be hopelessly complicated even before it could be designed to include other variables central to the study of small group communication. Students must consequently settle for a less-comprehensive model but one that suggests the features and relationships critical to an understanding of small group communication.

Figure 2.1 represents such a descriptive model. This framework depicts small group communication as a constellation of variables, each related to every other. Communication—what you say and how you say it—establishes and maintains the relationships among these essential variables. This model thus reflects a systems approach to group and team communication. Chapters 3, 4, and 11 present an in-depth discussion of these variables; for now, note the brief discussion that follows.

Communication   At its essence, communication is the process of acting on information. Human communication comprises what people say, how they say it, and to whom they say it. This is the primary object of study in small group communication research.

Leadership   In Chapter 1, part of the definition of small group communication concerned mutual influence. Leadership is behavior that exerts influence on the group.

Goals   All groups have goals. A goal may be to provide therapy for members, to complete some designated task, or simply to have a good time. Individual group members also have goals. Often individual goals complement the group goal; sometimes, though, they do not.

Norms   Norms are rules that establish which behaviors are permitted or encouraged within the group and which are forbidden or discouraged. Every group, from your family to the president's cabinet, develops and maintains norms or rules. Some norms are formal, such as when a group must use parliamentary procedure. Others are informal, such as the fact that a group always begins meetings fifteen minutes late.

Roles   Roles are sets of expectations people hold for themselves and for others in a given context. People play different roles in different groups. Researchers have identified several roles that need to be filled in order for a small group to reach maximum satisfaction and productivity.

Figure 2.1 Constellation of Variables in Small Group Communication

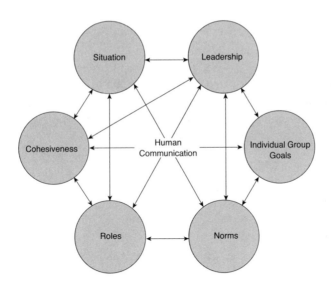

Cohesiveness   Cohesiveness is the degree of attraction group members feel toward one another and toward the group. Feelings of loyalty help unite the group.

Situation   The context in which group communication occurs is of paramount importance. The task is significant, but many other important situational variables exist, such as group size, the physical arrangement of group members, the location or setting, the group's purpose, even the amount of stress placed on the group by time constraints or other internal or external pressures. We will examine each of these situational variables later in the book.

The combined effect of these variables results in group outcomes. A group or team accomplishes something. Group and team outcomes include solving problems, making decisions, managing conflict, or even making money. Small group communication theory seeks to explain the relationships among these and other variables and to make predictions about group outcomes. Thus, the theories presented in this book help manage most of the complexity and uncertainty that surface at every level of group and team interaction. A good theoretical understanding of small groups, coupled with an expanded repertoire of communicative behavior, is the recipe for developing group communication competence—the objective of this book.

Putting Principles into Practice

The theories discussed throughout this book explain consistencies in communicative behavior that researchers have observed within small groups. If you can attain a theoretical grasp of small group communication, you can more successfully predict and control behavior.

As you observe groups of which you are a member, keep the following in mind:

▶ Theories provide explanations of behaviors that let us predict the likely consequences of various actions. Use the theories discussed in this chapter to help predict the probable consequences of various actions.

▶ Social exchange theory describes how satisfaction with a group relates to the relationship between the rewards and costs of group membership. Do a simple cost–benefit analysis to help you understand group members' behaviors.

▶ Systems theory can help you organize your observations into input variables, process variables, and output variables. Its primary application to small group communication is as an organizational strategy. Use systems theory to help you understand how your group's system relates to individual systems within it and the broader systems of which it is a part.

▶ Symbolic convergence theory reminds us that groups, like individuals, have personalities that we must understand and adapt to in order to be most effective. Explore the ways in which your group's "personality" relates to other variables such as rules, roles, and decision making.

▶ Structuration theory directs us to the power of rules and resources to structure interaction and outcomes. Identify existing rules and resources to enhance your influence in any group.

▶ Functional theories explain the connections between behaviors and their consequences in groups.

▶ One descriptive model for small group interaction is composed of seven variables: communication, leadership, goals, norms, roles, cohesiveness, and situation. Use these categories to help structure your thinking about groups.

As you read the rest of the book, continue to seek ways to apply what you're learning. The practicality of our theories is measured only by how we can use them to be more effective group leaders, members, and scholars.

PRACTICE

1. Make a list of informal theories you have about an ordinary day (for example, Professor X is boring, I'm afraid of speaking in class, etc.). On what basis did you formulate these theories? How do they affect your behavior? What might cause you to alter them?

2. Take a few minutes to reflect on rules that govern your behavior in groups. Write four or five of these as *if. . . . then* (condition/action) statements (for example, "*if* someone in the group addresses me directly, then it is my responsibility to respond"). Share and discuss your rules with others in your group. See if others in your group agree with your list. How do these rules contribute or detract from effective group communication?

Notes

1. Frank E. X. Dance and Carl E. Larson, *The Functions of Human Communication: A Theoretical Approach* (New York: Holt, Rinehart & Winston, 1976) 4.

2. George A. Kelly, *A Theory of Personality: The Psychology of Personal Constructs* (New York: Norton, 1963) 18.

3. Dean Barnlund, *Interpersonal Communication: Survey and Studies* (Boston: Houghton Mifflin, 1968).

4. Dean Barnlund, "Toward a Meaning-Centered Philosophy of Communication," in Kenneth G. Johnson et al., eds., *Nothing Never Happens* (Beverly Hills, CA: Glencoe Press, 1974) 213.

5. Stephen W. Littlejohn, *Theories of Human Communication,* 7th ed. (Belmont, CA: Wadsworth, 1996).

6. John K. Brilhart, *Effective Group Discussion,* 8th ed. (Dubuque, IA: Brown, 1995) 26.

7. Ernest Bormann, *Small Group Communication: Theory and Practice,* 3rd ed. (New York: HarperCollins, 1990).

8. Ernest Bormann, "Symbolic Convergence Theory and Communication in Group Decision Making," in R. Y. Hirokawa and M. S. Poole, eds., *Communication and Group Decision Making,* 2nd ed. (Beverly Hills, CA: Sage, 1996) 221.

9. Kathleen M. Propp and Gary Kreps, "A Rose by Any Other Name: The Vitality of Group Communication Research," *Communication Studies* 45 (1994): 7–19.

10. See Anthony Giddens, *New Rules of Sociological Method,* 2nd ed. (Palo Alto, CA.: Stanford University Press, 1993), and Anthony Giddens, *Studies in Social and Political Theory* (New York: Basic Books, 1979).

11. Marshall Scott Poole, David R. Seibold, and Robert D. McPhee, "A Structurational Approach to Theory Building in Group Decision-Making Research," in R. Y. Hirokawa and M. S. Poole, eds., *Communication and Group Decision Making,* 2nd ed. (Beverly Hills, CA: Sage, 1996).

12. Pooler, Seibold, and McPhee, "A Structurational Approach to Theory Building in Group Decision-Making Research."

13. Diane F. Witmer, "Communication and Recovery: Structuration as an Ontological Approach to Organizational Culture," *Communication Monographs* 64 (1997): 324–49.

14. Sunwolf and David R. Seibold, "Jurors' Intuitive Rules for Deliberation: A Structurational Approach to Communication in Jury Decision Making," *Communication Monographs* 65 (1998): 282–307

15. Marshall Scott Poole, "Group Communication Theory," in Lawrence R. Frey, ed., *The Handbook of Small Group Research* (Thousand Oaks, CA: Sage, 1996).

16. Dennis Gouran and Randy Y. Hirokawa, "Functional Theory and Communication in Decision-Making Groups: An Expanded View," in R. Y. Hirokawa and M. S. Poole, eds., *Communication and Group Decision-Making* (Thousand Oaks, CA: Sage, 1996).

17. Leonard M. Jessup and Joseph S. Valacich, eds., *Group Support Systems* (New York: Macmillan, 1992).

18. M. Scott Poole and Michele H. Jackson, "Communication Theory and Group Support Systems," in Leonard M. Jessup and Joseph S. Valacich, eds., *Group Support Systems* (New York: Macmillan, 1992).

19. M. Scott Poole and G. L. DeSanctis, "A Study of Influence in Computer-Mediated Group Decision Making," *MIS Quarterly* 12 (1988): 625–44.

Objectives:

After studying this chapter,
you will be able to:

► Discuss two classification systems of
interpersonal needs and describe how
they relate to group formation.

► Explain the potential conflict between
individual goals and group goals.

► Suggest ways of establishing mutuality of
concern in a work group.

► Identify and explain four factors that are
elements of interpersonal attraction.

► Identify and describe three factors in
group attraction.

► Facilitate a group's movement through
the initial stages of its formation.

► Apply your knowledge of group
formation toward greater effectiveness
as a communicator.

Group
Formation

"Coming together is a beginning; keeping together is progress; working together is success."

— Henry Ford, Sr.

Are you considering or being considered for membership in any particular group right now? A fraternal organization? A sports club? A political-action group? Are you thinking about getting married? Granted, a marriage starts with only two people, but it has a way of becoming a group of three or more.

To which groups do you already belong? Can you identify a circle of friends you might refer to as "your group"? Do you belong to clubs? Teams? You can probably generate a rather long list of groups that you either belonged to in the past or are involved with in the present. From the moment you are born into your first group—your family—you belong to a succession of groups. Some are formally organized, some are loosely structured; some you choose, others you are assigned to. But membership in groups does not happen randomly. Groups meet specific needs and perform special functions. To understand group formation, then, requires that you examine the needs and functions around which groups form.

On learning of the subject for this book, a friend remarked, "I don't know how you can even stand to think about it. I hate committee work. I'll do anything I can to avoid working in groups. I'd rather do things my own way." This fairly prevalent attitude toward groups ignores the pervasive influence that groups have on people's lives (discussed in Chapter 1). When asked if there wasn't at least one group in his life that provided him with some pleasure, the friend faltered, "There is my bowling team . . . and, come to think of it, I enjoyed working with a group of political strategists in the last election. My book club is pretty interesting, . . . and of course there is my family." He added, "But there's a difference between *those* groups and the committees I have to serve on as part of my job." Although this person might be in the wrong job, groups people choose to belong to differ from those to which they are assigned. Even the groups and committees people are assigned to at work or in school are the result of choices they have made. Professors do not enjoy every university committee on which they serve, but these committees are a part of the larger group that they *did* choose—the academic community. You may not have selected the group you work with in class, but you *did* select that class. Therefore, it is safe to say that all of the groups people belong to reflect *personal decisions*. Some groups they chose directly; others resulted from prior choices they made.

Why Do People Join Groups?

Understanding the many reasons that draw people to groups can help explain the complexity of small group interaction. Groups are many things to many people. To one member of a committee, the group's problem is an exciting vehicle toward greater self-understanding. To another member, it is merely an uninteresting but necessary obstacle on the way to reaching a personal goal. To all, the formation of groups—from families to teams to corporate boards—is part of a biological imperative that is simply part of our species; we are, all of us, social animals by nature.[1] Be that as it may, individuals differ dramatically in their motivation for joining the group and in their commitment and contribution to it. This chapter will first examine the needs and goals that lead individuals to join small groups; then it will explore the impact of these needs and goals on small group communication.

The answer to the question "Why do people join groups?" has many dimensions. These can be placed into five broad categories: (1) **interpersonal needs**, (2) individual goals, (3) group and team goals, (4) interpersonal attraction, and (5) group attraction.

Interpersonal Needs

Maslow's Theory

Abraham Maslow has asserted that all humans have basic needs and that these needs can be arranged in a hierarchy; that is, people do not concern themselves with higher-level needs until lower-level needs are satisfied.[2]

Physiological Needs   Maslow termed the first level of needs at the bottom of the hierarchy physiological needs. People's physiological needs are for air, water, and food.

Safety Needs   Safety needs are for security and protection. Maslow called these two levels *survival needs;* satisfaction of these needs is necessary for basic human existence. During childhood years, the family satisfies these needs. The formation of street gangs may also be a response to these needs.[3]

Once survival needs are fulfilled, the higher-level needs that Maslow called *psychological needs*—the need to belong, the need for esteem, and the need for self-actualization—become more important. These needs may affect people's group memberships throughout their lives. See Figure 3.1 to understand how interpersonal needs form a hierarchy.

Belongingness Need   People need to feel that they are a part of some group. Here again, the family provides a sense of belonging for children, but as they get older they begin to look outside the family to satisfy this need. Peer groups gain special importance during adolescence. At that time, people's need for affiliation is at its strongest.

Esteem Need   Once people have developed a sense of belonging, Maslow says that they have a need for respect or esteem. They need to feel not only that they are accepted, but also that they are worthwhile and valued by others.

Self-Actualization Need   The need for self-actualization differs from the other four needs. The former needs Maslow calls *deficiency needs* because individuals perceive them as a void to fill by drawing on the resources of other people. Maslow calls self-actualization a *being* need. It involves people trying to be all that they can be and living life to its fullest. They are ready to function as autonomous beings, operating independently in quest of their own full potential. They no longer need groups to take care of their deficiencies; instead, they need groups in which to find and express their wholeness. Although this need level is perhaps the most difficult to grasp conceptually, Maslow's hierarchy is consistent: People need groups to satisfy interpersonal needs. People also clearly differ from one

Figure 3.1 Hierarchy of Interpersonal Needs

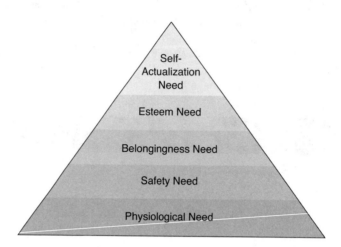

another in their motivations for joining groups. Their differing motivations may be reflected in their communicative behavior in the group. Those who simply want to belong may interact differently from those who need the group's esteem and respect. The higher we move up Maslow's hierarchy, the greater is the importance of communication in our need satisfaction.[4]

Schutz's Theory

In an elaborate theory of interpersonal behavior. William Schutz suggests that three basic human needs influence individuals as they form and interact in groups: **Inclusion, control, and affection**.[5] Individuals' needs vary, but groups often provide them with settings in which such needs can be satisfied.

Inclusion Need   Just as Maslow postulates in his belongingness need, Schutz says people join groups to fulfill their need for inclusion. They need to be recognized as unique individuals and to feel understood. When people try to understand someone, the implication is that the individual is worthy of their time and effort. In this respect, Schutz's inclusion need is also related to Maslow's esteem need.

Control Need   The need for control is a need for status and power. People need to have some control over themselves, and others, and sometimes to give others some control over them, such as when they seek guidance and direction.

Affection Need   The need for affection drives people to give and receive emotional warmth and closeness.

In a broad sense, groups are more than collections of people with common goals; they are arenas in which individual needs are satisfied or frustrated. Schutz asserts that people join groups to satisfy needs for inclusion, control, and affection and that these needs influence group process throughout the life of the group. He has observed that in the initial stages of group formation, communication aims primarily toward inclusion needs. Group members are friendly but cautious as they try to evaluate one another and try to be accepted by other members. As the group develops, control needs become more evident: Members contest issues and vie for leadership. Schutz observes that as conflicts are resolved, people turn toward affection needs. Members characteristically express positive feelings in this phase. The progression, Schutz says, is cyclical.

Continuing Cycle of Group Process From Schutz's perspective, group formation is a process not limited to the initial coming together of the group. Rather, formation patterns repeat themselves as the group develops over time. Group decision making involves a series of smaller decisions on the way toward achieving the group's primary goal. For example, a group of engineers planning a bridge must make decisions about the location and frequency of their meetings as well as the design and materials for the bridge. A group progresses through developmental phases throughout its life (as will be discussed in Chapter 8), and this cyclical pattern of formation and reformation occurs whenever the group approaches a new meeting and a new decision. If this process could be visualized, it might look something akin to a large jellyfish moving through the water. The jellyfish floats in the water in a relatively disorganized state until it needs to move forward. Then it organizes itself, contracts, and propels itself through the water until it returns to a restful, less-organized state. Group process moves through a similar series of contractions until it reaches its ultimate goal.

A group is defined, in part, by a common purpose. Within that purpose are several smaller goals. As a group reaches each of these goals, it momentarily loses a bit of its definition until a new goal replaces the old. As people accomplish each new goal, they begin a new cycle of inclusion, control, and affection behaviors. The following example illustrates this point:

Harv: Well, it's been hard, but we've finally found a date for the banquet that we can all agree on.

Juanita: For sure. For a while I thought we'd never agree, but I think we've made the best decision now.

Betsy: Yeah. We're over the major hurdle. Feels good, doesn't it?

Phil: Amen. We're organized now and ready to go for it! This is getting to be fun.
               (Laughter, followed by a pause)

Juanita: Well, here we are. What do we do next?

Phil: I guess we ought to talk about the theme and the speakers.

Harv: Hold on there! The speakers are irrelevant if no one is there to hear them. We've got to talk first about how we're going to publicize.

Phil: C'mon. Harv. How can we publicize if we don't even have a theme?

Betsy: Here we go again.

In this example you can see the end of one cycle and the beginning of the next. Members expressed positive feelings about the group and its accomplishments and halted a little in their conversation before regrouping for another attack on a new facet of their problem. The sense of cohesiveness peaks during the affection phase and then falls off, only to rebuild around the next task. Like the jellyfish, which coordinates its process around its task of propulsion, the small group does not end up back where it started. The whole process moves

People cluster in groups to meet interpersonal needs and goals. Why do you interact in groups?

forward. To say that the phases are cyclical, then, is somewhat misleading. Certain types of communicative behaviors recur, but the whole process moves forward. Frank E. X. Dance captured the essence of this process when he described human communication as being like a helix.[6] Like a bedspring, the helix is both linear and circular. It turns in on itself and yet always moves forward. Seen in this light, group formation does not cease but pulses throughout the life of the group.

REVIEW

Schutz's Theory

INDIVIDUALS JOIN GROUPS IN PART TO SATISFY THREE NEEDS:

▶ Inclusion: They want to be recognized and feel included. They also have needs to share and include others in their activities.
▶ Control: People have varying needs to control or to be controlled that groups can satisfy.
▶ Affection: Individuals satisfy their affection needs through giving and receiving emotional support in groups.

Groups pass through observable, cyclical phases of these needs.

Individual Goals

Theories of psychological and interpersonal needs provide some of the bases for group formation. So, too, do individual goals. Goals have a more tangible and obvious effect on your

People often form groups simply because they enjoy the same activities. What groups do you belong to like this?

selection of group memberships. What is it that you want out of life? Prestige? Status? Power? Anonymity? Recreation? Education? Personal growth? In other words, what goals do you have that exist apart from any particular group membership?

Individual goals are instrumental in determining which groups people join. Obviously, if people enjoy arranging flowers and wish to improve their skills, they may join garden clubs. If personal growth is an aim, people will join a support group. If they desire status and power, they will seek membership in an elite social or professional group. Sometimes the prestige associated with a particular group is enough to make membership attractive. This is often a motivation for joining a particular sorority or fraternity. Whatever their individual goals may be, people bring those goals with them when they join groups.

Group and Team Goals

Group and team goals are identifiable accomplishments that transcend the group members' individual goals. Certain professional and fraternal organizations serve community needs. For example, the Lions Club is well known for its sponsorship of research devoted to finding cures for eye diseases and preventing blindness. Individual members have many goals for joining the club: The chance to rub elbows with other professionals from the community, camaraderie and fellowship, the prestige of membership, the sense of belonging, or a genuine interest in serving the community. Whereas individual goals may vary, the group goal takes precedence over them.

Of course, somewhere along the way an individual or small group of individuals proposed the group goals, which suggests some initial commonality of purpose among individual goals. Once individuals adopt group goals, however, their individual goals are superseded. The many needs and goals that individuals bring to small groups may be incompatible with the group's goal. This is a potential source of problems in small group communication. Consider the following situation:

A CASE STUDY

The First Church of Roseville has a building-and-grounds committee. This committee, charged with overseeing the regular maintenance and upkeep of the church building and surrounding property, makes sure that the lawns are mowed, the hedges trimmed, the furnace maintained, the roof patched, and so forth. The committee consists of the following members:

Roberto Bomblast. Roberto has been an accountant for a local firm for twenty-three years. He has never felt that his firm has given him a chance to show his true leadership ability. He sees the church committee, of which he is chairperson, as his big chance to prove himself and show the world what a truly fine administrator he is. He has another ulterior motive: He wants very much to be the new part-time business manager for the church when "Old George," the present manager, dies or retires. This committee, then, is Roberto's stepping-stone to greatness.

Marmalade. No one is sure of Marmalade's real name. He was found ten years ago wandering around the sanctuary saying, "Wow . . . wow . . . wowwwww . . . wowwwwwwwwww." The church members took him under their wing, and he has been sweeping floors and doing other odd jobs around the church since then. The pastor thought it would "do Marmalade some good" to get involved with a responsible committee, so he assigned him to this one.

Latasha Greene. Latasha is a young attorney who joined the church last year because she enjoys its outstanding music program. She has been dismayed, though, to find church governance dominated by white males. "What decade are we in?" she wonders "Don't they know it's a new century?" She is continually annoyed when men like Roberto Bomblast and Thurman Jester act as if they are in charge of everything.

Merry Placid. In all of her forty-seven years, Merry has not been outside of her home state. She loves her country, her state, her community, her home, and her family. She especially loves her church because of the sense of warmth and community she feels there. She has served on every committee in the church, and when she is not serving on a committee she misses a sense of community. Merry has high needs for inclusion. She is pleased to be on this committee.

Thurman Jester. Ever since his vacation trip to Dallas, Thurman wears a white belt and off-white shoes to work every day (and strongly urges his employees at the insurance office to do the same). He is committed to keeping up with the trendsetters, and Dallas, he feels, is where trends are set. Thurman was also impressed by a 40-foot neon cross he spotted outside a church in Dallas. Thurman is highly motivated by control needs.

Imagine that this group has come together for its first monthly meeting, that the church custodian has just resigned, and that the roof of the church leaks. The group's goal is to maintain the building and grounds. All the members are, to some degree, committed to the goal. However, this commitment means different things to different members. An individual need or goal shapes each person's perception of what the group should be doing. Group members are aware of their personal goals, but most members are not aware that their behavior is also motivated by desires to satisfy interpersonal needs. Merry Placid may interpret her own behavior as a desire to serve, while her underlying, unconscious motive may be her need for inclusion. Thurman Jester wants to put a neon cross outside the church, but he may not be aware of his need to control others.

Needs and goals influence individuals' perceptions of group members and the group's task. Some individual goals are likely to overlap with group goals, while other individual goals will emerge from the group's focus. If a group goal is the desired end result of a group, and an individual goal is the desired end result of an individual, then individual and group goals will likely overlap in any given group. Differences between these goals may help or hinder the group. The conflict between individual and group goals is often the reason why some groups can't get off the ground.

This is the paradox of group membership: We often join groups to help us reach personal goals—which must be set aside, in part, for the group to succeed. Returning to the case of the church committee, try to imagine what the first meeting or two might be like. Each group member has a personal agenda—an individual goal—that will have a profound effect on his or her behavior in the group. Roberto seeks personal gain; Marmalade is being rehabilitated; Latasha wants to serve the church and be treated with the same respect afforded more experienced members; Merry just wants to feel a part of something; and Thurman wants to make his mark on the world with a 40-foot neon cross. Each of these characters will direct his or her communication in the group toward a particular goal, but none of their five goals is fully compatible with the more immediate need for fixing the leaky roof and hiring a new custodian. Although all the characters have come together ostensibly for the same purpose, each has a different idea of what the group should be doing. If each member pulls in a different direction, the results could be disastrous. The group may go nowhere, and, to compound matters, each member will probably perceive the others as being uncooperative. For this reason, groups must question their members' **mutuality of concern**—the degree to which members share the same level of commitment to a group—during the initial stages of group formation.[7]

Collaborating

E T H I C A L L Y

We often join groups to satisfy personal needs or reach personal goals. But is it ethical to join groups to promote personal objectives? Is it selfish?

In Chapter 1 we defined ethics as the beliefs, values, and moral principles by which we determine what is right and wrong. One test you can use as to whether it's right for you to join a group is the "win/win" test: Will both you and the group benefit from your membership and participation? If the answer is yes, everyone's a winner. If not, think twice before you head into an experience that may bring negative results.

Establishing Mutuality of Concern

When people join groups, they often assume that other group members share their commitment to the group's task. If a problem is to be solved, they take for granted that others view the problem in much the same way they do. However, as in the example of the building-and-grounds committee, each person brings a different perspective to the group.

Groups can also be frustrated because people bring different levels of commitment or concern to them. Suppose you have been appointed to a student-government group whose task is to recommend whether your college should institute a plus/minus grading system or continue with a straight A, B, C, and D grading policy. If you are a first- or second-year student, this policy change could have a direct effect on your grade-point average over your four years in college. If you are a graduating senior, a policy change would have little or no effect on you. Hence the level of concern over the problem can vary from member to member. Once again, individual goals interact with a group goal. Those affected directly by the problem will probably become more active in the group than those who are not as concerned with the problem. This can lead to needless conflict, as when some members resent having to carry the bulk of the workload.

The degree to which members are concerned with the group's task needs to be clarified at the outset. All group members should clearly state their personal needs and goals regarding the topic area. Clarifying mutuality of concern can resolve a lot of misunderstanding and avoid needless conflict.

Although individual needs and goals may bring a group together in the first place, they can also break a group apart. The success or failure of a group depends, in part, on the degree to which its goal is assumed by individuals as their own. Unsatisfied or unclarified individual needs and goals can become hidden agendas—private goals toward which individuals work while seeming to work toward the group goal. Such hidden agendas can be extremely disruptive to the group. Establishing mutuality of concern can help reduce this negative influence.

Culture is another important factor in balancing individual and group needs and goals. The value placed on individuality or conformity varies widely. In Japan, China, Israel, and Russia, for example, individuals tend to acquiesce to the will of the group, as a high degree of conformity is expected. As we noted in Chapter 1, North Americans and Europeans are thought to be more individualistic.[8] When we come to the group, our cultures—whatever they may be—come with us. These differing cultures, as well as individual differences, can contribute to a kind of tension in the group that communication scholars J. Kevin Barge and Lawrence Frey describe as "the product of two ideas being equally valid when considered alone, but contradictory when paired."[9] They give the following pairs of statements as examples:

I need to behave consistently in a group.

I need to adapt my behavior to changes in the group situation.

It is important to fit in with and be like other group members, even when doing so goes against my personal beliefs.

It is important to maintain my individuality when I am in a group.

Good group members defer their own needs to the larger needs of the group.

Good group members act independently within the group and pursue their personal agendas.[10]

In any given situation the interaction of individual and group needs will cause one of four possible outcomes:

✗ (1) Individual and group needs may be so diverse that they interfere with each other with no positive effects accruing either to individuals within the group, such as smokers, or to the group as a whole. (2) Group interaction may result in the realization of goals desired by the group as a whole, while individual needs are not met. (3) Individual needs may be realized by one or more group members to the detriment or destruction of the group. (4) Individual and group needs may blend so completely that the needs realized by the group as a whole are the same needs individuals wish to realize.[11]

©The New Yorker Collection 2000 Leo Cullum from cartoonbank.com

In the ideal, fully integrated group this fourth alternative is realized. Mutuality of concern can merge individual and group needs and goals.

Aside from the relationships among interpersonal needs, personal goals, and group goals, two other factors have an influence on people's selection of groups: Interpersonal attraction and group attraction.

Interpersonal Attraction

Often people are attracted to groups because they are attracted to the people who compose them. Of the many factors that influence interpersonal attraction, four of these are especially significant: Similarity, complementarity, proximity/contact/interaction, and physical attractiveness.

Similarity

One of the strongest influences in interpersonal attraction is similarity. Remember your first day on campus? That feeling of newness, strangeness, and aloneness? You needed a friend, and with luck you found one. Who did you look for to be your friend? Did you seek out someone you perceived to be very different from you? Probably not. If the principle of similarity in interpersonal attraction applies here, you probably looked for someone to talk to who appeared to be in the same situation—another lonely newcomer, or perhaps someone dressed in a style similar to yours.

Who are your closest friends? Do you share many of the same attitudes, beliefs, and values? Do you enjoy the same activities? More than likely you do. People are often attracted to those they consider to be like them. A probable explanation for this is that similar backgrounds, beliefs, attitudes, and values make it easier to understand one another—and all people like to feel that they are understood.

One danger of the similarity factor in group formation is that our tendency to be attracted to people like ourselves may result in a group that is too homogeneous to approach a complex task effectively. Indeed, research on classroom groups found that by a two-to-one margin, students reported their worst experiences occurred in groups they had formed themselves. Their best experiences occurred in groups to which professors had assigned them.[12]

Complementarity

In reading the previous section on similarity, some of you probably shook your heads and said, "No, that's not the way it is at all. My best friend and I are about as similar as an orchid and a fire hydrant!" No generalization is entirely true, and so it is with the principle of similarity. Although there is some truth to the statement that birds of a feather flock together, it is also true that opposites attract. Thibaut and Kelley suggest that some interpersonal relationships are based primarily on similarity, whereas others are based on **complementarity**.[13] At times people may be attracted to others who exhibit qualities that they do not have but that they admire. Although the principle of similarity seems to be the more pervasive phenomenon, everyone can cite instances of complementarity. For at least a partial explanation of attraction through complementarity, consider Schutz's theory of interpersonal needs, discussed earlier in this chapter. According to this theory, a person who has a high need to control would be most compatible with a person who has a high need to be controlled. The same would be true of needs to express and to receive inclusion and affection. These are complementary needs rather than similar needs.

Proximity, Contact, and Interaction

You tend to be attracted to people who are physically close to you, who live or work with you, and whom you see or communicate with often. If you know that you have to live or work close to another person, you may ignore that person's less desirable traits in order to minimize potential conflict. Furthermore, proximity, contact, and interaction breed familiarity, and familiarity has a positive influence on interpersonal attraction.[14] Interaction with another person helps you get to know that other person, and through this process the two of you may uncover similarities and discover ways in which you can satisfy each other's interpersonal needs. The actual physical distance between people, then, does not influence attraction, but the interpersonal possibilities illuminated by proximity, contact, and interaction do.

Physical Attractiveness

At least in the initial stages of interpersonal attraction, physical attractiveness influences people. If a person is physically beautiful, others tend to want to affiliate with him or her.[15] However, evidence indicates that this factor diminishes in importance over time and that—at least in North American cultures—physical beauty is more important to males than to females.[16]

When the telephone was first introduced, its designers believed it would be used only for brief business-to-business communications. The widespread use of telephones for personal conversations was something the designers had not envisioned; it was an invention of the users of the new technology.

Increasing use of computer-mediated communication will, no doubt, reshape the process of group formation in ways we're only beginning to understand as more and more interpersonal communication shifts to this medium. Some research already suggests that norms guiding the use of technology develop locally within particular groups and that those norms are limited by the boundaries of that particular group.[17] While forming new groups, we are also pioneers and inventors in computer-mediated communication!

For additional information about group formation and development, check out the Website at

http://www.san.orglip/cds/cmp/hwgroup.htm

In sum, people seem to be attracted to others who are likely to understand them, who can fulfill their needs, who complement their personalities, and who are physically appealing. Those individuals constitute a powerful influence on people's selection of groups.

Group Attraction

Although individuals may be attracted to a group because they are attracted to the members who compose it, they may also be attracted to the group itself. Such attraction usually focuses on the group's activities or goals, or simply on the desirability of group membership.

Group Activities

Although research is not extensive in this area, it seems fairly clear that people who are interested in the same activities tend to form groups.[18] People who enjoy intellectual pursuits may join literary-discussion groups. Bridge players may join bridge clubs. Beyond these obvious examples, people may be attracted to the activities of a group in a more general sense. Some may join groups simply because they enjoy going to regular meetings and joining in group discussions, regardless of the group's specific aims or goals. The structure and human contact provided by groups are potentially rewarding in and of themselves.

Group Goals

Another factor that may attract people to a group is the goal to which it is dedicated. If, for example, people believe that the spread of nuclear power must be curtailed, they may join a group dedicated to making it illegal. If they are committed to preserving and protecting the natural environment, they may join American Forests, the Sierra Club, the Audubon Society, or any organization that professes a goal similar to their own.

Group attraction includes elements that have already been mentioned: Similarity in interpersonal attraction and the relationship between individual and group goals.

Group Membership

Sometimes it is not a group's members, activities, or goals that attract people but membership itself. Potential members may perceive that membership in an exclusive club or honor society will bring them prestige, acceptance, or professional benefits outside of the group. For example, company officials may expect a young executive to belong to some civic group because such memberships provide good public relations for the firm.

The need for affiliation—Maslow's belongingness need and Schutz's inclusion need—can make group membership attractive. You probably know of professional committee members who move from group to group because their lives seem incomplete without some type of group membership. The need for affiliation is basic to human nature. Group membership can help satisfy that need.

Homogeneity and Diversity in Groups

Earlier in the chapter we noted the dynamic tension between individual goals and group goals. Each of us seeks to be independent and autonomous, while depending on the groups to which we belong. We need to influence and control, and also need to be influenced and controlled by others. Even in the most homogeneous groups, varying levels of these needs coupled with differing views toward the group and its goals can make for an interesting time and a fascinating field for study.

As we join or are assigned to groups, we are likely to find that those groups include increasing diversity. Research showing that 75 percent of new, entry-level workers in the United States are women and/or minorities is but one indication of this trend.[19]

What if we have a choice? Are groups that are more homogeneous in terms of race, gender, culture, and general ability more effective or less effective than more-diverse groups? Which should we choose? Perhaps not surprisingly, there are advantages and disadvantages to each. There is some evidence that over time diverse groups can be more effective, because they include more potential in terms of skills and approaches coupled with the ability to address the needs of an equally diverse base of clients or customers.[20]

When comparing homogeneous work groups with diverse work groups, researchers find that diverse work groups often have more trouble at the outset, but over time become more productive than homogeneous groups. This makes sense. We are more comfortable with people whom we think are similar to us. This makes for easier interaction in the initial stages of group formation. With a little effort, though, diverse groups can find the common ground to make interaction work; their diversity is ultimately very positive in that it produces more flexibility, more options, and more ways of looking at a problem.[21]

Group Formation over Time

Once a group is formed, it continues to grow and develop over time. Many researchers have observed that group development follows fairly predictable stages. Perhaps the best-known scheme for these stages was advanced by Tuckman.[22] The initial stage is *forming*, a period characterized by anxiety and uncertainty about belonging to the group and a resulting cautiousness in behavior. The second stage, *storming*, competition, individuality, and conflict emerge as group members try to satisfy their individual needs. *Norming*, the third stage, is characterized by attempts to resolve earlier conflicts, often by negotiating clear guidelines for the group. *Performing* is the fourth stage. Cooperation and productive work are the hallmarks of this stage. Although not all groups neatly cycle through these stages, you will probably be able to detect forming, storming, and performing behaviors in many of the groups and teams in which you participate.

These stages are important to remember as you read this book. Developmental changes in the life of a group are related to many important group dynamics including conflict management, and leadership. We will revisit these phases of group development when we discuss a descriptive approach to group and team problem solving in Chapter 8.

REVIEW

Factors in Interpersonal Attraction

FACTORS	DEFINITION	COMMENTS
Similarity	The degree to which two people are alike	You tend to like people who resemble you in their thinking and experiences; it is reinforcing, and they are more likely than most to understand you.
Complementarity	The degree to which two people are compatibly different from each other	You tend to be attracted to people who possess qualities that you admire but do not yourself possess.
Proximity, contact, and interaction	The actual, physical availability of other people	Talking with others reveals their similar and complementary traits and, thus, their attractiveness to you.

Physical attractiveness	The perception of physical beauty or handsomeness	Especially important in the early stages of a relationship; less important after you get to know someone.

Factors in Group Attraction

FACTORS	DEFINITION	COMMENTS
Group activities	People interested in the same activities tend to group together	The mere structure and human contact of group activities may provide rewards.
Group goals	Attraction based on mutually shared goals	Civic groups, parent/teacher organizations, and environmental groups are examples.
Group membership	Attraction based on the rewards of membership per se	Membership is often seen as having prestige or status.

Putting Principles into Practice

The dynamic interrelatedness of all the variables that affect small group processes makes the study of small group communication challenging and exciting. As you continue through the rest of this book, it is important that you retain what you have previously learned. Only when you have fit all the puzzle pieces together can you see a clear picture of small group communication.

This chapter has zoomed in on one part of the puzzle: Those needs and goals that motivate people to join groups and that influence their behavior within those groups. In the initial stages of group development, uncertainty is at its peak—uncertainty about the group, about its goals, and about each member's place in it. How you communicate at this sensitive stage of group development provides the basis for future interaction. As you join new groups, keep in mind the following:

▶ At the first meeting of any new group, you may feel anxious. You may be uncertain about who the other members are, what each person's role is to be, and what to say to whom. At this stage, share a little information about yourself and encourage others to do the same. Many group leaders will ask participants to say a few words about themselves. This strategy breaks the ice and provides some familiarity on which to base further discussion. In short, it reduces people's uncertainty and helps them relax.

▶ Sometimes you do not choose the groups you belong to but are assigned to them, perhaps by a teacher, a supervisor, or an employer. When you are assigned to a group, look carefully at the group's goal. Then assess the resources that you can bring to accomplishing that goal. Evaluate the benefits that you can derive from the experience. Decide what your level of commitment is to the goal and the group.

Talk about it with the group, and begin establishing mutuality of concern.

▶ When you join a new group, ask yourself what attracts you to it: "Why am *I* a part of this group? What do *I* want to accomplish here? What are *my* goals? What do I *want* from these people . . . and what can I *give* to them?" Never assume that everyone in your group shares your level of commitment to the group and its task. Clarify this potential uncertainty by telling the group openly and honestly how you feel about the group and its task, with the clear expectation that others will do the same.

▶ You may find that you are attracted to a group only because you are attracted to its members. If that is so, think twice before you join. When a group is dedicated to a common purpose, its members will probably resent someone being there for purely social reasons.

▶ Once you have joined a group, watch to see if it passes through several stages of development.

▶ Diversity in a group's membership can provide real strength.

In sum, people are attracted to groups for different reasons and join groups to satisfy a variety of needs. An understanding of these factors in group formation should guide your communicative behavior in groups.

PRACTICE

1. Select two groups in which you are an active member—a study group, a club, or your family, for example. For each group, indicate as follows the importance to you of the various factors in group formation. What attracts you to these groups? What are their rewards? Use a scale of 1 ("very important") to 5 ("not at all important to me").

	GROUP 1	GROUP 2
Interpersonal needs		
Inclusion	_____	_____
Control	_____	_____
Affection	_____	_____
Interpersonal attraction		
Similarity	_____	_____
Complementarity	_____	_____
Proximity	_____	_____
Physical attractiveness	_____	_____
Group attraction		
Group activities	_____	_____
Group goals	_____	_____
Group membership	_____	_____

Compare your ratings of the two groups. Do you now have a better understanding of the roles these groups play in your life?

2. Make a list of the groups you are affiliated with. For each one, identify its members, its activities, and its goals. Then note your individual goals in regard to each group. Examine the results. What is your primary attraction to each group? Are your individual goals compatible with the group's goals? Do you have any hidden agendas? Do your answers to these questions explain any of your attitudes about or behaviors within these groups?

 Your companion Website has more practice activities, questionnaires, and checklists!
www.ablongman.com/beebe

Notes

1. For an illuminating discussion of this topic, see Steven Pinker, *How the Mind Works* (New York: Norton, 1997).

2. Abraham Maslow, *Toward a Psychology of Being,* 2nd ed. (Princeton, NJ: Van Nostrand, 1982).

3. Dwight Conquergood, "Homeboys and Hoods: Gang Communication and Cultural Space," in L. R. Frey, ed., *Group Communication in Context: Studies of Natural Groups* (Hillsdale, NJ: Erlbaum, 1994) 23–55.

4. Don Stacks, Mark Hickson III, and Sidney R. Hill, Jr., *Introduction to Communication Theory* (Chicago: Holt, Rinehart & Winston, 1991).

5. William Schutz, *The Interpersonal Underworld* (Palo Alto, CA: Science & Behavior Books, 1958).

6. Frank E. X. Dance, "A Helical Model of Communication," in Frank E. X. Dance, ed., *Human Communication Theory* (New York: Holt, Rinehart & Winston, 1967) 294–98.

7. For a full discussion of mutuality of concern, see Bobby Patton and Kim Giffin, *Decision-Making Group Interaction,* 3rd ed. (New York: HarperCollins, 1990) 118–19.

8. L. Mann, "Cross Cultural Studies of Small Groups," in H. Triandis, ed., *Handbook of Cross-Cultural Psychology,* vol. 5 (Boston: Allyn and Bacon).

9. J. Kevin Barge and Lawrence R. Frey, "Life in a Task Group," in Lawrence R. Frey and J. Kevin Barge, eds., *Managing Group Life: Communicating in Decision-Making Groups* (Boston: Houghton Mifflin, 1997) 39.

10. Barge and Frey, "Life in a Task Group" 39.

11. Charles S. Palazzo. "The Social Group: Definitions," in Robert S. Cathcart and Larry A. Samovar, eds., *Small Group Communication: A Reader,* 6th ed. (Dubuque, IA: Brown, 1991) 11–12.

12. Susan Brown Feichtner and Elaine Actis Davis, "Why Some Groups Fail: A Survey of Students' Experiences with Learning Groups," in Anne Goodsell, Michelle Maher, and Vincent Tinto, *Collaborative Learning: A Sourcebook for Higher Education* (University Park, PA: National Center on Postsecondary Teaching, Learning, and Assessment [NCTLA], 1997) 59–67.

13. John Thibaut and Harold Kelley, *The Social Psychology of Groups* (New Brunswick, NJ: Transaction Publishing, 1986).

14. Robert Zajonc, "Attitudinal Effects of Mere Exposure," *Journal of Personality and Social Psychology* 9 (1968): 1–29.

15. Marvin Shaw, *Group Dynamics: The Psychology of Small Group Behavior* (New York: McGraw-Hill, 1981) 93.

16. D. M. Buss, "Sex Differences in Mate Preferences: Evolutionary Hypotheses Tested in 37 Different Cultures," *Behavioral and Brain Sciences* 12 (1989): 1–49.

17. Tom Postmes, Russell Spears, and Martin Lea, "The Formation of Group Norms in Computer-Mediated Communication," *Communication Monographs* 26 (2000): 341–371.

18. Shaw, *Group Dynamics* 85.

19. J. H. Boyett and H. P. Conn, *Workplace 2000: The Revolution Reshaping American Business* (New York: Dutton, 1992).

20. John E. Farley, *Majority–Minority Relations* (Englewood Cliffs, NJ: Prentice Hall, 1995).

21. Kathy Fritz, "The Diversity Dilemma: Dealing with Difference," paper presented at the Vocation of a Lutheran Institution Conference, Selinsgrove, Pennsylvania, 1999.

22. B. W. Tuckman, "Developmental Sequence in Small Groups," *Psychological Bulletin* 63 (1965): 384–399.

Objectives:

After studying this chapter, you will be able to:

▶ Describe how an individual develops and defines self-concept.

▶ Identify the task, maintenance, and individual roles that group members assume.

▶ Identify several group norms that often develop in small group discussions.

▶ Recognize and adjust to cultural differences in group communication.

▶ Describe several effects of status differences on small group communication.

▶ Describe how five power bases affect relationships in small groups.

▶ Identify factors that foster trusting relationships with others.

▶ Apply guidelines for appropriate self-disclosure in small groups.

▶ Describe how relationships develop over time among group members.

Relating to Others in Small Groups

"No member of a crew is praised for the rugged individuality of his rowing."
—Ralph Waldo Emerson

D o you consider yourself to be a leader or a follower in small group meetings? Do you usually talk a lot or a little when you serve on a committee? Do you think you are a good or mediocre group member? Perhaps your answers depend on the quality of your relationships with others in the group.

Relationships are the ongoing connections you make with another person. In groups and teams, relationships are the feelings, roles, norms, status, and trust that both affect and reflect the quality of communication between you and others. If the members of your group are old friends, your relationships with them will obviously be different than if you have just met for the first time. Have you served on a committee with three or four other people that you felt were much better qualified than you were to contribute to the discussion? Your feeling of inferiority undoubtedly affected your relationship with the other group members. In small groups, and in other communication contexts as well, the quality of interpersonal relationships often determines what people say to one another.

Communication scholar Joann Keyton notes that

> "Relational communication in groups refers to the verbal and nonverbal messages
> that create the social fabric of a group by promoting relationships between and
> among group members. It is the affective or expressive dimension of group communi-
> cation as opposed to the instrumental, or task-oriented dimension."[1]

Relational communication theorists assert that every message people communicate to one another has both a content dimension and a relationship dimension. The content dimension of a message includes the specific information conveyed to someone. The relationship dimension involves message cues that provide hints about whether you like or dislike the person with whom you are communicating. For example, the formality of their language and nonverbal cues provide important information about the relationship between two individuals having a conversation. Whether you are giving a public speech, talking with your spouse, or communicating with another member of a small group, you are providing information about the feelings you have toward your listener as well as about *ideas* and *thoughts*.

This chapter will emphasize the relational elements that affect the quality of the relationships you establish with other group members. Specifically, it will concentrate on six variables that have an important effect on the relationships you establish with others in small groups: (1) the roles you assume, (2) the norms or standards the group develops, (3) the status differences that impact the group's productivity, (4) the effects of cultural differences, (5) the power some members have, and (6) the trust that improves group performance.

Roles

Stop reading this chapter for just a moment, and reflect on the question "Who are you?" A simple question, you probably think. Perhaps you took little time to answer it. Maybe you responded by saying your name. Maybe you said you are a student—a label that summarizes your current status. Ask yourself the question again. Get a pen and write ten different responses.

Who Are You?

1. I am _____

2. I am _____

3. I am _____

4. I am _____

5. I am _____

6. I am _____

7. I am _____

8. I am _____

9. I am _____

10. I am _____

Some of you may have had little trouble coming up with a detailed profile of who you think you are. Others, however, may have had more difficulty labeling multiple aspects of your self-concept. As you relate to others in small groups, your concept of self—who you think you are—affects your communication and relationships with other group members. In addition, your self-perception will have an impact on how others relate to you.

In trying to reduce the uncertainty that occurs when communicating in groups, people quickly assess the behaviors of others. They assign others roles, or sets of expectations. For example, Gloria seems like a leader: She usually takes charge and delegates responsibility. In contrast, Hank doesn't talk much. He will probably follow the recommendations of others rather than introduce ideas of his own—or at least this is the behavior others expect of him. In a small group, roles result from (1) people's expectations about their own behavior—their *self-concepts,* (2) the perceptions others have about individuals' positions in the group, and (3) people's actual behavior as they interact with others. Because their self-concepts largely determine the roles people assume in small groups, it is important to understand how self-concepts develop—how people come to learn who they think they are.

Self-Concept Development: Gender, Sexual Orientation, Culture, and Role

How do you know who you are? Why did you respond as you did when you were asked to consider the question, "Who are you?" A number of factors influence your self-concept.

First, other people influence who you think you are. Your parents gave you your name. Perhaps a teacher once told you that you were good in art, and consequently you think of yourself as artistic. Maybe your music teacher or your brother or sister told you that you cannot sing very well. Because you believed that person, you may now view yourself as not being very musically inclined. Thus, you listen to others, especially those whose opinions you respect, to help shape your self-concept.

One important part of everyone's self-concept is *gender*.[2] Whether you have experienced life as male or female affects your communication with others. While it is natural to assume that there are communication differences based on aspects of gender defined biologically, recent research suggests that the psychological aspects of gender may be at least as important a variable.[3] Although psychologically a person can be placed anywhere on a scale ranging from stereotypically female, through androgynous, to stereotypically male, the important point to remember is that psychological gender affects our behavior in groups.[4] Research has supported gender differences that "characterize women as using communication to connect with, support, and achieve closeness with others, and men as using communication to accomplish some task and to assert their individuality."[5]

A person's sexual orientation is another factor that is important in affecting his or her sense of self-concept as well as how he or she relates to others. Although there are increasingly more acceptance and tolerance toward gays and lesbians, nonetheless negative prejudice continues to exist.[6] These negative attitudes have an effect on how a gay or lesbian perceives him- or herself.

Whether you approve or disapprove of another person's sexual orientation should not reduce your effectiveness when communicating in groups and teams. Chances are there will be gays or lesbians in your work group at school or where you are employed. But because you cannot typically determine whether someone is gay or lesbian unless he or she tells you, you may not always be aware of whether people in your group are gay or lesbian. You already know that it is inappropriate to use racially charged terms that demean a person's race or ethnicity; we suggest it is equally important not to use derogatory terms that degrade a person's sexual orientation. Telling stories or jokes at the expense of a person because of his or her sexual orientation may lower your credibility not only among gay and lesbian members of your group but also among group members who do not approve of bias against gays or lesbians. Being sensitive to issues and attitudes about sexual orientation is part of the role of an effective group communicator.

Another important component of self-concept is *culture of origin.* Different cultures foster different beliefs and attitudes about communication, status, nonverbal behavior, and all the interpersonal dynamics discussed throughout this book. The development of selfhood takes place very differently from culture to culture. For example, Japanese and North American social lives flow from different premises. In Japan, the group or the collective is the measure of all things, but in the West—and in the Unites States in particular—the individual is the measure and arbiter of all things.[7] Many North Americans prize the image of the "rugged individualist"; the Japanese, in contrast, view this image as suggestive of egotism and insensitivity. To the Japanese, the line where self ends and others begin is far less clearly defined than it is for most North Americans.

Culture influences self-concept and thus such behaviors as the willingness to communicate in a group.[8] There is ample evidence that individuals from different cultures interpret situations and concepts very differently from one another.[9] Therefore, understanding cultural differences is essential to understanding behavior in small groups.

The various groups with which one affiliates also help to define one's self-concept. If you are attending college now, you may describe yourself as a student. If you are a member of a fraternity or sorority, you may consider that that association sets you apart from others. Your religious affiliation, your political party, and your membership in civic and social organizations all contribute to the way you perceive yourself.

You also learn who you are by simply observing and interpreting your own behavior. Just before leaving your dorm, house, or apartment, you may look in the mirror to see if your hair is okay and if your clothes are wrinkle-free. You try to see yourself as others will see you. You stand back and look at yourself, almost as if you were looking at someone else, evaluating what you see and forming an impression of who you are. Of course, as both the observer and the observed, your impressions are subject to bias. You may be too critical in evaluating who you are. Your high expectations for your own behavior, when compared with your perceptions of your actions, may give you a distorted view. For example, you may want to be a great opera singer, yet your only opportunity to sing comes in the shower. Even though you may have an excellent voice, your expectations have not been fulfilled, so you tell others that you are not a very good singer. The contradiction between your expectations and your actual experiences affects your self-concept and self-worth.

Diversity of Roles in Small Groups

As a member of a small group, you bring with you the perceptions, expectations, and experiences you have had with other people. Your self-expectations thus provide a foundation for the roles you will assume in a group. Yet your role is also worked out between you and the other group members.[10] As you interact with others, they form impressions of you and your abilities. As they reward you for your actions in the group, you learn what abilities and behaviors they will reinforce. These abilities and behaviors may, in turn, become part of your self-concept. Consider the following example:

> Mohammed has long had an interest in physics and nuclear energy. When his small group in the group communication class considers a discussion of peaceful uses of nuclear energy, Mohammed is enthusiastically supportive. Other group members soon recognize Mohammed's knowledge and interest in the subject. Mohammed enjoys providing resources and information for the group, soon emerging as the group member who provides most of the information and coordinates the group's research efforts. It is a role he enjoys, and the rest of the group appreciates his contributions.

Mohammed's role as an initiator of ideas, a contributor of information, and a coordinator of research resulted from his interest and ability (which were reflected in his self-concept). The group's need and desire to have him serve as a leader also helped determine his role.

People assume roles because of their interests and abilities and because of the needs and expectations of the rest of the group. At times, however, some roles are formally assigned to group members. When police officers arrive on the scene of an accident, bystanders do not generally question their leadership roles. In a task-oriented small group, a member may be assigned the role of secretary, which includes specific duties and responsibilities. A chairperson may be elected to coordinate the meeting and delegate responsibilities. Assigning responsibilities and specific roles reduces uncertainty. A group can sometimes get on with its task more efficiently if some roles are assigned. Of course, even if a person has been elected

Both group task roles and group-building and maintenance roles are important to a group's success. What roles do you usually take in a group?

stereotyping individuals can lock them into roles. Bormann has extensively studied role behavior in groups and notes that participants, when asked to analyze group roles, often categorize members into roles corresponding to the category labels.[12] As you identify the roles adopted by group members, be flexible in your classifications. Realize that you and other members can assume several roles during a group discussion. In fact, a group member rarely serves only as an "encourager," "opinion seeker," or "follower." Roles are dynamic; they change as perceptions, experiences, and expectations change. An individual can assume leadership responsibilities at one meeting and play a supporting role at other meetings.

Because a role is worked out jointly between you and the group, you will no doubt find yourself assuming different roles in different groups. Perhaps a committee you belong to needs someone to serve as a procedural leader to keep the meeting in order. Because you recognize this need and no one else keeps the group organized, you may find yourself steering the group back on to the topic, making sure all members have a chance to participate. In another committee, where others serve as procedural leaders, you may be the person who comes up with new ideas. Whether consciously or not, you develop a role unique to your talents and the needs of the group. Your role, then, changes from group to group.

If you understand how group roles form and how various roles function, you will be better able to help a group achieve its purpose. For example, groups need members to perform both maintenance and task functions. Task functions help the group get the job done, and maintenance functions help the group run smoothly. If no one is performing maintenance functions, you could point this out to the group, or assume some responsibility for them. If you notice individuals hindering the group's progress because they have adopted individual roles (blocker, aggressor, recognition seeker, etc.), you could bring this to the attention of the offending group member. Explain that individual roles can make the group less efficient and can lead to conflict among members. Although you cannot assume complete responsibility for distributing roles within your group, your insights can help solve some of the group's potential problems. Understanding group roles—and when to use them—is an important part of becoming a competent group communicator.

T E C H N O L O G Y

Technology development is not neutral, but reflects the values of the cultures in which it develops. A team of researchers at the University of California at Santa Barbara analyzed the structure of the Internet to determine the social impact of that technology. They found that with a critical mass of users and almost universal access in sight, the primary use (70%) of the Internet is information dissemination and gathering. Its decentralized structure makes government regulation extremely difficult and encourages open communication. These democratic values implicit in the technology reflect, say the authors, a North American cultural influence that will most certainly drive the future development of the Internet.

For more information, see Andrew Flanigan and Wendy Jo Mayard Farinola, "The Technical Code of the Internet/World Wide Web, *Critical Studies in Media Communication* 17 (2000): 409-428.

A useful Website for exploring more about interpersonal relationships in groups can be found at

http://www.umr.edu/~flsp/group.html

Norms

You have undoubtedly seen a movie or television show about the Old West in which townspeople feared villains who had no respect for the law. According to the way movies depict history, people such as Wyatt Earp were among the first to enforce the law and restore peace and order. In groups and teams as well as in the Old West, standards of acceptable behavior are necessary to keep peace and order. Although a small group of people does not need a Wyatt Earp to enforce order, it probably does need certain norms to help its members feel comfortable with their roles and their relationships.

Identifying Group Norms

Norms are rules or standards that determine what is appropriate and inappropriate behavior in a group. They establish expectations of how group members should behave. Norms reduce some of the uncertainty that occurs when people congregate. People's speech, the clothes they wear, or do not wear, and how and where they sit are all determined by group norms. Group norms also affect group-member relationships.

If you recently joined a group, how do you know what the group's norms are? One way to identify norms is to observe any repeated behavior patterns. Note, for example, any consistencies in the way people talk or dress. In identifying normative behavior in a group, consider the following questions:

1. How do group members dress?

2. What are group members' attitudes toward time? (Do group meetings begin and end on time? Are members often late to meetings?)

3. What type of language is used by most group members? (Is swearing acceptable? Is the language formal?)

4. Do group members use humor to relieve tension?

5. Do group members formally address the group leader?

6. Is it proper to address group members by their first names?

Answering these questions will help you pinpoint a group's norms. Some groups even develop norms for developing norms. For example, members may discuss the type of clothing that will be worn to meetings or talk about what should be done with absent or tardy members.

Noting when someone breaks a rule can also reveal group norms. If a member arrives late and other members frown or grimace at that person, they probably do not approve of the violation of the norm. If, after a member uses obscene words, another member says, "I wish you wouldn't use words like that," you can be certain that for at least one person a norm has been broken. Thus, punishable offenses indicate violated norms. Often the severity of the punishment corresponds to the significance of the norm.[13] Punishment can range from subtle nonverbal expressions of disapproval (which may not even be noticed by the person expressing them) to death. The hangman's noose was commonly the ultimate punishment for those who violated the norms or laws of the Old West.

How Do Norms Develop?

Have you noticed that in some classes it is okay to say something without raising your hand, but in others the instructor must call on you before you speak? Raising your hand is a norm. How did different norms develop for two similar activities? At least two key reasons account for this: (1) People develop norms in new groups based on those of previous groups they have belonged to, and (2) norms develop based on what happens early in a group's existence.

Poole suggests that a group organizes itself based, in part, on norms members encountered in previous groups.[14] As we noted in Chapter 2, Poole calls this process *structuration*. Groups do things (become structured) based on the ways those things were done in other groups. If many of your classmates previously had classes in which they had to raise their hands before speaking, then they will probably introduce that behavior into other groups. If enough people accept it, a norm is born—or, more accurately, a norm is reborn.

Norms also develop from the kinds of behavior that occur early in a group's development. Because of member uncertainty about how to behave when a group first meets, members are eager to learn what is acceptable behavior. If, for example, on the first day of c¹ student raises his or her hand to respond to the instructor, and another stude⸱ same, that norm is likely to stick. However, if several students respond w ⸱ ⸱ng a hand, chances are that raising hands will not become a norm in the class.

Conforming to Group Norms

What influences how quickly and rigidly people conform to the rules and standards of the group? According to Reitan and Shaw, at least five factors affect conformity to group norms.[15]

NON SEQUITUR ©1995 Wiley Miller. Dist. By UNIVERSAL PRESS SYNDICATE. Reprinted with permission. All rights reserved.

1. *The individual characteristics of the group members:* In summarizing the research on conformity, Shaw makes the following observation:

   > More intelligent persons are less likely to conform than less intelligent persons; women usually conform more than men, at least on traditional tasks; there is a curvilinear relationship between age and conformity; persons who generally blame themselves for what happens to them conform more than those low on self-blame; and authoritarians conform more than nonauthoritarians.[16]

   Thus, group members' past experiences and unique personality characteristics influence how they conform to established norms.

2. *The clarity of the norm and the certainty of punishment for breaking it:* The more ambiguous a group norm, the less likely it is that members will conform to it. The military spells out behavior rules clearly so that little if any ambiguity remains. A new recruit is drilled on how to talk, march, salute, and eat. Failure to abide by the rules results in swift and sure corrective sanctions. Thus the recruit quickly learns to conform. In some small groups, particularly when groups first meet, members have a great deal of uncertainty about how to act. Yet as soon as rules become clear and norms are established, members will usually conform. The clearer the norms, the more likely group members will conform.

3. *The number of people who have already conformed to the norm:* Imagine walking into a room with five or six other people. Three lines have been drawn on a blackboard. One line is clearly shorter than the other two. One by one, each person is asked which line is shortest, and each says that all the lines are the same length. Finally, it is your turn to judge which of the lines is shortest. You are perplexed because your eyes tell you that one line is definitely shorter. Yet can all the other members of your group be wrong? You answer that all of the lines are the same length—you conform. You do not want to appear odd to the other group members.[17] Factors such as the size of a group, the number of people who agree with a certain policy, and the status of those who conform contribute to the pressure for conformity in a group.

4. *The quality of the interpersonal relationships that have developed in the group:* A group whose members like one another and respect one another's opinions is more likely to support conformity than is a less cohesive group. Employees who like their jobs, bosses, and coworkers and take pride in their work are more likely to support group norms than those who have negative or frustrating relationships with their employers or colleagues.

5. *The sense of group identification that members have developed:* If group members can readily identify with the goals of the group, they are more likely to conform to standards of behavior. For example, church members who support the doctrine of a church are probably going to conform to the wishes of those in leadership positions. In addition, group members who feel they will be a part of a group for some time are more likely to conform to group norms.

   Although violating a group norm usually results in group disapproval and perhaps chastisement, such a violation can occasionally benefit a group. Just because members conform unanimously to a rule does not mean that the rule is beneficial. For example, in some situations the opinion of group members may matter more to decision-making than the facts they exchange.[18]

Collaborating

E T H I C A L L Y

Relational communication is the process of building relationships between and among group members. But what happens when you see another group member behaving unethically? What does *your* sense of ethics tell you to do?

Researchers Granville King III and Amy Hermodson studied the conditions under which registered nurses would report unethical behavior to an authority outside their group. Conditions included the personal ethics of the observer, situational factors (such as the severity of the wrongdoing), and organizational issues such as policies and procedures.[19]

Consider how you would react if you found someone in your workgroup in this class committing unethical acts such as plagiarism. What are the conditions under which you would or would not report him or her to the instructor?

Establishing Ground Rules and a Mission Statement

Norms often develop in a group without explicitly identifying what is or is not acceptable behavior. A group or team may decide to develop more precise rules to help accomplish the task. According to communication researcher Susan Shimanoff, a rule is "a followable prescription that indicates what behavior is obligated, preferred, or prohibited in certain contexts."[20] Group or team **ground rules** are explicit, agreed-on prescriptions of what is acceptable and appropriate behavior. Undoubtedly your school has rules as to what constitutes appropriate behavior: Don't cheat on a test, plagiarize a paper, carry a gun to campus, or consume alcohol in class—these are typical college and university rules. Rules help keep order so that meaningful work can be accomplished. Rules also state what the group or organization values. Honesty, fairness, freedom of speech, and personal safety are typical values embedded in rules.

Because teams are usually more structured and coordinated than a typical group discussion, most training sessions that teach people how to become an effective team stress that and high-performing team needs clear ground rules.[21]

How does a team develop ground rules? The team leader may facilitate a discussion to establish the ground rules. If a group has no designated leader, any team member can say, "To help us stay organized and get our work done, let's establish some ground rules." Groups and teams operate better if its members develop their own ground rules rather than having them imposed from "on high" or from the leader.

To help your group or team develop ground rules, consider the following questions:

▶ How long should our meetings last?

▶ Should we have a standard meeting place and time?

▶ What should a member do if he or she can't attend a meeting?

▶ How we will follow up to ensure that each member is doing his or her assigned work?

▶ Who is going to organize the agenda for our meetings?

▶ How will we manage conflict?

▶ How will we make our decisions—by majority vote or consusus?

▶ What kind of climate do we want in our meetings?

▶ What other kinds of guidelines do we need to develop?

Typical team ground rules include:

▶ Everyone will attend all meetings.

▶ Meetings will start on time.

▶ Each team member will follow through on individual assignments.

▶ Each team member will be prepared for every meeting.

▶ We will make decisions by consensus rather than majority vote.

▶ We will work together to manage conflict when it arises.

Another component related to team ground rules that is usually taught in team training is that each team should develop a mission statement. A team **mission statement** is a concise description of the goals or desired outcomes of the team. A mission statement helps not only in accomplishing your task but also lets you know when you've completed your task. Your work is finished when you've accomplished your mission. As author Stephen Covey suggests, begin with the end in mind.[22] A well-worded team mission statement should be (1) specific—it should be brief and clearly describe what the team should accomplish, (2) measurable—the team must be able to determine whether the mission was achieved, (3) attainable—the mission should be realistic, (4) relevant—whatever the mission, it should be appropriate to the larger organization and the overall purpose of the team, (5) time bound—teams should set a deadline or time frame for achieving the missions, and (6) stretch the team a bit—if the mission is too simple it won't inspire the team to do its best work; as we noted in Chapter 1, a team should have a "clear and elevating goal." A good team mission statement should pass the SMARTS test.[23] SMARTS is the acronym for the six criteria of an effective mission statement: Specific, Measurable, Attainable, Relevant, Time bound, and Stretch the team.

Often teams are given their "marching orders" by someone from outside the group. Even when the team is given its goal, sometimes called a charge—the purpose of the team, group, or committee—the team should take some time to discuss the mission so that each person clearly understands and agrees to it. Also, discuss whether it passes the SMARTS test.

REVIEW

Conformity to Group Norms Depends On

▶ Culture

▶ The individual characteristics of group members

▶ The clarity of the norm and the certainty of punishment for breaking it

▶ The number of people who already conform to the norm

▶ The quality of interpersonal relationships in the group

▶ The sense of group identification that members have developed

Culture

Earlier in the chapter, we noted the powerful effect of culture on self-concept and behavior. To be effective leaders and members in multicultural groups, you must develop understanding and sensitivity to cultural differences.

A complete treatment of this subject would require volumes. Nevertheless, we can provide an introduction to get you started. We will divide cultural differences into three general categories: (1) *individualism*, (2) *conversational style*, and (3) *time*.

Individualism and Collectivism

Groups often have difficulty establishing norms and roles because of cultural variations in individualism among group members. As we discussed in Chapter 1, in some cultures (such as the Anglo-American) individual autonomy and initiative are valued; in others (Japanese, for instance) collective well-being takes precedence over individual achievement. People from collectivist cultures are therefore more likely to view assertive individualists as self-centered, while individualists may interpret their collectivist counterparts as weak. Collectivists are more likely to conform to group norms, and to value group decisions more highly.[24] We caution you, though against overgeneralization. Although different cultures clearly foster different orientations, there is also ample evidence for vast differences *within* cultures. Thus it is nearly impossible to predict with certainty an individual or collectivist orientation based on culture alone.[25, 26]

Although differences in individualism always exist in groups, these differences can be extreme in the presence of cultural diversity, resulting in low group satisfaction and productivity. To establish and maintain norms with which all members can feel comfortable, groups need to understand and be sensitive to the cultural expectations of all participants.

Conversational Style

Conversational norms vary by culture.[27] If not understood, these differences can cause misunderstanding, anxiety, and group conflict.

The white middle-class North American norm that has one group member quietly awaiting a turn to speak may cause him or her to wait a very long time when those from other cultures do not share that norm. People from some cultures love a good argument, whereas others, such as the Japanese, revere harmony and the ability to assimilate differences to build consensus.[28] Some cultures are put off by North Americans' frankness and relative lack of inhibition about sharing negative information. In Western cultures, control is exerted through speaking; in Eastern cultures, control is expressed through silence and in the outward show of reticence.[29]

The topics we address and our willingness to talk about personal matters vary by culture. Whereas Mexicans may talk about a person's soul or spirit, such talk may make North Americans uncomfortable. Persons from Hispanic cultures often begin conversations with inquiries about one's family, even with casual acquaintances or in a business meeting. Many North Americans view family matters as too personal to be discussed casually.[30]

Time

Thomas Fitzgerald recounts an anecdote that illustrates cultural differences in the temporal dimension. While interviewing a group of Brazilian students, Fitzgerald asked his subjects how they felt about a person who was consistently late. He was surprised to find that the students view such a person as probably more successful than those who are on time. A person of status, they reasoned, is *expected* to be late.[31]

North Americans are arguably the most time bound culture in the world. Even the Japanese view North American businesspeople as much too driven by schedules and deadlines, which in turn interfere with the smooth development of human relationships. North Americans tend to view time as **monochronic**—linear and segmented; they value precision in time. Many other cultures, including the African-American subculture, take a more **polychronic** view. Polychronic time is partly characterized by a more *laissez-faire* attitude about what constitutes being "on time" or "late." People who have a polychronic sense of time do not expect human activities to proceed like clockwork. After all, humans were here on Earth long before the invention of clocks.[32]

A New and Growing Culture: People with Disabilities

As physical spaces are built and renovated to be increasingly accessible, full participation by people with disabilities in all aspects of social and professional activity is finally becoming a reality. Able-bodied (or, as a friend of ours puts it, "temporarily able-bodied") indi-

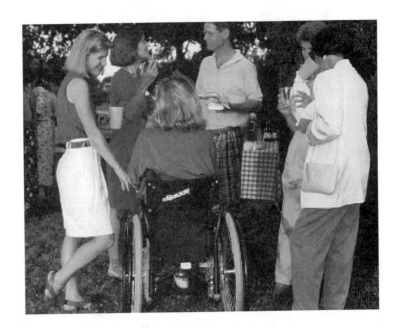

Disabilities can be viewed as cultural variables that can affect communication. What can various groups do to facilitate effective group communication?

viduals who have little or no experience communicating with people with disabilities sometimes feel uncomfortable and/or do and say things that are inappropriate.

People with physical disabilities see themselves as members of a culture. Dawn Braithwaite offers some do's and don'ts to assist in this form of intercultural communication that includes being aware that people with disabilities can speak and do things for themselves and will let you know when they want help. Most importantly, she advises, recognize that you are not dealing with a disabled person but a person who has a disability. That is, deal with the person—the disability is secondary.[33]

Despite great variety in physical appearances, we are all more alike than different. Try not to fear differences; get past them to see the person inside and communicate as you always do—with patience, concern, and self-assurance.[34]

Welcoming People with Disabilities

Marilyn E. Bishop, director of the Center for Ministry with Disabled People at the University of Dayton, offers many tips for relating to people with disabilities. Here is an abbreviated version.[35]

BLINDNESS AND VISUAL IMPAIRMENT

DO   When you greet a person who is blind, identify yourself .

When assisting, offer your arm, the same way an usher does at a wedding.

Talk normally, using customary and typical expressions of speech, such as "see you later."

Provide oral cues for the blind person when it is his or her turn to speak.

DON'T   Don't gesture about the person who is blind. He or she will often sense that some nonverbal communication is taking place and feel excluded.

Don't be protective. Encourage people who are blind, and let them set the pace for their own involvement.

Don't assume that the blind person needs Braille; many do not read it.

PHYSICAL OR MOBILITY IMPAIRMENT

DO Speak directly to a person in a wheelchair, not to a companion or attendant.

Ask directly how you may assist.

Sit down so that you are at eye level.

Shake hands or touch people who are physically impaired in the same way that you would any other person.

Remember that walkers, wheelchairs, and other equipment are part of the identity of the owner and are included in the imaginary boundary of personal space.

DON'T Don't ask personal questions about a person's disability.

Don't touch or move a wheelchair without the occupant's permission.

Don't talk about the person as if he/she is not present.

SPEECH IMPAIRMENT

DO Be patient with people who have difficulty speaking or pronouncing words. Let them talk at their own pace.

If you cannot understand the person's communication, ask questions that require only a short answer or shake of the head.

Repeat or paraphrase to confirm that you understand.

If you really can't grasp the message, encourage the person to "say it a different way."

Wait patiently for the person to go on after a pause.

If the person appears shy, invite him or her to contribute to the group's discussion.

DON'T Don't pretend to understand when you don't. It's better to ask the person to repeat the sentence or ask a friend of the person to interpret for you.

Don't confuse mental impairment with speech impairment; a person who has difficulty speaking may also have highly developed mental abilities not readily apparent.

Most of the research conclusions reported in this book are based on studies of the predominantly white, able-bodied, North American culture. When groups are multicultural (as is increasingly the case), the dynamics of the group will change, if only slightly. Where relevant information about cultural differences exists, we have included it in the remaining chapters of this book, with a special section on culture and nonverbal communication in Chapter 6. Remember that when cultural differences are present, the importance of interpersonal communication skills in groups increases.

"My dad can run faster than your dad."

"Oh, yeah? Well, my dad is smarter than your dad."

"No, he's not!"

"Oh, yes he is!"

"Says who?"

"Says me. Wanna make something of it?"

Children as well as adults are concerned about status—who is better, brighter, and more beautiful. **Status is an** individual's importance. People with higher social status generally have more prestige and command more respect than do people of lower status. Many people want to talk to and talk about, see and be seen with those with high status. They are interested in the lives of high-status individuals. Fan magazines and weekly tabloid newspapers are filled with features about the famous and near famous—status achievers and status seekers. The president of the United States, television personalities, authors, and athletes often provide the names that make name-dropping the pastime of status seekers.

Privileges Accorded to High-Status Group Members

Most people like to be perceived as enjoying some status within a group. Because occupying a position of status fulfills a need for attention, it also builds self-respect and self-esteem. Bormann explains why high-status positions are pleasant:

> The group makes a high-status person feel important and influential. They show him deference, listen to him, ask his advice, and often reward him with a greater share of the group's goods. He gets a bigger office, more secretaries, better furniture, more salary, a bigger car, and so forth. Even in communication-class discussion groups, the high-status members receive considerable gratification of their social and esteem needs. One of the most powerful forces drawing people into groups is the attraction of high status.[36]

Perhaps you have participated in small groups in which the status of an individual afforded him or her certain privileges that were not available to the rest of the group. The chairperson of the board may have a private dining room or an executive washroom, while other members must eat in the company cafeteria and use public washrooms.

Effects of Status Differences

In groups and teams, a members' status exerts a significant effect on interpersonal relationships. Status affects who talks to whom and how often a member speaks. The status or reputation an individual has before joining a group certainly affects the role he or she assumes. In addition, norms that help groups determine how they will deal with status differences and what privileges they should allow those with greater prestige develop quickly. Several researchers have observed how status differences affect the relationships among members of a small group. Consider the following research conclusions:

1. High-status group members talk more than low-status members.[37]

2. High-status group members communicate more with other high-status members than they do with those of lower status.[38]

3. Low-status group members tend to direct their conversation to high-status group members rather than to those of lower or equal status.[39]

4. Low-status group members communicate more positive messages to high-status members than they do to those of equal or lower status.[40]

5. High-status group members are likely to have more influence on the group's decision making than low-status members.[41]

6. High-status group members usually abide by the norms of the group more than do low-status group members. (The exception to this research finding occurs when high-status members realize that they can violate group norms and receive less punishment than low-status group members would receive; thus, depending on the situation, they may violate certain group norms.)[42]

7. Group members are more likely to ignore the comments and suggestions made by low-status members than those made by high-status members.[43]

8. Low-status group members communicate more irrelevant information than do high-status members.[44]

9. High-status members are less likely to complain about their jobs or their responsibilities.[45]

10. Communication with high-status group members can replace the need for the upward movement of low-status members in the group's status hierarchy.[46]

11. High-status group members tend to talk to the entire group more than members of lower status do.[47]

12. The leader of a small group is usually the member with the highest status. (The exception to this conclusion occurs when the leader emerges because of capability and competence and not necessarily because of popularity. That kind of leader holds a lower status than does a more popular and well-liked group member.)[48]

REVIEW

Effects of Status Differences in Groups

Group members with high status:

Talk more

Communicate more often with other high-status members

Have more influence

Generally abide by group norms

Are less likely to be ignored

Are less likely to complain about their responsibilities

Talk to the entire group

Are likely to serve in leadership roles

Group members with low status:

Direct conversation to high-status rather than low-status members

Communicate more positive messages to high-status members

Are more likely to have their comments ignored

Communicate more irrelevant information

Talk to high-status members as a substitute for climbing the social hierarchy in the group

Observing Status Differences to Predict Group Dynamics

Knowing how status affects the relationships among group members helps you predict who will talk with whom. If you can perceive status differences, you can also predict the type of messages communicated in a small group discussion. These research conclusions suggest that the social hierarchy of a group affects group cohesiveness, group satisfaction, and even the quality of a group's solution. One of the benefits of increased status within a group is the relative increase in the group member's influence or power.

Power

Sociologist Robert Bierstedt once observed that in the "entire lexicon of sociological concepts, none is more troublesome than the concept of **power**. We may say about it in general only what St. Augustine said about time, that we all know perfectly well what it is—until someone asks us."[49] Although scholars debate definitions of power as well as its relationship to other variables such as status and authority, they generally agree that power, at its core, involves the ability of one person to control or influence some other person or decision.[50] Power in a small group, then, is reflected in an individual's ability to get other members to conform to his or her wishes. Power is about influence.

Certain group members may have more power in the group than others. Sometimes the sources of their power are clear to members, such as in groups with large status differences; but in other cases, the sources of power are not so clear. In order to map out the territory of social power in small groups, you need to look at power bases and the effects of power on group processes.

Power Bases

Your power base in a group is the sum of the resources that you can use to control or influence others. Because no two group members have exactly the same resources, each member operates from a different power base. What are some of these power bases? French and Raven identified five power bases in their study of small groups: (1) legitimate power, (2) referent power, (3) expert power, (4) reward power, and (5) coercive power.[51]

Legitimate power stems from a group member's ability to influence others because of being elected, appointed, or selected to exert control over a group. Legitimate power comes from occupying a position of responsibility. The principal of a school has the legitimate power to control school policy; the senators from your state have legitimate power to represent their constituents. Many of the benefits reported in the previous section for high-status group members reflect this kind of power base. A small group member who has been elected chairperson is given legitimate power to influence the group's procedures.

Referent power is the power of interpersonal attraction. Recall from Chapter 3 that people are attracted to others whom they admire and want to emulate. Put simply, people we like have more power over us than those people we do not like.

Expert power stems from a group member's ability to influence others based on the knowledge and information the member possesses. As the saying goes, knowledge is power. Suppose you are a member of a group studying ways to improve the environment of the river in your community. If one of your group members has a Ph.D. in aquatic plant life, that person's knowledge and access to information give him or her expert power. More than likely, that person can influence the group. However, just because a group member has knowledge does not mean that he or she will exert more influence in the group. The group must find the knowledge credible and useful.

Reward power is based on a person's ability to provide rewards for behaviors. If you are in a position to help another member gain money, status, power, acceptance, or other rewards, you will have power over that person. Of course, group members are motivated by different needs and goals. What is rewarding to one may not be rewarding to others. Reward power is effective only if a person finds the reward satisfying or valuable. Others must also believe that a person actually has the power and resources to bestow the reward.

Coercive power, the negative side of reward power, is based on the perception that another can punish you for acting or not acting in a certain way. A person's ability to demote others, reduce their salaries or benefits, force them to work overtime hours, or fire them are examples of resources that can make up this power base. Even though coercive power may achieve a desired effect, group members usually resent threats of punishment intended to make them conform. Punished group members often try to win the next round or escape from heavy-handed efforts to accomplish a group goal.

Effects of Power on Group Process

Members who have power influence the group process. Whether their influence will be positive or negative depends on how wisely the members use their influence. The following principles summarize the impact of power on group deliberations:

▶ The struggle for power among group members can result in poor group decisions and less group cohesion.

▶ Members who overtly seek dominance and control over a group often focus attention on themselves rather than on achieving group goals. They typically serve as aggressors, blockers, recognition seekers, dominators, or special-interest pleaders. (These individual roles were discussed earlier in this chapter.) Individuals who seek power make the group less cohesive, and power struggles emphasize individual rather than group agendas.

▶ Group members with little power often talk less frequently in a group.

▶ Charles Berger observed that "persons who talk most frequently and for the longest periods of time are assumed to be the most dominant group members. In addition, persons receiving the most communication are assumed to be most powerful."[52] While not all powerful members dominate group conversations, a relationship exists between verbal contributions to the group and influence. The exceptions to this principle are members who talk so frequently that they are ignored by the group. Cultural variations can influence this perception as well.

▶ Group members can lose power if other members think they use power for personal gain or to keep a group from achieving its goals.

▶ Group members usually expect individuals with greater power to have high-status privileges. However, if members believe that powerful members are having a detrimental effect on the group, their credibility and influence are likely to diminish. Too many perks and privileges given to some members sap a group's ability to do its job and can result in challenges to the influential group members.

▶ Too much power in one individual can lead to less group decision making and more autocratic decision making.

▶ Autocratic decision making occurs when one person with several power bases (for example, one who can reward and punish, has needed information, is well liked, and has been appointed to lead) makes a decision alone rather than with the group as a whole. Group members may not speak their minds for fear of reprisals.

▶ Increasing your level of activity in a group can increase your power and influence.

▶ Groups with equal power distribution show higher quality group communication than do groups with unequal power distribution.[53]

▶ In corporate work teams, individual power is related to the task-based interdependencies represented by the different team members.[54]

If you are participating in a group and sense that your influence is diminishing, try to participate more and to take an active role in helping the group achieve its goal. Volunteering to help with tasks and increasing your knowledge about group problems, issues, or decisions can also enhance your influence. If you see other group members losing influence, you can give them specific tasks that will bring them back into the group's mainstream (assuming that they are willing to accept the responsibility).

REVIEW

Power Bases

TYPE OF POWER	INFLUENCE BASED ON:
Legitimate	Being elected, appointed, or selected to lead the group
Referent	Being well liked
Expert	A member's knowledge and information
Reward	Providing rewards for desired behavior
Coercive	The ability to punish another

Power and Gender

Stereotypes portray women as being more easily influenced than men and as having less power over others than their male counterparts. However, although results are mixed, recent research tends to dispel these illusions.[55, 56] In one study, when women were placed in positions of power, they were just as likely as men to use strategies associated with power. Because men typically occupy roles of higher power in society, the opportunity for them to use power strategies is greater than for women. This observation led the researcher to conclude that this unequal distribution of power results in the illusion of gender differences, which are really the result of women's and men's relative social status. Thus, apparent gender differences must be understood within a context of status and power.[57]

Clearly inequities exist in the workplace. But social and organizational expectations for men and women have changed and will continue to do so. Indeed, there is evidence that more and more firms value diversity in the ranks of management and believe that such diversity provides a competitive advantage. As these changes unfold, more and more women managers will likely feel free to "be themselves" without compromising their organizational image.[58]

Status and Power: A Cultural Footnote

It is important to remember that status is primarily in the eye of the beholder. Frequently status is meaningless when we cross cultural boundaries; a Ph.D. will not be revered in a country-and-western bar. Communication scholar Marshall Singer offers this observation:

> The Ph.D. holder and the famous athlete have acquired high status and the ability to influence their respective "constituents." Because high status—whether ascribed or acquired—depends so much on its being perceived as such, it may be the least transferable, across cultural barriers, of all the components of power we are discussing.[59]

Cultural differences in perceptions of status are revealed pointedly in the following letter. On June 17, 1744, the commissioners from Maryland and Virginia negotiated a treaty with the Indians of the Six Nations at Lancaster, Pennsylvania. The Indians were invited to send young men to William and Mary College. The next day they declined the offer as follows.

> We know that you highly esteem the kind of learning taught in those Colleges, and that the Maintenance of our young Men, while with you, would be very expensive to you. We are convinced, that you mean to do us Good by your Proposal; and we thank you heartily. But you, who are wise must know that different Nations have different Conceptions of things and you will therefore not take it amiss, if our ideas of this kind of Education happen not to be the same as yours. We have had some Experience of it. Several of our young People were formerly brought up at the Colleges of the Northern Provinces: They were instructed in all your Sciences; but, when they came back to us, they were bad Runners, ignorant of every means of living in the woods . . . neither fit for Hunters, Warriors, nor Counsellors, they were totally good for nothing.
>
> We are, however, not the less oblig'd by your kind Offer, tho' we decline accepting it; and, to show our grateful Sense of it, if the Gentlemen of Virginia will send us a Dozen of their Sons, we will take Care of their Education, instruct them in all we know, and make Men of them.

What do used-car salespeople, politicians, and insurance agents have in common? They are often stereotyped as people whose credibility is suspect. The untrustworthy images such people evoke are not always justified; but when they want something from you, whether it is money or a vote, you are often suspicious of the promises they make. When you trust people, you have faith that they will not try to take advantage of you and that they will be mindful of your best interests. In developing interpersonal relationships in small groups, the degree of trust you have in others affects your relationships with them. The following sections consider how trust in relationships affects group members and suggests how you can elicit more trust as you interact with others.

Developing Trusting Relationships

Why do you trust some people more than others? What is it about your closest friend that enables you to confide your most private feelings? How can group members develop trusting relationships? First, developing trusting relationships in a group takes time. Just as assuming a role in a group discussion requires time, so does developing confidence in others. Second, you base trust on the previous experiences you have had with others. You probably would not give a stranger your bank account number. You would, however, more than likely trust this number to your spouse or to a friend you have known for several years. As you communicate with other people, you gradually learn whether you can trust them. First you observe how an individual completes various tasks and responsibilities. Then you decide whether you can rely on him or her to get things done.

Trust, then, develops when you can predict how another person will behave under certain circumstances. Put another way, trust helps you reduce uncertainty as you form expectations of others. As you participate in a group, you trust those who, because of their actions and support in the past, have given you reason to believe that they will support you in the future. Group members establish trusting relationships as they develop mutual respect and as the group becomes more cohesive.

However, even time and experience cannot guarantee trust. A certain amount of risk is always involved whenever you trust another person. As Reichert suggests, "Trust is always a risk, a kind of leap in the dark. It is not based on any solid proof that the other person will not hurt you . . . trust is always a gamble."[60] Sometimes the gamble does not prove profitable. For example, if you have recently worked in a small group with several people who proved untrustworthy, you may be reluctant to trust others in future groups. Thus your good and bad experiences in past groups affect the way in which you relate to people in future groups.

Self-Disclosure

One of the most important ways to establish and maintain trusting relationships with others is through self-disclosure—the deliberate communication of information about yourself to others. Self-disclosure, like trust, involves a certain degree of risk. When you reveal personal, private information, you open yourself to the possibility that others might reject you. John Powell, author of the book *why am i afraid to tell you who i am?*, says that people hesitate to disclose much about themselves because "if I tell you who I am, you may not like who I am, and it's all that I have."[61]

Self-disclosure should be timed to suit the occasion and the expectations of the individuals involved. Telling all too soon may violate what the other person expects. In Western cultures, it would not be appropriate to talk about the intimate aspects of your life (for example, your financial net worth or your romantic endeavors) when you first introduce yourself to someone. The other person may feel uncomfortable and want to terminate the relationship. Thus when you first meet someone, you usually reveal information that is not too threatening or personal. As you establish a trusting relationship with an individual, you may feel more comfortable about discussing private feelings and concerns. Powell notes that the information you reveal about yourself often progresses through several predictable levels:

Level 5: *Cliché communication.* Standard phrases such as "Hi, how are you?, Nice to see you, Beautiful weather, isn't it?," and "How's it going?" signal the desire to initiate a relationship.

Level 4: *Facts and biographical information.* You reveal nonthreatening information about yourself, such as your name, hometown, or occupation.

Level 3: *Personal attitudes and ideas.* After introducing yourself and getting down to business, you then respond to various ideas and issues, noting where you agree and disagree with others.

Level 2: *Personal feelings.* Talking about your personal feelings makes you more vulnerable than discussing attitudes and ideas, particularly when you talk about feelings regarding yourself or others.

Level 1: *Peak communication.* People seldom reach this level. Only with your closest friends or people you have known for some time will you share personal insights that may result in rejection. This level of self-disclosure takes much time and trust to develop.[62]

These five levels are merely a means of describing the self-disclosure process, so do not try to classify all your personal communication with others into one of these categories. Such thinking may detract from an otherwise spontaneous conversation. Although self-disclosure should not be used as a tool to manipulate others into trusting relationships, you should develop greater awareness of the self-disclosure process to help evaluate your relationships with others in small groups.

One researcher has described five characteristics of appropriate self-disclosure.[63]

1. *Self-disclosure is a function of the ongoing relationship.* This means that self-disclosure is not something you do just once; you continually share information about yourself with others.

2. *Self-disclosure is reciprocal.* When you disclose something to another person, that person will probably disclose something to you—at least, if you give him or her an opportunity. If you rarely give others a chance to talk, they probably will not respond to you. If you want to create a climate of trust in your group, you must be willing to share with others.

3. *Self-disclosure is timed to what is happening in your group.* For example, if your group is discussing where a new highway should be located, it would not be appropriate for you to talk about how much you enjoy playing with your cat. In other words, do not

disclose just for the sake of disclosing. Your comments should be relevant to the discussion at hand.

4. *Self-disclosure should deal with what is happening among the people present.* Not only should your self-disclosure be appropriate to an occasion, but it should also be appropriate for the people in your group. You need not talk about a troubled relationship if it clearly is of no concern to the others present. You may find someone who will listen to you, but if the others present have no interest in your confessions, keep them to yourself.

5. *Self-disclosure usually moves by small increments* (it takes time). Establishing trusting relationships with others cannot be rushed. If a group of people will meet for only two or three sessions, do not feel compelled to enter into a self-disclosure session. If you ask others to disclose personal information too quickly, group members may interpret your efforts to establish trust as prying into their personal lives. Although you should not disclose too much too soon, you should persevere in trying to get to know other group members. Self-disclosure is a useful way to improve relationships.

The Development of Group Relationships over Time

We noted in Chapter 3 that group formation takes place over time. It takes time for relationships to develop. You experience some tension and anxiety the first time you participate in a small group. You are uncertain what your role in the group will be. The group has not met long enough for norms to develop. True, in some groups, certain standards of behavior already exist because of the common culture that group members share, but these expectations provide only skeletal guidance for behavior. Status differences among group members can also create tension. Bormann has defined this initial uneasiness as **primary** tension, which is

> the social unease and stiffness that accompanies getting acquainted. Students placed in a discussion group with strangers will experience these tensions most strongly during the opening minutes of their first meetings. The earmarks of primary tensions are extreme politeness, apparent boredom or tiredness, and considerable sighing or yawning. When members show primary tension, they speak softly and tentatively. Frequently they can think of nothing to say, and many long pauses result.[64]

Expect to find some primary tension during initial meetings. It is a normal part of group development. A group leader can minimize this tension, however, by helping members get to know one another. Get-acquainted exercises and brief statements of introduction can ease primary tension. While members of groups that meet only once might deem getting to know one another impractical, using a few minutes to break the ice and reduce some of the primary tension can help create more satisfying relationships among group members.

After a group resolves primary tension and its members become more comfortable with one another, another type of tension develops. Secondary tension, according to Bormann, occurs as conflicts arise and as differences of opinion emerge. Whether recognized as a personality conflict or simply as a disagreement, secondary tension surfaces when group members try to solve the problem, accomplish the task, or resolve specific issues facing the group. Secondary tension also is the result of power struggles. Secondary tension usually establishes group norms. Joking or laughing often helps manage secondary tension. However cohesive a group may be, some conflict over procedure will normally develop as relationships among members form. Chapter 7 will discuss the phases of a group's growth and development in more detail, and Chapter 10 will consider some suggestions for managing the conflict and controversy that result from secondary tension.

REVIEW

Group Tension

Primary tension:	Uneasiness and uncomfortableness in getting acquainted and managing initial group uncertainty about the group task and group relationships
Secondary tension:	Tension that occurs as group members struggle for influence, develop roles and norms, and explore differences in approaching the group task

Putting Principles into Practice

Five variables affect and reflect individuals' relationships with others in small groups: (1) roles, (2) norms, (3) status, (4) power, and (5) trust. An understanding of how these concepts affect your performance and the performance of other group members will help you explain and predict the types and quality of relationships that form in small groups. As you attempt to apply the information presented in this chapter, consider these suggestions:

ROLES

▶ Roles grow out of self-concept, which is based on a composite of life experiences. These experiences are influenced by gender, sexual orientation, and culture, as well as by the significant groups to which we have belonged. Work to understand your own self-concept to help understand your role in small groups.

▶ If no one performs important group roles, point this out to the group or assume the responsibility for performing them yourself.

▶ If you observe one or more group members hindering the progress of your group because they are adopting an individual group role (blocker, aggressor, recognition seeker, etc.), bring this to the attention of the group or the offending group member.

▶ Do not try to fit yourself or other group members into just one or two group roles. You and other group members can assume several roles during the course of a discussion.

NORMS

▶ Identify group norms by noting repeated patterns of behavior.

► Another way to identify group norms is by noting what kind of offenses group members punish.

► Consider the individual characteristics of group members, the clarity of norms and the certainty of punishment for breaking them, the number of people who have broken norms, the quality of relationships among group members, and the sense of group identification to help determine whether members will conform to the group norms.

CULTURE

Culturally diverse groups often have difficulty establishing satisfactory roles and norms because of differences in cultural expectations. Such groups require extra effort in group building and maintenance.

When group members do not share a common native language, some additional tactics may be necessary:[65]

► *Slow down* communication.

► *Repeat* or paraphrase when nonverbal expressions suggest that listeners do not understand.

► *Verify* common understanding by having others restate the argument or idea.

► If necessary (and possible), encourage *restatement* in the listener's native language.

Remember that cultures vary widely in conversational style as well as the appropriateness assigned to topics of conversation. Do not make the mistake of attributing such differences to impoliteness or insensitivity.

STATUS

► Identify the status of group members by the privileges that high-status group members receive.

► If you can spot status differences in small groups, you can predict who talks to whom.

► If you are aware of status differences, you can communicate more effectively and with greater influence.

POWER

► People develop power in a group because they can provide information, expertise, rewards, and punishment; because they have been elected or appointed; or because they are well liked or have status in the group.

► Consider the possible sources of power in your group to help you understand patterns of influence.

► Work to maximize the positive sources of power for all group members.

TRUST

► In most groups, don't expect trusting relationships to form too soon—it takes time for trust to develop.

► Self-disclosure is an important factor in developing trusting relationships with others. Self-disclosure and trust involve risk. Taking these risks with others helps them to do the same with you.

SELF-DISCLOSURE

▶ Do not think that self-disclosure just happens once when the group first gets together; it is a function of ongoing group relationships.

▶ Do not talk solely about yourself without giving other people a chance to talk about themselves.

▶ Appropriate self-disclosure should deal with what is happening among the people present. Your revelations should be relevant to the discussion at hand.

▶ Take your time self-disclosing; appropriate self-disclosure moves by small increments.

▶ Use get-acquainted exercises and brief statements of introduction during the first group meeting to help manage primary tension.

PRACTICE

Group Roles and Problem-Solving Competencies

In Chapter 1, we discussed six task and three relationship problem-solving competencies as essential skills required for effective group interaction in certain settings. In this chapter we introduced group roles—patterns of behavior that can move a group toward, and sometimes away from, its goal. Compare the two lists. Work with others in your group to reach consensus on which roles from Chapter 4 are best subsumed under the competencies from Chapter 1. Do any of the roles not fit into this scheme? If so, how do you explain that? Be prepared to report your results to the class.

Group-Role Inventory

When you see yourself differently from the way others see you, or when your expectations of people cloud your perceptions of them, there is a potential for uncertainty, confusion, frustration, and conflict in the group. This inventory was designed to help members become more aware of the roles they play and of how others perceive those roles. It is time-consuming (it takes at least 45 minutes) but worth the time and effort, particularly when a group is having trouble establishing norms. The group-role inventory can also be an effective means of dealing with one or two problem members by bringing everyone's role expectations into the discussion rather than by ganging up on the troublemakers.

Objectives: To become aware of the roles you play in your group and of how others perceive your roles

Materials: Group-role inventory sheet (attached)

Time: 45 minutes

Participants: Ongoing groups

Procedures: 1. Fill out group-role inventory sheet.

2. Go over the list and check the role you would like to have performed but did not perform.

3. Go over the list again and star (*) the role you performed but would rather not have performed.

4. Discuss results with your group.

Application: The exercise should make members aware of how roles are used in their groups.

Group-Role Inventory Sheet

Who in your group, including yourself, is most likely to

1. Take initiative, propose ideas, get things started?

2. Sit back and wait passively for others to lead?

3. Express feelings most freely, frankly, openly?

4. Keep feelings hidden, reserved, unexpressed?

5. Show understanding of other members' feelings?

6. Be wrapped up in personal concerns and not very responsive to others?

7. Interrupt others when they are speaking?

8. Daydream, be lost in private thoughts during group sessions, be "far away"?

9. Give you a feeling of encouragement, warmth, friendly interest, support?

10. Converse privately with someone else while another member is speaking to the group?

11. Talk of trivial things, engage in superficial chitchat?

12. Criticize, put people on their guard?

13. Feel superior to other members?

14. Be listened to by everyone while speaking?

15. Feel inferior to other members?

16. Contribute good ideas?

17. Contradict, disagree, argue, raise objections?

18. Sulk or withdraw when the group is displeasing?

19. Be the one you would like to have on your side if a conflict arose in the group?

20. Agree or conform with whatever is said?

21. Be missed, if absent, more than any other member?

 Your companion Website has more practice activities, questionnaires, and checklists!
www.ablongman.com/beebe

Notes

1. Joann Keyton, "Relational Communication in Groups," in Lawrence Frey, D. S. Gouran, and M. S. Poole, eds., *The Handbook of Group Communication and Research* (Thousand Oaks, CA: Sage, 1999) 192.

2. For a full discussion of gender and communication, see Julia T. Wood, *Gendered Lives: Communication, Gender and Culture,* 3rd ed. (Belmont, CA: Wadsworth, 1999) and Diana K. Ivy and Phil Backlund, "Exploring Gender Speak: Personal Effectiveness," in Pearson et al., eds., *Gender and Communication* (New York: McGraw-Hill, 1994).

3. Laura Stafford, Marianne Dainton, and Stephen Haas, "Measuring Routine and Strategic Relational Maintenance: Scale Revision, Sex versus Gender Roles, and Prediction of Relational Characteristics, *Communication Monographs* 67 (2000): 306–323.

4. J. C. Pearson and R. West, "An Initial Investigation of the Effects of Gender on Student Questions in the Classroom: Developing a Descriptive Base," *Communication Education* 40 (1991): 22–32.

5. Michael S. Woodward, Lawrence B. Rosenfeld, and Steven K. May, "Sex Differences in Social Support in Sororities and Fraternities," *Journal of Applied Communication Research* 24 (1996): 260.

6. M. E. Kite and B. E. Whitley, "Sex Differences in Attitudes Toward Homosexual Persons, Behaviors, and Civil Rights: A Meta-Analysis," *Personality and Social Psyhcological Bulletin* 22 (1996); 336–53; N. W. Pilkington and J. E. Lydon, "The Relative Effect of Attitude Simiarity and Attitude Dissimilarity on Interpersonal Attraction: Investigating the Moderating Roles of Prejudice and Group Membership," *Personality and Social Psychological Bulletin* 23 (1997): 107–22; T. P. Mottet, "The Role of Sexual Orientation and Predicted Outcome Value and Anticipated Communcation Behaviors," *Communication Quarterly* 48 (2000): 223–39.

7. Dean Barnlund, *Communicative Styles of Japanese and Americans: Images and Realities* (Belmont, CA: Wadsworth, 1989).

8. J. C. McCroskey and V. P. Richmond, "Willingness to Communicate: Differing Cultural Perspectives," *The Southern Communication Journal* 56 (1990): 72–77.

9. M. L. Hecht, S. Ribeau, and J. K. Alberts, "An Afro-American Perspective on Interethnic Communication," *Communication Monographs* 56 (1989): 385–410.

10. For a good review of role development in groups, see A. Paul Hare, "Types of Roles in Small Groups: A Bit of History and a Current Perspective," *Small Group Research* 25 (1994): 433–48 and Abran J. Salazar, "An Analysis of the Development and Evolution of Roles in the Small Group," *Small Group Research* 27 (1996): 475–503.

11. Kenneth D. Benne and Paul Sheats, "Functional Roles of Group Members," *Journal of Social Issues* 4 (Spring 1948): 41–49.

12. Ernest G. Bormann, *Discussion and Group Methods: Theory and Practice*, 3rd ed. (New York: Harper & Row, 1989) 209.

13. S. Schacter, "Deviation, Rejection, and Communication," *Journal of Abnormal and Social Psychology* 46 (1951): 190–207.

14. Marshall Scott Poole, "Group Communication and the Structuring Process," in Robert S. Cathcart and Larry A. Samovar, eds., *Small Group Communication: A Reader,* 6th ed. (Dubuque, IA: Brown, 1992) 275–87.

15. H. T. Reitan and Marvin E. Shaw, "Group Membership, Sex-Composition of the Group, and Conformity Behavior," *Journal of Social Psychology* 64 (1964): 45–51.

16. Marvin Shaw, *Group Dynamics: The Psychology of Small Group Behavior* (New York: McGraw-Hill, 1981) 281.

17. Solomon Asch, "Studies of Independence and Submission to Group Pressures," *Psychological Monographs* 70 (whole issue) (1956).

18. Michael G. Cruz, David Henningsen, and Mary Lynn Miller Williams, "The Presence of Norms in the Absence of Groups? The Impact of Normative Influence Under Hidden-Profile Conditions," *Human Communication Research* 26 (2000): 104–124.

19. Granville King III and Amy Hermodson, "Peer Reporting of Coworker Wrongdoing: A Qualitative Analysis of Observer Attitudes in the Decision to Report versus Not Report Unethical Behavior," *Journal of Applied Communication Research* 28 (2000): 309–329

20. Susan B. Shimanoff, "Group Interaction via Communication Rules," in Robert S. Cathcart and Larry A. Samovar, eds., *Small Group Communication: A Reader*, 6th ed. (Dubuque, IA: Brown, 1992).

21. Peter R. Scholtes, Brian L. Joiner, and Barbara J. Streibel, *The Team Handbook*, 2nd ed. (Madison, WI: Joiner, 1996); Jon R. Katzenbach and Douglas K. Smith, The *Wisdom of Teams: Creating the High-Performance Organization* (New York: HarperCollins, 1993); Dennis A. Romig, *Breakthough Teamwork: Outstanding Results Using Structured Teamwork*® (Chicago: Irwin, 1996).

22. Stephen R, Covey, *The Seven Habits of Highly Effective People* (New York: Simon & Schuster, 1989).

23. Scholtes, Joiner, and Streible, *The Team Handbook*.

24. Charles R. Bantz, "Cultural Diversity and Group Cross-Cultural Team Research," *Journal of Applied Communication Research* 21 (1993): 1–20.

25. Hee Sun Park and Timothy R. Levine, "The Theory of Reasoned Action and Self-Construal: Evidence from Three Cultures, *Comunication Monographs* 66 (1999): 199–218.

26. Min-Sun Kim, John E. Hunter, Akira Miyahara, Ann-Marie Horvath, Mary Bresnahan, and Hei-jin Yoon, "Individual- vs. Culture-Level Dimensions of Individualism and Collectivism: Effects on Preferred Conversational Styles," *Communication Monographs* 63 (1996): 29–49.

27. T. Katriel, Communicative Style in Cross-Cultural Perspective: Arabs and Jews in Israel. Paper presented at the annual meeting of the Western Speech Communication Association, Sacramento, California, 1990.

28. Barnlund, *Communicative Styles of Japanese and Americans*.

29. Satoshi Ishii and Tom Bruneau, "Silence and Silences in Cross-Cultural Perspective: Japan and the United States," in Larry A. Samovar and Richard E. Porter, eds., *Intercultural Communication: A Reader,* 6th ed. (Belmont, CA: Wadsworth, 1991).

30. John Condon, ". . . So Near the United States: Notes on Communication between Mexicans and North Americans," in Larry A. Samovar and Richard E. Porter, eds., Intercultural Communication: A Reader, 6th ed. (Belmont, CA: Wadsworth, 1991).

31. Thomas K. Fitzgerald, *Metaphors of Identity: A Culture-Communication Dialogue* (Albany: SUNY P, 1993).

32. Condon, "So Near the United States" 11.

33. Dawn O. Braithwaite, "Viewing Persons with Disabilities as a Culture," in Larry A. Samovar and Richard E. Porter, *Intercultural Communication* (Belmont, CA: Wadsworth, 1991).

34. Russell D. Hart and David E. Williams, "Able-Bodied Instructors and Students with Physical Disabilities: A Relationship Handicapped by Communication," *Communication Education* 44 (1995): 140–54.

35. Marilyn Bishop, "Do's and Don'ts: Welcoming People with Disabilities," *Church Magazine*, published by National Pastoral Life Center (1994).

36. Bormann, *Discussion and Group Methods* 215.

37. J. I. Hurwitz, A. F. Zander, and B. Hymovitch, "Some Effects of Power on the Relations among Group Members," in D. Cartwright and A. Zander, eds., *Group Dynamics: Research and Theory* (New York: Harper & Row, 1953), 483–92.

38. Hurwitz, Zander, and Hymovitch, "Some Effects of Power."

39. Hurwitz, Zander, and Hymovitch, "Some Effects of Power."

40. D. C. Barnlund and C. Harland, "Propinquity and Prestige as Determinants of Communication Networks," *Sociometry* 26 (1963): 467–79.

41. Shaw, *Group Dynamics* 246.

42. George C. Homans, *The Human Group* (New York: Harcourt Brace & World, 1992).

43. John K. Brilhart and Gloria J. Galanes, *Effective Group Discussion* (Dubuque, IA: Brown, 1997) 36.

44. H. H. Kelly, "Communication in Experimentally Created Hierarchies," *Human Relations 4* (1951): 36–56.

45. Kelly, "Communication in Experimentally Created Hiearchies."

46. Kelly, "Communication in Experimentally Created Hiearchies."

47. Bormann, *Discussion and Group Methods* 215.

48. Bormann, *Discussion and Group Methods* 215.

49. Robert Bierstedt, "An Analysis of Social Power," *American Sociological Review* 6 (1950): 7–30.

50. Randal S. Franz, "Task Interdependence and Personal Power in Teams," *Small Group Research* 29 (1998): 226–53.

51. J. R. P. French and B. H. Raven, "The Bases of Social Power," in D. Cartwright and A. Zander, eds., *Group Dynamics* (Evanston, IL: Row, Peterson, 1962) 607–23.

52. Charles R. Berger, "Power in the Family," in Michael Roloff and Gerald Miller, eds., *Persuasion: New Direction in Theory and Research* (Beverly Hills, CA: Sage, 1980) 217.

53. Marshall R. Singer, *Intercultural Communication: A Perceptual Approach* (Englewood Cliffs, NJ: Prentice Hall, 1987) 118.

54. Randal S. Franz, "Task Interdependence and Personal Power in Teams," *Small Group Research* 29 (1998): 226–53.

55. Kathleen M. Propp, "An Experimental Examination of Biological Sex as a Status Cue in Decision-Making Groups and Its Influence on Information Use," *Small Group Research* 26 (1995), 451–74.

56. Lindsey M. Grob, Renee Meyers, and Renee Schuh, "Powerful/Powerless Language Use in Group Interactions: Sex Differences or Similarities?" *Communication Quarterly* 45 (1997): 282–303.

57. Linda M. Sagrestano, "Power Strategies in Interpersonal Relationships: The Effects of Expertise and Gender," *Psychology of Women Quarterly* 16 (1992): 481–95.

58. William L. Gardner III, Joy Van Eck Peluchette, and Sharon K. Clinebell, "Valuing Women in Management: An Impression Management Perspective of Gender Diversity," *Management Communication Quarterly* 8 (1994): 115–64.

59. Shu-Chu Sarrina Li, *"Power and Its Relationship with Group Communication,"* Ph.D. dissertation, U of Iowa, 1993.

60. Richard Reichert, *Self-Awareness Through Group Dynamics* (Dayton, OH: Pflaum/Standard, 1970) 21.

61. John Powell, *why am i afraid to tell you who i am?* (Niles, IL: Argus Communications, 1990) 12.

62. Powell, *why am i afraid to tell you who i am?*, 54–58.

63. Joseph Luft, *Of Human Interaction* (Palo Alto, CA: National Press, 1969) 132–33.

64. Bormann, *Discussion and Group Methods* 181–82.

65. Adapted from Charles R. Bontz, "Cultural Diversity and Group Cross-Cultural Team Research," *Journal of Applied Communication Research* 21 (1993): 12.

5

Chapter Outline:

Objectives:

After studying this chapter,
you will be able to:

▶ Observe a group discussion and iden-
    tify behaviors that contribute to a
    defensive or supportive group climate.

▶ Identify examples of confirming and
    disconfirming interpersonal responses.

▶ Explain three types of listening in
    small groups.

▶ Describe two major barriers to effec-
    tive listening.

▶ Observe, identify, and describe at least
    four factors in group cohesiveness.

▶ Explain communication networks and
    their effects on group climate and
    individual satisfaction.

▶ Describe the relationships among
    group size, composition, climate, and
    productivity.

▶ Communicate in ways that are more
    likely to improve group climate.

Improving
Group Climate

> *"All for one, and one for all."*
> — Alexander Dumas

What does the word *climate* call to mind? If you've taken a course in geography or meteorology or have studied weather patterns, you may think of temperature gradients, barometric pressure, and how bodies of water, latitude, ocean currents, and mountains affect the weather of a particular region. Look out your window. What is the weather like? Does today's weather make you want to curl up with a book? Go to the beach? Go skiing? Would you say that climate affects your desire to engage in certain activities? How do you feel about a cold, snowy night spent in front of a roaring fire in a cozy room?

Group climate is roughly analogous to geographic climate. A variety of factors interact to create a group feeling or atmosphere. How group members communicate, to whom they communicate, and how often they communicate influence their satisfaction as well as productivity. You may have participated in groups where there was a genuine sense of warmth, trust, camaraderie, and accomplishment. This chapter examines how people communicate in ways that help the group establish a positive climate.

A CASE STUDY

Not long ago I received a rather mysterious telephone call from a good friend. He said that he and his wife had a business proposition for me and my wife, which they would like to discuss as soon as they could. No, he really didn't want to discuss any details over the phone. When could we meet? Tuesday evening? At my place? They'd see us then.

Our curiosity piqued, we anxiously awaited the Tuesday evening rendezvous. What could our friends possibly have up their sleeves? The appointed hour arrived. Right on time, the doorbell rang. ("Unusual," we thought, "they're usually a half-hour late.") Our next surprise was that our friend George was dressed in a three-piece suit, his wife Margaret in a tailored dress. My wife and I looked at each other in our jeans, bare feet, and T-shirts, then returned our gaze to George and Margaret and asked whether they had just returned from a funeral. They laughed nervously, marched past us, and began to set up a small demonstration board on our dining room table. Turning down our offer of wine, they asked if we could begin the meeting. This was becoming stranger by the moment. My wife, Nancy, and I were beginning to feel as if we had invited insurance agents into our home even though we had gone camping, hiking, canoeing, and spent many an evening with George and Margaret. Something didn't fit, but our curiosity was aroused so we decided to play along.

It wasn't long before the experience began to get frustrating. George and Margaret asked us what we wanted out of life. We suggested that they probably ought to have some idea of that by now—that most of our goals were inward, state-of-being kinds of goals, like having a greater awareness of ourselves and others, peace of mind, and so forth. This answer agitated our guests, who responded by suggesting that it might be nice if we never again had to worry about money. We agreed that it would, indeed, be pleasant. At this, they seemed to breathe a little more easily and proceeded to haul out charts, graphs, and illustrations which, they claimed, proved that we could double our present income in a little over a year—in our spare time, of course.

After an hour, George and Margaret were still refusing to tell us what it was we would have to sell (we'd figured out *that* much) or to whom we'd have to sell it. ("Please bear with us until the end," they said.) Something was definitely wrong. Here I was sitting in my own dining room with my wife, my friends, and a glass of wine, yet I felt as if I were back in junior high being asked to please hold all my questions until the end. I've had the same experience with life insurance and encyclopedia salespeople. They were treating us not as people, but as faceless members of the great mass of consumers.

George and Margaret were still making their pitch. They had finally revealed the name of the company and its line of products and were now setting about the task of showing how rapidly the company had grown due to its unique marketing concepts, fine products which sell themselves (of course), and so forth. It didn't matter, I had already decided not to do it. I felt dehumanized, abused by my friends. Why hadn't they simply told us that they were involved with the company (which we had heard of long before) and that they'd like to explore the possibilities of our becoming involved as well? With friends, it would be a much more effective approach—certainly a more honest one.

The formal part of the presentation was over. They were asking for our comments and questions. I was ready. As a communication professor, I am well versed in the art of critiquing oral presentations and visual aids. I proceeded to evaluate their entire presentation, emphasizing their failure to adequately analyze their audience and to adapt their communication style accordingly. George and Margaret were shocked and hurt. They had not, they said, come into our home to be criticized. They had come in good faith with an honest proposal from which we all stood to benefit. If they had offended us, they were sorry. No, they still did not care for a glass of wine. We'd get together again sometime soon.

Defensive Communication

Pause for a moment and ask: What was wrong with this picture? How many causes can you identify for the deterioration of the situation described? This case study illustrates many of the principles discussed in this text. Clearly, some group norms were being violated, particularly the interpersonal expectations of openness and honesty. Likewise, group roles to which all the participants had adjusted were altered dramatically as new roles of "salesperson" and "critic" were introduced. Messages, both verbal and nonverbal, were interpreted differently (for example, their "professional" attire seemed out of place to us). The scenario is a particularly good example of the type of communication that fosters a *defensive climate* in the small group.

A closer look at the case study reveals that from the first telephone call, information was withheld—a pattern that repeated itself throughout the entire episode. When George and Margaret arrived they were dressed in a very businesslike fashion, suggesting a change in what had become a typical pattern of interaction for the two couples. George and Margaret took *control* of the conversation. They maintained control of information and, to an extent, controlled others' choices (through limiting alternative responses). The response to George and Margaret was defensive, verbal aggression. I gave an evaluative critique of the presentation that aroused further defensiveness, hurt, and anger in a cyclical process that left old questions unanswered and new ones unasked. In short, it was a very uncomfortable and unproductive evening. The specific examples of **defensive communication** we find occurring here are *strategy, control,* and *evaluation.*

Defensive and Supportive Climates

For several years Dr. Jack Gibb observed the communicative behavior of people in groups and identified the types of behaviors that contribute to defensive climates and supportive climates. Gibb suggests that a defensive climate is clearly counterproductive in any group.

> The person who behaves defensively, even though he also gives some attention to the common task, devotes an appreciable portion of his energy to defending himself. Besides talking about the topic, he thinks about how he appears to others, how he may be seen more favorably, how he may win, dominate, impress, or escape punishment, and/or how he may avoid or mitigate a perceived or an anticipated attack.[1]

More recent research continues to reinforce the relationship of a supportive climate to productivity.[2] Indeed, supportive communication in the workplace has been found to reduce stress and burnout for many employees. Supportive communication provides links among employees or group members characterized by self-disclosure (see Chapter 4) and a shared definition of the relationship. Often, the key to building a supportive climate lies not only in *what* we communicate but in *how* we communicate it.[3] A message can be delivered in ways that evoke support or defense. Consider some examples based on Gibb's categories.

Evaluation versus Description

Problem solving in small groups involves generating and evaluating ideas. Unfortunately, not all ideas are perfect, and the group needs to discover this if it is to reach the most effective decision. When someone puts forth a less-than-perfect idea, you can respond by saying, "You idiot, that's the most ridiculous idea I've heard in a decade," or you can say, "As I think through that idea and apply it to our problem, I run up against some other problems. Am I missing something?" Imagine yourself on the receiving end of the first comment. How do you feel? You have just been put down and are likely to be defensive. This is an example of evaluation (albeit an extreme one). The second response, an example of description, is much more effective and supportive. Your idea may, in fact, be terrible, but at least the second response allows you to save face. It also keeps the door open for further discussion of your idea. Quite possibly, further investigation into your bad idea may lead to a better idea.

In a nutshell, *evaluation* is "you" language: It directs itself to the other person's worth or the worth of that person's ideas. As a result, it can provoke much defensiveness. *Description,* in contrast, is "I" language: It describes the speaker's thoughts about the person or idea. This type of response leads to more trust and cohesiveness in groups.

Control versus Problem Orientation

Communicative behavior that aims at controlling others can produce much defensiveness in group members. This pattern characterizes many aggressive salespeople who, quite intentionally, manipulate others into answering trivial questions that lead up to the final question of whether or not they want to buy a product. Various persuasive tactics aim at controlling behavior (as any student of television commercials can observe). Implicit in attempts to control lies the assumption that the controller knows what is good for the controllee—the "I know what's good for you" assumption. When people become aware of this attitude, they frequently get defensive.

In a group, *problem orientation* is a more effective approach. If others perceive you as a person who genuinely strives for a solution that will benefit all concerned (rather than just yourself), this perception will contribute to a supportive climate, greater cohesiveness, and increased productivity.

Strategy versus Spontaneity

Like controlling behavior, strategy suggests manipulation. The effects of strategy on the group's climate can be seen in the case study that began this chapter. Because we perceived George and Margaret to be withholding information and acting with hidden motivations, we became defensive. We felt used and manipulated. Again, this sort of behavior places the self before the group and does not lead to the most effective solutions to group problems.

If others perceive you as a person who acts *spontaneously* (that is, not from hidden motivations or agendas) and as a person who immediately and honestly responds to the present situation, you are likely to create a more supportive climate.

Neutrality versus Empathy

If you behave in a detached, uncaring fashion, as if the people in your group and the outcome of the group's process do not concern you in the least, your behavior will probably

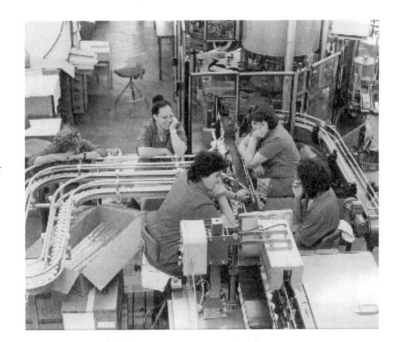

Communication that is spontaneous is perceived as more supportive than communication that appears planned. Why might workers at this factory appreciate spontaneous communication?

arouse defensiveness. Involvement and concern for the group task and for other group members are perceived as supportive.

Superiority versus Equality

If you feel superior, a small group meeting is not the place to show it. You probably know people who approach you in class after tests have been returned and ask, "What'd ya get?" Frequently these students use this question merely as a preface to showing you their superior grade. Most people think such behavior is obnoxious. It makes them feel defensive. In groups, some people preface their remarks with words such as "obviously" or point out their greater knowledge, experience, or some other attribute that makes them superior to other members. Most likely, their behavior will meet with some resistance. People create more supportive climates when they indicate a willingness to enter into participative planning with mutual trust and respect.

Certainty versus Provisionalism

Do you know people who always have all the answers, whose ideas are truths to be defended, who are intolerant of those with the wrong (that is, different) attitudes? These highly dogmatic people are well known for the defensiveness they produce in others. The usual response is to want to prove them wrong. This behavior is counterproductive in groups. Individuals are likely to be more effective if their attitudes appear to be held provisionally; that is, if they appear flexible and genuinely committed to solving problems rather than to simply taking sides on issues. If people leave themselves open to new information and can admit that, from time to time, they may be wrong about something, they will be more effective group members and will help build more supportive group climates.

As a communicator, you control your own actions. Your knowledge of defensive and supportive behaviors will help you make your group work more effectively. Another area of research and application in group climate is interpersonal confirmation and disconfirmation. This research deals not with communicative behaviors that you initiate, but with the ways in which you respond to other group members.

REVIEW

Defensive and Supportive Climate

DEFENSIVE COMMENTS

Evaluation: "You" language; calls into question the worth of the person.

Control: Aims at getting others to do what you want them to do.

Strategy: Planned communication— for example, saying something nice before criticizing someone.

Neutrality: Emotional indifference; "You'll get over it."

Superiority: Attitude that you're better than the other person.

Certainty: Taking dogmatic, rigid positions; "Don't bother me with facts, my mind is made up." Usually more interested in winning an argument than in solving a problem.

SUPPORTIVE COMMENTS

Description: "I" language; describes your own feelings and ideas.

Problem orientation: Communication aimed at solving problems: "Let's find a solution that works for both of us."

Spontaneity: Here-and-now orientation; being honest rather than planning how to manipulate.

Empathy: Emotional involvement; nonverbal behavior is important.

Equality: Communication based on mutual respect; "I'm okay, you're okay."

Provisionalism: Openness to receiving new information; showing some flexibility in the positions you take.

Collaborating

ETHICALLY

Defensive behaviors described by Gibb and disconfirming responses as identified by Sieburg and Larson are often not effective communication, but are they also unethical? If I interrupt you, or ignore you, or act superior, am I behaving unethically? Why or why not? Can you identify the basis for your response?

Group process often seems to go nowhere. Questions are left unanswered and ideas remain ignored. One of the most frequent complaints among group members is that communication in the group seems disconnected and disjointed, fostering vague feelings of uneasiness, as if the members are being disregarded.[4] Unfortunately, this is a common phenomenon and one that does not satisfy task, process, or individual needs. While attending a series of committee meetings, one observer noted that hardly anyone directly acknowledged what anyone else said. Rather, the meetings proceeded as a series of soliloquies. Not surprisingly, most group members expressed dissatisfaction with the group's process and frustration with their inability to reach decisions.

In an investigation of communication in effective and ineffective groups, Evelyn Sieburg examined the ways in which group members responded to the communicative acts of others. In this seminal study and in later work with Carl Larson, Sieburg identified several types of responses that she classified as *confirming* or *disconfirming*. Simply stated, **confirming responses** are those that cause people to value themselves more, while **disconfirming responses** are those that cause people to value themselves less.[5] Sieburg's identification of confirming and disconfirming responses has been one of the most salient contributions to the understanding of group climate.

Some interpersonal responses are obvious examples of confirmation and disconfirmation—for example, when a person responds to another with overt praise or sharp criticism. However, group members confirm and disconfirm one another in more subtle ways. Goldberg and Larson identify some of those behaviors as follows.

Disconfirming Responses

1. *Impervious response:* One speaker fails to acknowledge, even minimally, the other speaker's communicative attempt.

2. *Interrupting response:* One speaker cuts another speaker short or begins while the other is still speaking.

3. *Irrelevant response:* A speaker responds in a way that seems unrelated to what the other has been saying, or introduces a new topic without warning or returns to his or her earlier topic, apparently disregarding the intervening conversation.

4. *Tangential response:* A speaker acknowledges another person's communication but immediately takes the conversation in another direction. Occasionally individuals exhibit what may appear to be direct responses to the other, such as "Yes, but . . ." or "Well, you may be right, but . . . ," and then respond with communicative content very different from what preceded. Responses such as these may still be called tangential.

5. *Impersonal response:* One speaker conducts a monologue, or exhibits speech communication behavior that appears intellectualized and impersonal, or contains few first-per-

son statements and many generalized "you" or "one" statements—and is heavily loaded with euphemisms or clichés.

6. *Incoherent response:* A speaker responds with incomplete sentences; with rambling, difficult-to-follow statements; with sentences containing much retracing or rephrasing; or with interjections such as "you know" or "I mean."

7. *Incongruous response:* A speaker engages in nonvocal behavior that seems inconsistent with the vocal content, which results in a response that may be called incongruous. For example, "Who's angry? I'm not angry!" (said in a tone and volume that strongly suggest anger), or "I'm really concerned about you" (said in a tone that suggests lack of interest or disdain).

Confirming Responses

1. *Direct acknowledgment:* A speaker acknowledges another person's communication and reacts to it directly and verbally.

2. *Agreement about content:* A speaker reinforces information expressed by another.

3. *Supportive response:* A speaker expresses understanding of another person or tries to reassure or make the other feel better.

4. *Clarifying response:* A speaker tries to clarify another person's message or feelings. The usual form of a clarifying response is to elicit more information, to encourage the other person to say more, or to repeat in an inquiring way what was understood.

5. *Expression of positive feeling.* One speaker describes his or her own positive feelings related to prior utterances of another person. For example, "Okay, now I understand what you are saying."[6]

When you perceive others' behavior as threatening to your emotional security or position in a group, your uncertainty about your role in the group increases. Individual needs are elevated to a place equal to or even greater than the group's task and process needs. If you respond defensively, you are likely to evoke further defensiveness from the rest of the group. People do not trust one another in a defensive, disconfirming climate. The realization that you cannot trust another suggests that that person's behavior is unpredictable—that you do not know for sure how he or she will respond. Such uncertainty is counterproductive in a problem-solving group. In contrast, in a supportive, confirming climate, where mutual respect and trust prevail, you are more certain of your own well-being. This security, in turn, allows you to increase your concentration on the task and the process needs of the group.

The implication of this research for improving communicative effectiveness and thus the effectiveness of groups is this: By using confirming rather than disconfirming responses when communicating with other group members, people contribute toward a supportive, trustful climate and therefore promote greater group effectiveness and individual satisfaction.

Confirming responses cause us to value ourselves more. What responses from others make you feel good during your group activities?

Listening

Good listening skills are an important component of effective group leadership.[7] However, poor listening habits are one of the most common sources of defensiveness and disconfirmation. If you do not actively attend to what another person says, your responses will be perfunctory at best and apathetic, impervious, or tangential at worst. It is even easier to be a poor listener in groups than it is in interpersonal situations, because you do not have to respond to the speaker. After all, the other group members can always pick up the conversation. However, groups cannot reach their maximum effectiveness unless all members listen actively to one another.

Listening is a skill that can be improved with practice. It is an active process through which people select, attend, understand, and remember. To listen effectively, people must actively select and attend to the messages they receive. This involves filtering out the other stimuli that compete for their attention: The hunger pangs they're starting to feel, reminders of the groceries they need to pick up on the way home, curiosity about the attractive person nearby. Improving any skill takes knowledge and practice. This section will provide some knowledge. The practice is up to you. Are you listening?

Types of Listening

Allan Glatthorn and Herbert Adams suggest that there are three types of listening: (1) hearing, (2) analyzing, and (3) empathizing.[8]

Hearing   Hearing is the fundamental type of listening on which the other two types are built. "Hearing is receiving the message as sent."[9] Glatthorn and Adams point out that achieving this seemingly simple objective involves several complex operations. You must

Receive the sounds as transmitted

Translate these sounds into the words and meanings that were intended

Understand the relationship of those words in the sentences spoken

Note the relevant nonverbal cues that reinforce the message

Comprehend the entire message as intended[10]

Viewed in this way, hearing becomes a great deal more than a physiological response to stimuli. To say "I hear you" takes on new meaning.

Analyzing   Analyzing is the use of critical or creative judgment to discern the purpose of the speaker. Analyzing is based on hearing but goes far beyond; it includes making judgments about unspoken messages, as well as the broader context in which messages were received. For example, many messages in small groups are aimed at persuading other group members. Often these messages contain emotional appeals, such as "Our group's failure to stand up in support of anti-abortion laws is tantamount to murder!" Hearing this message is not difficult, particularly if the speaker's nonverbal behavior reinforces it. Analyzing it is a bit trickier. An appropriate response requires that you analyze the content of the message, the intent of the speaker, and the context within which the transaction takes place. You need to consider the persuasive strategy the speaker is employing, his or her degree of commitment to the issue, the nature and objectives of the group, and the probable positions other group members hold on the issue. In short, to respond with maximum effectiveness, you need to consider multiple factors instantaneously. Glatthorn and Adams claim that analyzing involves the following steps:

Hearing the message accurately

Identifying the stated purpose

Inferring the unstated purpose

Determining if a critical or creative judgment is required

Responding accordingly[11]

Empathizing   Empathizing is the most complex and difficult type of listening. It requires concentration, a sensitivity to the emotional content of messages, an ability to see the world from the speaker's viewpoint, and a willingness to suspend judgment. Empathizing involves hearing and analyzing but again moves beyond them. It involves these steps:

Hearing the message accurately

Listening to the unstated purpose

Withholding judgment

Seeing the world from the speaker's perspective

Sensing the unspoken words

Responding with acceptance[12]

Often problems that affect a group are expressed obliquely——not in the words themselves, but in the feelings behind the words.

Cindy: You all can do whatever you want to do. I'll go along with anything.

Toni: You sound as if you're not all here tonight. Is it something you can talk about?

Cindy: Oh, I'm having some problems at home. It'll all work out, but I can't get it out of my mind. I'm sorry if I'm a little distant tonight.

Floyd: That's okay. We understand.

Cindy has a problem that she brought with her to the group. Although her problem does not affect the group directly, it can be a potential source of misunderstanding and conflict. Her seeming lack of interest in the group may be a cause for unwarranted anger:

Cindy: You all can do whatever you want. I'll go along with anything.

Lou: Dammit, Cindy, I'm not going to let you get away with that. This group needs your ideas as much as anyone's, and you just can't sit back and let us do all the work.

This insensitive response reflects Lou's failure to empathize, which results in a disconfirming response to Cindy. Toni's empathizing response in the first dialogue, however, was accepting and supporting. It promoted the group's understanding of the situation, which led to a more positive group climate.

There are many good reasons to listen effectively, among them that listening is related to leadership: Group members perceived as poor listeners are not typically perceived as occupying leadership positions. People seen as leaders are also seen as good listeners.[13]

Barriers to Effective Listening

As explained earlier, listening is the process of selecting, attending, understanding, and remembering. The previous discussion suggests that this process can take place at a number of levels. To fully attend to, understand, and remember what another is saying at any of these levels requires that you overcome the common obstacles to effective listening. There are many such barriers—outside distractions, an uncomfortable chair, a headache—but the focus here will be on two prevalent and serious barriers: Prejudging and rehearsing.

Prejudging the Communicator or the Communication   Sometimes you simply dislike some people or always disagree with them. You anticipate that what these people will say will be offensive, and you begin to tune them out. An example of this is many people's tendency not to listen carefully to the speeches of politicians who hold political beliefs different from their own. In a group, you must overcome the temptation to ignore those you think are boring, pedantic, or offensive. Good ideas can come from anyone, even from people you do not like. Likewise, you should not prejudge certain topics as being too complex, boring, or controversial. This can be difficult, especially when a cherished belief is criticized or when others say things about you that you might not want to hear. These are precisely the times when communication needs to be clear, open, honest, and confirming. To communicate in that way, you need to listen.

It is especially important not to prejudge others on the basis of culture, ethnicity, or race. As far as our society has progressed, however, such prejudices linger.[14] In one study, college students indicated that racial stereotypes are alive and well. African Americans said that whites were "demanding" and "manipulative," whites reported that blacks are "loud" and "ostentatious."[15] Such prejudices inhibit our ability to listen effectively and also foster defensiveness in groups.

Rehearsing a Response   This barrier is perhaps the most difficult to overcome. It is the tendency people have to rehearse in their minds what they will say when the other person is finished. One of the reasons for this barrier is the difference between speech rate and thought rate. Most people speak at a rate of about 100 to 125 words per minute, but they have the capacity to think or listen at a rate of 400 or more words per minute! This gives them the mental time and space to wander off while keeping one ear on the speaker. The thought–speech differential is better used, though, to attend fully to what the speaker is saying—and not saying. When people learn to do this, their responses can be more spontaneous, accurate, appropriate, confirming, and supportive.

A Guide to Active Listening

Supportive, confirming communication focuses not only on verbal messages but on the emotional content of nonverbal behaviors as well. Learning to quiet one's own thoughts and to avoid prejudging others is a first step. Fully understanding others, though, involves considerable effort.

Active listening is an attempt to clarify and understand another's thoughts and feelings. To listen actively involves several steps:

1. *Stop:* Before you can effectively tune in to what someone else may be feeling, you need to stop what you are doing, eliminate as many distractions as possible, and focus fully on the other person.

2. *Look:* Now look for nonverbal clues that will help you identify how the other person is feeling. Most communication of emotion comes through nonverbal cues. The face provides important information about how a person is feeling, as do that person's voice quality, pitch, rate, volume, and use of silence. Body movement and posture clearly indicate the intensity of a person's feelings.

3. *Listen:* Listen for what another person is telling you. Even though that person may not say exactly how he or she feels, look for cues. Match verbal with nonverbal cues to decipher both the content and the emotion of the person's message. In addition, ask yourself, "How would I feel if I were in that person's position?" Try to interpret the message according to the sender's code system rather than your own.

4. *Ask questions:* As you try to understand another person, you may need to ask some questions. Most of these will serve one of four purposes: (1) to obtain additional information ("How soon will you be ready to give your part of our presentation?"); (2) to find out how someone feels ("Are you feeling overwhelmed by this assignment?"); (3) to ask for clarification of a word or phrase ("What do you mean when you say you didn't realize what you were getting into?"); and (4) to verify your conclusion about your partner's mean-

ing or feeling ("Are you saying that you can't complete the project without some additional staff assistance?").

5. *Paraphrase content:* Paraphrasing is restating in your own words what you think another person is saying. Paraphrasing is different from parroting back everything that person has said. After all, you can repeat something perfectly without understanding what it means. Rather, from time to time quickly summarize the message another person has given you so far.

Emily: I think this job is too much for me; I'm not qualified to do it.

Howard: You think you lack the necessary skills.

Note that at this point Howard is dealing only with the content of Emily's message. The goal of active listening, though, is to understand both the feelings and the content of another person's message.

6. *Paraphrase feelings:* In the example just given, Howard could follow his paraphrase of the content of the message with a question such as "You're probably feeling pretty frustrated right now, aren't you?" Such a paraphrase would allow Emily either to agree with Howard's assessment or to clarify how she's feeling. For instance, she might respond, "No, I'm not frustrated. I'm just disappointed that the job's not working out."

Effective listening skills can contribute a great deal to building a supportive, cohesive group. Effective listening is also the cornerstone of critical thinking—the skill required to make decisions and solve problems effectively, as we shall see in later chapters.

Verbal Dynamics in the Small Group

The most obvious yet elusive component of small group communication is the spoken word. Words lie at the very heart of who and what people are. Their ability to represent the world symbolically gives humans the capacity to foresee events, to reflect on past experiences, to plan, to make decisions, and to consciously control their own behavior. Words are the tools with which people make sense of the world and share that sense with others.

Words as Barriers to Communication

Although words can empower people and can influence attitudes and behaviors, they can also impede a process. Speech communication gives individuals access to the ideas and inner worlds of other group members, but it can also—intentionally or unintentionally—set up barriers to effective communication. Words affect group climate.

If you grew up in the United States, you can probably remember chanting defensively, "Sticks and stones can break my bones but names can never hurt me." Even as you uttered these lines you knew you were using a lie to protect yourself. You often unwittingly communicate in ways that threaten and make others feel defensive. When group members feel a need to protect themselves, they shift their attention from the group's goal to their own personal goal of self-protection, thus creating a barrier to effective group process. Some more subtle but pervasive word barriers are (1) bypassing, (2) allness, and (3) fact-inference confusion.

Bypassing   The meanings of the words you use seem so obvious to you that you assume those words suggest the same meanings to others. Nothing could be further from the truth. **Bypassing** takes place when two people assign different meanings to the same word. Many words are open to an almost limitless number of interpretations. Consider, for example, the words *love, respect,* and *communication.* Or you may know precisely what you mean when you say that the department's account is "seriously overdrawn," but how are others to interpret that? How serious is "seriously"?

According to some estimates, the 500 most frequently used words in the English language have over 14,000 dictionary definitions. Considering that a dictionary definition reflects only a tiny percentage of all possible meanings for a word and that people from different cultures and with different experiences interpret words differently, it is amazing that people can understand one another at all.

In groups, the problem of bypassing is compounded by the number of people involved; the possibility for multiple misunderstandings is always present. This points to the importance of good feedback among group members. Feedback is any response by listeners that lets speakers know whether they have been understood accurately. To overcome word barriers, people must understand that words are subjective. They need to check that what they understand from others is really what those others intend.

Allness   **Allness statements** are simple but untrue generalizations. You have probably heard such allness statements as "Women are smarter than men," "Men can run faster than women," and "Football players are stupid." These statements are convenient, but they simply are not accurate. The danger of allness statements is that you may begin to believe them and to prejudge other people unfairly based on them. Therefore, be careful not to overgeneralize; remember that each individual is unique.

Fact–Inference Confusion   **Fact–inference confusion** occurs when people respond to something as if they have actually observed it when, in reality, they have merely drawn a conclusion. Although statements of fact can be made only after direct observation, inferences can be made before, during, or after an occurrence. No observation is necessary. The key distinction is that in statements of inference people can speculate about and interpret what they *think* occurred. Suppose, for example, that you heard someone comment, "Men are better than women at math." If this statement were true, it would mean that *all* men and women were tested and that the results indicated that men are better in math than women. The statement is, in reality, an inference. If the speaker is summarizing research that has investigated the issue, he or she should say, "Some studies have found that . . ." rather than "It's a fact that . . . ." The first statement more accurately describes reality than does the second. Like bypassing and allness statements, fact–inference confusion can lead to inaccuracy and misunderstanding.

A Summary of Word Barriers and Their Solutions

BARRIER	DESCRIPTION	SOLUTION
Bypassing	Occurs when the same word is used to mean different things	Use specific language; be aware of multiple interpretations of what you say; clarify.
Allness statements	Simple but untrue generalizations	Don't overgeneralize; remember that all individuals are unique.
Fact-inference confusion	Mistaking a conclusion you have drawn for an observation	Clarify and analyze; learn to recognize the difference between fact and inference, and communicate the difference clearly.

Group Cohesiveness

Historically, cohesiveness has been considered to be the most important small group variable.[16] If this were a textbook in introductory physics, it would define cohesion as the mutual attraction that holds together the elements of a body. This, of course, is a small group communication textbook, but it offers a very similar definition of **group cohesiveness**—the degree of attraction members feel toward one another and the group. It is a feeling of deep loyalty, of "groupness," of *esprit de corps,* and the degree to which each individual has made the group's goal his or her own. It is a sense of belonging and a feeling of morale.[17] Cohesiveness results from the interaction of a number of variables, including group composition, individual benefits derived from the group, task effectiveness, and, first and foremost, communication. The productivity of groups and teams is strongly related to their cohesiveness.[18, 19]

Composition and Cohesiveness: Building a Team

As noted in Chapter 3, people often join groups because they feel an attraction toward the people in that group. Factors discussed earlier, such as the similarity of group members or the degree to which group members' needs complement one another, are influential in the development of group cohesiveness.

To borrow a metaphor from the sports world, the best team has the right players at the right positions—and good coaching. Based on their size, speed, aggressiveness, reaction time, and so forth, different players are suited for different positions. So it is with groups. For maximum effectiveness, they need participants with different talents that complement one another.

Cohesiveness develops around both the task and relationship dimensions we discussed in Chapter 4. Building a group solely on the basis of similarity in interpersonal attraction (Chapter 3) predicts strong cohesiveness based on relationships but mediocrity as a task group. This is why self-selected groups are often less cohesive—and less productive—than groups in which membership has been assigned carefully, with the group's task in mind. The characteristics we find most attractive in a friend may not be those best suited to help us do a job. Evidence from college classroom groups suggests strongly that self-selection is not the best policy, as we noted in Chapter 3. In one study, by a nearly two-to-one margin students who formed their own groups reported that group as one of their worst group experiences.[20] However, extreme diversity within a group brings stimulating perspectives to problem solving but may strain the relational aspects of group process. Likewise, negative emotions such as envy can have a detrimental effect on cohesiveness and productivity.[21]

Most work groups today are culturally and racially diverse in addition to reflecting a range of talents and expertise. As we noted in Chapter 4, such diversity can be a source of strength because of the multiple perspectives it brings to problem solving if the group can work together to minimize misunderstandings that can derive from diversity.[22] That takes leadership.

We will discuss leadership further in Chapter 11. Chapter 12 will address team building.

Individual Benefits and Cohesiveness

Cohesiveness is a combination of forces that holds people in groups. Depending on the nature of the group, its members can derive benefits of affiliation, power, affection, and prestige. People like to be with groups in which these needs are satisfied. Such groups can become important reference groups in that they allow people to validate their judgments about themselves and others.[23] An important determinant of group cohesiveness, then, is the degree to which a particular group is capable of meeting members' needs in comparison to the ability of any other group to meet those same needs. If people perceive that they derive benefits from a group that no other group could provide, their attraction toward that group will strengthen considerably. This factor partially accounts for the intense attraction most people feel toward their families or closest friends.

Task Effectiveness and Cohesiveness

The relation of personal and interpersonal variables to group cohesiveness has already been discussed. The performance of the group as a whole has considerable influence as well; success fosters cohesiveness. The mutuality of concern for the group's task, which provides the focal point for working toward that task, becomes socially rewarding when the task is completed successfully. Here is another example of the interrelatedness of the task and social dimensions: Reaching a particular goal provides a common, rewarding experience for all group members. This commonality, or shared experience, further sets a group apart from other groups.

Communication and Cohesiveness

None of the factors described so far is enough, in and of itself, to build a cohesive group. Rather, the interaction of these variables determines the degree of cohesiveness. Communication is the vehicle through which this interaction takes place. Through communication, individual needs are met and tasks are accomplished. In other words, "the communication networks and the messages that flow through them ultimately determine the attractiveness of the group for its members."[24]

Recall from Chapter 2 our discussion of the role of communication in creating symbolic convergence through which a cohesive group identity evolves. According to symbolic convergence theory, the group develops a unique identity through the sharing of fantasies or stories. A feeling of cohesiveness is likely to increase as group members share stories and other group members respond to those stories. A fantasy chain occurs when one story leads to another story, thus creating a bond among group members and the revelation of common fantasies.

Most of this book is devoted to the study of how communication affects small group process. The earlier discussion of defensive and supportive communication, for example, suggests some ways in which people can adjust their communicative behavior to improve group cohesiveness. In addition to the quality of communication, the amount of communication in the group also affects cohesiveness. George Homans states that if "the frequency of interaction between two or more persons increases, the degree of their liking for one another will increase, and vice versa."[25] Free and open communication characterizes highly cohesive groups. The more people interact with one another, the more they reveal themselves to others and the more others reveal themselves to them. Through communication, people negotiate group roles, establish goals, reveal similarities and differences, resolve conflict, and express affection. It makes sense, then, that as the frequency of communication increases, so does the group's cohesiveness. Communication is also the foundation for interpersonal trust within the group.

Communication Networks

Another influence on group climate is the **communication network**—the pattern of interaction within a group, or who talks to whom. If you think about the group meetings in which you participate, it may seem that although some people talk more than others, most of their communication is addressed to the group as a whole. Next time you are in a group, note who is talking to whom. You will find that people address relatively few comments to the group as a whole and that they direct most of what they say in groups toward specific persons. In some groups, people find that communication tends to be distributed equally among group members. Figure 5.1 represents such a distribution.

In some groups, members address most comments to one central person, perhaps the designated leader or chairperson. Figure 5.2 represents this type of communicative pattern.

Other patterns may emerge. These include circular patterns, in which people talk primarily to those sitting next to them, or linear patterns, in which people communicate in a kind of chain reaction. These patterns may be built into the group from the outset, or they may emerge spontaneously. Either way, networks tend to stabilize over time. Once people establish channels of communication, they continue to use these same channels. This network of channels influences group climate as well as group productivity.

A review of research suggests that, in general, "groups in which free communication is maximized are generally more accurate in their judgments, although they may take longer to reach a decision."[26] People also tend to feel more satisfied in groups in which they participate actively.[27] When interaction is stifled or discouraged, people have less opportunity to

Figure 5.1 Equal Distribution of Communication

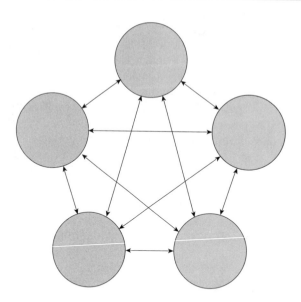

satisfy their needs through communication. Groups with centralized communication networks (see Figure 5.2) are certainly more efficient. That efficiency enhances group cohesiveness, but considerable evidence suggests that free and open communication networks, that include everyone in the group (see Figure 5.1) are more likely to lead to more accurate group judgments as well as to more attractive group climates and greater individual satisfaction.

Figure 5.2 Leader–Addressed Communication

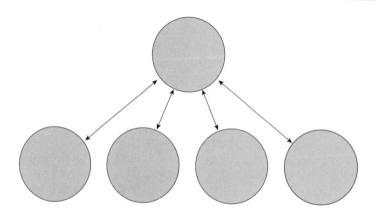

Collaborating via

TECHNOLOGY

Trust in Teams

Can trust exist in global virtual teams? Noting the lack of shared social context in such teams, much of the theoretical and empirical literature on interpersonal and organizational trust would suggest a negative response to this question. But trust among group members is important to a healthy group climate, open information sharing, and effective decision-making.

We discussed in Chapter 4 some of the factors that build trust in face-to-face groups. But what happens in virtual teams whose members are separated in time, space, and culture?

For a partial answer, go to this website:

http://www.ascusc.org/jcmc/vol3/issue4/jarvenpaa.html

You will find there an interesting article entitled "Communication and Trust in Global Virtual Teams" by Sirkka L. Jarvenpaa and Dorothy E. Leidner. The article discusses characteristics of virtual teams, and the development of what the authors term "quick trust" in such teams. Here is an abstract of the article, quoted from the website:

"This paper explores the challenges of creating and maintaining trust in a global virtual team whose members transcend time, space, and culture. The challenges are highlighted by integrating recent literature on work teams, computer-mediated communication groups, cross-cultural communication, and interpersonal and organizational trust. To explore these challenges empirically, we report on a series of descriptive case studies on global virtual teams whose members were separated by location and culture, were challenged by a common collaborative project, and for whom the only economically and practically viable communication medium was asynchronous and synchronous computer-mediated communication. The results suggest that global virtual teams may experience a form of 'swift' trust but such trust appears to be very fragile and temporal. The study raises a number of issues to be explored and debated by future research. Pragmatically, the study describes communication behaviors that might facilitate trust in global virtual teams."

Group Size

In a group, there is a positive relationship between the level of people's participation and the degree of their individual satisfaction. Obviously, as the size of a group increases, the opportunity to interact with other members decreases. What size should a group be in order to achieve maximum cohesiveness and productivity? Three heads are better than one, but are twenty heads better than three?

No one knows the precise number of people that will maximize the effectiveness of your group, but some observations may provide guidance. As a group's size increases, the principle of diminishing returns sets in. Imagine a long rope attached to a heavy weight. By yourself, using all your strength, you may not be able to move that weight. As more people join you in your effort, the weight begins to move and the task becomes easier. But as the group size increases, individuals use smaller and smaller percentages of their total strength; group information sharing tends to decrease.[28] One study found that cohesiveness is positively related to the opportunity for interaction afforded by group size: As group size increases, the opportunity for interaction decreases.[29] Cohesiveness is also related to productivity. More cohesive groups render poorer-quality decisions as group size increases.[30] What, then, is the optimum size?

Herbert Thelen has suggested the principle of "least group size." Clearly people want groups small enough to encourage maximum participation yet large enough to generate the maximum number of ideas. Thelen says that "the group should be just large enough to include individuals with all the relevant skills for problem solutions."[31] Although this principle provides no firm rule about group size, it does at least provide a guideline. In small group communication, bigger is not necessarily better. Groups of five to seven members are just about right in size.

Group Climate and Productivity

Thus far this chapter has discussed many variables that affect group climate—defensive behavior, confirming and disconfirming responses, group cohesiveness, group size—and has made some suggestions about how to improve the climate of groups. As already suggested, when communication is free and open and when everyone participates, people tend to feel more attraction toward the group and consequently receive more personal satisfaction. Another reason for developing and maintaining a positive group climate is that climate affects productivity. There is substantial evidence that factors discussed in this chapter—such as strong work norms and cohesiveness—interact in groups and teams to increase productivity.[32]

As we noted in Chapter 4, trusting relationships are those in which we feel we can count on others to behave in certain ways and in which there is mutual respect. Communication scholars Judy Pearson and Paul Nelson note two kinds of trust that are relevant to small group communication: "Having trust regarding the task means members can count on each other to get things done. A common source of conflict for many groups is having a member who doesn't contribute a fair share of the work, so others have to pick up the slack. That makes members angry and the climate tense. Having interpersonal trust means that members believe the others are operating with the best interests of the group in mind and not from hidden agendas"[33] (see Chapter 3). When a group has a trusting, open atmosphere and a high level of cohesiveness, members "do not fear the effects that disagreement and conflict in the task dimension can have on their social fabric. *Cohesive groups have strong enough social bonds to tolerate conflict.*"[34] Chapters 7 and 9 explore the function of conflict in groups. Here it is enough to say that through constructive conflict, groups deal with the difficult issues confronting them. When there is no conflict, it is usually because people do not trust one another enough to assert their individuality. Avoiding the issues does not lead to clarity concerning those issues. An absence of clarity does not help the group reach the most effective solutions.

It is a mistake to view positive group climate or group cohesiveness as a condition in which everyone is nice all the time. Quite the contrary. In a highly cohesive group, members know that they will not be rejected for their views and are therefore more willing to express them—even though expressing them may provoke disagreement. Ernest Bormann notes,

> At a point where someone in a cohesive group would say, "You're wrong!" or "I disagree!" an individual in a less cohesive group will say, "I don't understand," or "I'm confused." Members of groups with little cohesion have yet to create much of a common social reality.[35]

This common "social reality," which includes group roles and group norms, gives people the freedom to assert their individuality within a predictable context. In a cohesive group, people already know that they are accepted in the group.

Another aspect of this social reality is the degree to which group members make the group's goal their own. In highly cohesive groups, individuals personally commit themselves to the group's well-being and to accomplishing the group's task. In part, this personal commitment can be attributed to the feeling that this particular group meets people's needs better than any other group. When this is the case, as it often is in a cohesive group, people have a degree of *dependence* on the group. This dependence increases the *power* the group has over individuals. To put this in a less intimidating way, "There can be little doubt that members of a more cohesive group more readily exert influence on one another and are more readily influenced by one another."[36] These factors—personal commitment to the group, personal dependence on the group, group power over individuals within the group—come together in a positive group climate. The result is that cohesive groups work harder than those groups with little cohesiveness, regardless of outside supervision.[37]

With few exceptions, building a group climate in which cohesiveness can grow results not only in greater individual satisfaction but in greater group productivity as well.[38]

Putting Principles into Practice

Chapters 4 and 5 have focused on knowledge and skills associated with **communication competence**—communicative behavior that is both effective and appropriate in a given context. *Effectiveness,* says communication scholar Brian Spitzberg, is "the successful accomplishment of valued goals, objectives, or rewards relative to costs. *Appropriateness* means that the valued rules norms, and expectancies of the relationship are not violated significantly."[39]

Successful group communication requires communication competence: "The competent communicator knows how and when to communicate (cognitive ability) and is able to do so (behavioral ability)."[40] This chapter has provided principles that, when put into practice, can help you become a more competent communicator in groups.

▶ To the extent that you engage in supportive—rather than defensive—communication, you will foster a positive group climate in which people are free to focus their attention on the group and its task.

▶ If you can develop a sensitivity to your own confirming and disconfirming behaviors, you can become more confirming in your group behavior, thus contributing to a more positive group climate.

► Effective listening is crucial to maintaining a positive group climate. Only by listening attentively can people gain the understanding necessary to respond accurately, appropriately, and supportively to others. To do this, they need to overcome the barriers of prejudging and rehearsing a response. Listen actively. Remember to stop, look, listen, ask questions, and paraphrase.

► Cohesiveness is the result of the interaction of a number of variables, including the group's composition, individual benefits derived from the group, and task effectiveness and communication. Be aware of these factors to help foster group cohesiveness.

► If you are forming a group, include just enough people to ensure the presence of all the relevant skills for problem solving—and no more.

► A positive group climate is essential if you are to reach your maximum potential as a working group. A trusting and open climate allows all members the freedom to be themselves: To agree or disagree, or to engage in conflict without fear of rejection. The ability of a group not only to withstand but to benefit from constructive conflict is crucial to a group's productivity. To build such a climate, learn to communicate more supportively and confirmingly: Avoid defensive, disconfirming behavior.

PRACTICE

Confirmation/Disconfirmation

In your discussion group, stage a discussion in which group members attempt to use all of the disconfirming responses listed in this chapter. Choose a familiar topic about which everyone has something to say. Have observers keep a record of the number and type of disconfirming responses and the reactions (especially nonverbal) to them. Now repeat the discussion, covering as many of the same topics as possible, but this time concentrate on using only confirming responses. Again, have observers keep records. When you have completed both rounds of discussion, have group members discuss their reactions and have observers report their findings.

Observing Communication Networks: Interaction Diagrams

Communication networks—who talks to whom—have an effect on group cohesiveness, leadership patterns, and group productivity. A few minutes spent observing small group interaction will show you clearly that members infrequently address the group as a whole; instead, they tend to address specific group members. An **interaction diagram** can reveal a lot about the interaction patterns in your group. It tells you who is talking to whom and how often. You can identify the most active and the most reticent members. You can pattern the relationships that form among group members. By combining an interaction diagram with a **category system**, such as the confirming and disconfirming responses described in this chapter, you can recognize the contributions each member makes to the group. Interaction diagrams are extremely useful tools. This is how to make one:

1. Draw a circle for each member of the group, arranging your circles in the same relative positions as those in which group members are seated (Figure 5.3).

2. Refer to Figure 5.3. If Nancy were to open the meeting by asking Phil for the minutes from the last meeting, you would draw an arrow from Nancy's circle to Phil's, indicating the direction and destination of Nancy's communication. Each subsequent remark Nancy makes to Phil would then be indicated by a short crossmark at the base of the arrow.

3. Repeat this process each time someone in the group addresses someone else. If Phil were to address the minutes to Nancy, you would put an arrowhead at the other end of the line that connects the two.

4. Indicate communication addressed to the group as a whole with a line pointing away from the center of the group. Again, note subsequent remarks with crossmarks.

5. Figure 5.4 is an example of what a completed interaction diagram might look like.

Figure 5.3   Interaction Diagram

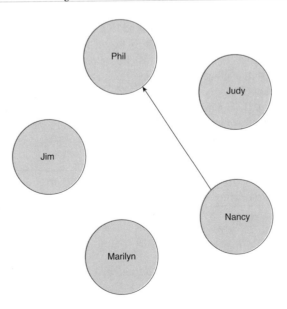

Figure 5.4 Completed Interaction Diagram with Category System

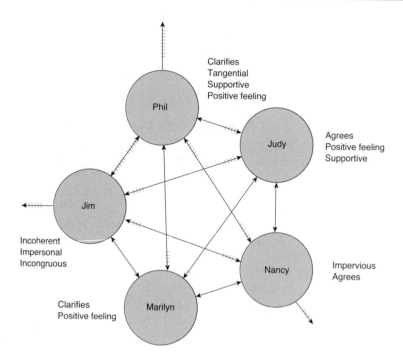

Clarifies
Tangential
Supportive
Positive feeling

Phil

Judy

Agrees
Positive feeling
Supportive

Jim

Incoherent
Impersonal
Incongruous

Nancy

Impervious
Agrees

Clarifies
Positive feeling

Marilyn

If you take a few moments to examine Figure 5.4, you will see some patterns beginning to emerge. For example, Phil seems to be the most vocal member of the group. Furthermore, most members address their remarks to Phil, which suggests that they perceive Phil to be the group's leader. The frequency with which Phil addresses the group as a whole supports this observation. The amount of communication between Phil and Jim indicates a strong relationship there, perhaps that of a leader and his "lieutenant."

The interaction diagram is an easy way to describe graphically the interaction patterns in a group. Also, this method of observation can be used without seriously disrupting the regular workings of the group. By updating the interaction diagram during several meetings, you can observe changes in group interaction. The addition of a category system to the interaction diagram renders this a most powerful descriptive tool.

 Your companion Website has more practice activities, questionnaires, and checklists!
www.ablongman.com/beebe

Notes

1. Jack R. Gibb, "Defensive Communication," *Journal of Communication* 11 (September 1961): 141.

2. Charles H. Tandy, "Assessing the Functions of Supportive Messages," *Communication Research* 19 (1992): 175–92.

3. Eileen Berlin Ray, "The Relationship Among Communication Network Roles, Job Stress, and Burnout in Educational Organizations," *Communication Quarterly* 39 (1991): 91–100.

4. Alvin Goldberg and Carl Larson, *Group Communication: Discussion Processes and Applications* (Englewood Cliffs, NJ: Prentice Hall, 1975) 105.

5. Evelyn Sieburg and Carl Larson, "Dimensions of Interpersonal Response," paper delivered at the annual conference of the International Communication Association, Phoenix, April 1971, 1.

6. Goldberg and Larson, *Group Communication* 103–104.

7. Scott D. Johnson and Curt Bechler, "Examining the Relationship Between Listening Effectiveness and Leadership Emergence: Perceptions, Behavior, and Recall," *Small Group Research* 29 (1998): 452–71.

8. Allan A. Glatthorn and Herbert R. Adams, *Listening Your Way to Management Success* (Glenview, IL: Scott, Foresman, 1984).

9. Glatthorn and Adams, *Listening Your Way to Management Success* 1.

10. Glatthorn and Adams, *Listening Your Way to Management Success* 2.

11. Glatthorn and Adams, *Listening Your Way to Management Success* 2.

12. Glatthorn and Adams, *Listening Your Way to Management Success* 3.

13. Curt Bechler and Scott D. Johnson, "Leadership and Listening: A Study of Member Perceptions," *Small Group Research* 26 (1995): 77–85.

14. Brenda J. Allen, "Diversity and Organizational Communication," *Journal of Applied Communication Research* 23 (1995): 143–55.

15. R. Leonard and D. C. Locke, "Communication Stereotypes: Is Interracial Communication Possible?" *Journal of Black Studies* 23 (1993): 332–43.

16. Albert V. Carron and Lawrence R. Brawley, "Cohesion: Conceptual and Measurement Issues," *Small Group Research* 31 (2000): 89–106

17. Kenneth A. Bollen and Rick H. Hoyle, "Perceived Cohesion: A Conceptual and Empirical Examination," *Social Forces* 69 (1990): 479.

18. Barbara A. Wech, Kevin W. Mossholder, Robert P. Steel, and Nathan Bennett, "Does Work Group Cohesiveness Affect Individuals' Performance and Organizational Commitment? A Cross-Level Examination," *Small Group Research* 29 (1998) 472–94.

19. Harry Prapavessis and Albert V. Carron, "Cohesion and Work Output," *Small Group Research* 28 (1997): 294–301.

20. Susan Brown Fiechtner and Elaine Actis Davis, "Why Some Groups Fail: A Survey of Students' Experiences with Learning Groups," in Anne Goodsell, Michelle Maher, and Vincent Tinto, *Collaborative Learning: A Sourcebook for Higher Education* (University Park, PA: National Center on Postsecondary Teaching, Learning, and Assessment (NCTLA), 1997) 59–67.

21. Jason D. Shaw, "The Salieri Syndrome: Consequences of Envy in Groups," *Small Group Research* 31 (2000): 3–23.

22. Clint A. Bowers, James A. Pharmer, and Eduardo Salas, "When Member Homogeneity is Needed in Work Teams," *Small Group Research* 31 (2000): 305–327

23. A. Paul Hare, *Handbook of Small Group Research,* 2nd ed. (New York: Free Press, 1976) 10.

24. Ernest G. Bormann, *Discussion and Group Methods: Theory and Practice,* 2nd ed. (New York: Harper & Row, 1975) 162–63.

25. George C. Homans, *The Human Group* (New York: Harcourt Brace, 1992).

26. Hare, *Handbook of Small Group Research,* 345.

27. Joseph A. Bonito, "The Effect of Contributing Substantively on Perceptions of Participation, *Small Group Research* 31 (2000): 528–553.

28. Michael G. Cruz, Franklin W. Boster, and Jose I. Rodriguez, "The Impact of Group Size and Proportion of Shared Information on the Exchange and integration of Information in Groups," *Communication Research* 24 (1997): 291–313.

29. B. Mullen, T. Anthony, E. Salas and J. E. Driskell, "Group Cohesiveness and Quality of Decision Making," *Small Group Research* 25 (1994): 189–204.

30. Stanley Seashore, *Group Cohesiveness in the Industrial Work Group* (Ann Arbor: University of Michigan Press, 1954); reprinted by Ayer Publishing, 1977.

31. Herbert A. Thelen, "Group Dynamics in Instruction: Principle of Least Group Size," *School Review* 57 (1949): 139–48.

32. Claus W. Langfred, "Is Group Cohesiveness a Double-Edged Sword? An Investigation of the Effects of Cohesiveness on Performance," *Small Group Research* 29 (1998): 124–143.

33. Judy C. Pearson and Paul E. Nelson, *An Introduction to Human Communication* (Madison, WI: Brown and Benchmark, 1997).

34. Bormann, *Discussion and Group Methods* 145.

35. Bormann, *Discussion and Group Methods* 144–45.

36. Dorwin Cartwright and Alvin Zander, *Group Dynamics: Research and Theory,* 3rd ed. (New York: Harper & Row, 1968) 104.

37. Hare, *Handbook of Small Group Research* 340.

38. C. Burningham and M. A. West, "Individual, Climate, and Group Interaction Processes as Predictors of Work Team Innovation," Small Group Research 26 (1995): 106–17.

39. Brian H. Spitzberg, "Intercultural Communication Competence," in Larry A. Samovar and Richard E. Porter, *Intercultural Communication* (Belmont, CA: Wadsworth, 1997) 354.

40. Carolyn M. Anderson and Matthew M. Martin, "The Effects of Communication Motives, Interaction, Involvement, and Loneliness on Satisfaction: A Model of Small Groups," *Small Group Research* 26 (1995): 119.

Understanding Nonverbal Dynamics

Objectives:

After studying this chapter,
you will be able to:

▶ Explain why nonverbal communication is important to the study of
   groups.

▶ Apply research findings about
   nonverbal communication to groups
   and teams.

▶ Describe how nonverbal cues should
   be interpreted in light of gender and
   cultural differences.

▶ Identify guidelines for interpreting
   nonverbal communication in small
   groups.

> " As I grow older, I pay less attention to what people say:
> I just watch what they do."
> —Andrew Carnegie

It was day three of *Apollo XIII's* mission in April 1970. All was going well for Lovell, Haise, and Swiggert, the crew of yet another U.S. trip to the moon, an event that for many Americans was becoming a common occurrence. Then Mission Control heard those now famous words from Commander Jim Lovell, "Houston, we have a problem." Something had gone terribly wrong. An unexplained malfunction in the oxygen tanks caused the cabin to vent precious life-sustaining oxygen into space. The astronauts and Mission Control soon learned that if a solution to the problem could not be found, the crew would not return alive.

At the first news conference following the accident, members of Mission Control faced an intensely interested press corps. A small group of officials from NASA sought to put a positive spin on the situation by claiming all was under control. But as one member of the control team later commented, "All you had to do was look at our grim faces and you knew that we had a tremendous problem." The nonverbal message of the group telegraphed the anxiety that their words were attempting to overshadow. The unspoken messages on the team's faces, the stress in their voices, and the edginess in their posture and gestures let the world know that Houston, indeed, had a serious problem. The nonverbal message, as is often the case in group meetings and presentations, told the real story.

Nonverbal communication is communication behavior that does not rely on written or spoken words. In the context of a small group, this definition includes body posture and movement, eye contact, facial expression, seating arrangement, spatial relationships, personal appearance, use of time, and even tone of voice. Although the words someone utters are not classified as nonverbal communication, the pitch, quality, rate, intonation, and use of silence can speak volumes; thus vocal tone is considered part of nonverbal communication.

Every message contains both content and information about relationships. Nonverbal messages, particularly facial expression and vocal cues, are often the prime source of information about interpersonal relationships. Thus they play important functions in **metacommunication**—which literally means communication about communication. The nonverbal aspects of a message communicate information about its verbal aspects.

The purposes of this chapter are (1) to identify the importance of nonverbal communication to the study of groups and teams, (2) to discuss the application of research in nonverbal communication to groups and teams, (3) to identify how culture and gender differences influence nonverbal communication in groups, and (4) to identify guidelines for interpreting nonverbal communication in small groups and teams.

The Importance of Nonverbal Communication in Groups

You have undoubtedly participated in group and team meetings that were dull and boring. Although not all unexciting group discussion results from poor or inappropriate nonverbal communication, group members' posture, facial expression, tone of voice, and unspoken enthusiasm (or lack of enthusiasm) dramatically affect a group's climate and members' attitudes toward the group. We'll examine three reasons why nonverbal-communication variables are important to group discussion.

More Time Is Spent Communicating Nonverbally Than Verbally

In a group or team discussion, usually only one person speaks at a time. The rest of the members can, however, emit a host of nonverbal cues that influence the deliberations. Eye contact, facial expression, body posture, and movement (some cues are controlled consciously, others are emitted less intentionally) occur even when only one person is speaking. Because group members are usually within just a few feet of one another, they can easily observe most nonverbal cues. Viewing nonverbal communication from the broadest perspective, it is safe to say that "you cannot not communicate."

Emotions and Feelings Are Typically Expressed Nonverbally Rather Than Verbally

In the past several chapters we have identified factors that influence the climate of a group, what it feels like to be a group member. If a group member is frustrated with the group or disenchanted with the discussion, more than likely you will detect those feelings by observing that person's nonverbal behavior—even before he or she verbalizes any frustration. If a member seems genuinely interested in the discussion and pleased with the group's progress, this, too, can be observed through nonverbal behavior. Albert Mehrabian and some of his colleagues devised a formula that suggests how much of the total emotional meaning of a message is based on verbal components and how much on nonverbal components.[1] According to his research, only 7 percent of the emotional meaning of a message is communicated through its verbal content. About 38 percent of the impact of the emotional content is derived from the voice (from such things as the rate, pitch, quality, and volume). The largest source of emotional meaning, 55 percent, is a speaker's facial expression. Generalizing from this formula, approximately 93 percent of emotions are communicated nonverbally. Although these percentages cannot be applied to all situations, Mehrabian's research suggests that when inconsistencies exist between people's verbalized emotional states and their true emotions, expressed nonverbally, nonverbal cues carry more clout in determining how receivers interpret speakers' emotions.

Vincent Brown and his colleagues suggest that the expression of feelings and emotions during group discussion can have a negative effect on group members' brainstorming ideas.[2] During a freewheeling brainstorming session, group members are not supposed to evaluate others' ideas; yet because of nonverbal expression of feelings, it's almost impossible not to let true positive or negative feelings leak out.

Nonverbal Messages Are Usually More Believable Than Verbal Messages

Nonverbal communication affects how others interpret our messages. Nonverbal cues are so important to communication that when a verbal message (either spoken or written) contradicts a nonverbal message, people are more inclined to believe the nonverbal message. The group member who sighs and, with a sarcastic edge, says, "Oh, what a great group this is going to be," communicates just the opposite meaning of that verbal message. One researcher estimates that people communicate 65 percent of the social meaning of messages nonverbally.[3]

An understanding of nonverbal communication, then, is vital to even a cursory understanding of communication in general and of group communication in particular. As you become a more skillful observer of nonverbal behavior, you will understand more thoroughly the way people interact in small groups.

Applications of Nonverbal Communications Research to Groups and Teams

Relatively few research studies have investigated nonverbal behavior in groups. Despite the unchallenged importance of nonverbal group dynamics to group discussion, researchers have found this aspect of communication difficult to observe and investigate. When group members simultaneously emit a myriad of nonverbal behaviors, it is difficult to systematically observe and interpret these cues. Nonverbal messages are considerably more ambiguous than verbal messages. No dictionary has definitive meanings for nonverbal behaviors. We suggest that you exercise caution, then, when you attempt to interpret the nonverbal behavior of other group members. Yet research conclusions about nonverbal communication in a variety of contexts do help us increase our awareness and sensitivity to the rich display of information and feelings in groups.

The following sections describe some research so that you can become more sensitive to your own nonverbal behavior and to the role nonverbal communication plays in group discussions. Specifically, the sections will discuss the following aspects of research in nonverbal communication in small groups: (1) physical posture, movement, and gestures, (2) eye contact, (3) facial expression, (4) vocal cues, (5) territoriality and personal space, (6) personal appearance, (7) the communication environment, and (8) use of time.[4]

Posture, Movement, and Gestures

To observe and analyze movement, posture, and gestures, Paul Ekman and Wallace Friesen have identified five major types of nonverbal behavior: (1) emblems, (2) illustrators, (3) affect displays, (4) regulators, and (5) adaptors.[5]

Emblems are nonverbal cues that have specific verbal counterparts and are shared by all group members. Emblems often take the place of spoken words, letters, or numbers. Group leaders who place index fingers vertically in front of their lips use a nonverbal emblem to take the place of the words "Shhhh, let's be quiet now." A hitchhiker's raised thumb and a soldier's salute are other examples of emblems. Group members who point to their watches to indicate that the group should get on with it because time is running out, or who use their index fingers and thumbs to signify all is okay, also depend on nonverbal emblems to communicate their messages.

Illustrators are nonverbal behaviors that add meaning to accompanying verbal messages. In a group you may see a gesture illustrating emphasis. For example, a group member who emphasizes a spoken message while shaking a fist in the face of another member

Eye contact, posture, facial expression, and vocal clues tell other people how involved or uninvolved you are in the discussion. What do the nonverbal cues tell you about the people in this picture?

illustrates conviction and determination. Several researchers have observed that people synchronize many of their body movements to their speech.[6] A blink of the eyes, a nod of the head, and a shift in body posture accent spoken messages.

An **affect display** is a nonverbal cue that communicates emotion. As mentioned before, the face is the primary source of emotional display. Research suggests that the body indicates the intensity of the emotion, or affect, that is being expressed. For example, the faces of group members may indicate that they are bored. If they are also slouched in their chairs, they are probably more than just moderately apathetic about the discussion.

Regulators are nonverbal behaviors that help a group control the flow of communication. They are very important to small group discussions because people rely on them to know when they should talk and when they should listen. Regulators also provide cues to indicate when other group members want to contribute to the discussion. Eye contact, posture, gestures, facial expression, and body position all help regulate communication in a group discussion. Generally, large groups operate with a rather formal set of regulators; participants raise their hands so that the chairperson will recognize them before they speak. In a less-formal discussion, group members rely on direct eye contact (to indicate that a communication channel is open), facial expression (raised eyebrows often signify a desire to talk), and gestures (such as a raised index finger) as cues to regulate the flow of communication. When nonverbal regulators are absent, such as during electronic collaboration when team members are not physically present, team members have a more difficult time of coordinating their conversation.

Adaptors are nonverbal acts that satisfy personal needs and help people adapt to their immediate environment. Adaptors are also important for learning to get along with others and for responding to certain situations. Generally, people are not aware of most of their adaptive nonverbal behavior. Self-adaptors, for example, are things people do to their own bodies, such as scratching, biting their nails, or twirling their hair. Researchers have noted that when people become nervous, anxious, or upset, they frequently display more self-adaptive behaviors.[7]

REVIEW

Categories of Nonverbal Communication

CATEGORY	DESCRIPTION	EXAMPLE
Emblem	Movements and gestures that replace spoken messages	Group members shake their heads to communicate no
Illustrators	Nonverbal behaviors that add meaning to accompany verbal communication	Group members say "it was this long," holding their hands 3 feet apart
Affect displays	Expressions of feeling	Frowning, smiling, grimacing, smirking
Regulators	Nonverbal behaviors that control the flow of communication within a group	Eye contact, raising a hand or a finger to signal you want to talk
Adaptors	Nonverbal acts that satisfy personal needs and help group members adapt to their environment	Scratching, yawning, adjusting your glasses

Eye Contact

Have you ever felt uncomfortable because the person you were talking to seemed reluctant to establish eye contact? Maybe you've wondered, "Why doesn't she look at me when she's talking to me?" Perhaps you've had just the opposite experience—the person you were talking to seemed to stare constantly at you. Although you become uneasy in these situations because they violate norms of eye contact. Although you may think that you do a pretty good job of establishing eye contact with others, researchers estimate that most people look at others only between 30 and 60 percent of the time.[8] Eye contact usually lasts less than 10 seconds.

Researchers have identified several factors that determine when you look at another person:[9] You are listening rather than talking; you like the other person; you are farther away from someone; you want to persuade or influence someone; you have a high need for approval or affiliation; you seek a response from someone.

Other circumstances will dictate when you are less likely to have eye contact with someone: You are from a culture where people tend not to look directly at others; you are embarrassed; you do not want to talk or participate in the discussion; you don't like someone; you are shy or introverted; you have a low need for approval.

When eye contact does occur in a small group setting, it may serve one or more important functions: (1) cognitive, (2) monitoring, (3) regulatory, and (4) expressive.[10]

Cognitive Function   This function of eye contact indicates thought processes. For example, some people look away when they are thinking of just the right word to say. Others look away before they speak so they won't be distracted by the person to whom they are talking.

Monitoring Function   Monitoring is the way you seek feedback from others when communicating with them. You look to monitor how your message is being received. For example, if you say something that other members disagree with, you may observe a change in facial expressions, body posture, or restless movement. Because you've monitored their nonverbal expression, you may then decide that you need to spend more time explaining your point.

Regulatory Function   Eye contact plays a vital role in regulating the back-and-forth flow of communication; it signals when the communication channel is open or closed. You can invite interaction simply by looking at others. If the chair of the committee asks for volunteers and you don't want to participate, you are more likely to not establish eye contact. Nonverbally this says: "I don't want to talk. I don't want to participate."

Expressive Function   Although eyes generally do not provide clues about specific emotions, the immediate area around the eyes provides quite a bit of information about feelings, emotions, and attitudes.

Eye contact or lack of it thus reveals information about thought processes, provides feedback, regulates communication channels, and expresses emotions. Eye contact also provides clues about status and leadership roles in small groups. One researcher has documented that group members who talk more receive more eye contact.[11] In addition, research suggests that eye contact is the predominant cue that regulates when you want to speak and when you want to stop speaking during group discussion.[12] In the next small group meeting you attend, determine who receives the most eye contact in the group. Where do group members look for information and guidance? They probably look at the group leader. If, as in many groups, several members share leadership, participants may look toward any of those leaders, depending on the specific problem or level of uncertainty facing the group.

REVIEW

Functions of Eye Contact

Cognitive function	Provides cues about thought processes
Monitoring function	Seeks feedback from others
Regulatory function	Signals when the communication channel is open and closed
Expressive function	Provides information about feelings, emotions, and attitudes

Facial Expressions

As discussed before, the face is the most important revealer of emotions. Sometimes you can cleverly mask your emotional expressions, but the face is usually the first place you look to determine someone else's emotional state. Facial expressions are particularly significant in interpersonal and small group communication because of the close proximity of communicators to one another. You can readily detect emotions displayed on a person's face. Even though some researchers estimate that the face can produce thousands of different expressions, Ekman and Friesen have identified six primary emotions displayed on it: Happiness, anger, surprise, sadness, disgust, and fear.[13]

Ekman and his colleagues have also developed a method of identifying which areas of the face play the most important roles in communicating emotion.[14] According to this research, people communicate happiness with the area around their eyes and with smiles and raised cheeks. They reveal disgust with raised upper lips, wrinkled noses, lowered eyelids, and lowered brows. They communicate fear with the area around their eyes, but their mouths are also usually open when they are fearful. When they are angry, people are likely to lower their eyebrows and stare intensely. They communicate surprise with raised eyebrows, wide-open eyes, and often open mouths. They communicate sadness in the area around the eyes and mouth.

Facial expressions are important sources of information about a group's emotional climate, particularly if several members express similar emotions. Their faces may suggest that they are bored with the discussion or that they are interested and pleased. Remember that group members may attempt to mask their facial expressions in an effort to conceal their true feelings.

Vocal Cues

"John," remarked a group discussion member, obviously upset, "it's not that I object to what you said; it's just the way you said it." The pitch, rate, volume, and quality of your voice (also called **paralanguage**) play important parts in determining the meanings of your messages.

From a speaker's paralanguage cues, then, you can make inferences about how that person feels toward you. You may also base inferences about a person's competence and personality on vocal cues. A speaker who mispronounces words and uses "uhs" and "ums" is probably going to be perceived as less credible than a speaker who is more articulate.[15] In addition to determining how speech affects a speaker's credibility, researchers have studied the communication of emotion via vocal cues.[16]

At times you can distinguish emotional states from vocal cues, but as a group member you should beware of drawing improper inferences and labeling someone negatively just because of vocal cues. As this chapter has emphasized, nonverbal cues do not operate in isolation. They should be evaluated in the context of other communicative behaviors.

Territoriality and Personal Space

The next time you are sitting in class, note the seat you select. Even though no one instructed you to sit in the same place, chances are that you tend to sit in about the same general area, if not in the same seat, during each class. Perhaps in your family each person sits at a certain place at the table. If someone sits in your chair, you feel your territory has been invaded and you may try to reclaim your seat.

Territoriality is a term used in the study of animal behavior to note how animals stake out and defend given areas. Humans, too, stake out and defend areas.

Understanding territoriality may help you understand certain group behaviors. For example, the readiness of group members to defend personal territory may provide insights about their attitudes toward the group and toward individual members. At the

Group members often stake out their territory with objects to mark their space. How might this affect other group members?

next meeting you attend, observe how members attempt to stake out territories. If the group is seated around a table, do members place objects in front of and around themselves to signify that they are claiming territory? Higher-status individuals generally attempt to claim more territory.[17] Notice how group members manipulate their posture and gestures if their space is invaded. Lower-status individuals generally permit greater territorial invasion. Note, too, how individuals claim their territory by leaving markers—such as books, papers, or a pencil—when they have to leave the group but expect to return shortly.

A classic area of study is called **small group ecology**—the consistent way in which people arrange themselves in small groups. As you interact with others in a small group, see if you can detect relationships among participants' seating arrangements and their status, their leadership roles, and the amount of communication they direct toward others. B. Stenzor found that when group members are seated in a circle, they are more likely to talk to those across from them than to those on either side.[18] Other researchers suggest that more-dominant group members select seats at the heads of rectangular tables or select seats that maximize their opportunity to communicate with others.[19] In contrast, people who sit at the corners of tables generally contribute the least to a discussion. Armed with this information, if you find yourself in a position to prepare the seating for a discussion or conference, you should be able to make choices to maximize group interaction. If, for example, you know that Sue (who always dominates the discussion) will be attending the next meeting, you may suggest that she sit in a corner seat rather than at the head of the table.

Did you know that an individual's position relative to other group members in a small group discussion can influence his or her chances of becoming the leader of the group? In a study by Howells and Becker, five people sat around a table, three on one side and two on the other. The researchers discovered that the participants had a greater probability of becoming leaders if they sat on the side of the table facing the three discussion members.[20] More direct eye contact with numerous group members, which can subsequently result in a greater control of the verbal communication, may explain why the two individuals who faced the other three emerged as leaders.

Additional research suggests that where you sit in a group may determine whether you initiate or receive information during deliberations. One team of researchers who observed groups of three people in snack bars, restaurants, and lounges found that more-visible group members (people who received more eye contact) tended to receive communication whereas more centrally located members usually initiated communication.[21] Another research team came to a similar conclusion: Group members who were in the center of other group members spoke most often.[22] As noted previously, eye contact seems to be an important factor in determining who speaks, who listens, and who has the greatest opportunity to emerge as group leader.

Other researchers have discovered that such variables as stress, gender, and personality also affect how people arrange themselves in small groups. Some people prefer greater personal space when they are under stress.[23] If you know that an upcoming discussion will probably produce anxiety, hold the meeting in a room that permits members to have more freedom of movement. This will allow them to find their preferred personal distance from other group members.

Robert Sommer found that women in North America tend to sit closer to others (whether those others are men or women) than men tend to sit to other men (that is, men generally prefer greater personal space when sitting next to other men).[24] In a study to find out whether personality characteristics affect seating arrangements, M. Cook discovered that extroverts tend to sit across from another person more than do introverts.[25] Introverts generally prefer distance between themselves and others. Collectively, these studies suggest that people arrange themselves with some consistency in small group discussions. A discussion leader who understands seating preferences should provide a comfortable climate for small group discussions.

REVIEW

Summary of Small Group Ecology Principles and Practices

▶ Whom you have eye contact with during group discussion usually affects whom you talk with.

▶ People who are more centrally located in a group often received more oral messages from other group members than people who were less centrally visible in the group.

▶ You are more likely to talk with people seated directly across from where you are seated.

▶ We usually expect the person seated at the head of a rectangular table to be the leader.

▶ More outspoken, dominant individuals often choose to sit at the head of the table.

▶ People who sit at the corner of a rectangular table often contribute less to the discussion.

- During times of stress, people prefer more space around them.
- People who are more outgoing (extroverts) choose to sit where they can see and be seen in a group; less outgoing people (introverts) often choose more distance between themselves and others.

Personal Appearance

How long does it take to determine whether or not you like someone? Some researchers claim that within seconds after meeting another person you complete your initial judgment of whether you should continue to communicate with him or her or try to excuse yourself from the conversation. You base many of your initial impressions of others primarily on personal appearance. The way people dress, their hairstyles, weight, and height affect your communication with them.

Research suggests that women who are thought attractive are more effective in changing attitudes than are women thought less attractive.[26] In addition, more attractive individuals are often thought by others to be more credible than less attractive people. They are also perceived to be happier, more popular, more sociable, and more successful than are those rated as being less attractive.

It is important to note we are not advocating that you purposely make stereotypical judgments of others based on personal appearance. We are suggesting, however, that *your* personal appearance may affect how others perceive you. And *yes*, you may be influenced by others' personal appearance. Monitor your appearance and also monitor how you may inappropriately discount good ideas from others because their appearance distracted you.

Communication Environment

Five students have been assigned to work together on a project for their group communication class. Their task is to formulate a policy question and solutions to it. Their first problem is finding a place to meet. Apparently, the only available place is a small, vacated office in Smythe Hall, the oldest building on campus. No one seems happy about holding meetings in the old office, but the students are relieved to have found a place to meet. When they arrive for their first meeting, they find a dirty, musty room with peeling paint, only three hardback wooden chairs, and a gray metal desk. The ventilation is poor, and half of the light bulbs have burned out. Such a dismal environment will undoubtedly affect the group's ability to work.

People can generally comprehend information and solve problems better in a more attractive environment. Research does not suggest, however, that one environment is best for all group communication situations. The optimal environment for any group depends on its specific task as well as the needs and expectations of its members. Some students need absolute quiet to read or study, while others can be productive while listening to music. Group members or leaders should attempt to find the best environments for their group based on the group's needs and the types of tasks confronting it. Group leaders could ask members which type of environment they prefer. If a group must solve problems that require considerable thought, energy, and creativity, it might work best in a quiet, comfortable room.

Time

The memo said the meeting was to start at 10 A.M. You arrive shortly before ten with your agenda, notepad, and pen, ready to participate. But at 10 no one has arrived except you. You check your watch and double-check to make sure you are in the right place. Finally, at 10:15, a couple of people arrive; most of the group comes in by 10:20. "Oh, we don't usually start right on time," said one of the latecomers. "Most people drift in by a quarter after the hour." Attitudes toward time may not seem like a nonverbal variable, yet a group's use of time and norms that develop about deadlines and efficiency are important unspoken aspects of a group's approach to work and productivity.

As we noted in Chapter 4, some people are **monochronic**. They are most comfortable doing only one thing at a time, like to concentrate on the job at hand, are more serious and sensitive to deadlines and schedules, like to plan how to use their time, and stress the importance of starting and ending meetings on time.[27] Other people are **polychronic**. Such individuals can do many things at once, are less enslaved by deadlines and schedules, feel that relationships are more important than producing volumes of work, frequently change plans, and are less concerned about punctuality than are monochronic individuals.

Communication researchers Dawna Ballard and David Seibold confirmed what scholars have suspected: Groups have different approaches to how they use time. Ballard and Seibold found that groups they investigated had three general approaches to time: (1) flexible, (2) separation, and (3) concurrency.[28] Groups with a flexible approach to time set fewer deadlines and provided groups and group members more autonomy. Groups with a separation approach to time preferred to literally separate themselves from others when working on a group task; they were more likely to keep the door closed and get away from others. Concurrency groups were more likely to attempt to do several things at once (multitask); they would look for ways to combine projects and activities. Being aware of how groups and teams in which you participate use time can help the group better understand why your group behaves as it does. If you're in a flexible group, you may need to monitor deadlines more closely. Separation groups may need to ensure they don't separate themselves so far from the organization that they lose sight of the overall organizational goal. Because concurrency groups have a tendency to do several things at once, such groups may need added structure and a system to keep track of the various projects undertaken.

The use of time and expectations about time can cause conflict and frustration if group members have widely differing perspectives. Time use and expectations vary from culture to culture.[29] People from the United States and Northern Europe tend to be more monochronic; attention to deadlines and punctuality are important. Latin Americans, Southern Europeans, and Middle Easterners are more often polychronic; they give less attention to deadlines and schedules. Western cultures tend to approach problems in a linear, step-by-step fashion. How events are structured and sequenced is important. Eastern cultures (Chinese and Japanese) approach time with a less-structured perspective. The observations of several researchers have been summarized in Table 6.1.[30]

Intercultural researcher Donald Klopf found that North Americans tend to think about time as a linear progression with a definite beginning and ending and believe that only one thing can be done at a time.[31] This is consistent with the monochronic approach to time discussed earlier. People from other cultures (for example, Latin American cultures) prefer working on multiple tasks and projects at the same time. And some Southeast Asians view time as a cyclical rather than a linear phenomenon.

Table 6.1 Cultural Differences in the Use of Time

In Western Cultures	In Eastern Cultures
Time is something to be manipulated	Time simply exists
The present is a way-station between the past and the future.	The present is more important than the past or the future.
Time is a resource that can be saved, spent, and wasted.	Time is a limitless pool.
Time is an aspect of history rather than part of an immediate experience.	Events occur in time; they cause ripples, and the ripples subside.

Source: Adapted from Donald W. Klopf, *International Encounters: The Fundamentals of Intercultural Communication* (Englewood, CO: Morton Publishing, 1998, and Edward T. Hall and Mildred R. Hall *Understanding Cultural Differences* (Yarmouth, ME: Intercultural) 1989).

Even if your group does not have members from widely different cultures, you may notice that people have different approaches to time. Groups develop their own norms about time. It may be useful to explicitly discuss and clarify norms related to the group's use of time. The importance of deadlines, expectations for group productivity, and general attitudes about punctuality may need to be discussed to manage any uncertainty about time that may exist. How a group approaches time is only one nonverbal variable that is strongly influenced by cultural backgrounds. Now we will focus on other ways in which cultural differences in interpreting nonverbal messages can affect group dynamics.

REVIEW

Sources of Nonverbal Cues

Posture, gestures and movement	Provides information regarding status, intensity of attitude, warmth, approval seeking, group climate, immediacy, deception
Eye contact	Provides cognitive, monitoring, regulatory, and expressive functions
Facial expression	Communicates emotion, especially happiness, anger, surprise, sadness, disgust, and fear
Vocal cues	The pitch, rate, volume, and quality of the voice communicate emotion, credibility, and personality perceptions
Territoriality	Staking out, claiming, and defending a given space
Personal space	Use of individual space, which communicates power, status, and intimacy
Personal appearance	Clothing, body shape, and general attractiveness influence others' perceptions and reactions
Communication environment	The general attractiveness or unattractiveness of a space, which contributes to the group's productivity and overall group climate
Time	Responses to deadlines, beginning and ending times, and use of time during group meeting

Now that we've seen how specific cues contribute to understanding messages in group discussion, you may still wonder what are some of the more general effects or functions of nonverbal messages. Unspoken messages play a significant role in how leaders are perceived, group members are persuaded, body posture and movement are synchronized, and group-member lying is detected.

Nonverbal Messages Influence Perceived Leadership

To lead is to influence. Nonverbal cues have a major affect on how leaders are perceived in groups and teams. Communication researcher John O'Connor discovered someone's frequent gesturing was highly correlated with other members' perception that the person was a leader in the group.[32] In a follow-up study, John Baird found that group members who other members thought of as group leaders used shoulder and arm gestures more often.[33] Although leaders may gesture more frequently than do followers, this does not mean that frequent gesturing causes a person to emerge as a leader. The evidence does not suggest a cause-and-effect relationship. It simply suggests that people in leadership roles may use more nonverbal gestures, perhaps to coordinate or regulate message flow.

Nonverbal Messages Influence Persuasion Skills

Do individuals in small groups use certain nonverbal cues during their attempts to persuade others? Albert Mehrabian and M. Williams found that persuasive communicators exhibit more animated facial expressions, use more gestures to emphasize their points, and nod their heads more than do those who are less persuasive.[34] Another team of researchers found that people trying to project warm, friendly images will be more likely to smile, less likely to fidget with their hands, and more likely to shift their postures toward others.[35]

One team of researchers found that we rely extensively on nonverbal cues to signal when we want to speak or change topics. Typically, a group member signals topic change by leaning forward, smiling, making a head nod, shifting posture, having a foot make contact with the floor, or breaking eye contact to signal a change in the direction of thought.[36]

DILBERT Copyright ©United Features Syndicate

Nonverbal Messages Help Syncronize Interaction

An excellent book by Judee Burgoon and her colleagues reports that nonverbal cues play a central role in adapting and relating to others.[37] We tend to mirror the posture and behavior of others; it seems to get us in sync with those with whom we interact. At your next group meeting, note how one member tends to unconsciously mirror the posture of another. This is especially true of members seated across from each other or within each other's line of vision. You may find, for example, that a person sitting across from someone with folded arms may assume a similar posture. Like partners in an intricate dance, people reflect each other's movements, eye contact, gestures, and other nonverbal cues. The rhythm of life is thus constantly conveyed as we respond and adapt to others through nonverbal cues.

We respond not only to physical posture and movement but also to the rhythm and sound of human speech. W. S. Condon and others, using slow-motion films, documented a distinct relationship between facial expressions and head movements and speech.[38] A. Kendon observed that people may shift their body positions in response to verbal messages.[39] Davida Navarre and Catherine Emihovich report similar evidence that group members may respond in synchrony to the movements and postures of others.[40] These authors suggest that during group interactions people may adopt poses similar to those of others they like or agree with. Thus coalitions of group members may be identified not only by their verbal agreement but also by their synchronized nonverbal behavior. It is probably more than just coincidence that group members consistently fold their arms and cross their legs in the same way. Just as religious services use singing and group litanies to establish unity and a commonality of purpose, small groups may unwittingly use common nonverbal behaviors to foster cohesiveness. Counselors report that they can help clients self-disclose by adopting body postures similar to those of their clients. By synchronizing body position, counselors believe they can better empathize and establish rapport with their clients. In your small group discussions, observe the similarity and dissimilarity of members' postures, positions, and gestures. Such cues may provoke interesting insights about group climate, leadership, and cohesiveness.

In one of the few studies that examined nonverbal behavior in groups, Edward Mabry sought to discover whether group members' nonverbal behavior changes from one meeting to the next. After observing a group that met five times, he found that during the second and third meetings group members were more likely to have the palms of their hands in more open positions. Group members also tended to lean back more in the first and fifth sessions of their deliberations. Participants also made more direct eye contact with one another after they had met together once. What do these differences mean? Mabry's study suggests that group members' nonverbal behavior changes from one group meeting to the next. Groups do not develop a static way of behaving nonverbally; nonverbal communication may depend on the topic and how group members feel toward one another as they become more comfortable after meeting together over several sessions.[41]

Nonverbal Messages Provide Information About Perceived Honesty or Dishonesty

In addition to categorizing movement, posture, and gestures, researchers have studied whether nonverbal behavior provides clues as to whether someone is lying. Sigmund Freud said, "He that has eyes to see and ears to hear may convince himself that no mortal can keep a secret. If his lips are silent, he chatters with his fingertips; betrayal oozes out of him at every pore." Paul Ekman and W. V. Friesen found that feet and legs often reveal people's true feelings.[42] They theorized that while people consciously manipulate their facial expressions to hide deception, they are not so likely to monitor their feet. At your next group meeting you may more readily detect anxiety or restlessness by observing nervous movement of people's feet and legs than by looking for clues in their faces or other areas of the body that they are more likely to control consciously. One team of researchers suggested that the following behaviors (some which involve posture, movement, and gesture), listed in order from most to least important, can provide clues as to whether someone is lying.[43]

Greater time lag in response to a question

Reduced eye contact

Increased shifts in posture

More hand/shrug emblems

More adaptors

Unfilled pauses

Less smiling

Slower speech

Higher pitch in voice

More deliberate pronunciation and articulation

Simply because a group member exhibits one or more of these nonverbal behaviors does not mean that he or she is lying. Although a person trying to hide something or lie may exhibit some of the cues listed above, not everyone who displays such behavior is deceptive. The ambiguity of nonverbal cues prevents you from drawing such definitive conclusions about the motives of other people based on nonverbal cues alone.

Culture and Nonverbal Communication

Culture is a learned system of knowledge, behavior, attitudes, beliefs, values, and norms that is shared by a group of people.[44] We often think of cultural differences as existing between ethnic groups or nations, but they can also exist between families, organizations, or even different parts of the same country or state. When individuals of different cultures interact, it is not surprising that cultural differences interfere with effective communication. Culture is a difference that *makes* a difference. As we mentioned in our discussion of how some cultures view time, unspoken cultural differences may contribute to underlying tension in small groups.[45]

One obvious cultural difference is language—it would be challenging indeed to participate in a group without a common language! But it can also be challenging to work with others where there are nonverbal cultural differences. Differences in how people from different cultures respond to context and attitudes toward personal contact have a direct bearing on nonverbal communication in small groups. We will explore differences between high-context and low-context cultures as well as high-contact and low-contact cultures.

We will also note examples of how cultural differences in nonverbal communication can provide insight into how people interact in small groups.

High-Context and Low-Context Cultures

In some cultures the surrounding context or the unspoken, nonverbal message plays a greater role than in others.[46] A **high-context culture** is one in which more emphasis is placed on nonverbal communication. In high-context cultures, the physical context is important to help communicators interpret the message. The environment, the situation, and the communicator's mood are especially significant in decoding messages. A **low-context culture** places more emphasis on verbal expression. Figure 6.1 shows cultures arranged along a continuum from high to low context.

People from high-context cultures may be more skilled in interpreting nonverbal information than people from low-context cultures. Individuals from high-context cultures may also use fewer words to express themselves. Because individuals from low-context cultures place greater emphasis on speech, they may talk more than those from high-context cultures. People from a low-context culture typically are less sensitive to the nonverbal cues in the environment, and the situation in interpreting the messages of others.[47]

In a small group, high- or low-context orientation can play a role in the amount of time a person talks and his or her sensitivity in responding to unspoken dynamics of a group's climate. Sometimes people from a high-context culture will find those from a low-context culture less credible or trustworthy. Someone from a low-context culture may be more likely to make explicit requests for information by saying, "Talk to me," "Give it to me straight," or "Tell it like it is." In contrast, a person from a high-context culture expects communication to be more indirect and to rely on more implicit cues.

High-Contact and Low-Contact Cultures

People from some cultures are more comfortable being touched or being in close proximity to others; these are said to be **high-contact cultures**. Individuals from **low-contact cultures** tend to prefer more personal space, typically have less eye contact with others and are much more uncomfortable with being touched or approached by others. Edward Hall offers the classification of high- and low-contact cultures shown in Table 6.2.[48]

Whether group members are from high- or low-contact cultures can affect preferred seating arrangements and other aspects of small group ecology that we discussed earlier. For example, some cultural groups, such as the Chinese, prefer sitting side-by-side rather than directly across from one another.[49] In Middle Eastern countries, Fathi Yousef and Nancy Briggs found that it is appropriate, if not expected, to stand close enough to someone to smell their breath.[50] North Americans usually prefer more space around them than do Latin Americans, Arabs, and Greeks.[51] Cultural differences can be found among ethnic groups within the same country. In a study conducted in the United States, whites maintained greater distances from African-Americans than whites did from other whites or than African-Americans did from whites.[52]

It may be tempting to make stereotypical inferences about all people within a given culture based on some of the research conclusions we have cited. We caution you to resist assuming that someone from a given culture will behave in a certain way simply because you have categorized him or her as from a high- or low-context, or high- or low-contact culture. Robert Shuter cautions against making broad, sweeping generalizations about a

Figure 6.1 *Where Different Cultures Fall on the Context Scale*

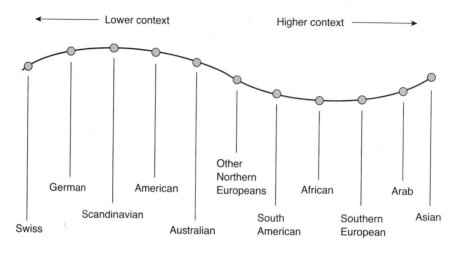

High/Low Contexts
Where different cultures fall on the context scale.

← Lower context   Higher context →

German   American   Other Northern Europeans   African   Arab

Scandinavian

Swiss   Australian   South American   Southern European   Asian

Low-context cultures
(Information must be provided explicitly, usually in words.)

• Less aware of nonverbal cues, environment, and situation
• Lack well-developed networks
• Need detailed background information
• Tend to segment and compartmentalize information
• Control information on a "need to know" basis
• Prefer explicit and careful directions from someone who "knows"
• Knowledge is a commodity

High-context cultures
(Much information drawn from surroundings. Very little must be explicitly transferred.)

• Nonverbal cues important
• Information flows freely
• Physical context relied upon for information
• Environment, situation, gestures, and mood all taken into account
• Maintain extensive information networks

Source: Adapted from Donald W. Klopf, *International Encounters: The Fundamentals of Intercultural Communication* (Englewood, CO: Morton Publishing, 1998) 33; and *Meeting News,* June 1993.

---

specific culture.[53] His research suggests that significant variations in nonverbal behavior exist *within* a culture. Thus the conclusions we have just cited are offered to document the existence of cultural differences and to warn that such differences may hamper effective communication in small groups.

No list of simple suggestions or techniques will help you manage the cultural differences that you will encounter in groups. However, a basic principle can help: *When interacting with people from a culture other than your own, note differences you think may be culture-based and adapt accordingly. Become other-oriented.* We are not suggesting that you abandon your cultural norms, traditions, and expectations—only that you become more flexible, thereby minimizing the communication distortion that cultural differences may cause. Carley Dodd suggests that if you think you have offended someone or

Cultural differences and similarities will influence nonverbal interaction when people communicate. How would you manage cultural differences in a group?

Table 6.2 Comparing High- and Low-Contact Cultures

HIGH-CONTACT CULTURES	LOW-CONTACT CULTURES
Tend to be from warmer climates:	Tend to be from cooler climates:
Arab, Mediterranean, Hispanic, Indonesian, European and Middle Eastern Jews, eastern European, Russian	Norway, Finland, Sweden, Germany England, Japan, United States

Source: Edward T. Hall, *Beyond Culture* (Garden City, NY: Doubleday, 1976).

acted inappropriately, ask the other person what you did that was wrong.[54] Being aware of and responding to cultural differences in small groups can enhance your ability to interact with others.

Gender and Nonverbal Communication

Deborah Tannen's best-selling book *You Just Don't Understand* struck a responsive chord by identifying gender differences in verbal communication. Her work popularized a research conclusion that most of us already knew: Men and women have different communication patterns. Evidence indicates that men and women sometimes use language differently, and that they also interpret nonverbal behavior differently. Clara Mayo and Nancy Henley[55] as well as Diana Ivy and Phil Backlund [56] are among the scholars who provide excellent reviews of how males and females use and respond to nonverbal cues differently. Note some of the following conclusions that identify gender differences in sending and receiving nonverbal messages:

People of both sexes tend to move closer to women than to men.[57]

Women tend to move closer to others than do men.[58]

Men tend to have less eye contact with others than do women.[59]

Women seem to use more expressive facial expressions than do men.[60]

Men tend to use more gestures than do women.[61]

Men initiate touch more often than women.[62]

Women speak with less volume than men.[63]

Besides differing in their use of nonverbal behaviors, there is evidence that women tend to be more accurate in receiving and interpreting nonverbal messages. Why are there differences in the way males and females use and respond to nonverbal messages? Some theorize that the answer lies in physiological differences between men and women. But the leading explanation seems to focus on how we, as men and women, are socialized into society. Men typically have higher status in our culture and many other cultures throughout the world. Women seem to have learned how to respond to others' emotions. Status differences, the need for approval, and the value placed on interpersonal relationships and emotional needs are identified as differences between the sexes that may explain how males and females learn to use nonverbal cues.

The research conclusions reviewed here can help explain some of the differences in the way that men and women communicate in groups and teams. We emphasize, however, that these are research generalizations; do not expect all men and all women to exhibit these differences. Contrary to a popular book title by John Gray, *Men Are from Mars, Women Are from Venus*, men and women do not live on different planets. Therefore, in your group deliberations, be cautious about always expecting to see these differences. But knowing that there are gender differences in nonverbal behavior may help you become both more flexible and tolerant when communicating with others in groups.

Interpreting Nonverbal Communication

Nonverbal cues do not create meaning independently of other communication cues (for example, message content, language style, and message organization). Also, there is much we still do not know about nonverbal communication. After reading the research conclusions reported here, you may be tempted to interpret someone else's body language, but you should remember several principles when ascribing meaning to the posture and movement of others.

Interpret Nonverbal Communication in Context
Just as you can misunderstand the meaning of a sentence taken out of context, so can you make an inaccurate inference about a nonverbal behavior when it is interpreted out of context. Simply because a group member sits with crossed legs and folded arms does not necessarily mean that person does not want to communicate with others. Other variables in the communication system may be affecting the person's posture and position.

TECHNOLOGY

COLLABORATING ONLINE: FEWER NONVERBAL CUES CAN HAVE BOTH POSITIVE AND NEGATIVE CONSEQUENCES

If you've participated in an online chat room, you know that it's sometimes difficult to catch the subtle and sometimes not so subtle meaning of messages because nonverbal cues are lost. Electronic meetings and other e-collaborations have both positive and negative consequences. The lack of nonverbal cues can result in missed meaning, especially missing emotional and relational cues. On the positive side, however, electronic collaboration often results in more equal participation. Without the opportunity of seeing someone frown or grimace, you may be more likely to offer your ideas to the group. Electronic collaborators are also more honest because often their contributions are anonymous.[64] There is usually more expressed disagreement in face-to-face group and team deliberations than in electronic discussion. Why? Because the nonverbal reactions in face-to-face group meetings result in increased nonverbal expressions of conflict and disagreement. If there is unresolved conflict and expressions of disagreement, such emotional displays can have a negative impact on a group.[65]

Look for Clusters of Cues   Look for a pattern of cues to help you interpret what a specific behavior means rather than considering only one gesture, expression, or use of personal space. Seek corroborating cues that can help you reach a more accurate conclusion about what a specific behavior means. Besides noting whether someone makes eye contact, also note whether you find complementary vocal cues, posture, and gestures to confirm your conclusion.

Recognize That People Respond Differently to Different Stimuli   Not all people express emotions in the same manner. It may take considerable time before you can understand the unique, idiosyncratic meaning underlying another person's specific nonverbal behaviors.

Consider Cultural and Gender Differences   Keep the person's cultural background or gender in mind when you draw an inference from his or her nonverbal behavior. As we have stressed in several places in this chapter, nonverbal behaviors have no generally held universal meanings. Even though some evidence indicates that common facial expressions can be interpreted across several cultures with up to 92 percent accuracy, there are subtle as well as dramatic differences in the way nonverbal behaviors may be interpreted. In small group interactions, it is especially interesting to observe cultural differences in how people use space and territory. In Chapter 8, we'll offer additional tips for being sensitive to cultural differences.

Consider Your Past Experience with Someone When Interpreting Nonverbal Cues

As you spend time working with group members, chances are you will learn how to interpret their nonverbal cues. For example, when you first met Lee you weren't sure why he seemed so distant and aloof. His lack of eye contact suggested that he was not interested in being a productive member of the group. After you had spent several meetings getting to know him better, you realized that Lee is simply shy. He has good ideas but needs to be drawn out. Working with him convinces you that you should not make snap judgments of other group members. First impressions are not always accurate.

Look for Cues That Communicate Liking, Power, and Responsiveness

Albert Mehrabian has developed a three-dimensional model that identifies how people respond to nonverbal messages. Even though this framework was not designed exclusively for small groups, his research can be useful in helping to interpret the meaning of messages. Although his conclusions cannot be applied universally, they do reflect the way many North Americans interpret nonverbal messages. His research suggests that people derive meaning from nonverbal behavior based on: (1) immediacy or liking, (2) power, and (3) responsiveness.[66]

1. *Immediacy: Behaviors that communicate liking and disliking.* As defined by Mehrabian, immediacy refers to whether people like or dislike others. The immediacy principle states that, "People are drawn toward persons and things they like, evaluate highly, and prefer; and they avoid or move away from things they dislike, evaluate negatively, or do not prefer." According to Mehrabian, such nonverbal behaviors as touching, leaning forward, reducing distance and personal space, and maintaining direct eye contact can communicate liking or positive feelings. Based on the immediacy principle, group members who consistently sit closer to you, establish more eye contact with you, and, in general, are drawn to you probably like you more than group members who generally do not look at you and who regularly select seats away from you.

2. *Power: Behaviors that communicate influence and status.* People of higher status generally determine the degree of closeness permitted in their interactions. A person of higher status and influence, for example, usually is surrounded by more space. A boss who sits at the head of the table is more likely to have empty chairs around him or her; subordinates are more likely to give the boss more space. A person of higher status generally has a more relaxed body posture when interacting with a person of lower status. High status members also tend to have less eye contact with others, a louder voice, make more expansive movements and postures, and may reflect their status by the way they dress.

3. *Responsiveness: Behaviors that communicate interest and attention.* Body movements, facial expressions, and variation of vocal cues (such as pitch, rate, volume, and tone) all contribute to our perceptions of others as responsive or unresponsive. A group member who communicates energy and enthusiasm would be rated highly responsive.

Develop the Skill of Perception Checking

People judge you by your behavior, not your intent. You judge others the same way—by what you see, not by what they are thinking. Unless you are a mind reader, the only way to check your perception of others' nonverbal behavior is to ask them. **Perception checking** is the skill of asking someone whether your interpretation of his or her unspoken message is accurate. There are three steps to this skill. First, observe the nonverbal cues we have discussed. Next, mentally draw a conclusion about what the nonverbal behavior may mean. Finally, ask the other person if your inference was accurate.

Suppose you offer a solution to a problem your group has been discussing. After you announce your proposal, the group is silent, your colleagues break eye contact, and you see one person frown. To find out whether their nonverbal response means that your proposal has been rejected, you could ask, "Does your silence mean you don't like my idea?" You could also add, "From the look on your face, you don't seem to be pleased with my suggestion." Your colleagues may say, "Oh, no. Your idea is a good one. I just need some time to think about how we could put your suggestion into action." We do not recommend that you overuse this skill. Stopping to seek confirmation of every facial expression or vocal tone would be irritating. We do suggest that you consider using this skill when you genuinely do not understand how a group member is responding to you.

These principles point to a key conclusion: Nonverbal messages are considerably more ambiguous than verbal messages. No dictionary has definitive meanings for nonverbal behaviors. Exercise caution, then, when you attempt to interpret the nonverbal behavior of other group members.

REVIEW

Dimensions of Nonverbal Meaning

DIMENSION	DEFINITION	NONVERBAL CUES
Immediacy	Behaviors that signal liking, attraction, and interest	Touch, forward lean, close personal space, eye contact
Potency	Behaviors that communicate power, status, and influence	Protected space, increased distance, relaxed posture
Responsiveness	Behaviors that communicate active interactions and attention	Eye contact, varied vocal cues, animated facial expression

Collaborating

ETHICALLY

After reading research conclusions about the impact of nonverbal messages on team deliberations in his group communication class, Kosta realized how easy it can be to strategically manipulate other team members by using nonverbal cues to manage the group's emotional climate and regulate discussion. He also decided to apply some of the small group ecology principles of using seating arrangements to help control some of the more talkative members of the team. Is Kosta's use of nonverbal communication research ethical? Is it appropriate to intentionally use nonverbal communication principles and practices to advance a team member's individual agenda?

Perception Check

STEPS	FACTORS TO CONSIDER
1. Observe someone's nonverbal behavior.	What is her facial expression? Does she make eye contact? What is her posture? What is her tone of voice?
2. Think about what the behavior may mean.	Does she appear to be angry, sad, depressed? Is the nonverbal message contradicting the verbal message?
3. Check your perception by asking whether your interpretation is accurate.	"The expression on your face suggests you may be upset. Are you?"

Putting Principles into Practice

This chapter has noted that nonverbal communication variables have a profound impact on small group dynamics. Group members send more messages nonverbally than they do verbally—people cannot *not* communicate.

Nonverbal cues affect the meanings of messages; individuals generally believe these cues more than they believe verbal messages. Nonverbal cues are particularly important in communicating emotions.

We have discussed several applications of nonverbal communication research to small groups. Consider the following suggestions

Body Posture, Movement, and Gestures

▶ You may be more effective in persuading others when you use eye contact, maintain a direct body orientation, and remain physically close to others.

▶ You can often identify high-status group members (or at least those who perceive themselves as having high status) by such nonverbal cues as relaxed postures, loud speaking voices, territorial dominance, expansive movements, and, sometimes, their keeping themselves at a distance from others.

▶ Someone who is lying may speak with a higher-pitched voice, use less eye contact, show less enthusiasm, shrug his or her hands more often, nod less, speak more slowly and with more errors, and adopt a less immediate posture.

▶ Group leaders may gesture more than followers.

▶ Observing the similarity of group members' posture and gestures can reveal insights about group climate, leadership, and cohesiveness.

Eye Contact

- ▶ People sometimes interrupt eye contact with others because they are trying to think of the right words to say, not because they are uninterested.
- ▶ When talking with others in a small group, be sure to look at all members so that you can respond to the feedback they provide.
- ▶ You sometimes can draw a person into the conversation just by establishing direct eye contact.
- ▶ Because eye contact signals whether a communication channel is open or closed, you may be able to quiet an extremely talkative member by avoiding eye contact.
- ▶ By noting who looks at whom in a small group, you can get a good idea of who the leader is. Group members usually look at their leader more than they look at any other member (assuming that they respect their leader's ideas and opinions).

Facial Expression

- ▶ Look at group members' facial expressions to find out the emotional climate in the group.

Vocal Cues

- ▶ You may find that you dislike a group member not because of what he or she says but because of that person's vocal quality, pitch, or rate of speech. People's vocal cues affect your perceptions of them.

Territoriality and Personal Space

- ▶ Members probably will stake out their territory or personal space early on in group gatherings.
- ▶ When group members' territories are invaded, they probably will respond nonverbally (via posture or territorial markers) to defend their territories.
- ▶ If you want to increase your interaction with a group member, sit directly across from him or her.
- ▶ If you know that a group member generally monopolizes the conversation, try to get that person to select a corner seat rather than one at the head of a conference table.
- ▶ You are more likely to emerge as a group leader if you sit so that you can establish eye contact and a direct body orientation with most of the group members.
- ▶ Because people prefer greater personal space when they are under stress, make sure that group members have plenty of territory when you know that a meeting is going to be stressful.

Personal Appearance

▶ Your personal appearance will affect the way other group members perceive you. It can also influence your ability to persuade others.

Communication Environment

▶ Make sure that the physical environment for a group meeting is as comfortable and attractive as possible to enhance satisfaction and productivity.

Functions of Nonverbal Communications in Groups and Teams

▶ *Leadership function:* Nonverbal messages influence who is perceived as group or team leader.

▶ *Persuasion function:* Skilled persuaders use more animated facial expressions, more gestures, smile, are less likely to fidget with their hands, and lean forward when communicating.

▶ *Synchronization function:* Nonverbal cues help synchronize our communication with others.

▶ *Honesty function:* Nonverbal cues often provide cues about whether the communicator is honest or dishonest; dishonest communicators often speak slower and more distinctly with a higher pitch and have more pauses and hesitations, have less eye contact, and evidence more shrugs and postural shifts.

Time

▶ Talk with your group members about their expectations of punctuality, meeting deadlines, and work efficiency in order to avoid misunderstandings about use of time.

Gender

▶ Men and women may differ in the way they interpret and send nonverbal messages; avoid assuming that all males and all females behave in a certain way.

Culture

▶ If you are communicating with someone from a high-context culture (which places more emphasis on nonverbal than verbal information), realize that your unspoken signals will be especially important in the interpretation of your message. You don't have to say it to say it.

▶ Some people prefer greater closeness (high-contact culture) whereas other individuals prefer less physical contact (low-contact culture); monitor your use of personal space to assess the impact that your use of territory has on others.

▶ Interpret nonverbal messages from both the sender's and receiver's culture.

▶ Become other-oriented to minimize communication distortion that may result from cultural differences.

Interpreting Nonverbal Behavior

▶ Consider the context when making inferences about what a specific behavior may mean.

▶ Look for clusters of cues rather than focusing on just one nonverbal behavior when interpreting unspoken messages.

▶ Because not all people have the same reaction to the same situation, avoid interpreting one person's nonverbal expression in the same way as the identical expression displayed by another person.

▶ Factor in cultural and gender expectations that others may have when interpreting nonverbal messages.

▶ You will likely be more successful in interpreting nonverbal messages from people you know or have worked with over a long period of time. Therefore be cautious when drawing a conclusion about a new acquaintance's nonverbal behavior.

▶ Use eye contact, posture, touch, and personal-space factors to help determine whether you are liked or disliked by others.

▶ Use posture, appearance, personal space, and relaxation cues to help you interpret someone's perception of his or her power and influence.

▶ Use eye contact, vocal cues, movement, and facial expressions to help interpret someone's interest and responsiveness toward you.

▶ To check your interpretation of someone's nonverbal behavior, ask whether your understanding of his or her unspoken message is accurate.

PRACTICE

Receiving Nonverbal Reinforcement

Pair up with another student and take turns telling each other about an important idea, feeling, or experience. Your partner should give no nonverbal indications that he or she is paying attention while you speak: No smiles, nodding of the head, "um-hums," postural orientation, facial expressions. After each of you has talked for three to five minutes, discuss what it felt like (1) to receive no nonverbal attention and (2) to give no nonverbal attention. After you discuss the importance of nonverbal communication, talk again with your partner—this time providing genuine nonverbal feedback. Your instructor will lead you in a discussion of the differences between receiving and not receiving nonverbal reinforcement.

Nonverbal Group Observation

If you are working on a group project, videotape one of your group meetings or videotape your group trying to solve a case study. Replay the videotape with the sound turned off. Or, if you don't have video equipment, simply observe a group while you are some distance from it. Focus on group member' actions, not their words.

1. Notice group members' use of emblems, illustrators, affect displays, regulators, and adaptors.

2. Observe how nonverbal cues regulate the flow of communication.

3. How do body posture and movement communicate members' status and attitudes?

4. Try to identify the four functions of eye contact in your group.

5. Do group members communicate much emotion with their faces?

6. Note relationships among territorial behavior, seating arrangement, and leadership, status, and verbal interaction in the group.

7. If your group had to meet in a special room to videotape the session, how did the change in environment affect the group?

Redesign Your Meeting Room

Working with a group of others, how would you redesign your classroom? Or, if you're working on a small group project and you have a regular meeting place, how would you redesign that space for maximum meeting effectiveness? As you brainstorm suggestions, consider the architecture, lighting, colors, furniture, sounds, and any other features that would enhance the room's functional design for group deliberations.

 Your companion Website has more practice activities, questionnaires, and checklists!
www.ablongman.com/beebe

Notes

1. Albert Mehrabian, *Nonverbal Communication* (Chicago: Aldine Atherton, 1972) 108.
2. V. Brown, M. Tumeo, T. S. Larey, and P. B. Paulus, "Modeling Cognitive Interactions During Group Brainstorming," *Small-group Research* 4 (1998) 495–536.
3. R. L. Birdwhistell, *Kinesics and Context* (Philadelphia: U. of Pennsylvania, 1970); for a comprehensive review of nonverbal communication in small groups, see Sandra M. Ketrow, "Missing Link: Nonverbal Messages in Group Communication Research," paper presented at the annual meeting of the Speech Communication Association, November 1994.

4. For an excellent literature review of nonverbal communication and groups see S. M. Ketrow, "Nonverbal Aspects of Group Communication," in L. Frey, ed., *The Handbook of Group Communication Theory and Research* (Thousand Oaks, CA: Sage, 1999): 251–87.

5. P. Ekman and W. V. Friesen, "The Repertoire of Nonverbal Behavior: Categories, Origins, Usage, and Coding," *Semiotica* 1 (1969): 49–98.

6. W. S. Condon and W. D. Ogston, "Soundfilm Analysis of Normal and Pathological Behavior Patterns," *Journal of Nervous and Mental Disease* 143 (1966): 338–47.

7. P. Ekman and W. V. Friesen, "Hand Movements," *Journal of Communication* 22 (1972): 353–74. See also Pio Enrico Ricci Bitti and Isabella Poggi, "Symbolic Nonverbal Behavior: Talking Through Gestures," in Robert S. Feldman and Bernard Rime, eds., *Fundamentals of Nonverbal Behavior* (Cambridge, England: Cambridge, 1991).

8. M. Argyle and A. Kendon, "The Experimental Analysis of Social Performance." In L. Berkowitz, ed., *Advances In Experimental Social Psychology,* vol. 3 (New York: Academic Press, 1967), 55–98.

9. Mark L. Knapp and Judith A Hall *Nonverbal Communication in Human Interaction* (Fort Worth, TX: Harcourt Brace, 1997), 297.

10. A. Kendon, "Some Functions of Gaze-Direction in Social Interaction," *Acta Psychologica* 26 (1967): 22–63.

11. A. Kalma, "Hierarchisation and Dominance Assessment at First Glance," *European Journal of Social Psychology* 21 (1991): 165–81.

12. A. Kalma, "Gazing in Triads: A Powerful Signal in Floor Apportionment," *British Journal of Social Psychology* 31 (1992): 21–39.

13. P. Ekman and W. V. Friesen, *Unmasking the Face* (Englewood Cliffs, NJ: Prentice Hall, 1975).

14. P. Ekman and W. V. Friesen, and S. S. Tompkins, "Facial Affect Scoring Technique: A First Validity Study," *Semiotica* 3 (1971): 35–38; Eckman and Friesen, *Unmasking the Face.*

15. K. K. Sereno and G. J. Hawkins, "The Effect of Variations in Speakers' Nonfluency upon Audience Ratings of Attitude toward the Speech Topic and Speakers' Credibillity," *Speech Monographs* 34 (1967): 58–64; G. R. Miller and M. A. Hewgill, "The Effect of Variations in Nonfluency on Audience Ratings of Source Credibility," *Quarterly Journal of Speech* 50(1964): 36–44.

16. J. R. Davitz, *The Communication of Emotional Meaning* (New York: McGraw-Hill, 1964). See also Arvid Kappas, Ursula Hess, and Klaus R. Scherer, "Voice and Emotion," in Robert S. Feldman and Bernard Rime, eds., *Fundamentals of Nonverbal Behavior* (Cambridge, England,: Cambridge, 1991).

17. Albert Mehrabian, "Significance of Posture and Position in the Communication of Attitude and Status Relationships," *Psychological Bulletin* 71 (1960): 363.

18. B. Stenzor, "The Spatial Factors in Face-to-Face Discussion Groups," *Journal of Abnormal and Social Psychology* 45 (1950): 552–55.

19. F. Strodtbeck and L. Hook, "The Social Dimensions of a Twelve Man Jury Table," *Sociometry 36* (1973): 424-29; A. Hare and R. Bales, "Seating Position and Small-Group Interaction," *Sociometry 26* (9163): 480–86.

20. L. T. Howells and S. W. Becker, "Seating Arrangements and Leadership Emergence," *Journal of Abnormal and Social Psychology* 64 (1962): 148–50.

21. Ronald L. Michelini, Robert Passalacqua, and John Cusimano, "Effects of Seating Arrangements on Group Participation, "*Journal of Social Psychology* 99 (1976): 179–86.

22. C. Harris Silverstein and David J. Stang, "Seating Position and Interaction in Triads: A Field Study, " *Sociometry* (1976): 166–70.

23. M. Dosey and M. Meisels, "Personal Space and Self Protection," *Journal of Personality and Social Psychology* 11 (1969): 93–97.

24. R. Sommer, "Studies in Personal Space," *Sociometry* 22 (1959): 247–60.

25. M. Cook, "Experiments on Orientation and Proxemics," *Human Relations* 23(1970): 61–70.

26. J. E. Singer, "The Use of Manipulative Strategies: Machiavellianism and Attractiveness," *Sociometry* 27 (1964): 128–51; J. Kelly, "Dress as Non-Verbal Communication," paper presented at the annual conference of the American Association for Public Opinion Research, May 1969; M. Lefkowitz, R. Blake, and J. Mouton, "Status Factors in Pedestrian Violation of Traffic Signals," *Journal of Abnormal and Social Psychology* 51 (1955): 704–06; J. Mills and E. Aronson, "Opinion Change as a Function of the Communicator's Attractiveness and Desire to Influence," *Journal of Social Psychology* 1 (1965): 73–77. See also Dale Leathers, *Successful Nonverbal Communication* (Boston: Allyn and Bacon, 1997).

27. Edward T. Hall and Mildred Reed Hall, *Understanding Cultural Differences* (Yarmouth, ME: Intercultural Press, 1989).

28. D. I. Ballard and D. R. Seibold, "Time Orientation and Temporary Variation Across Work Groups: Implications for Group and Organizational Communication," *Western Journal of Communication* 64 (Spring 2000): 218–42.

29. Ballard and Seibold, "Time Orientation and Temporary Variations Across Work Groups."

30. Adapted from Donald W. Klopf, *Intercultural Encounters: The Fundamentals of Intercultural Communication* (Englewood, CO: Morton, 1998) and Hall and Hall, *Understanding Cultural Differences.*

31. Klopf, *Intercultural Encounters.*

32. J. O'Connor, "The Relationship of Kinesics and Verbal Communication to Leadership Perception in Small Group Discussion" (Ph.D. dissertation, Indiana, 1971).

33. John Baird, "Some Nonverbal Elements of Leadership Emergence," *Southern Speech Communication journal* 40 (1977): 352–61; see also Laurence M. Childs et al., "Nonverbal and Verbal Communication of Leadership," paper presented at the annual meeting of the American Psychological Association, Los Angeles, 1981.

34. Albert Mehrabian and M. Williams, "Nonverbal Concomitants of Perceived and Intended Persuasiveness," *Journal of Personality and Social Psychology* 13 (1969): 37–58.

35. M. Reece and R. Whitman, "Expressive Movements, Warmth, and Verbal Reinforcement." *Journal of Abnormal and Social Psychology* 64 (1962): 234–36.

36. Mark L. Knapp, Roderick P. Hart, Gustav W. Friedrich, and Gary Schulman, "The Rhetoric of Goodbye: Verbal and Nonverbal Correlates of Human Leave-Taking," *Speech Monographs* 40(1975): 182–98.

37. Judee K. Burgoon, Lesa A. Stern, and Leesa Dillman, *Interpersonal Adaptation: Dyadic Interaction Patterns.* (Cambridge, England; Cambridge, 1995); see also Judee K. Burgoon, David Buller, and W. Gill Woodall, *Nonverbal Communication: The Unspoken Dialogue* (New York: McGraw-Hill, 1996).

38. W. S. Condon and L. W. Sander, "Neonate Movement Is Synchronized with Adult Speech: Interactional Participation and Language Acquisition." *Science* I (January 1974): 99–101; W. S. Condon and W. D. Ogston, "Soundfilm Analysis of Normal and Pathological Behavior Patterns," *Journal of Nervous and Mental Disease* 143 (1996): 338–47.

39. A. Kendon, "Some Relationships between Body Motion and Speech: An Analysis of an Example," in A. W. Siegman and B. Pope, eds., *Studies in Dyadic Communication* (Elms-

ford, NY: Pergamon, 1972). See also Frank J. Bernieri and Robert Rosenthal, "Interpersonal Coordination: Behavior Matching and Interactional Synchrony," in Robert S. Feldman and Bernard Rimes, eds., *Fundamentals of Nonverbal Behavior* (Cambridge, England: Cambridge, 1991).

40. Davida Navarre and Catherine A. Emihovich, "Movement Synchrony and Self-Analytic Group," paper presented at the Eastern Communication Association, Boston, 1978.

41. Edward A. Mabry, "Developmental Aspects of Nonverbal Behavior in Small Group Settings," *Small Group Behavior* 20 (May 1989): 190–202.

42. Paul Ekman and W. V. Friesen, "Nonverbal Leakage and Clues to Deception," *Psychiatry* 32 (1969): 88–106.

43. Knapp and Hall, *Nonverbal Communication* 313.

44. Definition based on one by A. G. Smith, ed., *Communications and Culture* (New York; Holt, Rinehart & Winston, 1966).

45. B. J. Broome and L. Fulbright, "A Multistage Influence Model of Barriers to Group Problem Solving: A Participant-Generated Agenda for Small-Group Research," *Small Group Research* 26 (1995): 25–55.

46. Edward T. Hall, *Beyond Culture* (Garden City, NY: Doubleday, 1976).

47. Hall, *Beyond Culture*.

48. Hall, *Beyond Culture*.

49. Carley H. Dodd, *Dynamics of Intercultural Communication* (Dubuque, IA: Brown, 1997).

50. Fathi Yousef and Nancy Briggs, "The Multinational Business Organization: A Schema for the Training of Overseas Personnel in Communication," *International and Intercultural Communication Annual* 2 (1975): 74–85.

51. Edward T. Hall, *The Silent Language* (New York: Anchor, 1973).

52. Melanie Booth-Butterfield and Felecia Jordan, "Communication Adaptation Among Racially Homogeneous and Heterogeneous Groups," *The Southern Communication Journal* 54 (Spring 1989): 253–72.

53. Robert Shuter, "A Field Study of Nonverbal Communication in Germany, Italy, and the United States," *Communication Monographs* 44 (1977): 298–305.

54. Dodd, *Dynamics of Intercultural Communication*.

55. Clara Mayo and Nancy Henley, *Gender and Nonverbal Behavior* (New York: Springer, 1981).

56. Diana K. Ivy and Phil Backlund, *Exploring Gender Speak: Personal Effectiveness in Gender Communications,* 2d ed. (New York: McGraw-Hill, 2000).

57. Gloria Leventhal and Michelle Matturro, "Differential Effects of Spatial Crowding and Sex on Behavior," *Perceptual Motor Skills* 50 (1980): 111–19.

58. Robert Sommer, "Studies in Personal Space," *Sociometry* 22 (1959): 247–60.

59. Phoebe C. Ellsworth and Linda M. Ludwig, "Visual Behavior in Social Interaction," *Journal of Communication* 22 (1972): 375–403.

60. Mehrabian, *Nonverbal Communication*.

61. Nancy M. Henley, *Body Politics: Power, Sex and Nonverbal Communication* (Englewood Cliffs, NJ: Prentice-Hall, 1977).

62. Henley, *Body Politics*.

63. Norman N. Markel, Joseph Long, and Thomas J. Saine, "Sex Effects in Conversational Interaction: Another Look at Male Dominance," *Human Communication Research* 2 (1976): 35–64.

64. J. Siegel, V. Dubrovsky, S. Kiesler, and T. W. McGuire, "Group Processes in Computer-Mediated Commination," *Organizational Behavior and Human Decision Processes* 33 (1986): 157–187; P. Bordia, N. DiFonzo, and A. Chang, "Rumor as Group Problem Solving: Development Patterns in Informal Computer-Mediated Groups," *Small Group Research* 30 (1999): 8–28.

65. S. G. Straus, "Testing Typology of Tasks: An Empirical Validation of McGrath's (1984) Group Task Circumplex," *Small Group Research* 30 (1999): 166–87.

66. Albert Mehrabian, *Silent Messages* (Belmont, CA: Wadsworth, 1981) 108.

Chapter Outline:

Developing a Discussion Plan

Formulating Discussion Questions

Using Electronic Resources and the
Library

Using Logic and Reasoning

Using Evidence in Group Discussion

Using Critical-Analysis Skills: Avoiding
Reasoning Fallacies

Putting Principles into Practice

Practice

Notes

Objectives:

After studying this chapter,
you will be able to:

▶ Develop a plan for preparing for a group
discussion.

▶ Formulate a question of fact, value, or
policy for a group discussion.

▶ Identify three criteria for a well-phrased
policy-discussion question.

▶ Identify appropriate methods for
researching group discussion questions.

▶ Use appropriate logic and reasoning to
develop sound conclusions.

▶ Identify appropriate ways to use facts,
examples, opinions, and statistics in
group discussions.

▶ Avoid reasoning fallacies by critically analyzing the reasoning and evidence presented in group discussions.

▶ Identify the characteristics of an ethical
group communicator.

Preparing
for Discussion

"To solve a problem it is necessary to think.
It is necessary to think even to decide what facts to collect."
— Robert Maynard Hutchins

The primary message of this chapter can be summarized with the Boy Scout motto "Be prepared!" Have you ever spent an hour or two at a group or team meeting only to find no one was ready to make a meaningful, informed contribution? Many wasted meetings boil down to the fact that group members just haven't done their homework. GIGO is the acronym that computer programmers use for the expression "Garbage in, garbage out." If you put poor information (garbage) into developing a computer program, you get poor results when you're finished. It works the same way in group discussion.[1] To achieve a quality decision, a group needs quality information gleaned from research as well as effective reasoning and critical-thinking skills.[2] In this chapter we focus on how to prepare effectively for group discussion and how to use research and critical-thinking skills to enhance the quality of group discussion.

The Greek philosopher Socrates believed the primary goal of dialogue and discussion was the search for truth. Today group discussion continues to be a trusted method of seeking answers to tough questions. Our legal system is based on a jury of men and women who, after hearing evidence and using their best critical-thinking and analysis skills, discuss whether someone is or is not guilty of a crime. In corporations, teams and task forces churn out key decisions. Regardless of a group's composition, goal, or context, its discussion will be more productive if group members have appropriately prepared and if they know how to critically evaluate information used to reach reasoned conclusions.

Developing a Discussion Plan

Imagine you've been assigned to a group or committee. Perhaps the instructor in your group communication class has assigned you to a group to make a recommendation, solve a problem, or make a decision. What should you do first? How do you develop a plan to get your work accomplished? What should you not do? It's tempting for groups to jump in with both feet and start deciding what to do without adequate research or preparation. The most effective groups develop a plan for accomplishing their goal. Suggesting solutions or making final recommendations at your first meeting is not a good idea. Effective groups prepare for discussion in their search for truth. We'll outline the general parts of a discussion plan and then spend the rest of the chapter describing these strategies in detail.

Get Acquainted with Your Group Members

Most North Americans are task oriented. "Let's get down to business. What are we supposed to do? Get to the point." are typical statements heard at most first team or group meetings. It's important, however, to take a few minutes to get better acquainted with group members before focusing on the task. A consistent conclusion from teamwork research is the importance of ensuring that group members know each other in order to develop appropriate roles and responsibilities.[3] In fact, often the most serious problems group and team members encounter are not caused by task issues; problems occur because people have difficulty relating to each other. Taking time to establish good working relationships and trust can help a group or team be more productive in the long run.

Do more than just announce your name to the group. Perhaps you can provide information about how much experience you have with the topic or, if no specific task has been articulated, you can talk about your experience in working on group and team projects. You may want to exchange phone numbers and e-mail addresses so that you can contact each other. You need not artificially prolong this initial orientation period, but it will be useful to spend some time learning about group or team members.

Clarify the Goals of the Group

Once you've completed introductions, make sure you know what the group's purpose, goal, and assignment is. You should be able to summarize the group goal in your own words. Most work-group goals boil down to three tasks: (1) generating ideas, information, or options, (2) making a choice often to solve a larger problem, and (3) putting an idea into action. Your team may be involved in only one of these tasks, or all three. Later in this chapter, we'll suggest that you formulate a discussion question as either fact (something did or did not happen), value (something is better or worse than something else), or policy (something should be done). Consider writing your question or group goal on a chalkboard or flipchart for all team members to see. When the group starts to wobble or get off track, point group members back to the central reason for the discussion—to achieve the goal of the group. As we noted in Chapter 1, having a clear, elevating goal is one of the essential requirements for an effective team.

Develop a Plan for Gathering Information and Analyzing Issues

Once you have formulated your discussion question and clarified your goal, you need to collect information and data to help you answer your question. In this chapter we'll talk about how to conduct research by using electronic searches and the traditional resources of the library, and by developing a survey.

But before you launch out for the library or surf the Internet, find out what you and your group members already know about the topic and issues. Are any group members already experts on the topic? After assessing your existing group's knowledge, figure out what kind of information you need. Identify who is most interested in specific aspects of your topic. Begin to divide and conquer. Assign or ask for volunteers to begin researching the topic. Coordinate your group's research efforts rather than having group members scatter and then plunge into the research process. Without coordination, you may needlessly duplicate your research efforts. Besides just divvying up the work, be sure to give yourselves specific deadlines when the information will be collected. Allow plenty of time for the group to discuss the information rather than just compiling the facts and data before your group is to make final recommendations. Do more than just make assignments; indicate when the information should be shared with the group. Develop a concrete plan for structuring the workload.

Several communication scholars have found that how much information group members share with each other has a major impact on the success of the group. Not surprisingly, more information shared is likely to result in a better solution or outcome.[4] James Larson concluded that group members usually first share information in group deliberations that most other group members already know.[5] It's important, however, to not just share obvious information but to share information that perhaps only you know. Having a plan for gathering and sharing information can ensure that group members can share their knowledge with other members. Communication researcher Kathleen Propp found that groups who begin their deliberations with conflict and contention need additional information to help them sort through their disagreements; so if you get off to a rocky start, perhaps your group needs to make a conscious effort to do additional research.[6] Carol Saunders and Shaila Miranda concluded that virtual groups who collaborate only via computer connections typically have access to more information, but face-to-face groups usually gather more information earlier in their deliberations.[7]

Follow a Structured Plan to Accomplish the Task

Once group members begin sharing information with the entire group (whether with written summaries, via e-mail, or with oral reports) you may need to fine-tune your team's goal or reword your discussion question. The new information may lead you into another direction or make you aware that you were pursuing the wrong goal. In Chapter 9 we will share several specific techniques and methods of organizing a problem-solving discussion. The most basic problem-solving structure includes these steps: (1) identify and define the problem, (2) analyze the problem, (3) generate several possible solutions, (4) select the best solution or combination of solutions, and (5) test and implement the solution. Organizing your meeting agenda around these steps can help keep your group on track.

In addition to preparing an agenda for each group meeting, your group may want to plot an overarching work plan. Consider developing deadlines for completing certain tasks. Stephen Covey, author of *Seven Habits for Highly Effective People*, suggests we should "Begin with the end in mind" for any project or task. When developing the work plan for your group or team, visualize what the completed project will look like. Is the goal to produce a written report or to deliver an oral presentation in which you will make recommendations? Once you have developed a clear, collective vision of your final work product, work back from the final deadline to develop a timeline for making the vision a reality.

Use Critical-Thinking and Analysis Skills

As the group begins to analyze the information and generate possible options or recommendations, test the validity of the logic and reasoning that you are using to reach your conclusions. Also examine the quality of the evidence you're using. In addition, be on guard for reaching a conclusion using a fallacious reasoning assumption. We will present some of the most typical reasoning fallacies later in the chapter.

Determine How to Present Your Information

Once you have developed your conclusions, you'll need to decide how to best present your information to others. In the Appendix to this book we describe three common formats for doing this: (1) a panel discussion, (2) a symposium presentation, and (3) a forum presentation. In addition to presenting your conclusions orally, you may need to prepare a written report.

Consider organizing your written report around the key group competencies that we've presented (definition of the problem, analysis of the problem, criteria, possible solutions, best solution or solutions). Most written reports are prepared for a specific individual or group. Keep your reader in mind as you develop the written report. Follow any specific guidelines or structure that have been prescribed for you.

In most groups, time to participate in a group discussion is limited. Developing a plan of action and talking about it with the entire group can be a productive way to use your time wisely and take advantage of the variety of skills and talents in your group or team. The rest of this chapter will present specific details on developing discussion questions, conducting research, reaching logical conclusions from evidence, avoiding reasoning fallacies, and deciding on a format to share your information with others. In Chapter 12 we describe basic principles and strategies of running a meeting, including how to develop a meeting agenda. You may want to review this material to give your group some ideas about how to efficiently work together to develop a discussion plan.

REVIEW

Developing a Discussion Plan

1. *Get acquainted with your group or team members.*
   - ▶ Spend some time learning about the background and interests of group members.
   - ▶ Exchange phone numbers and e-mail addresses.

2. *Clarify the goals of the group or team.*
   - ▶ Determine how you will know when you are finished with the task at hand, by clearly stating the final objective

3. *Develop a strategy for gathering information and researching your topic.*
   - ▶ Determine which group members may be experts on the topic.
   - ▶ Identify what you and your group already know.
   - ▶ Identify what information you need to answer your discussion question.
   - ▶ Divide and conquer; volunteer or assign group members to gather appropriate information and evidence.
   - ▶ Decide on a specific place and time when you will share your information with the rest of the group.
   - ▶ Share information with other group or team members.

4. *Follow a structured plan to accomplish your task.*
   - ▶ Develop deadlines for the group.
   - ▶ Consider using a classic problem-solving structure for your report or presentation:
     Define the problem
     Analyze the problem
     Identify criteria

Generate solutions

Select the best solutions(s)

Test and evaluate the solution

5. *Develop logical arguments and sound reasons to support your ideas.*

   ▶ Evaluate the quality of your evidence and the evidence of other group members.

   ▶ Don't confuse the volume of information you gather via the web with the quality of information you collect.

   ▶ Guard against uncritical-thinking or reasoning fallacies as you develop conclusions.

   ▶ Use critical listening skills.

6. *Decide on the best format (oral, written, or both oral and written) to present your findings.*

Formulating Discussion Questions

Before most scientists begin an experiment or conduct scholarly research, they have some idea of what they are looking for. Some researchers start with a *hypothesis*, a guess based on previous theory and research about what they will find in their search for new knowledge. Other investigators formulate a research question that provides a direction for their research. Like scientific research, problem solving seeks answers to questions. It makes sense, then, for group members to formulate a question before searching for answers. By identifying a specific question that they must answer, members can reduce some of the initial uncertainty that accompanies their discussion.

Phrasing a discussion question should be done with considerable care. It is an important part of initiating and organizing any group discussion, particularly problem-solving discussions, because the quality and specificity of a question usually determine the quality of the answer. The better a group prepares a discussion question, the more clearly articulated will be the group's goal, and the greater will be the chances for a productive and orderly discussion.

For Better or For Worse®   **by Lynn Johnston**

FOR BETTER OR FOR WORSE ©United Features Syndicate

In some group discussions and conferences, the question has been predetermined. Government committees and juries exemplify such groups. But usually groups are faced with a problem or need and are responsible for formulating a specific question to guide their deliberations. There are basically three types of discussion questions: (1) questions of fact, (2) questions of value, and (3) questions of policy. To help you determine which type is most appropriate for your various group discussions, we will discuss each.

Questions of Fact

In summarizing the responsibilities of the jury during a criminal court case, the judge provides a specific **question of fact** to help guide the jury in its discussion. "Your job," instructs the judge, "is to decide whether the defendant is guilty or not guilty of the charges against him." A question of fact asks whether something happened or did not happen; its answer determines what is true and what is false.

A well-worded question of fact can ultimately be answered by one of two responses—either yes or no. Either something did or did not occur. (Although, of course, a yes or no response can be qualified in terms of the probability of its accuracy.) The question "Did the Diamondbacks win the World Series in 2001?" is a question of fact; either they did or they did not. "Are there more incidents of terrorism in the United States today than in the 1990s?" Again, the answer is either yes or no, depending on the evidence. But questions of fact often appear deceptively simple. In trying to answer a question of fact, define the critical words or phrases in the question. In the preceding question, for example, what is meant by "incidents of terrorism"? Does it mean any act of violence is an incident of terrorism? By reducing the ambiguity of a question's meaning, a group can save considerable time in agreeing on a final answer.

Your group's objective will determine whether or not you should investigate a question of fact. If the group needs to discover what is true and what is false, then formulate a question of fact and define the key words in the question to give it greater focus and clarity. If the group needs to make a less objective value judgment or to suggest solutions to a problem, choose one of the types of questions discussed below.

Questions of Value

A **question of value** generally produces a lively discussion because it concerns attitudes, beliefs, and values about what is good or bad or right or wrong. Answering a question of value is more complicated than simply determining whether an event did or did not occur. "Which political party in the United States produced the best presidents?" is an example of a question of value. Group members' responses to this question depend on their attitudes toward Democrats, Republicans, or other political parties.

An **attitude** is a learned predisposition to respond to a person, object, or idea in a favorable, neutral, or unfavorable way. In essence, the attitudes you hold about the world determine whether you like or dislike what you experience and observe. A favorable attitude toward Democrats will affect your response to the value question, "Which political party in the United States produced the best presidents?"

A **belief** is the way in which you structure what is true and false. Put another way, it is the way you structure reality. If you believe in God, you have structured your reality to assume that God exists. If you do not believe in God, you have structured your perception of what is true and false so that God is not part of your reality.

Problem solving groups must formulate their research questions carefully. Why?

A **value** is often defined as an enduring conception of good and bad. Your values affect your perceptions of right and wrong. A value is more resistant to change than an attitude or a belief.

What are your values? Which of your values have the most influence on your behavior? Because values are so central to how you respond in the world, you may have trouble coming up with a tidy list of your most important values. You may be able to list things you like and do not like (attitudes) or what you believe is true and not true (beliefs), but your values are sometimes difficult to identify as the guiding forces affecting your behavior.

Understanding the differences among attitudes, beliefs, and values helps you better understand what happens when a group discusses a value question. You base your response to a value question on your own attitudes, beliefs, and values, as do other group members. If you can identify the underlying attitudes, beliefs, and values that influence the responses to a value question, you can examine and discuss them.

In looking at relationships between attitudes (likes and dislikes), beliefs (what is true or false), and values (what is perceived to be good or bad), it is important to note that values change less frequently and attitudes are most susceptible to change.

Figure 7.1 shows values in the center of the diagram because they are central to how you make sense out of what you experience; if you valued honesty yesterday you will probably still value honesty today and in the future. Beliefs, the next ring, may change depending on your experiences and your perception of what is true and false. Attitudes are shown in the outer ring because they are likely to change more often. Although our values are less likely to change, our attitudes may change daily. For example, one day you may like your small group communication class, and the next day you don't. Yet the underlying value of obtaining a good education probably will not vary.

Figure 7.1 Interrelationships of Values, Beliefs, and Attitudes

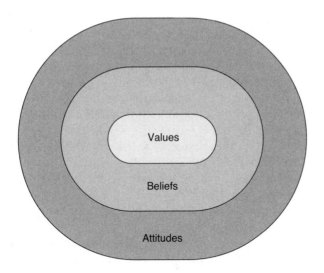

You base your response to a value question on your own attitudes, beliefs, and values, as do other group members. If you can identify the underlying attitudes, beliefs, and values that influence the responses to a value question, you can examine and discuss them.

Questions of Policy

Most problem-solving discussions revolve around **questions of policy**—questions that help groups determine what course of action or policy change would enable them to solve a problem or reach a decision. "What should be done to improve the quality of education in U.S. colleges and universities?" and "What can Congress do to reduce America's trade deficit?" are examples of policy questions. These questions can be identified easily because answers to them require changes of policy or procedure. Discussion questions including phrases such as, "What should be done about . . .?" or "What could be done to improve . . .?" are policy questions. Most legislation in the U.S. Senate and House of Representatives is proposed in response to specific policy questions. A well-written policy question should adhere to three criteria: It should imply a problem exists, it should be limited in scope, and it should be controversial enough to spark discussion.

1. *A policy question should imply that a specific problem must be solved.* The question "What should be done about UFOs?" is not an appropriate policy question, because it does not provide enough direction to a specific problem. Do not confuse a discussion *topic* with a discussion *question*. If your group is going to discuss UFOs, it has a topic, but it is not trying to solve a problem. The group could rephrase the discussion question to make it more policy-oriented: "What could be done to improve the way the government handles and investigates UFO sightings in the United States?" The rephrased

question more clearly implies that there is a problem in the way the government investigates sightings of UFOs. The latter question provides clearer direction for research and analysis.

2. *A policy question should be limited in scope.* Do not try to tackle a complex problem unless your group has the time and resources to solve it. For example, a group of students was assigned the task of formulating a policy question, discussing it, and then reporting the results of the discussion to the class. The students had three weeks to analyze and suggest possible solutions to the problem they had chosen to investigate "What should be done to deal with Social Security?" Although the question clearly implies a specific problem, its lack of focus frustrated the group. A more limited discussion question, such as "What should be done to improve the tax base in our community?" would have been more manageable. You would do better to consider a simple, clearly worded question that can be analyzed in the time period allotted to your group than a question that would keep the U.S. Congress busy for several months or even years. On the other hand, a group should not phrase a policy-discussion question so that it requires only a yes or no answer or so that it limits the group's options for solutions. Given this criterion, "Should safety belts be required by law?" is a less-satisfactory policy discussion topic than "What can be done to ensure greater highway safety?"

3. *A policy question should be controversial.* It should be an important issue worth discussing. An issue is a question about which individuals disagree. If group members disagree about how to solve a problem, they should not necessarily select another issue. Conflict, controversy, and disagreement should not always be viewed negatively. If group members agreed on how to solve a problem at the beginning of a discussion, they would have nothing to discuss. The purpose of a group discussion is to consider all alternatives and to agree on the best one. Therefore, do not reject a discussion question because other group members may hold contrasting points of view. Your discussion will be more interesting and you will probably reach a better solution if the group examines all sides of an issue.

The three types of discussion questions (fact, value, and policy) may not appear to overlap, but as one researcher has observed, you must concern yourselves with questions of fact and value when considering questions of policy.[8] They must judge evidence as true or false (question of fact). Your attitudes, beliefs, and values (questions of value) will influence the decisions you make on policy changes (questions of policy). A discussion question serves a valuable function in providing direction to group deliberations. Once groups devise discussion questions, however, they can still modify them.

Decide whether your group is considering a question of fact, value, or policy. Identifying the type of question helps you understand the dynamics of the issue under discussion. If you realize that the question "Should we legalize casino gambling in our community?" involves value judgments, you will be less likely to condemn group members who disagree with you. Even in the face of disagreement, frustration and defensiveness can yield to understanding and compromise. Remember, too, that even though a discussion question may be clearly identified as one of fact, value, or policy, your discussion probably will include other types of questions. Once your group has a well-defined problem to discuss, members should begin researching and analyzing it.

Three Types of Group-Discussion Questions

QUESTION TYPE	DEFINITION	EXAMPLE
Question of fact	A question that asks whether something is true or false	Did the university have a freshman-admission policy last year?
Question of value	A question that considers the worth of or desirability of something	What are the virtues of a democratic form of government?
Question of policy	A question that considers whether a change in procedure should be made	What should be done to curtail gang violence?

Using Electronic Resources and the Library

You undoubtedly already know how to go about finding information in your library. Although some libraries still have the traditional card catalog to help you find books, most libraries today have computer-assisted or electronic indexes of both books and periodicals. In many libraries, you can now use your personal computer in your home to find out what books and articles are in your library. Check to see if your library has facilities for you to conduct computer searches of scholarly journals through the Educational Resources Information Center (ERIC), business journals through the ABI/Inform, or general works through the *Readers' Guide to Periodical Literature*. Do not overlook other useful sources of information that your library may have, such as collections of government documents or audiovisual materials.

Using the Web

In addition to the books and journals in the physical space in your library, a wealth of information exists in cyberspace and on the Internet—the network of information in computers stored around the world. Started as a network of only four computers in 1969, today the Internet consists of thousands of computer networks and is accessed by millions of users in every country in the world.

The Internet can be a challenging place on the information superhighway. It provides many wonderful opportunities but there are possible drawbacks, such as figuring out how to access all the information that is available. The Internet is an ever-evolving system; the procedures for finding information may change overnight. An Internet address that you find today may be obsolete within a short period. In addition, the multitude of networks and subnetworks makes it difficult to know where to go to get what you need. If you are not yet electronically literate, your college librarian or perhaps a member of your group can help you gather information from this valuable source.

There is no single index to all the information available to you on the World Wide Web (usually just called "the Web"). The two most prevalent systems to help you access the Web are (1) *Netscape Navigator* and (2) *Internet Explorer*. Once you have accessed the Internet with one of these programs, you can find the information you need through a search engine, which is really nothing more than a large index organized by subject of literally millions of Websites. Some of today's more popular search engines include Altavista (www.altavista.digital.com), Yahoo! (www.yahoo.com), Google (www.google.com), and Excite (www.excite.com), in addition to a score of others. *Lexis-Nexis* is another powerful electronic research tool available through many university libraries; it can provide complete texts of periodicals and newspapers, as well as legal and government documents. Although a single search engine may not be the magic bullet for finding what you need, through diligence and detective-like persistence you are likely to find help for what you are looking for.

Several other useful sources of information or resources that might be useful in your research are your professors, your school's own Web page, and the staff in the library and information technology department. Never underestimate the value in asking others about their experience in Web research; people that you already know may be your best lead for a great Website. As technology continues to progress, it will likely become easier to locate resources. You will be able to locate more complete texts of books and articles on the Web rather than just finding references sites. Search engines will continue to expand and improve in accuracy. Of course, the Internet is only a tool to help you find information. You will need to use your skill in identifying which information is most useful to you.

Another challenge in electronic research is deciding which data are relevant to your question. Although you can now access hundreds of libraries and end up with a ream of documents, the volume of information is not nearly as important as your ability to use the information you gather. In the medical profession, triage is the process of making decisions about which patients need the most attention or medical care, in an emergency room, for example. **Information triage** is the process of sorting through information you have gathered from your search to determine what is most useful or needs the most critical attention. Later in this chapter we present some tests of using evidence to help you wade through the evidence that you retrieve. You will also need to cite the sources that you find on the Internet. Most of the new style manuals will tell you how to prepare a bibliographical entry to document an Internet citation.

Evaluating Web Sources

As with any source of information, just because you find it "in print" or on the Web does not mean the information is accurate or reliable. Anyone with a computer and software can construct a Website. Information on the Web may not have gone through an editorial process to check for accuracy. For example, information that you glean from the Website of the *New York Times* is more credible than someone's personal Website or the Website of an organization with a particular political or profit-based agenda. When evaluating information you retrieve from the Web, consider the following criteria:

1. *Accountability*. Who is responsible for the Website? What can you find out about the sponsor? To whom do the sponsors of the Website owe allegiance? Knowing who is

placing the information on the site can help you evaluate whether the information is biased or unbiased. If there is no way for you to determine who is putting the information on the Web, it will be difficult to evaluate the authenticity of the information presented.

2. *Objectivity.* Related to the accountability of the Website is the objectivity of the information presented. Consider the interests and philosophical or political biases of the organization or individual responsible for the site. If the site is sponsored by a for-profit organization, the information may be biased in favor of the organization's financial gain. The more objective the author of the site, the more credible the facts and information presented.

3. *Accuracy.* Is the information accurate? Is the information verifiable by other sources? Web resources should also be relatively free of common grammar, spelling, and punctuation errors. A site containing such errors may also contain errors in content. Just as the sources for facts in a print document should be cited, so too should they be identified in a Web document.

4. *Recency.* How current and up to date is the information on the Website? Look for clues that the site was recently posted or is kept current. Many sites include a description of when the site was posted and when it was last updated. As a general rule of thumb, the more recent the information (especially facts, statistics, and other data) the better.

5. *Usability.* Is there information that you can actually use? Does it relate to the group or team's goal? Also consider the overall layout and design of the site which should facilitate its use. The site may have outstanding graphics but an overdone, multimedia-laden site can slow down the speed with which you load or access the information; in the worst-case scenario it could cause your computer to freeze.

Developing a Survey

Not all the information you need can be found on the Internet. If you are investigating a local campus or community problem, you may need to conduct a **survey** to describe the attitudes, beliefs, values, or behavior of people affected by the problem you are solving. Surveys can also help a group understand the seriousness of a problem or its probable causes, effects, and symptoms.

John W. Bowers and John Courtwright suggest that anyone attempting to conduct a survey faces several problems, including (1) developing clear, unbiased questions, (2) selecting a large-enough sample to be representative of the entire population being sampled; (3) writing a questionnaire so that it is clear to the reader and efficient for the interviewer; (4) deciding on whether to interview people face-to-face, over the phone, or by mail; (5) making sure that the questionnaire will answer the questions that need answers; and (6) testing the clarity of the questionnaire by administering a pilot study or minisurvey.[9]

First, the group must determine a survey's objectives. What does the group want to know that it does not know now? Once a group determines its objectives, it can then decide how best to ask questions that will give clear answers. **Open-ended questions**, such as essay questions, permit respondents to answer freely without any constraints. **Closed-ended**

The Internet can be a useful source of data and information to help your group analyze issues and accomplish your task. The following Websites offer a wealth of information to help you conduct your research.

Electronic Encyclopedias
You can search by word or phrase for information; you'll also find links to research articles.
www.encyclopedia.com

With this link you can access the *Encyclopedia Britannica*.
www.Britannica.com

This completely online encyclopedia includes information on a broad range of topics.
www.encyberpedia.com

Statistical Abstracts from the U.S. Census Bureau
This powerful site presents information from the last census.
www.census.gov/dmd/www/2khome.htm

Information Exchange
www.info.gov

questions ask respondents to choose answers from among several responses supplied by the interviewer. Examples of closed-ended questions include multiple-choice and true–false questions and questions that require respondents to rank items of importance or indicate agreement or disagreement. The answers to closed-ended questions can be more easily tabulated, but open-ended questions allow for a wide range of responses. The type of questions your group asks depends on what you want to know.

After developing and organizing questions, you need to decide on a survey method. If you primarily ask open-ended questions, it may be best to conduct face-to-face interviews so that you can probe and clarify respondents' answers. Interviewing requires listening and recording skills. If you have the time and resources, you may want to mail questionnaires. Including a self-addressed, stamped envelope with each questionnaire improves your response rate. You can also stop people on campus or in your community to have them respond to a brief written questionnaire. (Make sure you have permission to do this from whomever owns the property on which you distribute questionnaires.) In addition, most universities have rules about conducting research on campus. If you are working on a class project, consult your instructor before making final decisions about survey methods and distribution.

Table 7.1   Examples of Closed-Ended Survey Questions

1. Are you in favor of raising property taxes?

   _____Yes   _____No

2. Local property taxes should be increased to support our local school. Circle your response:

   Strongly agree   Agree   Undecided   Disagree   Strongly disagree

3. Select the statement that most closely reflects your feelings about tax increases.

   a. Property taxes should be increased to support local schools.

   b. Property taxes should not be increased to support local schools.

   c. I am uncertain whether property taxes should be increased to support local schools.

   d. Taxes other than the property tax should be increased to support local schools; indicate which taxes should be increased to support local schools.

4. Rank the following sources of potential tax revenue increases to support local schools from most desirable (1) to least desirable (6).

   _____ Property tax   _____ Cigarette tax

   _____ Sales tax   _____ Alcohol tax

   _____ Gasoline tax   _____ Income tax

   Before administering your questionnaire, survey a very small sample to make sure your questionnaire is clear. Have your instructor or other members of your class examine its format and wording to see that it makes sense. This step can save you time, energy, money, and embarrassment.

   An example of an open-ended question is the following: "What are your feelings about increasing property taxes to support local schools and other services?" Examples of closed-ended questions are as shown in Table 7.1.

   Once you have designed and tested a questionnaire, you must make sure that you survey a broad sample of people to justify your conclusions. If, for example, you want to know if students support a 5 percent increase in university tuition, it would not be wise to ask only graduating seniors. A random sample of the entire student population at your school would provide the best basis for making a decision about the acceptability of a tuition increase. You would also need to ask enough people to gauge the attitude of your entire student body. If you survey only 20 students out of 15,000, you have a greater potential for error.

Using Logic and Reasoning

In the search for truth in the crucible of a group discussion, you will need to develop logical arguments and reach reasoned conclusions. **Reasoning** is the process of drawing a conclusion from evidence. Your evidence will consist of the facts, examples, statistics, and opinions that are used to support the point you wish to make. For over two thousand years, students have studied the principles of critical analysis that we now present. Although you may have been introduced to a discussion of logic, reasoning, and evidence in another course (such as public speaking, argumentation, or philosophy), we think it's important to apply these important principles to group and team deliberations. First we will provide an overview of reasoning strategies and then we'll describe how to use evidence effectively. There are three major ways of structuring an argument to reach a logical conclusion: (1) inductive reasoning, (2) deductive reasoning, and (3) causal reasoning.

Inductive Reasoning

Inductive reasoning is a method of arriving at a general or bottom-line conclusion through the use of specific examples, facts, statistics, and opinions. For example, suppose you recently bought a used personal computer that didn't work the way it was supposed to when you got it home. You learn that one of your classmates also bought a used computer that didn't work well. Your uncle also bought a used computer from someone who ran an ad in the paper; his computer didn't work properly either. Based on those three examples, you reach a conclusion that buying used computers will give you trouble. You've reached a general conclusion based on the specific examples you know about.

As you reach a conclusion to help you answer your group-discussion question, you need to make sure you are reaching a valid or logical conclusion. When you reason inductively (from specific examples to a general conclusion), keep the following questions in mind:

1. *Are there enough specific examples to support the conclusion?* Are three examples of problems with used computers enough to prove your point that all used computers don't work well? There are millions of used computers; three is not a very large sample. If you coupled your examples with additional statistical evidence that over 30 percent of people who purchased a used computer experienced computer problems, then your evidence would be more convincing.

2. *Are the specific instances typical?* Were the three examples you cited representative of all used computers? How do you know? Perhaps you, your classmate, and your uncle bought computers that were not typical of most used computers. For example, maybe you all bought them from the same guy, who sells them out of the trunk of his car, whereas most people buy them from a reputable retail outlet. If the examples you are using to develop your point aren't representative of the entire population, you run the risk of reaching a flawed conclusion.

3. *Are the instances recent?* How long ago did you purchase your used computers? If you made your purchase three years ago, conditions may have changed. Perhaps used computers on the market today have better technology and are more reliable.

Deductive Reasoning

Deductive reasoning is the process of going from a general statement or principle to a specific conclusion. This is the reverse of inductive reasoning. Deductive reasoning can be presented in the form of a **syllogism**—a way of organizing or structuring an argument in three parts: (1) a major premise, (2) a minor premise, and (3) a conclusion. To reach a conclusion deductively, you start with a generalization that serves as the **major premise.** "All students who take a course in small group communication will have a successful career" is an example of a major premise. The **minor premise** is a more specific statement about an example that is linked to the major premise. "Mark Arnold has taken a course in group communication" is an example of a minor premise. The **conclusion** is based on the major premise and the more specific minor premise. In reasoning deductively, you should ensure that the major and minor premises are true and can be supported with evidence. The conclusion to our syllogism is "Mark Arnold will have a successful career."

To test the truth or validity of an argument organized deductively, consider the following questions.

1. *Is the major premise (general statement) true?* Will all students who take a course in small group communication necessarily have a successful career? What evidence exists to support that generalization? The most important part of making a deductive argument hinges on whether your major premise is true. It takes evidence to document the soundness of your major premise. Obviously, just asserting that a statement or generalization is true and labeling it a major premise is not enough. You need facts, examples, statistics, or expert opinion to support your generalization.

2. *Is the minor premise (the particular statement) also true?* If your minor premise is not true, your syllogism will fall apart. In our example, it is easy to confirm whether Mark Arnold has had a course in small group communication. But not all minor premises can be verified as easily.

Causal Reasoning

The third way to reach a logical conclusion is through **causal reasoning**—the process of relating two or more events and concluding that one event caused the other. For example, you might reason that in 2000 the use of a confusing "butterfly ballot" in some counties in Florida resulted in voter error.

You can structure a causal argument in two ways. First, you can reason from cause to effect, moving from a known fact (cause) to predict a result (effect). You know that the number of drug arrests in your community has increased; you know this is a fact because you have researched the police records. You reason that crime will decrease in your community if the drug offenders are locked up. Weather forecasters use the same method of reasoning when they predict the weather. They base a conclusion about what will happen tomorrow on what they know about today's weather.

The second way to structure a causal argument is to reason backward, from a known effect to an unknown cause. You know, for example, that interest rates have decreased in the past six months. You hypothesize that the decrease has occurred because of a healthy economy. You can't be absolutely sure of your analysis, but you do know that interest rates have decreased (the effect). As with other forms of reasoning, you develop strong causal arguments by using evidence to link something known with something unknown. If you understand how to use evidence effectively, you can enhance your use of inductive, deductive, and causal reasoning.

Using Evidence in Group Discussion

As discussed, after you formulate your discussion question you need to define key terms and gather information on the issues it involves. Members should also know something about the four kinds of evidence available: (1) facts, (2) examples, (3) opinions, and (4) statistics. Group members who use evidence effectively make better decisions. A research study found that the key element in swaying a jury is the quality and quantity of the evidence presented.[10]

Facts

A *fact* is any statement proven to be true. A fact cannot be a prediction about the future, because such a statement cannot be verified; it must be a report of something that has already happened or that is happening. "It will rain tomorrow" cannot be a fact, because the statement cannot be verified. "The weather forecaster predicts rain" may be a fact if the weather forecaster has made such a prediction; the accuracy of the forecast has nothing to do with whether the statement is a fact. Ask yourself these questions to determine whether a statement is a fact:

1. Is it true?

2. Is the source reliable?

3. Are there any contrary facts?

Examples

An *example* is an illustration of a particular case or incident and is most valuable when used to emphasize a fact. An example may be real or hypothetical. A real example can also be called a fact; it actually exists or has happened. A hypothetical example is of little use in proving a point but can add color and interest to illustrate an otherwise dry or boring factual presentation. Apply the following tests to examples:

1. Is it typical?

2. Is it significant?

3. Are there any contrary examples?

Opinions

An *opinion* is a quoted comment. Opinions of unbiased authorities who base opinions on fact are most valuable as evidence. Like examples, opinions can dramatize a point and make it more interesting. Opinions are most effective when used in conjunction with facts or statistics. The following questions can help you determine the usefulness of opinions:

1. Is the source reliable?

2. Is the source an expert in the field?

3. Is the source free from bias?

4. Is the opinion consistent with other statements made by the same source?

5. Is the opinion characteristic of opinions held by other experts in the field?

Statistics

Because they cannot present dozens of facts or examples in a given time limit, people often rely on statistics. A *statistic* is simply a number: 10,000 people, 132 reported cases of child abuse, 57 Western nations. Statistics provide firm support for important points. Pay special attention, though, to the tests of statistics listed next, because statistics are probably the most frequently misgathered and misinterpreted type of evidence.

1. Is the source reliable?

2. Is the source unbiased?

3. Are the figures recent? Do they apply to the time period in question?

4. How were the statistics drawn? If from a sample, is the sample representative of the total population? Is the sample big enough to be reliable?

5. Does the statistic actually measure what it is supposed to measure?

6. Are there contrary statistics?

Once you have located and collected your evidence, keep in mind a couple of guidelines for applying it effectively. First, never take evidence out of context. Even if you find a statement that seems to be exactly the evidence you need, do not use it if the next sentence following it says something like, "However, this idea has recently been proved false." Second, try to gather and use evidence from as many sources as possible. Finally, use many types of evidence to support a point.

Using Critical Analysis Skills: Avoiding Reasoning Fallacies

It's not enough just to have evidence or to be able to label the kind of reasoning that you're using to reach conclusions. On talk radio shows, you'll hear both callers and hosts reach some amazing and stupefying conclusions. If you want to critically analyze information and ideas, you must evaluate both the logic and the evidence used to reach a conclusion. Critical thinkers who are members of groups and teams need to develop key technical skills:

Discovery: The ability to seek and find relevant information

Organization: The ability to categorize and structure information

Analysis: The ability to break information down into pieces and interpret the information

Synthesis: The ability to combine information, to see new patterns and put information together in new and meaningful ways

Clarification: The ability to help the group focus on the important and to differentiate between key and secondary information.[11]

In addition to identifying and analyzing information, groups need to avoid inappropriate **fallacies**—false reasoning that occurs when someone attempts to research a conclusion without adequate evidence or with arguments that are irrelevant or inappropriate. Avoiding reasoning fallacies in your own arguments will enhance your critical-thinking skills. Being able to spot reasoning fallacies that others are using will make you a more discriminating and effective listener. Here are some of the most common fallacies.

Causal Fallacy

This fallacy is the inappropriate assumption that one event is the cause of another when there is little evidence to connect two events. The Latin phrase used to summarize this fallacy is *post hoc, ergo propter hoc*, which translates as "after this, therefore because of this." Superstitions illustrate causal fallacy. Assuming that your "lucky" rabbit's foot will help you perform better on a math test is a relationship that probably can't be demonstrated with facts and evidence. It's your ability to study and learn math that predicts your math test, not whether you have a rabbit's foot in your pocket. Be on the lookout for group members who inappropriately try to connect one event to another without adequate cause and effective evidence.

Either/Or

This fallacy occurs when someone argues that there are only two approaches or solutions to a problem; it oversimplifies the options by suggestions we must do either X or Y. "It's either vote for new school taxes or we will have to send our kids to the next county to be educated," claims a parent at a school-board meeting. Usually there are a range of options to consider in any discussion. In fact, one hallmark of successful groups is the ability to identify several options to solving a problem.

Bandwagon Fallacy

"Everybody is in favor of expanding the city park, so you should favor it too," is an example of the bandwagon fallacy. Someone using this fallacy tries to convince you that an idea is good simply because "everybody" else thinks it's a good idea; hence, you should jump on the bandwagon and support the idea. Judge an idea on its merits, not just because of a popular opinion poll. As we noted in Chapter 1, one disadvantage of group discussion is that the group may give in to pressure from others.

Hasty Generalization

A person reaching a conclusion from too little evidence or evidence that doesn't exist is making a hasty generalization. As we noted when we discussed tests of evidence or tests of inductive reasoning, one or two examples do not prove your point. For example, because a friend of yours got ripped off by a service station when vacationing in Texas doesn't mean that you should avoid all service stations in Texas. Here's another example: "We don't need to spend more money on music education in our schools; my son listens to classical music at home, and so can other students."

It is a fallacy to attack someone's personal characteristics rather than examining the idea they are proposing. How can you improve your group discussion skills?

Attacking the Person

This fallacy—also known as *ad hominem*, Latin for "to the man"—involves attacking irrelevant personal characteristics about someone rather than examining the idea or proposal he or she is advancing. "We all know that Sue's idea won't work because she's been in local politics for years and we just can't trust her" does not really deal with the soundness of the idea, which may be a great idea.

Red Herring

This fallacy, which occurs when someone undermines an idea by using irrelevant facts or arguments as distractions, gets its name from the old trick of dragging a red herring across the trail to divert the sniffing dogs who may be following. Someone uses a red herring fallacy to divert attention or distract listeners from the real issues. For example, someone who claims, "The real problem is not sexual harassment in the military, but the fact that we need to pay our military personnel more money." This speaker is trying to divert attention from the issue of sexual harassment and change the subject to the salary of military personnel. A group member who is a critical listener will recognize this distraction and return the discussion back to the issue at hand.

If in the course of your discussion you detect that someone is reaching a conclusion using a reasoning fallacy, how do you bring it to his or her attention? We don't suggest that you use your best accusatory voice and pounce on someone for the lousy logic. As we learned in Chapter 5, making someone defensive doesn't do much for maintaining a quality group climate. Your first effort to draw attention to a reasoning fallacy should be to

E T H I C A L L Y

When preparing for a group discussion or a team meeting, consider the following ethical obligations.

1. *Use sound evidence and reasoning.* As we have discussed in this chapter, using appropriate evidence and reasoning will help ensure that your group will reach a quality decision. It is unethical to claim you have found "the truth" without adequately researching the issues you are discussing. Furthermore, a discussion peppered with reasoning fallacies can lead to inaccurate conclusions and an insensitivity to the ideas and positions of others. Asserting your conclusions without evidence and overrelying on emotional appeals at the expense of rational, logical reasoning are also unethical.

2. *Give credit to your sources.* Avoid **plagiarism**—taking the words and ideas of others as your own without giving proper credit to the source. Don't use quotes or paraphrase the ideas of others without acknowledging them. Give proper credit to ideas and information that are not your own, both when speaking and writing. In group discussions you can provide an oral footnote: Simply tell your listeners where you got the idea or information you are using. In your written work, use footnotes or references to document the original source of the ideas.

3. *Follow through on commitments.* Working in a group means that others are depending on you to fulfill your assignments and workload. When you don't follow through on work you have promised to perform, you are not being an ethical group communicator. Don't promise to do more than you can accomplish, but accomplish all that you promise to do. Others are counting on you to do your part.

calmly and tactfully describe how the evidence offered does not support the point. Consider using an "I" statement: "I'm not sure I follow that argument . . . ." Describing how you don't see the logic of their point is a better way to challenge fellow group members than immediately labeling their logic as a "fallacious argument" and trying to belittle them. "You" statements ("You're wrong! Your evidence is terrible!") tend to raise the hackles of your listener and create a defensive, disconfirming climate.

Putting Principles into Practice

If you understand how to go about the process of preparing for group discussion, your group interactions will be not only more informed but also more productive. The following suggestions should help you apply the concepts presented in this chapter.

Develop a Discussion Plan

▶ Group members should try to get to know each other; exchange phone numbers and e-mail addresses.

▶ Develop a strategy for gathering information and researching your topic.

▶ Determine whether you have expert group members who can help address the issues confronting your group.

▶ Divide and conquer. Volunteer or assign group members to gather appropriate information.

▶ Give your group interim deadlines; don't wait until the last minute to share your information; pool your information and ideas early in the process.

▶ Put your discussion plan in writing rather than relying on memory as to who will do what by a specific date.

Formulate Discussion Questions

▶ To focus and direct the deliberations of your group, formulate a discussion question.

If your group is trying to decide whether something is true or false or whether something did or did not occur, formulate a question of fact.

If your group is trying to decide whether one idea or approach to an issue is better than another, formulate a question of value.

If your group is trying to develop a solution to a problem, formulate a question of policy.

Using Electronic Research Resources

▶ Use electronic resources such as ERIC, ABI/Inform, or the *Readers' Guide to Periodical Literature* to find articles that may relate to your discussion topic.

▶ Use the Internet (such as, *Netscape Navigator* or *Internet Explorer*) to search for information on the World Wide Web (WWW).

▶ Develop the skill of information triage; sort out useful from less important ideas and data that you retrieve from your computer or Internet searches.

Test Your Use of Logic and Reasoning

▶ When using inductive reasoning, make sure you have enough examples that are typical or representative of other examples, and that are recent.

▶ When using deductive reasoning, make sure that the general premise is true and that you have evidence to support it.

▶ When using causal reasoning, make sure that there is in fact a cause-and-effect relationship between the events you link together; simply because two things hap-

pen at the same time (because they are correlated) does not mean one event causes the second event.

Test the Quality of the Evidence You Use

▶ When relying on facts to prove a point, ask yourself three questions: Are the facts true? Is the source of the facts reliable? Are there any contrary facts?

▶ When relying on examples, determine if the examples are typical and significant and whether there are any contrary examples.

▶ When quoting opinions of others, determine if the source of the opinion is reliable, if the person is an expert, if the source is free from bias, and if the opinion is consistent with other statements made by the source and other experts in the field.

▶ When using statistics, determine if the source is reliable and unbiased, the information is up-to-date, the sampling method used to gather the statistics was sound, and whether there are any contrary statistics.

Use Critical-Thinking and Analysis Skills to Evaluate Reasoning

▶ Don't assume a cause-and-effect relationship without adequate evidence (causal fallacy).

▶ Don't suggest that options boil down to either one solution or another (either/or fallacy).

▶ Don't accept an idea or solution just because numerous people are in favor of it (bandwagon fallacy).

▶ Don't reach a conclusion without adequate evidence (hasty generalization).

▶ Don't criticize a person in order to attack an idea; focus on evaluating the quality of the idea, not the person (attacking-the-person fallacy).

▶ Don't let the group get away with diverting attention from the key issue under discussion (red herring fallacy).

PRACTICE

Identifying Questions of Fact, Value, and Policy

Read the following narrative, then identify and phrase the following questions: (1) the main discussion question (labeled as fact, value, or policy), (2) at least one question of fact, and (3) at least one question of value.

A new liberal divorce law has come up for discussion in the state senate. Senator Smith, who introduced the bill, has lobbied hard for it because she has found evidence to suggest that rather than deterring divorce, complications in the current law only result in lengthy delays and higher fees for divorce lawyers. Senator Williams also supports the new law; he was recently divorced and experienced much frustration and irritation in the process. Senator Schwartz, in contrast, is happily married and quite conservative; he leads opposition to the new law.

Critical-Thinking and Analysis: Identifying Reasoning Fallacies

Read the following statements. Working with your group members, determine whether there is a flaw in the analysis or logic. If there is fallacious reasoning, identify which reasoning fallacy is illustrated.

1. Everyone in our city drinks fluoridated water. Therefore it's safe to drink fluoridated water.

2. Your idea can't be a good one. You grew up in a small town in the rural area of Missouri where it would be impossible to get a good education.

3. We either increase tuition or tell 10 percent of the faculty that they are fired; those are the only ways to balance the budget.

4. Each year we have the El Niño weather effect, the economy improves; clearly El Niño has an impact on stock prices.

5. Of course we know that eating a good breakfast makes you smarter. My nephew Mike eats a good breakfast and he has an IQ of over 130.

6. A recent survey found that 52 percent of respondents approved of modifying a résumé to make credentials appear better than they actually are; therefore it would be appropriate for you to modify your résumé credentials.

7. The school board should either add a new class period at the end of the school day or leave the schedule the way it is now.

8. Everyone knows a talk-show host is primarily an entertainer and therefore couldn't make a meaningful comment about the proposal to salvage Social Security.

9. The university should plan for more parking spaces because when I arrive on campus I often can't find a place to park.

10. Even though we are discussing whether to raise admissions standards at our university, I think you will all agree that the real reason we don't have high-quality students is that many of them lack good oral communication skills.

 Your companion Website has more practice activities, questionnaires, and checklists!
www.ablongman.com/beebe

Notes

1. M. Schittekatte and A. Van Hiel, "Effects of Partially Shared Information and Awareness of Unshared Information on Information Sampling," *Small Group Research* 27 (1996): 431–49.

2. Dennis A. Romig, *Breakthrough Teamwork: Outstanding Results Using Structured Teamwork* (Chicago: Irwin, 1996); Peter R. Scholtes, Brian L. Joiner, and Barbara J. Streibel, *The Team Handbook*, 2nd ed. (Madison, WI: Joiner Associates, 1996)

3. D. D. Chrislip and C.E. Larson, *Collaborative Leadership* (San Francisco: Jossey-Bass, 1994); J. R. Katzenback and D. K. Smith, *The Wisdom of Teams: Creating the High-Performance Organization.* (New York: HarperBusiness, 1993); Romig, *Breakthrough Teamwork*.

4. D. D. Stewart and G. Stasser, "Expert Role Assignment and Information Sampling During Collective Recall and Decision Making." *Journal of Personality and Social Psychology*, 69 (1995): 619–28; also see D. D. Stewart. "Stereotypes, Negativity Bias, and the Discussion of Unshared Information in Decision-Making Groups." *Small Group Research* 29 (1998): 643–68.

5. J. R. Larson, Jr., "Modeling the Entry of Shared and Unshared Information into Group Discussion: A Review and BASIC Language Computer Program," *Small Group Research* 28 (1997): 454–79.

6. K. M. Propp, "Information Utilization in Small Group Decision Making: A Study of the Evaluative Interaction Model," *Small Group Research* 28 (1997): 424–53.

7. C. Saunders and S. Miranda, "Information Acquisition in Group Decision Making," *Information and Management* 34 (1998): 55–74.

8. Dennis S. Gouran, *Discussion: The Process of Group Decision-Making* (New York: Harper & Row, 1974) 72.

9. John Wait Bowers and John Courtright, *Communication Research Methods* (Glenview, IL: Scott, Foresman, 1984).

10. Ann Burnett Pettus, "The Verdict Is In: A Study of Jury Decision-Making Factors, Moment of Personal Decision, and Jury Deliberations—From the Jurors' Point of View," *Communication Quarterly* 38 (Winter 1990): 83–97.

11. Ellen K. Aranda, Luis Aranda, and Kristi Conlon, *Teams: Structure, Process, Culture, and Politics* (Englewood Cliffs, NJ: Prentice-Hall, 1998).

Objectives:

After studying this chapter,
you will be able to:

▶ Differentiate between group decision
  making and group problem solving.

▶ Describe the elements of group
  decision making.

▶ List and describe characteristics of
  effective group decision makers.

▶ Compare and contrast descriptive,
  functional, and prescriptive
  approaches to problem solving in
  small groups.

▶ Identify the four phases of the group
  process.

▶ Discuss the three types of group
  activity tracks.

8

Making Decisions
and Solving
Problems

> "There's nothing in the middle of the road but yellow stripes and dead armadillos."
> — Jim Hightower

As suggested by the chapter-opening quote by Jim Hightower, if you stay in the middle of the road you are likely to get run over. Most North Americans value decisiveness and action rather than indecisiveness and muddled thought. More research has been conducted about group problem-solving and decision-making communication than about any other group objective. Groups discuss issues to search for truth; groups make decisions; and groups solve problems. In this chapter and the next, we turn our attention to principles and strategies that provide structure and guide interaction to help groups do their work. That work often involves choosing among several options, or circumventing vexing obstacles to solve problems.

We build on the information we presented in the last chapter, which discussed how to focus on a discussion question, conduct research, think critically, and test and evaluate evidence and reasoning. Here we focus on the communication strategies that help groups make quality decisions. First we'll describe the process of group decision making by identifying elements, methods, and obstacles to quality decision making. Then we describe the nature of group problem solving, including three approaches to examining how groups solve problems: Descriptive, functional, and prescriptive. We end the chapter by identifying cultural assumptions about group problem solving and decision making. In Chapter 9 we continue our discussion of group problem solving with a look at strategies and techniques that can help groups do their work effectively and efficiently.

Group Decision Making: Choosing Among Alternatives

One critical task that groups are called on to do is **decision making** — the process of choosing from among several alternatives. For example, in deciding which college or university to attend, you probably considered several choices. Perhaps you started by gathering information about fifteen or twenty schools and then narrowed the alternatives as you considered the advantages and disadvantages of each institution. Eventually you narrowed your choice to two and made a final decision. Groups make decisions in essentially the same way. In this section we will consider the elements, methods, and characteristics of group decision making and also examine some of the obstacles that keep groups from making high-quality decisions.

Elements of Group Decision Making

According to Randy Hirokawa, Dennis Gouran, and several other group communication scholars, group decision making usually follows a predictable pattern.[1] Groups tend to make better decisions if the pattern is explicitly identified so that the group can structure its discussion. Group decision making includes the following steps.[2]

1. *The group assesses the present situation.* A group analyzes a situation based on available information and realizes that it needs to make a decision. For example, an airline's board of directors is trying to decide whether to lower fares. Thus, they look at competitors' fares and the number of passengers those competitors transport each day.

2. *The group identifies its goals.* After assessing the current situation, the group should identify its objectives. A group uncertain about its task will have difficulty making a quality decision. If its goal is clear, a group begins to identify alternatives or choices.

3. *The group identifies several alternatives.* The greater the number of alternatives a group generates, the greater the likelihood it will make a good decision. Poor decisions usually occur when a group fails to generate enough good possible choices.

4. *The group evaluates the positive and negative consequences of alternatives.* A group must do more than identify alternatives; it should also assess the positive and negative implications of each alternative before making a decision.

5. *The group selects the alternative (makes a decision).* The alternative selected should potentially have a maximum positive outcome with minimal negative consequences. A group is more likely to select the best alternative if it has carefully assessed the situation, considered group goals, identified several choices and noted the positive and negative implications of each.

Methods of Group Decision Making

After the alternatives have been narrowed and weighed, what methods can groups use to make a decision? Knowing these methods can give you and your group options to consider when a decision needs to be made.[3]

Decisions by Experts in Group
One person in a group may seem to be the best informed about the issue, and members can turn to this person to make the choice. This expert may or may not be a group's designated leader. Deferring to an expert from within a group may be an efficient way to make a decision, but without adequate discussion the group may not be satisfied with the outcome.

Decisions by Experts Outside Group
A group may decide that none of its members has the credibility, knowledge, or wisdom to make a particular decision, and it may feel unable or unwilling to do so. Members can turn to someone outside the group, someone with authority to make a decision. Although an outside expert may make a fine decision, a group that gives up its decision-making power to one person loses the advantages of the greater input and variety of approaches that come from being a group in the first place.

Averaging Individual Rankings or Ratings
Group members can be asked to rank or rate possible alternatives. After the group averages the rankings or ratings, it selects the alternative with the highest average. This method of making decisions can be useful to start discussions and to see where the group stands on an issue. However, it is not the best way to make a decision, because it does not take full advantage of the give-and-take of group discussion.

Random Choice   Sometimes groups become so frustrated that they make no decisions. They resort to coin tosses or other random approaches. These methods are not recommended for groups that take their decision making seriously. Groups that resort to random methods usually are desperate.

Majority Vote   This is the method of group decision making most often used. Majority rule can be swift and efficient but can also leave an unsatisfied minority. Unless it allots time for discussing an issue, a group may sacrifice decision quality and group cohesiveness for efficiency.

Decision by Minority   Sometimes a minority of group members makes a decision. The minority may yell the loudest or threaten to create problems for the group unless it gets its way. Members may ask, "Does anyone have any objections?" and, if no one answers immediately, consider the decision made. Minority members whose decision is adopted may temporarily rejoice, but over time the group will have difficulty implementing a decision that is not widely accepted.

Decision by Consensus   Consensus occurs when all group members can support a course of action. This method is time-consuming and difficult, but members are usually satisfied with the decision. If group members must also implement the solution, this method works well. To reach a decision by consensus, group members must listen and respond to individual viewpoints and manage conflicts that arise. Consensus is facilitated when group members are able to do such things as remain focused on the goal, emphasize areas of agreement, and combine or eliminate alternatives identified by the group. Several suggestions for reaching consensus and managing group conflict are identified in Chapter 10.

Obstacles to Quality Group Decision Making

Perhaps you have heard the saying that a camel is a horse that was designed by a committee. Groups sometimes make foolish decisions. Knowing some of the typical pitfalls groups encounter when choosing among alternatives can help your group avoid them. Consider the following obstacles.[4]

1. *The group fails to accurately analyze the present situation.* If a group improperly analyzes its current situation, it is likely to make a bad decision. To analyze something is to break it down into smaller parts. Having too little evidence—or none—is one of the reasons groups sometimes fail to analyze the present situation accurately. Even if group members do have ample evidence, it may be defective if they have not applied the proper tests of evidence, which we discussed in Chapter 7.

2. *The group fails to establish a clear and appropriate goal.* A group that has not clearly spelled out what it hopes to accomplish by making a decision has no way to assess the effectiveness of the decision. It will be more difficult for you to select the right college or university if you do not know what your major will be or what your future plans are.

3. *The group fails to identify the positive and negative consequences of the alternatives.* A group that is so eager to make a decision that it does not take time to consider the pros and cons of its actions is setting itself up to make a bad decision. A critical error of ineffective groups is failing to consider the consequences of their decision *before* they make it.[5]

4. *The group has bad information.* As we learned in the last chapter, if a group has flawed or outdated evidence the decision will also be flawed.[6]

5. *The group does not think critically about the data it has.* Just having information does not mean the group will use it well. **Reasoning** is the process of drawing conclusions from information. Flawed reasoning, like flawed data, can contribute to a bad decision. In Chapter 7 we reviewed several reasoning fallacies.

6. *Too few people are involved in the discussion.* One primary advantage of working in groups and teams is to tap the knowledge base of many people rather than just of a few individuals. Research by John Oetzel documents what makes intuitive sense: Groups make better decisions when there is more equal participation in the discussion.[7] If several members ororverbalize, decision quality suffers.

REVIEW

Comparing Effective and Ineffective Group Decision Making

EFFECTIVE GROUP DECISION MAKING	INEFFECTIVE GROUP DECISION MAKING
Accurately assesses the present situation	Improperly analyzes the present situation
Establishes clear and appropriate group goals	Does not establish clear and appropriate group goals
Accurately identifies positive and negative consequences of decision alternatives	Fails to identify enough positive and negative consequences of decision alternatives
Has accurate information	Works from too little information or faulty information
Draws reasonable conclusions from available information	Fails to think critically or logically about the available information
Many people involved	Few people involved

Group Problem Solving: Overcoming Obstacles to Achieve a Goal

The board of directors of a multinational corporation, a band-booster fund-raising committee, and a group of students doing a project for a group-communication class all have something in common—they have problems to solve. Have you ever been involved in group problem solving and thought to yourself, "If I weren't working in this silly group, I could be more productive"? Despite such frustrations, a small group of people has the potential of arriving at a better solution than do individuals working alone. As we noted in Chapter 1, groups have more information and more creative approaches to surmounting obstacles, which results in a higher-quality decision.

All decision making involves assessing a situation, identifying alternative solutions, and selecting the best alternatives. What group decision methods have worked well in your group?

Problem solving is the process of overcoming obstacles to achieve a goal. Whereas decision making involves making a choice from among alternatives. Problem solving usually requires a group to make many decisions or choices as it identifies a problem and determines how to solve it.

A problem consists of three elements: (1) an undesirable existing situation, (2) a goal a group wishes to achieve, and (3) obstacles that keep a group from achieving its goal.[8] Problem solving allows a group to eliminate or manage the obstacles that keep it from achieving its objective.

Like decision making, problem solving begins with assessing the present situation. What's wrong with what is happening now? *Almost every problem can be phrased in terms of something you want more of or less of.*[9] Problems often can be boiled down to such things as lack of time, money, information, or agreement. For example, a school board that decides a district needs a new high school yet realizes it lacks the money for one has a problem: The district has too many students for existing facilities. The board needs fewer students or more space. The goal the board wants to achieve is quality education for all district students. The board cannot achieve this goal with the existing undesirable situation. The obstacles that keep the board from reaching its goal include lack of classroom space and lack of money to build more space. Every problem can be identified by noting its three elements just mentioned: The undesirable present, the group goal, and the obstacles to achieving it.

Three Elements of a Problem

Undesirable existing situation: Something is wrong with the way things are.

Goal: What the group wants to achieve.

Obstacles: Something that keeps a group from achieving its goal.

Barriers to Group and Team Problem Solving

What keeps groups and teams from working at their full capacity? Knowing what these barriers are can help you spot them and eliminate them from your group or team. Thus, before we spend the bulk of this chapter and the next one suggesting principles and strategies to help groups work better, we lay out problems you and your group may face. Benjamin Broome and Luann Fulbright spent over six years asking people who participated in group discussions what barriers kept their group from operating at full capacity. What is significant about the following list is that these are problems that group members reported; they are not just problems that an observer noted. Here's their list of the top ten barriers. [10]

1. *Groups need help in structuring discussion.* Group members wanted specific methods to help their group function more efficiently.

2. *Groups sometimes had problems because group members weren't sensitive to issues of cultural diversity.* Some group members were put off by biases, prejudice, sexist comments, and the failure to take cultural differences into account when interacting with others.

3. *Groups sometimes didn't plan well.* Group members often weren't prepared or group members were unsure what the focus of the group was supposed to be.

4. *Groups didn't have all the resources they need to do their job.* Sometimes the group met in an inadequate physical space or just didn't have all the information and technical support to get the job done.

5. *Groups sometimes had the wrong people attending the meetings.* The key people with the authority or information weren't involved in the discussion.

6. *Groups sometimes felt pressure to provide any answer rather than providing the best answer.* There was also pressure for immediate results and pressure to tell those in authority what they wanted to hear.

7. *Groups had some difficulty communicating and listening to one another.* Misunderstandings, inattentiveness, and dominance by one group member or factions of members within the group were cited as reasons for ineffective communication.

8. *Groups did not have a supportive, positive, open climate.* Group members sometimes did not feel they were cohesively working together and they could not support or trust one another.

9. *Group members had a negative attitude toward the project or toward one another.* Some group members weren't flexible or were unwilling to compromise about procedures or where and when to meet, or they had unrealistic expectations about the group.

10. *Groups sometimes didn't use a process that helped define the problem or reach consensus.* Group members tended to focus on the solution before defining the problem or there was a lack of balanced participation.

Three Approaches to Group Problem Solving

Thus far we have defined group decision making and problem solving, noted the obstacles to and the characteristics of effective group decisions, and noted barriers that keep groups from working well. We will now examine three different approaches to the study of group problem solving: (1) **descriptive**, which focuses on how groups solve problems; (2) **functional**, which identifies key communicative behaviors that contribute to effective problem solving; and (3) **prescriptive**, which recommends specific agendas and techniques to improve group performance. In this chapter we will discuss the descriptive and functional approaches to group problem solving; we will introduce the prescriptive approach here but reserve a detailed discussion of it for Chapter 9.

Descriptive Approach

When you describe something, you use words to categorize, classify, and clarify your subject. A descriptive approach to group problem solving identifies how groups do solve problems, not how they should solve problems.[11]

A descriptive approach does not offer specific guidelines and techniques for solving problems in groups; rather, it outlines how most groups go about solving problems. B. Aubrey Fisher makes two assumptions about the descriptive approach: (1) There is a "natural" or normal process of group problem solving, and (2) a group will follow a normal problem-solving approach unless some external authority interferes with its freedom to solve its problem (for example, an agenda is handed to the group or a strong-willed group leader dictates how the group should approach its task).[12] One of the most fruitful areas of research from a descriptive perspective seeks to identify the normal phases or cycles that groups experience when solving problems.

Describing Group Phases.
"Don't worry, Mom, I'm just going through a phase." Think back. Does this sound like something you may have said at one time? Apparently you were trying to alleviate your mother's concern by assuring her that your behavior was not at all uncommon and that it surely would pass in time. Implicit here is an assumption that individuals pass through several identifiable developmental stages, each of which leads to the next. Problem-solving groups, like individuals, go through several stages. If you under-

stand these stages, you can learn to communicate in ways that expedite a group's passage from one stage to the next.

Does every group neatly cycle through the same phases of group discussion? The answer is no. As we will discuss later in the chapter, not all groups take the same path to solve a problem. Group discussion is often messy. Many groups do, however, go through phases. Knowing what these phases are can help you spot them if they occur in your group; it's like having a map that lets you know where you are in your group deliberations.

Several researchers have attempted to identify the phases of a problem-solving group. They have observed and recorded who speaks to whom and have categorized the comments group members exchange. Even though for the past fifty years researchers have used various labels to describe these phases, they have reached similar conclusions. Although some researchers describe five phases, most scholars identify four phases.

Of the research on developmental phases of groups, Fisher's is the most significant for small group communication. He focused primarily on what was said throughout the development of his test groups. We use his terminology in the following sections.

Phase 1: Orientation

In the first phase of small group interaction "group members break the ice and begin to establish a common basis for functioning."[13] Speech communication during this phase tends to be oriented toward members getting to know one another, sharing backgrounds, and tentatively approaching the group's task. You are not likely to say anything that might prompt the rest of the group to reject you. Fisher noted that "more ambiguous comments . . . are contained in Phase 1 than in any other phase except the third, which is also characterized by ambiguity."[14]

The research on the **orientation phase** suggests that your communication is directed at orienting yourself toward others as well as to the group's task, which can also be said about the other phases. What sets this phase apart from the others is the degree to which the social dimension is emphasized and the tentative, careful way in which the task dimension is approached.

Even the most efficient, task-motivated group will spend some time socializing and getting acquainted. Do not underestimate the importance of this type of interaction. Interpersonal trust—an essential ingredient for an effective working environment—does not happen all at once. You begin slowly, with small talk, to determine whether it is safe to move on to deeper levels of interaction. The orientation phase, then, develops trust and group cohesiveness, which are important for the group's survival in the second phase—conflict.

Phase 2: Conflict

During the orientation phase, group members begin to form opinions about their own positions in the group and about the group's task. By the second phase they start asserting these opinions. They have tested the water in the first phase and now are ready to jump in. On the process, or social, level, this is a period

©The New Yorker Collection 1997 Charles Barsotti from cartoonbank.com

in which individuals compete for status in the group. Two or more potential leaders may emerge, with the support for each dividing the group into camps. In a decision-making or problem-solving group, this division is reflected along the task dimension as well. During the first phase, members are hesitant to speak about the group's task, but in the second phase they begin to assert their individuality and respond favorably or unfavorably to the direction the group is taking. With such polarization of attitudes, disagreement or conflict naturally results.[15]

Communication during the **conflict phase** is characterized by persuasive attempts at changing others' opinions and reinforcing one's own position. Some participants relish the idea of a good argument, Whereas others see conflict as something to avoid at all cost. Avoiding conflict, however, means avoiding issues relevant and even crucial to the group's success. Just as individuals need to assert their own points of view, so do groups need to investigate all relevant alternatives in order to select the best solutions.

The conflict phase is necessary at both the task and the process dimensions of small group communication. Through conflict, you begin to identify the task issues that confront the group and clarify your own and others' roles. This clarification leads toward greater predictability, less uncertainty, and the establishment of group norms.

Phase 3: Emergence

In Phase 3, new patterns of communication indicate a group's emergence from the conflict phase. If a group is going to function as a cohesive unit, it must resolve the conflict of Phase 2. Although conflict is still a part of Phase 3, what sets the **emergence phase** apart from the preceding conflict phase is the way in which members deal with conflict. This shift is most apparent in the reappearance of ambiguity in task-related statements.

Task and process dimensions are interwoven at this stage. Although the group is divided, there is also clarity. Leadership patterns and roles have been established, the issues and problems confronting the group have been identified, and the need to settle differences and reach consensus has become apparent. Ambiguity appears to be the means by which you can comfortably shift your position toward group consensus.

In the emergence phase, a group settles on norms and moves toward consensus via ambiguous statements that gradually modify dissenting positions. Such ambiguous statements might take the form of qualifiers or reservations to the previous position: "I still would like to see our company merge with the Elector Electronics Corporation, but maybe we could consider a merger later in the year. Such a merger may be more appropriate next fall." Such a statement allows you to save face and still allows the group to reach consensus.

Phase 4: Reinforcement

A spirit of unity characterizes the final phase of group interaction. In the preceding three phases, group members struggle through getting acquainted, building cohesiveness, expressing individuality, competing for status, and arguing over issues. The group eventually emerges from those struggles with a sense of direction, consensus, and a feeling of group identity. Not surprisingly, then, the fourth phase is characterized by positive feelings toward the group and its decisions. Finally, members feel a genuine sense of accomplishment.

Reinforcement predominates in communication:

Jim: I may have been against it at first, but I've finally seen the light. We're going in the right direction now.

Marilyn: Yes, but don't shortchange your contribution, Jim. If you hadn't

opposed it so vehemently, we never would have developed the idea
so fully.

Fisher noted that ambiguous and unfavorable comments all but disappear in the
fourth phase, being replaced by uniformly favorable comments and reinforcement. At this
time, all the hassle of group decision making and problem solving seems worthwhile. The
group is at its most cohesive, individual satisfaction and sense of achievement are high,
and uncertainty is at a low.

The Process Nature of Group Phase

Although it may appear from our discussion that a group goes through four neat phases of
development in a predictable, easy-to-identify way, group deliberations are seldom that
orderly. Communication does not typically operate in such a linear, step-by-step manner.
The descriptive phases we've presented have been observed in some groups, but not all of
them. Group communication researchers have identified other models such as the spiraling model, punctuated equilibrium model, and multisequence model.

Spiraling Model.   Group-communication scholars Tom Scheidel and Laura Crowell's
research suggests that groups may not march through four clearly delineated phases but
rather cycle or spiral through them throughout the group or team's development.[16] For
example, the first issue confronting the group may be "What's the purpose of this group?"
A group will probably spend some time getting oriented to this task, conflict may follow as
members learn each person's objectives, and after discussion, a consensus may emerge
about the group's purpose. Finally, members may assure one another that their purpose
has been developed clearly. Perhaps the next issue to come before the group is "How will
we organize our work — should we have a subcommittee?" Again, the members may go
through orientation, conflict, emergence, and reinforcement about a specific issue.
Because group discussions tend to hop from topic to topic, a group may get bogged down
in conflict, abandon the issue, and move to another issue. Thus, groups may spiral through
phases for each issue, or group members may get sidetracked and abandon discussions
about a particular topic.

J. E. McGrath is another prominent small group researcher who suspects that groups
and teams cycle through their work rather than follow specific phases.[17] His theory
includes the dimensions of time, interaction, and performance, which he calls TIP theory.
McGrath suspects that groups do what they need to do at a given moment based on their
needs at the moment depending on what function the group needs to perform. Groups will
experience conflict when conflict arises. They will become oriented or focused on a task
when there is uncertainty, not just at the beginning of a group.

Punctuated Equilibrium Model.   C. J. Gersick also suggests that the phase model is
not always a realistic way of describing how groups do their work. He describes what he
calls a pattern of "punctuated equilibrium."[18] During the first half of a group's existence,
group members may experience uncertainty and indecision about what to do or how to
proceed. The group experiences inertia; nothing seems to be happening. And then to coun-
terbalance the inertia, a revolutionary transition or breakpoint, about midway through the
group's deliberation, punctuates the seeming equilibrium when "nothing happening"
changes to "something happening." The equilibrium is punctuated by a burst of activity.
Then there will be a second inertia phase—a phase where the group seems to stop and

again ponder which direction to go next before moving on to accomplishing the task. Gersick thinks this punctuated equilibrium model may only occur for groups with a specific time limit; it may be less likely to occur in a group with an unstructured or open-ended time frame.

Multisequence Model   Yet another descriptive, nonphase model of describing how groups and teams typically function is proposed by M. Scott Poole.[19] As the name Multisequence Model implies, groups and teams may be doing several things at once rather than cycling though predictable phases; Poole builds on Fisher's phase research by suggesting that groups engage in three types of activity tracks that do not necessarily follow logical step-by-step patterns.

The three types of activities that Poole believes best describe group interaction are (1) **task-process activities**, (2) **relational activities**, and (3) **topical focus**.[20] Task process activities are those activities that help the group accomplish its work such as analyzing a problem, becoming oriented to the issues of a problem, establishing criteria, and evaluating proposed solutions. Answering such questions as "What's the problem here?" "How can we better understand the problem?" and "How effective will our solution be?" are examples of task-process activities.

Verbal or nonverbal communication that indicates who is liked and disliked can be categorized as relational activity. Relational activities are activities that manage relationships and help maintain the group climate. As noted in Chapter 4, communication has both a task dimension and a relationship dimension. Relational activities are also commu-

Collaborating via

T E C H N O L O G Y

Developing a well-functioning team takes skill, patience, and information. Throughout the book we've noted similarities and differences between groups and teams. Teams have more clearly defined roles, rules, goals, and methods of collaboration. The following Websites provide information and additional links to help your team work effectively and efficiently.

www.coreroi.com/publica.htm
This site developed by a teamwork consulting firm, CORE R.O.I. Inc. includes tips and information about how to help your group operate as a team. The article "Why Teams Fail," by George Gates, president of CORE R.O.I., offers especially useful ideas for avoiding some of the problems that detract from team success.

www.Rampages.onramp.net/~bodwell/home.htm
How to develop a high-performing team is the focal point of this site; it's packed with several links to articles and ideas about enhancing team effectiveness.

www.workteams.unt.edu
This site is supported by the Center for the Study of Work Teams.

nication behaviors that sustain or damage interpersonal relationships among group members. Criticism, conflict, praise, and encouragement help group members understand their relationships with one another. Relational activities also affect a group's working climate.

The third type of activity, topical focus, deals with the "general themes, major issues, or arguments of concern to the group at a given point in the discussion."[21] Ernest Barman and other researchers have noted that groups often focus their conversations on given themes or topics that serve as the actual agendas for the groups.[22] This third type of activity, then, deals with major topics that do not relate to a group's specific task or to member relationships.

Poole's three **activity tracks** do not all develop at the same rate or according to the same pattern. Some groups may spend a considerable portion of their time developing relationships before discussing their tasks in great detail. In contrast, task-oriented groups often devote considerable energy to completing their tasks, letting relationships play minor roles in group deliberations. Groups switch activity tracks at various **breakpoints**, which occur as groups switch topics, adjourn, or schedule planning periods. Another type of breakpoint, called a delay, occurs because of group conflict or inability to reach consensus. Whereas groups may expect and schedule some breakpoints, they usually do not schedule delays. Poole notes, "depending on the nature of the delay and the mood of the group [a] breakpoint can signal the start of a difficulty or a highly creative period."[23] A disruption, the third type of breakpoint, results from a major conflict or a realization that a group may not be able to complete its task. To manage disruption, a group must be flexible.

Poole's analysis of group phases and group activity emphasizes the process nature of group communication rather than assuming that groups proceed through a linear, step-by-step approach. Although several researchers have documented chronological phases in a group's decision-making efforts, a group's communication can also be described by the three activities of task process, relational activity, and topical focus. A descriptive approach to group communication can help you better understand and explain why certain types of statements are made in groups and how a group develops over time. With an understanding of the process, you should be in a better position to evaluate and improve your participation in group meetings.

Functional Approach

The descriptive approach assumes that you can identify how groups solve problems and describes the phases and activities of groups, the **functional approach** suggests that to be effective, groups and group members should perform certain communication processes or functions. These processes enhance group and team performance. The functional approach assumes that groups are goal-oriented; to accomplish the goal, certain activities or communication functions need to be performed. Groups and teams are effective, argue functional theorists, not just by applying communication techniques (the prescriptive approach) but by communicating in ways that affect fundamental processes of how the groups achieves its goal.[24] Communication, according to functional theorists, is a tool that group members use to perform key functions that enhance group problem solving and decision making.[25]

The primary way researchers have identified the functions of effective problem solving is by examining the behaviors of both effective and ineffective groups. Certain types of communication and critical thinking distinguish effective groups from ineffective ones.

A Comparison of Descriptive Models of Group Process

PHASE MODELS	Groups go through predictable phases (such as orientation, conflict, emergence, reinforcement) when working on a task or solving a problem.
SPIRAL MODELS	Groups may go through several phases and then repeat the cycle again and again throughout the history of the group.
PUNCTUATED EQUILIBRIUM MODELS	Groups go through a period of uncertainty and indecision punctuated by a breakthrough, followed by more uncertainty until a pattern emerges.
MULTISEQUENCE MODELS	Groups switch from one activity to the next task-process activities, relational activities, and topic focus.

What are these key functions? According to Randy Hirokawa, groups must perform five key functions in order to develop a high-quality solution.[26]

1. *Develop an accurate understanding of the problem.* Specify precisely what the problem is. Identify the causes, symptoms, and history of the problem. Use data and information to help your group understand the problem.

2. *Develop requirements for an acceptable choice.* Establish criteria—explicit standards for an acceptable solution. Identify what a good solution will look like so you'll know one when you see it.

3. *Develop many alternatives to solve the problem.* The more high-quality alternatives you generate, the greater the chance that you will find a high-quality solution. Just suggesting one or two ideas early in the discussion will usually result in a less-effective solution.

4. *Assess the positive features of the alternatives or options for solving the problem.* Systematically identify the merits or benefits that will occur if the suggested solution or solutions are implemented.

5. *Assess the negative features of the alternatives or options for solving the problem.* Balance the positive benefits that the group identifies with negative features or disadvantages of the suggested solution or solutions.

Group communicators who incorporate these functions into their interactions with others are what Hirokawa and other researchers call **vigilant thinkers**. Vigilant thinkers are critical thinkers. They pay attention to the process of problem solving.

Of these five functions, is one more important than the others? Recent research finds support for all these functions, but the best predictors of quality group performance are points 1, 2, and 5. So, for best results, (1) analyze the problem; be sure to use data and information rather than just sharing opinions when analyzing the current situation; (2) establish criteria; know what a good solution looks like; and (3) evaluate the potential negative consequences of possible solutions; think about what might go wrong before implementing a solution. Discuss certain standards or expectations for a solution before hunting for a solution.[27]

Communication researcher Elizabeth Graham and her colleagues found that effective groups established and used clear criteria as well as make comments that positively evaluated alternative solutions that group members suggested; in essence, the group had a clear goal and said nice things about solutions.[28] The researchers suspected that the positive comments helped to establish a supportive group climate.

In contrast, Kevin Barge suggests that the following functions are essential for an effective problem-solving group. Group members should (1) network with others within and outside the group to gather effective information; (2) acquire the skill of **data splitting** —that is, analyze information effectively; (3) generate and evaluate solutions; and (4) manage their relationships effectively by means of listening, feedback, and negotiation skill.[29]

The vigilant-thinking functions suggested by Hirokawa and his colleagues as well as Barge are similar to those suggested by Irving Janis: Gather accurate information, analyze the information, draw reasonable conclusions from the data, generate solutions, evaluate the costs and risks of the solutions, and select the best one.[30]

Communication Functions of Effective Group Problem Solvers   The functional perspective assumes that groups will make a higher-quality decision if group members analyze information appropriately, generate an ample number of ideas, evaluate information and solutions, and remain sensitive to others. Based on the work of several groups-communication researchers, the following specific communication functions are considered essential to effective problem solving from a functional perspective.[31]

1. **Analysis function:** Group members who effectively analyze information and ideas have the following characteristics:

- *They establish clear criteria.* Groups and teams have their goal clearly in mind as they analyze the issues.

- *They see the problem from a variety of viewpoints.* One often looks at a problem as it affects oneself. A skilled problem solver considers how the problem affects others, too, and is able to think about an issue from other people's vantage points.

- *They gather data and research issues.* Good problem solvers do not rely on their own opinions. They spend time in the library or develop surveys to gather information and others' opinions about an issue.

- *They use evidence effectively to reach a valid conclusion.* Beyond just collecting evidence, a good problem solver needs to know how to use evidence to reach a conclusion.

- *They ask appropriate questions.* One big problem groups have is keeping the discussion focused on the issues. Members often bounce from one idea or topic to the next. Good problem solvers know this and use questions to help keep the group moving toward its goal. Questions such as "Where are we now?" or "What's the next step in solving our problem?" or "Aren't we getting off the track here?" can help the group get back to the task.

2. **Idea-generation function:** An essential aspect of a well-functioning problem-solving group is group members who are creative and inventive, who find ways to keep ideas flowing.

    - *Search for many alternatives or solutions to a problem.* Effective groups are not content to have just one or two approaches to a problem. Many solutions are identified, which may help overcome the obstacles keeping the group from reaching its goal.

    - *Make high-quality statements to the group.* According to several researchers, high-quality statements are precise rather than rambling and abstract. They are also consistent with previous evidence, relevant to the topic under discussion, and act to positively reinforce the comments of other group members.[32]

    - *Take a vacation from a problem to revitalize the group.* If the group gets bogged down and cannot reach agreement, postpone further discussion if possible. Sometimes you get a burst of creativity when you are not even thinking about a problem.[33] Have you ever had an idea come to you while you were jogging, driving a car, or taking a shower? Give your mind a chance to work on the problem by giving yourself a break from agonizing over a solution.

3. **Evaluation function:** Being able to separate good ideas from bad ideas is a critical function of a good problem-solving group.

    - *Examine the pros and the cons of potential solutions.* Give special attention to considering what might go wrong before implementing a solution.

    - *Evaluate the opinions and assumptions of others.* Do not just accept another person's conclusion or opinion at face value. One study found that groups that reach better solutions include members who take the time to test the assumptions of others.[34] Although you should not attack another person's credibility, all opinions and assumptions need to be supported by evidence. A group that tactfully examines the basis for an opinion can determine whether the opinion is valid.

According to the functional perspective, effective group members take breaks away from a problem instead of agonizing over a solution. What activities help you generate ideas?

▶ *Test solutions to see if they meet preestablished criteria.* Criteria are standards for acceptable solutions. Such criteria as "It should be within the budget" and "It should be implemented within six months" are important to problem solving. If a group has generated criteria for a solution, a good problem solver reminds the group what the criteria are and evaluates possible solutions according to standards previously identified.

4. **Personal-sensitivity function:** As we have emphasized throughout the book, groups have both a task and a relationship dimension. Members of successfully functioning teams or groups are other-oriented, empathic, sensitive to the needs of others, and listen thoughtfully.

▶ *Be concerned for both the group task and the feelings of others.* Being too task-oriented is not good for the overall group climate. As discussed in Chapter 5, sensitivity to the feelings of others can enhance the group climate and foster a supportive, rather than a defensive, approach to achieving a group goal.

▶ *Listen to minority arguments and opinions.* It is always tempting to disregard the voice of a lone dissenter. That individual may, however, have a brilliant idea or a legitimate complaint about the majority point of view. Assume that all ideas have merit; do not discount ideas because they come from members who are not supporting the majority at the moment.

Prescriptive Approach

When the doctor gives you a prescription, he or she is telling you to do something very specific: Take a measured dose of a particular medicine to treat your medical problem. A prescriptive approach to problem solving is a third approach based on the assumption that groups need more than a general understanding of how groups solve problems or what the key functions of group communication are. The prescriptive approach offers specific suggestions for structuring a group's problem-solving agenda. Prescriptive approaches invite group members to perform certain behaviors in a specific order to achieve a group goal. Fisher describes the prescriptive approach as providing "guidelines, a road map, to assist the group in achieving consensus. A prescriptive approach is based on an assumed 'ideal' process."[35]

According to Fisher, two assumptions underlie the prescriptive approach to problem solving: (1) Group members are consistently rational, and (2) the prescribed agenda or set of techniques will result in a better solution.

The descriptive approach to group problem solving and decision making helps a group understand *how* groups usually solve problems. The functional approach identifies key communicative behaviors that should be performed to enhance the group's effectiveness. The prescriptive approach offers specific recommendations for sequencing certain types of communication in a group. Which approach is best? Some scholars advocate the descriptive approach, pointing out that it does not constrain a group from its normal or natural process. These scholars reject the prescriptive approach as being too rigid. Others suggest that groups should consciously perform key functions to maximize effectiveness. Yet others contend that the prescriptive approach gives a group needed structure for solving problems, because working in groups often results in uncertainty and ambiguity.[36]

Arthur VanGundy categorizes problems as either structured or unstructured.[37] An unstructured problem is one in which we have little information and thus high uncertainty. The more unstructured the problem, the greater the need for a prescriptive technique of gathering and analyzing information to solve the problem. One study suggests that leaders who give the group a structure by setting goals, monitoring time, and providing suggestions about procedure enhance the group's perceived effectiveness.[38] VanGundy has identified over 70 techniques that help provide structure to the problem-solving process.

REVIEW

A Summary of Group Communication Functions

FUNCTIONS	CHARACTERISTICS OF AN EFFECTIVE GROUP PROBLEM SOLVER
Analysis functions	Sees the problem from variety of viewpoints
	Gathers data and researches the issues
	Knows how to use evidence
	Asks appropriate questions
Idea-generation functions	Searches for many solutions to a problem
	Makes high-quality statements
	Takes a vacation from the problem to revitalize the group

Evaluation Functions	Evaluates the pros and the cons
	Evaluates the opinions and assumptions of others
	Tests proposed solutions to see if they meet preestablished criteria
Personal sensitivity functions	Shows concern for both the group task and the feelings of others
	Listens to minority arguments.

Collaborating

E T H I C A L L Y

Ethical group communicators support an atmosphere of free choice. World history is full of examples of unethical leaders who used their power to take away the free choice of others. An ethical group communicator gives other group members the freedom to choose rather than unscrupulously limiting options. The power of group deliberations resides in the ability of a group to sort through information to make a reasoned choice. Unethically demanding that others believe what you believe violates your colleague's freedom to choose. It is appropriate to use valid evidence and reasoning to persuade others; it is inappropriate to demand that others do as you wish or to blackmail your group members. ("You do what I say, or I will not share my evidence with you.")

Clearly each approach has its unique advantages. Draw on all three approaches to help you be an effective problem-solving group participant. If the task is very simple, a group may not need a cumbersome, predetermined set of prescriptions. Research suggests, however, that if the task is complex (as many group tasks are) specific guidelines and procedures will help the group work more effectively.[39]

In this chapter, we have emphasized descriptive and functional perspectives. In Chapter 9, we will describe in more detail prescriptive approaches, formats, and techniques to give you some options in structuring group problem solving.

Cultural Assumptions About Group Problem Solving and Decision Making

As we conclude this chapter, we remind you that our assumptions about the descriptions, functions, and prescriptions of group and team problem solving and decision making should be filtered through the cultural perspective group members hold. As we noted in Chapter 1, some cultures assume an individualistic approach to accomplishing work (notably in the United States, Britain, and northern Europe) whereas other cultures assume a collaborative or collectivistic mind set (as in Asian cultures).

Table 8.1 North American and Japanese Decision-Making Assumptions Compared

NORTH AMERICAN	JAPANESE
Individual leader often takes control and directs the group.	Group leader assumes role of facilitator and shares responsibility for accomplishing the task.
Makes decisions quickly yet sometimes slow in implementing decisions.	Takes longer to make decisions, but implements decisions quickly.
More likely to reach a decision by either an individual recommendation or a majority vote.	More likely to make decisions by consensus.
Assumes a rational approach to solving problems and making decisions.	More likely to assume an intuitive approach to reaching group harmony.
More likely to directly confront problems in managing conflict.	Less likely to be direct in dealing with problems and managing conflict.
More likely to rely on one expert for information.	Less likely to rely on one expert for information; seeks information from several sources.

Source: From Teruyuki Kume, "Managerial Attitudes Toward Decision-Making: North America and Japan," in William B. Gudykunst, Lea P. Stewart, and Stella Ting-Toomey, eds., *Communication, Culture and Organizational Processes* (Newbury Park, CA: Sage, 1985). Reprinted by permission.

In addition to culture, gender differences also contribute to group differences that researchers suggest make a difference in how group members interact. For example, Karen Hawkins and Christopher Powell found that females tend to ask more probing questions during group deliberations than do males.[40]

One researcher has categorized and contrasted the assumptions North Americans hold toward decision making, compared with Japanese assumptions. Table 8.1 summarizes those assumptions.

Although Table 8.1 summarizes differences between only two cultures, it illustrates the point that you can't always assume your approach to working with others in groups will be compatible with approaches others have. You need not travel abroad to experience different cultural perspectives. In the United States you are likely to encounter individuals with a wide range of cultural and ethnic traditions. Even within regions of the United States group members may differ in their approaches and assumptions toward collective problem solving, collaboration, and teamwork.

What strategies can bridge these cultural differences? Consider the following suggestions.[41]

1. *Develop mindfulness.* To be mindful is to be consciously aware of cultural differences and to note that there are differences between your assumptions and the assumptions of others.[42] Consciously say to yourself, "These group members may have a different assumption about how to accomplish this task. Before I impose my strategies on them, I'll listen and make sure I understand what they are saying."

2. *Be flexible*. Realize that you may have to adapt and change according to the perceptions and assumptions others hold.

3. *Tolerate uncertainty and ambiguity*. Working with others from a culture or cultures different from your own is bound to create a certain amount of uncertainty and confusion. Being patient and tolerant will help you manage cultural differences when collaborating with others.[43]

4. *Resist stereotyping and making negative judgments about others*. Ethnocentrism is the assumption that your cultural heritage is superior. Assuming superiority when evaluating others typically produces defensiveness.

5. *Ask questions*. One way to learn about the assumptions others hold is to simply ask them what their preferences are for establishing norms and ground rules. An essential element in the development of any effective team is developing common ground rules; this can best be accomplished by asking others how they work and solve problems.

6. *Be other-oriented*. Empathy and sensitivity to others are keys to bridging cultural differences. Although simply considering an issue from someone else's point of view will not eliminate the difference, it will help enhance understanding. One of the seven habits of Stephen Covey nicely summarizes this principle: Seek to understand before being understood.[44]

Putting Principles into Practice

If you understand how groups go about the task of solving problems, you will be better able to manage the problem-solving process in small groups. The following suggestions should help you apply the concepts presented in this chapter.

Group Decision Making

▶ Start the decision-making process by accurately assessing the present situation.
▶ Establish clear and appropriate group goals to frame the decision-making objective.
▶ Identify positive and negative consequences of the alternatives identified.
▶ Ensure that group members have accurate information.
▶ Determine whether group members are drawing reasonable conclusions for the information that is available.

Group Problem Solving

▶ With other group members, answer the question "What do we want more or less of?" Analyze the problem by identifying: (1) the undesirable present, (2) your goal, and (3) obstacles that may keep you from achieving the goal.
▶ Give all group members the opportunity to help formulate appropriate group goals.

▶ Even when the first proposed solution seems reasonable or workable, examine other alternatives.

▶ Effective problem solvers:

Are vigilant thinkers; they appropriately analyze information and data.

Identify criteria; they define standards so they'll recognize a good solution when they see it.

Generate creative ideas; they search for many high-quality solutions.

Evaluate ideas and solutions; they examine the costs and benefits of solutions.

Are sensitive to others; they are concerned for both the task and the feelings of other group members.

▶ Interpret and evaluate the information you collect. Do not just accept the information at face value.

▶ Do not let yourself be satisfied after you have generated a few potential solutions. Keep searching unless the group needs a break.

Approaches to Group Problem Solving

▶ Adopt a functional approach to group problem solving by performing the functions of effective problem solvers.

▶ Adopt a prescriptive approach to problem solving if your group needs the structure that a problem-solving agenda provides.

▶ Do not be concerned if your group takes time to orient itself to the problem-solving process. It is a normal part of group work.

▶ Expect some conflict and differences of opinions after a group clarifies its task and passes through the orientation phase of problem solving.

▶ Even though conflict may appear to impede a group's efforts to solve a problem, expect a decision to emerge after a thorough discussion and analysis of the issues.

▶ Do not overlook the importance of the reinforcement phase of group problem solving. Group members need a sense of accomplishment after making a decision. Take time to celebrate.

Bridging Cultural Differences

▶ *Develop mindfulness*: Become consciously aware of cultural differences.

▶ *Be flexible*: Be ready to adapt to the cultural expectations and traditions of others.

▶ *Tolerate uncertainty and ambiguity*: Be patient when working with those who have a cultural background different from your own.

▶ *Avoid stereotyping and making negative judgments*: Avoid an ethnocentric mind set that assumes your cultural traditions are superior to those of others.

▶ *Ask questions*: Reduce your uncertainty by asking questions to help you and your team members develop common ground rules and norms.

▶ *Be other-oriented*: Cultivate the skill of empathy and seek to understand others before forcing your ideas and opinions on others.

PRACTICE

Description of Group Process

Attend a school board, city council, or other public meeting in which problems are discussed and solutions are recommended. Prepare a written analysis of the meeting by attempting to identify phases in the group's discussions. Also, try to identify examples of the three activity tracks discussed in this chapter (task process, relational, topical). In addition, provide examples of breakpoints in the discussion of the group.

Hurricane Preparedness Case

Although you have idly watched local meteorologists track Hurricane Bruce's destructive course through the Caribbean for several days, you have not given any serious thought to the possibility that the storm might directly affect your coastal city. However, at about seven o'clock this morning, the storm suddenly veered northward, putting it on course for a direct hit. Now the National Hurricane Center in Miami has posted a hurricane warning for your community. Forecasters are predicting landfall in approximately nine to twelve hours. Having taken no advance precautions, you are stunned by the amount of work you now have to do to secure your three-bedroom suburban home, which is about half a mile from the beach. You have enough food in the house for two days. You also have one candle and a transistor radio with one weak battery. You have no other hurricane supplies, nor have you taken any hurricane precautions. Your task is to rank the following items in terms of their importance for ensuring your survival and the safety of your property. Place number 1 by the first thing you should do, 2 by the second, and so on through number 13. Please work individually on this task.

Fill your car with gas   _____

Trim your bushes and trees   _____

Fill your bathtub with water   _____

Construct hurricane shutters for your windows   _____

Buy enough food for a week   _____

Buy batteries and candles   _____

Bring in patio furniture from outside   _____

Buy dry ice   _____

Invite friends over for a hurricane party   _____

Drain your swimming pool   _____

Listen to TV and radio for further bulletins before doing anything   _____

Make sure you have an evacuation plan   _____

Stock up on charcoal and charcoal lighter for your barbecue grill   _____

    After you have made your individual decisions, work in small groups with others and seek to reach consensus. Your group's task is to rank these items according to their importance.

Stranded in the Desert Situation[45]

You are a member of a geology club that is on a field trip to study unusual formations in the New Mexico desert. It is the last week in July. You have been driving over old trails, far from any road, in order to see out-of-the-way formations. At about 10:30 A.M. your club's specially equipped minibus overturns, rolls into a 20-foot ravine, and burns. The driver and the professional adviser to the club are killed. The rest of you are relatively uninjured.

    You know that the nearest ranch is approximately 45 miles east of where you are. There is no closer habitation. When your club does not report to its motel that evening, you will be missed. Several people know generally where you are but will not be able to pinpoint your whereabouts.

    The area around you is rather rugged and dry. There is a shallow waterhole nearby, but the water is contaminated by worms, animal feces and urine, and several dead mice. Before you left you heard from a weather report that the temperature would reach 108° F making the surface temperature 128°F. All of you are dressed in lightweight summer clothing and all have hats and sunglasses.

    Although escaping from the minibus, each group member salvaged a couple of items; there are twelve items in all. Your group's task is to rank these items according to their importance to your survival, starting with 1 for the most important and proceeding to 12 for the least important.

    You may assume that the number of club members is the same as the number of persons in your group and that the group has agreed to stick together.

_____ Magnetic compass

_____ A piece of heavy-duty, light-blue canvas, 20 square feet in size

_____ Book, *Plants of the Desert*

_____ Rearview mirror

_____ Large knife

_____ Flashlight

_____ One jacket per person

_____ One transparent, plastic ground cloth (6 feet by 4 feet) per person

_____ A .38-caliber loaded pistol

_____ One 2-quart plastic canteen of water per person

_____ An accurate map of the area

_____ A large box of kitchen matches

 Your companion Website has more practice activities, questionnaires, and checklists!
www.ablongman.com/beebe

Notes

1. D. S. Gouran and R. R. Hirokawa, "Functional Theory and Communication in Decision-Making and Problem-Solving Groups: An Expanded View," in R. Y. Hirokawa and M. S. Poole, eds., *Communication and Group Decision Making* (Thousand Oaks, CA: Sage, 1996) 55–80; D. S. Gouran, R. Y. Hirokawa, K. M. Julian, and G. B. Leatham, "The Evolution and Current Status of the Functional Perspective on Communication in Decision-Making and Problem-Solving Groups," in S. A. Deetz, ed., *Communication Yearbook* 16, Newbury Park, CA: Sage, 1993) 573–600; E. E. Graham, M. J. Papa, and M. B. McPherson, "An Applied Test of the Functional Communication Perspective of Small Group Decision Making," *The Southern Communication Journal* 62 (1997): 169–279.

2. Gouran and Hirokawa, "Functional Theory,": 69.

3. See John K. Brilhart and Gloria Galanes, *Communicating in Groups* (Madison, WI: Brown & Benchmark) 1997, 256; David W. Johnson and Frank P. Johnson, *Joining Together: Group Theory and Group Skills* (Englewood Cliffs, NJ: Prentice Hall, 1987) 99–104.

4. Randy Y. Hirokawa and Dirk R. Scheerhorn, "Communication in Faulty Group Decision-Making," in Randy Y. Hirokawa and Marshall Scott Poole, *Communication and Group Decision-Making* (Beverly Hills, CA: Sage, 1986) 67.

5. Hirokawa and Scheerhorn, *"Communication in Faulty Group Decision-Making."*

6. A. R. Dennis, "Information Exchange and Use in Small Group Decision Making," *Small Group Research* 27 (1996): 532–50. See also G. M. Wittenbaum, "Information Sampling in Decision-Making Groups: The Impact of Members' Task-Relevant Status," *Small Group Research* 29 (1998): 57–84; K. M. Propp, "Information Utilization in Small Group Decision Making: A Study of the Evaluation Interaction Model," *Small Group Research* 28 (1997): 424–53.

7. J. G. Oetzel, "Explaining Individual Communication Processes in Homogeneous and Heterogeneous Groups Through Individual-Collectivism and Self-Construal," *Human Communication Research* 25 (1998): 202–24.

8. Charles H. Kepner and Benjamin B. Treogoe, *The Rational Manager* (New York: McGraw-Hill, 1965); see also Brilhart and Galanes, *Effective Group Discussion* (Dubuque, IA: Brown, 1992) 232.

9. We thank Dennis Romig for this observation. For additional information about structuring problem solving in teams, see Dennis A. Romig, *Breakthrough Teamwork: Outstanding Results Using Structured Teamwork* (New York: Irwin, 1996).

10. Benjamin J. Broome and Luann Fulbright, "A Multistage Influence Model of Barriers to Group Problem Solving: A Participant-Generated Agenda for Small Group Research," *Small Group Research* 26 (February 1995): 24–55.

11. B. Aubrey Fisher, *Small Group Decision Making: Communication and the Group Process*, 2nd ed. (New York: McGraw-Hill, 1980) 132.

12. Fisher, "Small Group Decision Making," 130.

13. B. Aubrey Fisher, "Decision Emergence: Phases in Group Decision-Making," *Speech Monographs* 37 (1970): 60.

14. Fisher, "Decision Emergence," 130–31.

15. Fisher, "Decision Emergence," 61.

16. T. M. Scheidel and L. Crowell, "Idea Development in Small Discussion Groups, " *Quarterly Journal of Speech* 50 (1994): 140–45.

17. J. E. McGrath, "Time, Interaction, and Performance (TIP): A Theory of Groups," *Small Group Research* 22 (1991): 147–174.

18. C. J. Gersick, "Time and Transition in Work Teams: Toward a New Model of Group Development," *Academy of Management Journal* 32 (1989): 274–309; C. J. Gersick, and J. R. Hackman, "Habitual Routines in Task-Performing Groups," *Organizational Behavior and Human Decision Processes* 47 (1990): 65–97.

19. Marshall Scott Poole, "Decision Development in Small Groups, III: A Multiple Sequence Model of Group Decision Development," *Communication Monographs* 50 (December 1983): 321–41.

20. Poole, "Decision Development in Small Groups, III."

21. Poole, "Decision Development in Small Groups, III."

22. See Ernest G. Bormann, *Discussion and Group Methods* (New York: Harper & Row, 1975).

23. Poole, "Decision Development in Small Groups, III," 330.

24. Randy Y. Hirokawa, "Discussion Procedures and Decision-Making Performance: A Test of a Functional Perspective," *Human Communication Research* 12, no. 2 (Winter 1985): 203–24.

25. Randy Y. Hirokawa and Kathryn Rost, "Effective Group Decision-Making in Organizations: Field Test of the Vigilant Interaction Theory," *Management Communication Quarterly* 5 (1992): 267–88; Randy Y. Hirokawa, "Why Informed Groups Make Faulty Decisions: An Investigation of Possible Interaction-Based Explanations," *Small Group Behavior* 18 (1987): 3–29; Randy Y. Hirokawa, "Group Communication and Decision-Making Performance: A Continued Test of the Functional Perspective," *Human Communication Research* 14 (Summer 1988): 487–515; Marc O. Orlitzky and R. Y. Hirokawa, "To Err Is Human, to Correct for It Divine: A Meta-Analysis of Research Testing the Functional Theory of Group Decision-Making Effectiveness." Paper presented to the National Communication Association, Chicago, November 1997.

26. R. Y. Hirokawa and A. J. Salazar, "Task-Group Communication and Decision-Making Performance," in L. Frey, ed., *The Handbook of Group Communication Theory and Research*, (Thousand Oaks, CA: Sage, 1999) 167–191; D. Gouran and R. Y. Hirokawa, "Functional Theory and Communication in Decision-Making and Problem-Solving Groups: An Expanded View," in R. Y. Hirokawa and M. S. Poole, eds., *Communication and Group Decision Making* (Thousand Oaks, CA: Sage, 1996) 55–80.

27. Orlitzky and Hirokawa, "To Err Is Human, To Correct for It Divine."

28. Graham, Papa, and McPherson, "An Applied Test of the Functional Communication Perspective of Small Group Decision-Making."

29. K. Barge, *Leadership: Communication Skills for Organizations and Groups* (New York: St. Martin's, 1994).

30. I. L. Janis, *Victims of Groupthink* (Boston: Houghton Mifflin, 1973); I. L. Janis, *Critical Decision: Leadership in Policymaking and Crisis Management* (New York: Free Press, 1989).

31. See Randy Y. Hirokawa and Roger Pace, "A Descriptive Investigation of the Possible Communication-Based Reasons for Effective and Ineffective Group Decision Making," *Communication Monographs* 50 (December 1983): 363–79. The authors also wish to acknowledge Dennis A. Romig, Performance Resources, Inc., Austin, Texas, for his contribution to the discussion.

32. Dale G. Leathers, "Quality of Group Communication as a Determinant of Group Product," *Speech Monographs* 39 (1972): 166–73; Randy Y. Hirokawa and Dennis S. Gouran, "Facili-

tation of Group Communication: A Critique of Prior Research and an Agenda for Future Research," *Management Communication Quarterly* 3 (August 1989): 71–92.

33. See Frank J. Sabatine, "Rediscovering Creativity: Unlearning Old Habits," *Mid-American Journal of Business* 4 (1989): 11–13.

34. Graham, Papa, and McPherson, "An Applied Test of the Functional Communication Perspective of Small Group Decision-Making."

35. Fisher, *Small Group Decision Making*, 130.

36. Steven A. Beebe and John T. Masterson, "Toward a Model of Small Group Communication: Applications for Teaching and Research," *Florida Speech Communication Journal* 8, no. 2 (1980): 9–15.

37. See Arthur B. VanGundy, *Techniques of Structured Problem Solving* (New York: Van Nostrand Reinhold, 1981)4; see also Romig, *Breakthrough Teamwork*.

38. William E. Jurma, "Effects of Leader Structuring Style and Task Orientation Characteristics of Group Members," *Communication Monographs* 46 (1979): 282–95.

39. Susan Jarboe, "A Comparison of Input–Output, Process–Output and Input–Process–Output Models of Small Group Problem-Solving Effectiveness," *Communication Monographs* 55 (June 1988): 121–42; Randy Y. Hirokawa, "Group Communication and Decision-Making Performance."

40. K. Hawkins and C.B. Power, "Gender Differences in Questions Asked During Small Decision Making Group Discussions," *Small Group Research* 30 (1990): 235–256.

41. This discussion of bridging cultural differences is based on a discussion in: Steven A. Beebe, Susan J. Beebe, and Mark V. Redmond, *Interpersonal Communication: Relating to Others* (Boston: Allyn and Bacon, 2002).

42. See William B. Gudykunst, *Bridging Differences: Effective Intergroup Communication* (Newbury Park, CA: Sage, 1998).

43. Oetzel, "Explaining Individual Communication Processes in Homogeneous and Heterogeneous Groups Through Individualism-Collectivism and Self-Construal."

44. Stephen R. Covey, *The 7 Habits of Highly Effective People* (New York: Simon & Schuster, 1989).

45. Johnson and Johnson, *Joining Together*.

Chapter Outline:

Objectives:

After studying this chapter, you will be able to:

▶ Use the steps and tools of reflective thinking to solve a problem in a small group discussion.

▶ Apply brainstorming to a problem-solving group discussion.

▶ Apply the ideal-solution problem-solving method to a group discussion.

▶ Apply the single-question problem-solving approach to a group discussion.

▶ Determine which problem-solving approach is most suitable for a given group discussion.

Using Problem–Solving Techniques

> "The best way to escape from a problem is to solve it."
>
> — Anonymous

Imagine that you are the chairperson of a committee appointed to improve the quality of education in your community. Students' scores on standardized achievement tests have declined in the past two years. School administrators complain that they do not have the funds to develop new programs or to hire more teachers. Your committee must develop a plan to deal with the problem. The last chapter introduced three approaches to problem solving: Descriptive, functional, and prescriptive. As committee chairperson, you could adopt a descriptive problem-solving approach by cluing in group members on some of the processes and phases that groups experience when trying to solve problems. Although giving your committee an understanding of the process may be beneficial, you feel you need to provide more structure to help the group efficiently organize its approach to solving the problem. You could then approach your task from a functional perspective by ensuring that critical elements of problem solving are introduced in your discussion.

In addition, there is, as we have indicated, a third approach—the prescriptive approach to problem solving. Unfortunately, there is no one best way to solve problems in groups. Each group is unique, as is each group member. No single prescriptive problem-solving formula always works. Yet evidence indicates that guiding a group through a structured agenda can enhance its effectiveness.[1] This chapter will give you several suggestions for solving problems in groups, one of which should meet your group's need at any given time.

An Overview of Prescriptive Problem-Solving Strategies

There are a vast number of specific strategies and techniques that can help you facilitate group problem solving.[2] Some activities are common among almost all of them. Most include references to five key elements: (1) identify and define the problem, (2) analyze the problem, (3) identify possible solutions, (4) select the best solution, and (5) implement the solution. These steps outline the primary way most scientists in any discipline go about finding answers to puzzling questions. We will examine the origin of these steps as well as why they continue to be used to structure group problem-solving discussion.

The Origin of Prescriptive Problem-Solving Strategies

In 1910, philosopher and educator John Dewey, in his book *How We Think,* identified the steps most people follow to solve problems. According to Dewey, a reflective thinker considers these key questions.[3]

1. What is the "felt difficulty" or concern?

2. Where is it located, and how is it defined?

3. What are possible solutions to the felt difficulty?

4. What are logical reasons that support the solution?

5. What additional testing and observation need to be done to confirm the validity of the solution?

These five steps should look familiar. They are very close to the five steps we just mentioned. Even though Dewey did not focus specifically on small groups, the steps he outlined, called **reflective thinking**—a series of logical, rational steps based on the scientific method of defining, analyzing, and solving a problem—have been used by many groups as a way to structure the problem-solving process. As new courses in group discussion were being designed in the 1920s and 1930s, teachers and authors adapted Dewey's framework as a standard agenda that could be used to tackle any problem-solving group discussion. One of the first texts to adapt these steps explicitly was published in Alfred Dwight Sheffield's brief book *Creative Discussion: A Statement of Method for Leaders and Members of Discussion Groups and Conferences*, first published in 1926. Soon other scholars began making similar references to this sequence, and, as you will see in the discussion that follows, it has become a **standard agenda** for structuring group problem solving.[5]

The Importance of Structuring Problem-Solving Discussion

Communicating with others in small groups to solve a problem is often a messy and disorganized process. Even though we noted that some researchers have identified distinct phases in the course of a group's deliberation (orientation, conflict, emergence, reinforcement), others find that group discussion often bounces from person to person and can be an inefficient, time-consuming process. And as we discussed in Chapter 2, groups also develop fantasy themes that can trigger a chain of stories—some that are related to the group's task and some that are not. Although these stories and group fantasies are important to a group's identity, extended off-task "storytelling" can have a negative effect on the group's productivity.

To counteract the messiness of group interaction, researchers investigating groups have suggested that an agenda be used to structure the discussion. The purpose of an agenda is to help keep the discussion on track, not to stifle group interaction or consciousness raising. Robert Bales found that most task-oriented groups spend a little over 60 percent of their time talking about the task and almost 40 percent of their time talking about social, relational, or maintenance matters.[6] An agenda ensures that the time spent talking about the task is on target.

Researchers have found that groups and teams that have no planned structure or agenda have many more procedural problems. Here's a summary of what researchers have found during "naturally occurring" or unhindered discussion where there is little or no structure.

1. The group takes more time to deliberate; interaction is inefficient and often off task.

2. Groups members prematurely focus on solutions rather than analyze issues.

3. The group often jumps at the first solution mentioned.

4. Group members hop from one idea or proposal to the next without seeing the larger issues.

5. The group is more likely to be dominated by an outspoken group member.

6.   Conflict is likely to go unmanaged.[7]

The bottom line of this research: Groups and teams need help to keep them on track.

Of all the various ways to organize or structure discussion, which method seems to be the best? Many of the sequences have not been tested empirically. Among those sequences that have been compared in controlled studies, no single method seems to work best all of the time. One powerful conclusion, however, emerges from the research: *Any method of structuring group problem solving is better than no method at all.*[8]

Groups need **structure** because members have relatively short attention spans and uncertainty results both from the relationships among group members and from the group's definition of the task. In separate studies, researchers found that groups shift topics about once a minute.[9] As noted in the last chapter, Poole argues that group members consider task process, relational concerns, and topical shifts with varying degrees of attention. Thus groups benefit from an agenda that keeps the discussion focused on their task. And one research study found that some members need more structure than others. Group members who have a preference for using more rigid procedures arrived at higher-quality decisions than those using a less-structured approach to organizing their discussion.[10]

Think of the various steps and tools in this chapter as a way to impose a common structure on a group's deliberation. Without that structure, a group is more likely to wobble, waste time, and be less productive.

Can a group have too much structure? The answer is yes. Perhaps you have been to a meeting that was more like listening to someone give a speech. An overly structured group discussion occurs if one person—sometimes the designated leader but sometimes not—talks too much, which minimizes group **interaction**. By interaction we mean the amount of talk or dialogue that reflects the give-and-take contributions that group members make. As Figure 9.1 suggests, the goal is to find the right balance between structure and interaction. Based on his effective decision-making theory, John Oetzel has found that groups that have more equal participation enjoy better-quality results; this research supports the assumption that groups need balanced interaction to achieve their goals.[11] Some research studies suggest that groups that used networked computers to share information (a highly structured situation) generated lots of ideas but had difficulty reaching a decision.[12] A less-structured, interactive, face-to-face situation was better for discussing alternatives and reaching a final decision. The techniques we review in this chapter are designed to focus the discussion but still permit the interaction that helps the group achieve its goals. In addition, many of these prescriptive agendas incorporate the key functions of group effectiveness, as discussed in the last chapter.

Figure 9.1 The Balance Between Structure and Interaction

Reflective Thinking: The Traditional Approach to Group Problem Solving

Some researchers and numerous group-communication textbooks recommend reflective thinking (or one of its many variations) as the standard agenda for organizing or structuring group problem solving. However, many group-communication theorists today believe that it is more useful as a description of the way some people solve problems than as an ideal pattern for all groups to solve problems. We describe the procedures and tools that can assist you and your groups in organizing the sometimes uncertain and fractious process of problem solving. The steps we present here are not intended to be a one-size-fits-all approach that groups should use in solving every problem. They do, however, provide a logical, rational way of structuring group interaction.[13]

Step 1: Identify and Define the Problem

Perhaps you have heard the saying "A problem well stated is a problem half solved." A group first has to recognize that a problem exists. This may be the group's biggest obstacle. Before a PTA fund-raising committee can effectively consider suggestions for raising money, members must recognize that a need exists. Many groups do not bother to verbalize the problem facing them; each person merely begins by offering solutions to remedy the problem. A group must clearly and succinctly agree on the problem facing it. The problem should be limited so that members know its scope and size. After members identify and limit it, they should define key terms in light of the problem under consideration, so that they have a common understanding of the problem. For example, one student group recently decided to solve the problem of student apathy on campus. The students phrased their problem as a question: "What can be done to alleviate student apathy on campus?" They had identified a problem, but they soon discovered that they needed to decide what they meant by the word apathy. Does it mean poor attendance at football games? Does it mean a sparse showing at the recent fund-raising activity "Hit Your Professor with a Pie"? After additional efforts to define the key word, they decided to limit their problem to low attendance at events sponsored by the student-activities committee. With a clearer focus on their problem, they were ready to continue with the problem-solving process. Researchers have consistently found that groups develop better solutions to their problems if they take the time to analyze the issues *before* jumping in and listing possible solutions; groups and teams have a tendency, however, to leap to a solution before looking at and analyzing the issues.[14]

Consider the following questions when attempting to identify and define a problem for group deliberations:

1. What is the specific problem the group is concerned about?

2. What obstacles are keeping the group from its goal?

3. Is the question the group is trying to answer clear?

4. What terms, concepts, or ideas need to be defined?

5. Who is harmed by the problem?

6. When do the harmful effects of the problem occur?

Tools for Defining the Problem   In addition to using these questions to identify and define the problem, three tools or techniques that provide even more structure—the *is/is not* analysis, the *Journalist's Six Questions*, and *Pareto Charts*—may be useful when your group needs "super" structure to clarify and define the problem.

1. *Is/is not Analysis*. The **is/is not analysis** is a way to ensure that a group is, in fact, investigating a problem and not just a symptom of the problem.[15] Early in a group's deliberation group members consider such questions as What is the area or object with the problem? What is not the area or object with the problem? Where does the problem occur? Where does the problem not occur? The accompanying chart includes other *is/is not* questions that can help give the group the structure it needs to clearly identify and define a problem. To use this technique, you could ask group members to use the chart to focus on the specific problem under consideration. Members could first write down their answers and then share their responses one at a time. Having group members write before speaking is a way to help further structure their comments.

For example, one group was attempting to investigate the declining standardized test scores in one elementary school in their community. They thought the problem they were trying to solve was inadequate teaching that resulted in lowered scores. But when the group used the *is/is not* technique to identify when and where the problem is and is not observed, they discovered that the low test scores occurred in only three classrooms, which were in the same wing of the building and all controlled by the same air-conditioning system. On further investigation, they realized that the air-conditioning units were not functioning, resulting in uncomfortable classrooms, which in turn affected student performance on the examinations. The problem changed from trying to eliminate bad teaching to changing the air-conditioning system. The *is/is not* technique is a way to identify and define the problem rather than the symptoms of the problem.

Is/Is Not Analysis

	Is	Is Not
What	What is the area or object with the problem?	What is not the area or object with the problem?
Symptoms	What are the symptoms of the problem?	What are not the symptoms of the problem?
When	When is the problem observed?	When is the problem not observed?
Where	Where does the problem occur?	Where does the problem not occur?
Who	Who is affected by the problem?	Who is not affected by the problem?

2. *Journalist's Six Questions*: Most news reporters are taught to quickly identify the key facts when writing a news story or broadcasting a news event. The key elements of almost any newsworthy story can be captured by addressing a **journalist's six questions**: Who? What? When? Where? Why? How? Using these five W's and an H can help a group quickly structure how a problem is defined. Group members could be given a worksheet such

as the accompanying example and instructed to come to a meeting, having first attempted to answer these six questions.[16] The group could then pool the results and be well on the way to analyzing the problem. Or the group could brainstorm answers to these questions while the group leader records the responses on a flip chart or chalkboard.

Journalist's Six Questions

Who?	
What?	
When?	
Where?	
Why?	
How?	

3. *Pareto charts.* A Pareto chart is a bar graph that shows data that describes the cause, source, or frequency of the problem. The chart is arranged with the tallest bars on the left and the shortest bars on the right. A Pareto chart makes it easy to look at data and identify the source of the problem. The chart gets its name form the **Pareto Principle**. Perhaps you've heard it: *The source of 80 percent of the problem comes from 20 percent of the incidents.*[17] Here are some examples: Eighty percent of the dirt on your carpet is on 20 percent of the floor; 80 percent of the food you order comes from 20 percent of the menu; 80 percent of the conflict in a group is created by 20 percent of the group members. When looking at the source of problems, most groups find that the primary source of the problem comes from only a few examples. When the group or team is struggling to figure out exactly what the problem is, a Pareto chart can help the group spot the issue easily.

As shown in Figure 9.2, one group was interested in why there were so many errors on financial aid statements at their university; students weren't receiving their financial aid on time. They gathered data and found that 61 percent of the problem was caused by improperly completed financial-aid forms, 23 percent was related to errors in entering data into the computer, 4 percent of the mistakes were caused by reporting no phone number, and 3 percent arose because students did not report their e-mail address. When the group displayed these data on a Pareto chart, they could easily see the main source of the problem—the forms weren't being completed properly.

Step 2: Analyze the Problem

Ray Kroc, founder of McDonald's, was fond of saying that nothing is particularly hard if you divide it into small jobs. To analyze a problem is to break a problem into causes, effects, symptoms, and subproblems. During the analysis phase of group problem solv-

Figure 9.2   Pareto Chart: Source of Errors on Financial-Aid Statements

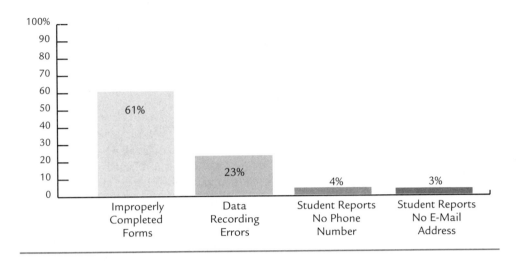

ing, members need to research and investigate the problem. In analyzing the problem, a group may wish to consider the following questions:

1. What is the history of the problem? How long has it existed?

2. How serious is the problem?

3. What are the causes of the problem?

4. What are the effects of the problem?

5. What are the symptoms of the problem?

6. What methods does the group already have for dealing with the problem?

7. What are the limitations of those methods?

8. How much freedom does the group have in gathering information and attempting to solve the problem?

9. What obstacles keep the group from achieving the goal?

10. Can the problem be divided into subproblems for definition and analysis?

Another element in the analysis step of the reflective-thinking process is to formulate **criteria**—standards or goals for acceptable solutions. Formulating such criteria may prevent future uncertainties and misunderstandings and may help your group sort through proposed solutions to arrive at the best possible one. Many groups begin listing solutions before they have properly analyzed problems or identified adequate criteria. If you adhere to the reflective-thinking format, you will identify criteria before offering possible solutions. In listing criteria for a solution, you may wish to consider the following questions:

1. What goal are we trying to achieve?

2. What are the minimum requirements of an acceptable solution?

3. Which criteria are the most important?

4. How should the group use the criteria to evaluate the suggested solutions?

Sample criteria for a solution may include the following:

1. The solution should be inexpensive.

2. The solution should be implemented as soon as possible.

3. The solution should be agreed on by all the group members.

Tools for Analyzing the Problem   Groups may need help in breaking a problem down into its subcomponents. Two techniques can help a group sort out factors contributing to the problem: (1) force-field analysis and (2) cause-and-effect (fishbone) diagram. Each of the techniques can help a group focus on data and facts rather than on vague impressions of what may be causing the problem.

1. *Force Field Analysis*. This technique is based on the assumptions of Kurt Lewin, often called the father of group dynamics.[18] To use **force-field analysis,** the group needs to have a clear statement of its goal, which can be stated in terms of what the group wants more of or less of (for example, "We need more money, more time, or less interference from others"). The group analyzes the goal by noting what driving forces make it likely to be achieved and what restraining forces make it unlikely to be achieved.

Follow these steps to complete the force field-analysis chart (Figure 9.3) on page 225.[19]

Step 1. Identify the goal, objective, or target the group is trying to achieve (such as more money, fewer errors).

Step 2. On the right side of the chart, list all the restraining forces: Those forces that currently keep the group from achieving its goal.

Step 3. On the left side of the chart, list all the driving forces: Those forces that currently help the group achieve its goal.

Step 4. The group now decides whether to do one of three things: (a) increase the driving forces; (b) decrease the restraining forces; (c) increase selected driving forces and decrease those restraining forces over which the group has control.

After the group has sorted through the facts and identified the driving and restraining forces, it will more likely be able to focus on the essential causes of the problem rather than on the problem's symptoms.

Say, for example, you are working in a group that has the goal of increasing teamwork and collaboration among faculty and students. Driving forces—or those forces that favor teamwork—include such factors as faculty members who are motivated to work with students, students who also want to work with faculty, an existing training program that teaches teamwork and collaboration skills to both students and faculty. These and other driving forces could be included on the left-hand side of the force-field chart. Restraining forces—or those forces that work against increased collaboration—include current lack of knowledge of teamwork principles, the negative attitudes of a small but vocal group of fac-

Figure 9.3 Force Field Analysis

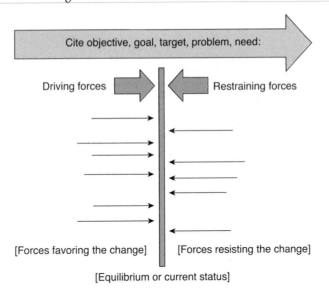

ulty members who want to use more individual approaches to education, and the lack of a tradition of collaboration. These obstacles are listed on the right side of the chart. Ideally, the group should work together on the force-field analysis diagram by using a flip chart or projecting the chart using an overhead projector. After generating additional driving and restraining forces, the group then turns its attention to the question "What can be done to increase the driving forces and decrease the restraining forces?" The group's force-field analysis of the problem can provide new insights for overcoming the obstacles and achieving the goal.

2. *Cause-and-Effect (Fishbone)* Diagram.   Another problem analysis tool often used in groups and teams is the **cause-and-effect diagram,** also often called a **fishbone diagram** because the diagram completed, looks like the skeleton bones of a fish. Developed by Kaoru Ishikawa, a Japanese specialist in quality management, this diagram helps groups and teams visually examine the relationship between causes and their probable effects.[20]

To develop a cause-and-effect diagram, first think of the possible effect you want to analyze. For example, imagine your group is trying to identify possible causes in the drop in students' standardized test scores in your community high school. The drop in test scores is the effect, but you aren't sure what's causing the drop. To prepare a cause-and-effect diagram, draw a line on a piece of paper, chalkboard, or flipchart. Then, angling out from the long line, draw lines to represent possible causes of the drop in scores. Here you must use your analytical-thinking skills. For example, as illustrated in Figure 9.4, the major causes could be as follows. The test-administration instructions are unclear, parents may not be involved, teachers may not have time to prepare students for the test, and students may have too many competing activities. Then, on each of the four angled lines, list possible contributing factors for each of the four main problem causes. For example, on

Figure 9.4 Cause-and-Effect (Fishbone) Diagram of the Reasons for Low Student Test Scores

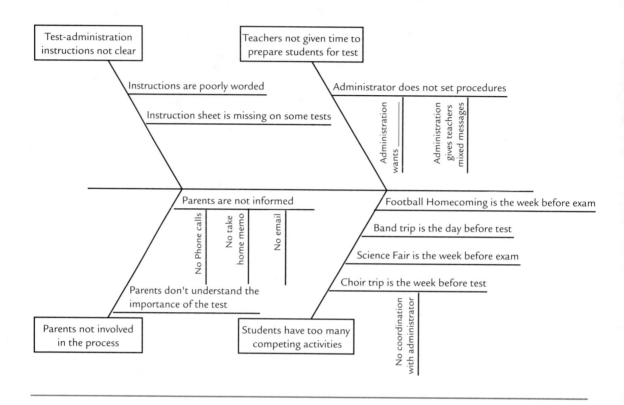

the line suggesting that students have competing activities, you could draw lines to specify those competing activities. If you're stumped for a way to get started analyzing the problem, Ishikawa suggested that almost all problems boil down to issues related to the 4 Ms: Manpower (people), Machines, Materials, and Methods. These four categories can represent major lines angling off the horizontal line.

The advantage of the cause-and-effect diagram is that all group members can work together to show relationships between causes and effects. For groups and teams to collaborate, they need a common format that helps them collaborate. A cause-and-effect diagram creates that shared space in which to work. You don't need to make your diagram complicated; you don't always need four lines angling off the center line. Often simpler is better. The key is to write down the potential causes so all group or team members can see the relationships among possible causes and the known effect. As suggested by management consultant Peter Scholtes, "One of the biggest challenges in creating a cause-and-effect diagram is to have the bones show cause-and-effect relationships."[21] He cautions that cause-and-effect diagrams only depict *potential* causes. Once you have a list of potential causes, your group will need to verify the relationship between the cause and the effect with data and evidence.

Step 3: Generate Several Possible Solutions

After analyzing a problem and selecting criteria for a solution, the group should begin to list possible solutions in tentative, hypothetical terms. Many groups suggest a variety of possible solutions without evaluating them. Later in the chapter, we will discuss how to use several brainstorming techniques as a way to generate several solutions.

Step 4: Select the Best Solution or Combination of Solutions

After a group has compiled a list of possible solutions to a problem, it should be ready to select the best solution. How do you narrow down a long list of proposed solutions? One way is to refer to the criteria proposed during the analysis stage of the discussion and consider each tentative solution in light of these criteria. The group should decide which proposed solution or combination of solutions best meets its criteria. Our discussion of how to facilitate consensus, presented in Chapter 10, offers several strategies for narrowing the number of options. The following questions may be helpful in analyzing the proposed solutions:

1. What are the advantages of each solution?

2. Are there any disadvantages to the solution? Do the disadvantages outweigh the advantages?

3. What would be the long-term and short-term effects of this solution if it were adopted?

4. Would the solution really solve the problem?

5. Does the solution conform to the criteria formulated by the group?

6. Should the group modify the criteria?

If group members agree, the criteria for a best solution may need to be changed or modified.[22]

Tools for Evaluating the Solutions   In addition to asking questions to guide discussion of the solutions or alternatives that the group has identified, the following tools can provide additional ways of focusing or structuring discussion.

1. *Analyze the pros and cons.* One of the most consistent findings of functional communication researchers is that when groups weigh the positive and negative outcomes of solutions they will make a better decision.[23] One method of facilitating such a discussion is to make a T-chart like the one shown on page 228 to evaluate solution pros and cons. A T-chart gets its name from that fact that when you draw a large "T" on a board or flipchart, you can list "Pros" on one side and "Cons" on the other. If the group is large and you want to make sure everyone participates, you can have members first silently write down pros and cons (or the risks and benefits) and then share their responses with the group. For example, if a group were trying to decide whether to purchase a new piece of property, one side of the center line might list positive aspects, such as good investment, property values increasing, good location, and so on. On the other side would be negative implications of the purchase: It will reduce our cash flow, it will increase property taxes, expensive lawyer fees, and so on. A thorough look at pros and cons can help a group consider alternatives before it makes a final decision.

2. *Average rankings and ratings.* It is usually easier for a group to identify possible solutions than it is to narrow the list of alternatives and select the best solution. If a group

T-Chart

Pros	Cons

has many solutions to evaluate, one way to narrow the list is to ask group members to either rank or rate the solutions and then average the rankings or ratings to see which solutions emerge as the most and least popular. Ranking or rating should be done after a group has discussed the pros and cons of the solutions. Ranking solutions works best if you have no more than five to seven solutions; group members often have a difficult time ranking more than seven items. If you have a very long list of solutions— a dozen or more—you may ask the group members to rank their top five choices, assigning a rank of 1 to their top choice, 2 to their next choice, and so on. One researcher has found that asking the group to rank-order a list of possible alternatives is a better procedure than asking the group to pick the best solution. By ranking each option, group members are forced to critically evaluate each alternative rather than just picking one solution.[24]

Besides ranking solutions, group members could also assign a rating score to each solution. Each solution could be rated on a five-point scale, with a rating of 1 being a very positive evaluation and 5 being a negative evaluation. Even a long list of 20 or more potential solutions could be rated. Averages for each solution could be calculated, and the most highly rated solutions could be discussed again by the entire group.

Step 5: Test and Implement the Solution

Group members should be confident that the proposed solution is valid—that it will solve the problem. After a group selects the best solution, it must determine how the solution can be put into effect. You may wish to consider the following questions:

1. How can the group get approval and support for its proposed solution?

2. What specific steps are necessary to implement the solution?

3. How can the group evaluate the success of its problem-solving efforts?

In many groups, those who choose a solution are not the same people who will implement it. If this is the case, members who select the solution should clearly explain why they selected it to members who will put the solution into practice. If they can demonstrate that the group went through an orderly process to solve the problem, they usually can convince others that their solution is valid.

Tools for Implementing a Solution There are two key tools for implementing a solution: (1) an action chart and (2) a flowchart. An **action chart** is a grid that lists the tasks that need to be done and identifies who will be responsible for each task. Such a chart is based on more elaborate diagrams and procedures, such as a PERT diagram. PERT (stands for Program Evaluation and Review Technique) was originally developed by the U.S. Navy in the late 1950s to assist with the production of the *Polaris* missile program.[25] The action chart presented below was developed by using the following steps:

1. Identify the project goal.

2. Identify the activities needed to complete the project.

3. Identify the sequence of activities (what should be done first, second, third, and so on).

4. Estimate the amount of time it should take to complete each task.

5. Determine which group members should be responsible for each task.

6. Develop a chart that shows the relationships among the tasks, times, people, and sequence of events that are needed to accomplish the project.

   One reason why solutions do not get implemented is that people are uncertain about who should do what. An action chart provides needed structure to reduce this uncertainty. An action chart also helps ensure that everybody is aware of what needs to be done and reduces the risk that nobody will do anything.

   A **flowchart** is a step-by-step diagram of a multistep process. One group was charged with improving the way textbooks were ordered for college classes. The chart in Figure 9.5 shows how the group described the essential steps involved in selecting, ordering, and purchasing a text. Flowcharts can help a group see whether the sequence of procedures they have identified to solve a problem are practical and fit together. A flowchart can also help your group work through logistics and identify practical problems of moving from an

An Action Chart

Names								
Ken	•	•			•	•		•
Darryl		•			•			
Steve			•		•			
Janice			•		•		•	
Carl				•	•	•	•	
Assignment	Conduct needs assessment	Write behavioral objectives	Develop training content outline	Write training facilitator guide	Develop audio-visual resources	Conduct training pilot test	Conduct training for client	Analyze evaluation data
Week	Week 1		Week 2		Week 3		Week 4	
Day	Monday	Friday	Monday	Friday	Monday	Friday	Monday	Frid

Figure 9.5   Process: Ordering a Textbook

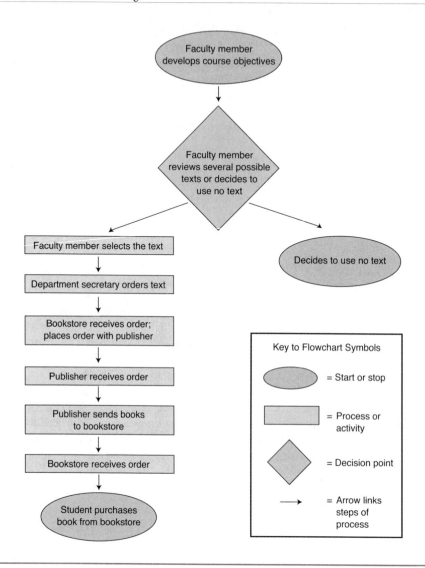

idea's conception to its implementation. Like an action plan, a flowchart is a way to give structure to group thought. Flowcharts can be simple, like our example, or very complex like those computer programmers use to identify sophisticated programs.

How detailed does a flowchart need to be? The level of detail depends on the needs of the group. We caution you, however, not to make the flowchart so detailed that your goal becomes developing a flowchart rather than describing and implementing a process. Use a flowchart as a tool to make sure all group members have a clear understanding of the critical parts of a more complex process.

How to Apply Reflective Thinking to Your Group or Team

Reflective thinking suggests that groups work best when their discussions are organized rather than disorganized or random. Remember that you should use reflective thinking as a guide, not as an exact formula for solving every problem. As noted earlier, several group-communication researchers have discovered that groups do not necessarily solve problems in a linear, step-by-step process.[26] The process by which groups solve problems goes through several phases of growth and development as members interact.[27] Reflective thinking is most useful in helping groups understand the phases of problem solving. As Ernest Bormann has noted, "Difficulties arise when [group] participants demand rationality from a group throughout its deliberations."[28] To add flexibility to the reflective-thinking steps, a group may return to an earlier problem-solving step to help clarify the discussion. For example, after researching and analyzing a problem, a group may decide to define it a little differently than it had been defined previously. Perhaps after carefully trying to apply criteria to select the best solution, a group may decide that it needs to revise the criteria. Reflective thinking can serve as a general guide to the problem-solving process. Randy Hirokawa's research suggests that a systematic approach to group problem solving and decision making is better than no organized approach at all.[29]

In trying to apply reflective thinking to group problem solving, consider the following suggestions.

1. *Clearly identify the problem you are trying to solve.* Make sure that you are not just discussing a topic. For example, one group decided to discuss the quality of the U.S. judicial system. The group selected a topic area, but it did not identify a problem. It should have focused clearly on a specific problem, such as "How can we improve the quality of the judicial system in the United States?" or "What should be done to improve the education and training of lawyers in the United States?"

2. *Phrase the problem as a question to help guide group discussion.* Identifying your group's problem as a question adds focus and direction to your deliberations. When formulating a problem-solving discussion question, keep in mind the guidelines discussed in Chapter 7.

3. *Do not start suggesting solutions until you have analyzed the problem.* Many group-communication researchers agree that until your group has researched the problem, you may not have enough information and specific facts to reach the best solution.[30] You will be tempted to think of solutions to your problem almost as soon as you have identified it. By deferring the search for a solution, you will gain a greater understanding of the causes, effects, and symptoms of the problem.

4. *In the definition-and-analysis steps of reflective thinking, do not confuse the causes of the problem with its symptoms.* A fever and headache are symptoms and not necessarily causes of a patient's ill health. The cause may be a cold or flu virus or a number of other things. A doctor tries to identify the cause of symptoms by running tests and analyzing a patient's medical history. In other words, a doctor needs to define, analyze, and solve a problem. You should try to clarify the differences between the causes and the symptoms (effects) of a problem. Perhaps your only goal is to alleviate the symptoms. However, you can better understand what your group is trying to accomplish if you can distinguish causes and symptoms.

5. *Constantly evaluate your group's problem-solving method.* For many years the only problem-solving method suggested to group-discussion classes was reflective thinking. Some communication theorists suggest, however, that for certain types of problems, alternative problem-solving methods work just as well, if not better, than reflective thinking. The final part of this chapter will discuss some of these other problem-solving strategies.

6. *Appoint one or more group members to remind the group to use a structured method of solving problems.* One study found that groups who have a trained group member to help the group be mindful of the procedures it is using will make high-quality decisions.[31] Trained raters were instructed to remind the group to use effective problem-solving and decision-making skills by asking the following questions at appropriate times:

Do we have enough evidence to support our choice of solution?

Have we looked at a sufficient number of alternatives?

Have we reexamined alternatives we rejected previously?

Have we avoided stereotypical thinking or premature judgments?

Because you're taking a course in small group communication and you now know the importance of helping a group stay on track and be vigilant thinkers, you can periodically ask these questions. Even if you're not the appointed leader of a group, you can have a positive impact on the quality of the group's discussion by helping the group examine its process.

Brainstorming: A Creative Approach to Generating Ideas for Problem Solving

Imagine that your employer assigns you to a task force whose goal is to increase the productivity of your small manufacturing company. Phrased as a question, the problem is "What can be done to increase efficiency and productivity for our company?" Your group is supposed to come up with ideas to help solve the problem. Assume that your boss has clearly identified the problem for the group and has provided you with several documents analyzing the problem in some detail. Your group may decide that reflective thinking, which focuses on identifying and analyzing problems, may not be the best process to follow. Your group needs innovative ideas and creative, original solutions. Perhaps your group could benefit from brainstorming.

Brainstorming is a problem-solving approach designed to help a group generate several creative solutions to a problem. It was first developed by Alex Osborn, an advertising executive who felt the need for a problem-solving technique that instead of evaluating and criticizing ideas would focus on developing imaginative and innovative solutions.[32] Brainstorming has been used by businesses, committees, and government agencies to improve the quality of group decision making. Although it can be used in several phases of many group discussions, it may be most useful if a group needs original ideas or has trouble coming up with any ideas at all. Research suggests that group members who are trained to use creative approaches to problem solving participate more, produce more ideas, are

A group may be more creative while brainstorming when they are comfortable and in a relaxed environment. What environmental factors are helping people in this picture have a creative brainstorming session?

less critical of others, are generally more supportive, and use humor more often than individuals who are not trained to brainstorm.[33]

What enhances group creativity? Listing many ideas, breaking out of traditional thinking, identifying seemingly wild and far-out ideas, building on the ideas of others, and initially withholding evaluation all contribute to group creativity.[34]

Traditional Brainstorming Steps

Here is a step-by-step description of how to conduct traditional brainstorming.

1. *Select a specific problem that needs solving.* Be sure that all group members can identify and clearly define the problem.

2. *Ask group members to temporarily put aside all judgments and evaluations.* The key to brainstorming is ruling out all criticism and evaluation. Osborn makes these suggestions:

   Acquire a "try anything" attitude.

   Avoid criticism, which can stifle creativity.

   Remember that all ideas are thought-starters.

   Today's criticism may kill future ideas.

3. *Ask group or team members to think of as many possible solutions to the problem as they can and orally share the ideas with the group.* Consider the following suggestions:

   The wilder the ideas, the better.

   It is easier to tame ideas down than to think ideas up.

   Think out loud and mention unusual ideas.

Someone's wild idea may trigger a good solution from another person in the group.

4. *Make sure that the group understands that "piggybacking" off someone's idea is useful.* Combine ideas; add to previous ideas. Adopt this philosophy: Once an idea is contributed to the group, no one owns it. It belongs to the group and anyone can modify it.

5. *Have someone record all the ideas mentioned.* Ideas could be recorded on a flipchart, chalkboard or an overhead projector so that each group member can see them. You could also tape-record your discussions.

6. *Evaluate ideas when the time allotted for brainstorming has elapsed.* Consider these suggestions:

   Approach each idea positively, and give it a fair trial.

   Try to make ideas workable.

   Encourage feedback about the success of a session. If only a few of the ideas generated by a group are useful, the session has been successful.

Nominal–Group Technique: Using Silent Brainstorming to Generate Ideas

Nominal-group technique (NGT) is a procedure that uses some of the same principles and methods of brainstorming but has members write their ideas individually before sharing them with the group.[35] Nominal-group technique gets its name from the principle that the group is nominal (in name only), in the sense that members work on problems individually rather than during sustained group interaction. This technique uses **silent brainstorming** to overcome some of the disadvantages researchers have discovered in exclusively oral brainstorming.

Why does silent brainstorming often produce better results than verbal brainstorming? During traditional brainstorming, the group and team members blurt out ideas. But when someone laughs at an idea or says, "That's cool," or "That won't work," then ideas have been evaluated. *The key to making brainstorming work is that the generation of ideas is separated from the evaluation of ideas.* In oral brainstorming it's hard not to evaluate ideas. Thus, during traditional brainstorming, ideas are often evaluated as soon as they are verbalized, so group members may be less likely to share ideas. Criticism and evaluation diminish creativity. Even if group members do not verbalize their evaluation, their nonverbal expression often leaks positive or negative evaluation of ideas. Such evaluation tends to stifle creativity, and fewer people participate. Because we know that some people are apprehensive or nervous about speaking up in a group, traditional oral brainstorming makes it less likely that the communication-apprehensive members will participate. Silent brainstorming overcomes that problem by encouraging even the communication apprehensive group and team members to participate by first writing their ideas. Once they have a written "script," they are more comfortable sharing their ideas. In addition, when one person talks during a group discussion (or if several people talk) other members may stop and listen to the ideas presented. Researchers also found that people work more diligently if they have an individual assignment than if they have a group assignment.[36] In addition, researchers have found that sometimes when using traditional brainstorming, the creative talents of some members seem to be restricted just by the very presence of oth-

Collaborating

E T H I C A L L Y

Dave has a great idea and likes to take the lead during group discussions. During traditional brainstorming sessions, he often suggests more than anyone else. But he also just can't seem to avoid evaluating and criticizing other people's ideas. Dave's presence in a group sometimes intimidates others, so they don't contribute. Group members have asked Dave to resist evaluating other people's suggestions, but he just can't seem to stop doing it. Should the group ask Dave to leave the group? He makes a considerable contribution to the group but also limits the contributions of others. What are the ethical responsibilities of group members to balance the concern for an individual member of the group against the needs of the entire group?

ers.[37] Group and team members may generate more ideas if members first work alone and then regroup. After they reconvene, group members can modify, elaborate on, and evaluate ideas. The generation of ideas (writing them down) has been separated from the evaluation of ideas. Even before a group meets for the first time, you could describe a problem and ask group members to brainstorm individually before assembling. E-mail makes this easier. In the pages ahead, we'll talk about electronic brainstorming as a separate technique of developing creative ideas.

Nominal-group technique adds structure to the brainstorming process. The following steps summarize how to use NGT:

1. All group members should be able to define and analyze the problem under consideration.

2. Working individually, group members write down possible solutions to the problem.

3. Group members report the solutions they have identified to the entire group one at a time. Each idea should be noted on a chart, chalkboard, or overhead projector for all group members to see.

4. Group members discuss the ideas gathered, not to advocate for one idea over another but to make sure that all the ideas are clear.

5. After discussing all proposed solutions, each group member ranks the solutions. If the list of solutions is long, the group members can rank the five solutions they like best. The results are tabulated.

6. The entire group discusses the results of the rankings. If the first round of ranking is inconclusive or the group is not comfortable with the results, the options can be ranked again after additional discussion. Research suggests that using this organized method of gathering and evaluating information results in better solutions than if the group attacks a problem in a disorganized fashion.[38] One researcher has found that nominal-group technique works better than other prescriptive approaches such as reflective thinking.[39]

This individual method of idea generation and evaluation has the advantage of involving all group members in deliberations. It can be useful if some group members are unwilling or uncomfortable in making contributions because of status differences in the group. Also, alternating group discussion with individual deliberation can be useful in groups plagued by conflict and tension.

Both traditional brainstorming and nominal-group technique can be used at any phase of the problem-solving process. For example, you could combine nominal-group technique with force-field analysis by asking group members to silently brainstorm, driving and restraining forces toward group goal attainment. Or you could ask members to brainstorm possible causes or symptoms of the problem during problem analysis. When seeking strategies to implement a solution, again, you could use brainstorming or NGT to generate possible strategies.

Ballard Street by Jerry Van Amerongen

SHORT, RAPID STROKES...A LONGER DAGGING MOTION...LET'S THINK OF SOME OTHER POSSIBILITIES!

Barry loves to go around brainstorming.

Delphi Technique

Whereas the nominal-group technique invites participants to contribute ideas by first writing them down and then sharing with the group, the **Delphi Technique** takes this idea one step further. This method, named after the ancient oracle at Delphi, has been called "absentee brainstorming," because individuals share ideas in writing or via e-mail, without meeting face-to-face. One person coordinates the information and shares it with the rest of the group. This approach is especially useful when conflict within the group inhibits effective group interaction. It also is used when time and distance constraints make it difficult for group members to meet. Here is a step-by-step description of the Delphi technique.[40]

1. The group leader selects a problem, issue, policy, or decision that needs to be reviewed.

2. The leader corresponds with group members in writing, informing them of the task and inviting their suggestions and input. Often a specific questionnaire is developed or the group members are asked to individually brainstorm suggestions or reactions to the issue confronting the group.

3. The respondents complete the questionnaire or generate a brainstormed list of responses and send them to the leader.

4. The leader then summarizes all the responses from the group and shares the summary with all group members, asking for additional ideas, suggestions, and reactions. Team members are asked to rate or rank the ideas and return their comments to the leader.

T E C H N O L O G Y

*E*lectronic brainstorming is a method that makes it possible for a group to generate solutions or strategies by typing ideas at a computer keyboard and having them displayed to the entire group. This high-tech method resembles nominal-group technique in that group members write ideas before sharing them with the group. By seeing the ideas as they are written, either at the individual workstation or on a large screen, group members can piggyback off the ideas of others. Electronic brainstorming can be performed with all group members in the same room or computer lab or when they are at their computers either in their offices or home.

Research suggests that groups using electronic brainstorming generate more ideas than traditional face-to-face brainstorming groups.[42] One group-communication research team found that when some groups include face-to-face members supported with ideas from group members not physically present but using electronic means to share information, more ideas are generated and are of higher quality than when only face-to-face groups generate ideas.[44] Some researchers theorize that this happens because the ideas are generated anonymously.[43] Members feel less fear or anxiety about being criticized for unconventional ideas because no one knows who suggested them. Thus, when group members move to the phase of evaluating ideas, they are not sure whether they are evaluating an idea coming from a boss or a group leader or a new intern. All ideas are considered, based not on who suggested them but on their merit and quality. Another reason more ideas may be generated is because of the "piggyback effect." Group members may be stimulated to build on the ideas of other group members.

One obvious disadvantage to electronic brainstorming is the need to have access to a computer network and appropriate software. But recent evidence strongly supports the value of this variation of the brainstorming method by using computers to add structure to the process.

5. The leader continues the process of summarizing the group feedback and asking for more input until general consensus emerges and decisions are made. It may take several rounds of soliciting ideas and evaluating ideas before consensus is achieved.

This method often produces many good ideas. All participants are treated equally, because no one is aware of who submitted which idea. It is, however, a time-consuming process. And because there is no face-to-face interaction, some ideas worth elaboration and exploration may get lost in the shuffle. Using the Delphi technique in combination with face-to-face meetings can help eliminate some disadvantages of the procedure.

Affinity Technique

Have you ever sat down at a desk cluttered with papers from a variety of projects and realized that you needed to sort the papers into piles to help you organize your desk? **Affinity**

technique is a method that uses Post-it notes to sort through and organize ideas that a group may generate.[41] Affinity technique is similar to the nominal-group technique but instead of listing ideas on paper, group members write ideas on Post-it notes. Like the other variations of brainstorming that we've discussed, the group is given the issue or problem about which to generate ideas. The entire group (or a smaller subcommittee) then organizes the ideas into categories that have an "affinity" or are similar to each other.

Affinity technique is a way to make brainstorming sessions more fun and incorporate movement into the meeting. You can ask group members to post their notes on the wall or other smooth surface such as a chalkboard or dry-erase board and then to move around the room, review the ideas, and group them into categories. If your group sticks the notes on a chalkboard, you could draw a circle around the notes and label the category using a word or terms that capture the theme of the suggestions. This technique will allow your group to quickly identify how many people have generated the same idea. The group will be able to see that one affinity category may have six or seven ideas whereas another category may have only one or two. After the categories are created, the group may then decide to combine categories. Someone should be assigned to record the ideas that have been developed. Affinity technique may take a bit longer than nominal-group technique, but for certain groups it may be the best way to develop a sense of collaboration in generating ideas.

REVIEW

Comparing Brainstorming Methods

	ADVANTAGES	DISADVANTAGES
Traditional brainstorming	Easy to use	High potential for group members to evaluate ideas while generating ideas
	No special materials needed	Takes more time than highly-structured methods
	Group members can piggy-back off of ideas suggested	Quiet members less likely to participate
Nominal-group technique	Can build on ideas of others	Needs good leader to organize the process
	Provides a written record of ideas suggested	Less time for free flow of ideas
	Controls more talkative, dominating group members	Difficult to implement with a large group
Delphi technique	Group does not have to meet face-to-face	No synergy created by hearing the ideas of others
	Provides a written record of ideas suggested	Minimizes opportunities or elaborating on ideas
	Helps group members prepare for upcoming meeting	Group members may be suspicious that someone has manipulated the results

Affinity technique	Builds acceptance	Need Post-it notes
	Provides for interaction and acceptance of ideas	Takes more time
	Preserves a written record of ideas presented	No accommodation for second round of generating ideas
Electronic brainstorming	Very efficient	Need special equipment
	Anonymity increases number of ideas	Need training in using computer software
	More ideas can be generated	Need more time to describe procedures of electronic brainstorming

Source: Adapted from Eileen K. Aranda, Luis Aranda, and Kristi Conlon, *Teams: Structure, Process, Culture, and Politics* (Upper Saddle River, NJ: Prentice Hall, 1998) 89.

How to Apply Brainstorming to Your Group or Team

Although you should now understand how brainstorming, in its various forms, works, you may still have some questions about how you can apply this method of creative problem solving to your group discussions. Consider the following suggestions:[45]

1. *Do not make the time limit for brainstorming too short.* Research suggests that groups that are given only a short time for brainstorming (four minutes) can be very productive, but not as creative as groups that have a longer time.[46] If you are brainstorming orally, do not worry about a little silence while people are thinking. If you are using silent brainstorming (nominal-group technique), it is okay if people are not writing furiously during the entire brainstorming period.

2. *Be certain that each group or team member understands the specific problem the group is trying to solve.* A problem must be clearly defined and understood and must also be limited in size and scope. A broad, vaguely worded problem must be clarified before a group attempts to identify possible solutions.

3. *Make sure that the brainstorming is part of an overall problem-solving strategy.* As with reflective thinking, group members need to define and analyze the problem under consideration, provided that it has not already been identified for them.[47] One difference between a creative problem-solving method such as brainstorming and traditional reflective thinking is that those using the brainstorming apply criteria for solutions *after* they generate possible solutions. Otherwise, criteria may put a damper on group creativity. Instead of developing solutions according to established criteria, when brainstorming members evaluate possible solutions after several options are generated.

4. *Make sure that each group member follows the brainstorming rules.* Brainstorming will be most effective if group members stop criticizing and evaluating ideas. Do not forget that group members can criticize nonverbally through tone of voice, facial expression,

or posture. Everyone in the group must feel completely free to communicate ideas that may solve the problem. What should you do if a few members just cannot stop evaluating the ideas that are suggested? You may have to (1) remind them courteously to follow the rules, (2) ask them to be quiet, (3) ask them to record the ideas of others, or (4) ask them to leave the group. You may also consider using another technique (nominal-group, affinity, or electronic brainstorming) as an alternative to oral brainstorming.

5. *If you are serving as the group's leader, try to draw less-talkative group members into the discussion.* Call people by name: "Curt, you look like you've got some good ideas. What do you suggest?" You can also compliment the entire group when members are doing a good job of generating ideas: "Good job, group! We've got thirty ideas so far. Let's see if we can come up with thirty more."

6. *Set aside a definite amount of time for brainstorming.* Decide as a group how much time you want to devote to brainstorming. As we have discussed, be sure to give yourself plenty—it is better to have too much time than too little. You may want to set a goal for a certain number of ideas that should be recorded: "We'll stop brainstorming when we get sixty ideas."

7. *Consider reverse brainstorming.*[48] This method asks group members to brainstorm ideas or solutions that would make the problem *worse*. After generating such a list, consider the implications of doing the opposite of what was identified.

8. *Consider rolestorming.*[49] This method asks group members to assume the roles of someone other than themselves to help unlock ideas and increase group creativity. If you are focusing on a problem in your community, ask group members to assume the role of the mayor, superintendent of schools, or city manager. If it is a government problem, have them imagine that they are the governor, a member of the legislature, or even the president of the United States.

9. *Tell the group what will happen with the ideas and suggestions that are generated.*[50] Do not just finish the brainstorming session with a long list of ideas that may be shelved. Perhaps a subcommittee can be formed to combine ideas and eliminate obvious overlapping suggestions. The subgroup might also be asked to evaluate the ideas or determine which ideas need further exploration or more information.

10. *Try the random-word technique.* One strategy to enhance the power of brainstorming that seems to work for some groups is the **random-word technique**. As described by Edward de Bono, while a group is brainstorming or pondering a problem, one person is assigned the task of saying a random word so others can hear it. The word is selected from a list of random words.[51] The spoken word is supposed to act as a trigger for new or creative ideas. This technique helps groups, say those who've tried it, "think outside the box."

Does using creative approaches to problem solving really work? Research strongly suggests the answer is a resounding yes. One study found that group members who were trained in creative problem solving, including brainstorming and other structured methods, came up with better ideas than groups whose members were not trained. In addition, group members who were trained to use such skills participated in the discussion more, criticized ideas less, were more likely to support ideas, laughed and smiled more, and produced more ideas than those who were not trained. Specifically, group members in the trained group were taught a six-stage model of creative problem solving:

Step 1. Mess finding: Isolating a concern or problem on which to work.

Step 2. Data finding: Generating and selecting the most important data regarding the mess.

Step 3. Problem finding: Generating and selecting a statement that captures the "essence" of the situation.

Step 4. Idea finding: Generating and selecting the best available alternative(s) for solving the problem.

Step 5. Solution finding: Using criteria to screen, select, and support ideas selected in idea finding.

Step 6. Acceptance finding: Generating ways to implement the solution and developing a plan for action.[52]

REVIEW

Traditional Problem–Solving Steps and Techniques

STEPS	TECHNIQUES
Identify and define the problem	Is/is not analysis Journalist's six questions Gather data Pareto charts
Analyze the problem	Is/is not analysis Cause-and-effect (fishbone) diagram Journalist's six questions Force-field analysis Develop criteria Identify history, causes, effects, symptoms, goals, obstacles
Generate solutions	Brainstorm Rolestorm Reverse brainstorm Nominal-group technique Delphi technique Affinity technique Electronic brainstorming
Select the best solution or combination of solutions	Compare pros and cons Apply solutions to criteria

	Appoint a subgroup
	Combine alternatives
	Average rankings and ratings
Test and implement the solution	Identify implementation steps
	Develop a group action plan
	Develop a flowchart

Question–Oriented Approaches to Problem Solving

As discussed earlier, a group adopts a problem-solving format mainly to organize its deliberations and reach its goal more efficiently. Thus far, the chapter has discussed a traditional problem-solving format (reflective thinking) and a method of generating creative ideas (brainstorming). A third approach to problem solving requires groups to consider a series of questions to keep them oriented toward their goal. Two such approaches will be discussed in the following sections: (1) the ideal-solution format and (2) the single-question format. Both formats have groups consider a series of questions to help identify the critical issues they need to resolve. The questions also provide an orderly sequence of thought to help groups formulate the best possible solutions.

Ideal–Solution Format

Obviously, problem-solving groups want to identify the best solutions to problems. In the **ideal-solution format**, groups answer questions designed to help them identify ideal solutions. Alvin Goldberg and Carl Larson have devised the following agenda of questions:

1. Do all members agree on the nature of the problem?

2. What would be the ideal solution from the point of view of all parties involved in the problem?

3. What conditions within the problem could be changed so that the ideal solution might be achieved?

4. Of the solutions available, which one best approximates the ideal solution?[53]

These questions help groups recognize the barriers that the problems under consideration have created. The questions also encourage groups to analyze their problem's cause and to evaluate proposed solutions. The advantage of the ideal-solution format over other problem-solving approaches is its simplicity. Group members simply consider each of the questions listed previously, one at a time. One expert recommends the ideal-solution format for discussions that involve people with varied interests; this format works best when acceptance of a solution is important.[54] The format enables group members to see the problem from several viewpoints in their search for the best solution.

Although the ideal-solution format is similar to reflective thinking, its chief value is that it uses questions to help a group systematically identify and analyze a problem, pinpoint the best possible solution, and formulate specific methods for achieving a solution. Like the other problem-solving formats presented in this chapter, it helps a group—particularly one with varying viewpoints and experiences—to focus on a problem and devise ways to solve it in a rational, structured way.

Single-Question Format

Like the ideal-solution format, the **single-question format** poses a series of questions designed to guide the group toward a best solution. Goldberg and Larson suggest that the answers to the following five questions can help a group achieve its goal:

1. What is the question whose answer the group needs to know in order to accomplish its purpose?

2. What subquestions must be answered before the group can answer the single question it has formulated?

3. Does the group have sufficient information to answer the subquestions confidently?

4. What are the most reasonable answers to the subquestions?

5. Assuming that the answers to the subquestions are correct, what is the best solution to the problem?[55]

Unlike the ideal-solution format, the single-question format requires a group to formulate a question to help obtain the information needed to solve a problem. The single-question format also helps a group identify and resolve issues that must be confronted before it can reach a solution. As Goldberg and Larson note, "An assumption of the single-question form seems to be that issues must be resolved, however tentatively."[56] Thus the single-question format would probably work best if a group is capable of reaching reasonable agreement on the issues and agreeing on how the issues can be resolved. A group characterized by conflict and contention would probably not find the single-question approach productive.

The success of the single-question format depends on a group's agreeing on the subissues before trying to agree on the major issues. If you are working with a group that has difficulty reaching agreement, the single-question format may not be the best approach. The group may become bogged down arguing about trivial matters while the major issues go unanswered. Decide whether your group will be able to reach agreement on the minor issues before you decide to use the single-question format. If your group cannot reach agreement, either the ideal-solution format or the reflective-thinking format may be a better method of organizing your group's deliberations.

How to Apply Question–Oriented Approaches to Your Group or Team

You may have noticed some similarities among the single-question, the ideal-solution, and the reflective-thinking formats. All these approaches suggest that a group should begin its deliberations by trying to define the problem or attempting to formulate a question that will focus the discussion. After a group zeroes in on key issues, members next must analyze the problem. The ideal-solution format suggests that the group formulate criteria to direct its search for a solution, whereas the single-question format asks a group to identify and answer subquestions to help formulate a solution.

By guiding groups toward their goals with questions, the ideal-solution and single-question formats help groups agree on minor issues before they try to agree on solutions to problems. Carl Larson tried to find out whether an ideal-solution, single-question, or

Recording group members' ideas on a flip chart can help provide necessary structure when the group is trying to solve problems. What other equipment might help solve group problems?

reflective-thinking format, or no format at all, would produce better solutions.[57] His study indicates that ideal-solution and single-question formats generated better solutions than did the reflective-thinking approach. All three approaches fared better than no approach at all. Whereas just one laboratory study does not prove that the single-question and ideal-solution formats are superior to the reflective-thinking format, it does suggest that under certain conditions goal-oriented approaches may have certain advantages. In Larson's study, when groups were given alternatives and told to choose the best solution to a problem, their discussions lasted only about twenty minutes. Thus, by considering specific questions, members were able to solve problems efficiently. Norman Maier also concluded that a problem-solving approach that has a group consider minor issues before major issues can improve group decisions.[58] Clearly, theorists need to conduct additional research before they can prescribe specific formulas to ensure efficiency in group problem solving.

If you are going to lead a group discussion, the following suggestions may help you apply the ideal-solution and single-question approaches to problem solving:

1. *If you are going to use the ideal-solution or single-question approach, provide group members with copies of the questions that will guide their discussion.* You can reduce some of the uncertainty that occurs normally in groups by making sure that each person knows the procedure. Tell the group to use the questions as a guide.

2. *Explain why you are using the format you have selected.* Most groups are willing to go along with a particular discussion agenda, especially if you give them reasons for having selected it. Tell the group that considering specific questions in a developmental format can keep the discussion on track. If your group has a specified time period

in which to meet, you can explain that using questions to guide the discussion can help make the discussion more efficient.

3. *Keep the discussion focused on the specific question under consideration.* If you have provided copies of the questions for either the ideal-solution or single-question format, some group members may be tempted to skip a question or may want to discuss an unrelated issue. You may have to help the group focus on one question at a time. Several studies suggest that groups with members who try to keep participants aware of the pertinent issues by summarizing the discussion and requesting clarification have a good chance of agreeing on a solution and of being satisfied with their discussion.[59]

4. *Agree to use a collaborative approach to solving the problem.* Frank LaFasto and Carl Larson suggest that the single-question format can be enhanced if group members explicitly consider the question "What principles should we agree on in order to maintain a reasonable and collaborative approach through the [problem-solving] process?"[60] Consider this question early in the problem-solving process. Making collaboration a problem-solving value can enhance teamwork and cooperation.

Beyond Technique

Throughout this book we've offered skills, strategies, tips, and techniques for improving group process. We conclude this chapter that is chock full of specific group techniques with a caution: Participating in groups and teams is more than applying simple "how to's." The zipping, buzzing, humming, halting, and cacophonous process of communicating in groups and teams is often complicated. Based on systems theory, which we discussed in Chapter 2, group communication is an interrelated, fragile process in which each person or element in the system affects the entire group. Groups and team research has not advanced to a state where we can certify that using the various techniques we've discussed will *always* result in high-quality solutions and decisions. Working in a group is more complicated than that.[61]

How do you know when to reach for a specific technique to help improve the group's process? The key, we believe, is to listen to your group, watch, observe, and identify what the group needs at a given time. In a word: Adapt. Adapt to the needs of the group rather than assuming that a predetermined strategy or technique will somehow miraculously help the group or team achieve a breakthrough. If the group seems confused, disoriented, or stuck when defining or analyzing the task in front of it then a more-structured technique such as the cause-and-effect diagram, or force-field analysis may be what the group needs. But if the group is making progress, we don't recommend that you haul out a group technique such as nominal-group technique, Delphi technique, a T-chart, or other structured technique. The power of a group does not reside in technique. In fact, group researchers have had some difficulty documenting precisely what makes a group successful in all situations. We don't believe groups will always be successful. There is no *one* approach or technique that always works. Use your knowledge of group problem-solving techniques in combination with your understanding of group process to assess whether your group needs the structure of a specific technique or tool. Effective groups and group members thoughtfully use techniques and strategies to help them make progress toward their goal depending on what is (or is not) happening in the group. Use techniques wisely.

Putting Principles into Practice

In this chapter we discussed several prescriptive approaches that a group or team can use to solve a problem. Groups often need some plan or structure to help their members define, analyze, and solve a problem. We described four kinds of problem-solving formats: (1) reflective thinking, (2) brainstorming, (3) ideal solution, and (4) single question. Review the following suggestions for applying these problem-solving approaches to the groups in which you participate.

Reflective Thinking: Traditional Problem Solving

▶ To help your group or team define and limit a problem, phrase it as a question.

▶ Do not start suggesting solutions until your group has thoroughly analyzed a problem.

▶ Consider using tools such as *is/is not* analysis, force-field analysis, journalist's six questions, Pareto charts, and cause-and-effect (fishbone) diagrams to help your group analyze the problem.

▶ Formulate criteria for a good solution before you begin suggesting solutions.

▶ Use brainstorming to help your group generate possible solutions.

▶ If the other group members agree, you may need to change the criteria you have selected during the analysis phase of reflective thinking.

▶ Make sure that reflective thinking is the best method for your group; another problem-solving approach may work better.

▶ To help make sure that everyone knows and follows through on his or her assignment, consider using an action chart or a flowchart.

Brainstorming

▶ Make sure all team members understand the ground rules for brainstorming. Do not evaluate solutions until you have finished brainstorming.

▶ If group members do not follow the brainstorming rules, you may have to (1) restate the rules, (2) ask them to keep quiet, (3) ask them to record the ideas of others, or (4) ask them to leave the group.

▶ If oral brainstorming does not work, consider having each member of the group work individually; consider using other brainstorming formats such as Delphi, nominal-group, affinity, and electronic brainstorming.

▶ Try to draw less-talkative group members into the discussion; compliment members when they come up with good ideas.

▶ Set aside a definite amount of time for brainstorming.

Ideal Solution and Single Question

▶ If you are the leader of the group, tell the group why you have selected either the ideal-solution format or the single-question approach to problem solving.

▶ Use the ideal-solution format to help the group come to an agreement on the nature of the problem.

▶ Use the single-question format if you are sure that your group is capable of agreeing on the issues and on how they can be resolved.

▶ Provide members with copies of the questions used in the ideal-solution format or the single-question format; this will help to keep your discussion on track.

▶ Remind group members to address only those questions and issues that are relevant to the discussion.

PRACTICE

A CASE STUDY: THE COMPANY LAYOFF[62]

In this case study, imagine that you are one of the managers of a department store in your community. You have just been informed by your supervisor that one of your employees will have to be laid off because of company cutbacks. You are now meeting with your managerial colleagues to decide which employee will be chosen. All employees listed work full-time, and all work the same number of hours. There is one formal rule you have to follow: The basis for laying a person off must be a job-related reason. Please make the best decision you can with the limited information you are given. Be prepared to discuss the reasoning behind your group's decision.

List of Employees

Masha   Aged 33, married, with two children, Masha has worked for the company for five years. She loves her job and works with little or no supervision. You have considered giving her a promotion when the opportunity arises. Other people go to Masha when they have questions, because she trains well. She has been going to school part time to get a management degree and will graduate in another year.

Bob   Aged 49, divorced, with one child, Bob has worked with the company for 22 years. He keeps to himself but always gets work done. You never have to give Bob instructions, because he knows his job so well. Others in the department call him "Pop" because he seems to parent everyone and is well liked. He really adds a great deal of stability to your department. He does not want to change his job at all because he is happy. You put Bob in charge in your absence.

Trent   Aged 19, single, a Navajo, Trent just began working for your company 11 months ago. He went to an accelerated school as a child and started college when he was 15 years old. He has since graduated with a business degree and shows promise of going far in your company. He is already the best salesperson in your department. Most people get along with him well. Because he is new, Trent needs a lot of training, but his sales are worth your extra time.

Madeline Madeline is 25, married, and three months pregnant. She transferred to your store only last month but has over three years total experience in the company. You have not been very well satisfied with her attendance because she is calling in sick a lot. However, she is the only person that you feel you can give your most difficult tasks to, because she is very thorough. She also has had more customer compliments than any other person in your department.

Catrina   Catrina is 40, single, has three children, and is a recovering alcoholic. She fulfills a very necessary function in your department by doing maintenance work, which no one else really has time for. Catrina is efficient and is never late; however, she does not really associate with the others. She has worked with the company for over 10 years but she cannot read or write; it is likely that this is one of the few places she could find work.

Antonio   Aged 27, single, with no children, Antonio has worked for two years in your department and, in that time, has won three awards for creating outstanding merchandise displays (the heart and soul of retail). He is your most conscientious worker and keeps your department looking great. You have wondered, though, whether he comes to work under the influence of drugs. Several customers have complained about poor grooming habits and language he used toward them. In the last month, however, he has made significant improvements.

Earthquake

According to the *Worst-Case Scenario Survival Handbook*, there are certain do's and don'ts if you experience an earthquake.[63] First, individually rank-order the following suggestions from most important to least important. Then work with a small group to compare and revise your answers based on the collective wisdom of the group. Your instructor will give you the experts' rankings.

1.   If you are driving, stop, but carefully.   _____

2.   Check food and water supplies.   _____

3.   Check for gas leaks and damaged electrical wires.   _____

4. Put on a pair of thick-soled shoes. ———

5. Be prepared for aftershocks. ———

6. If you are indoors, stay indoors. ———

7. Check for injuries and apply first aid. ———

8. Get out in the open if you are inside. ———

9. In you are in a mountainous area, watch out for landslides. ———

Assessing Problem-Solving Group Competencies[64]

Use the following evaluation form to assess the presence or absence of small group communication competencies in a group or team discussion. Competencies are specific behaviors that group and team members perform (review Chapter 1, pages 23 and 24). This assessment form includes nine competencies organized into four general categories. Here's how to use the form:

1. Observe a group or team that is attempting to solve a problem. Write the names of the group members at the top of the form. (If the group includes more than six group members, photocopy the form so that each group member can be evaluated.)

2. When using the form, first decide whether each group member has performed each competency. Circle "NO" if the group member was not observed performing the competency. Circle "YES" if you did observe the group member performing the competency,(e.g., defining the problem, analyzing the problem, identifying criteria, and so on.)

3. For each competency for which you circled "YES," determine how effectively the competency was performed. Use the scale, which ranges from 0 to 3.

    0 = This competency was performed, but it was inappropriately or inadequately performed. For example, the person observed tried to define the problem but did so poorly.

    1 = Overall, there was an adequate performance of this competency.

    2 = Overall, there was a good performance of this competency.

    3 = Overall, there was an excellent performance of this competency.

4. Total the score for each group member in each of the four categories.

    The first category, *Problem-Oriented Competencies*, consists of items 1 and 2. These behaviors help the group or team member define and analyze the problem. If the competency was performed, the total number of points will range from 0 to 6. The higher the number of points, the better the individual performed on this competency.

    Solution-Oriented Competencies include items, 3, 4, and 5, with a point range from 0–9. These competencies focus on how well the group or team member helped develop and evaluate a solution to the problem.

    Discussion-Management Competencies. Competencies that helped the group or team remain focused or helped the group manage interaction are items 6 and 7. The points for this category range from 0 to 6.

Competent Group Communicator

PROBLEM-SOLVING GROUP-COMMUNICATION COMPETENCIES	GROUP MEMBER		GROUP MEMBER	
PROBLEM-ORIENTED COMPETENCIES				
1. Defined the problem the group attempted to solve	NO	YES 0 1 2 3	NO	YES 0 1 2 3
2. Analyzed the problem the group attempted to solve. Used relevant information, data or evidence, discussed the causes, obstacles, history, symptoms, or significance of the problem.	NO	YES 0 1 2 3	NO	YES 0 1 2 3
SOLUTION-ORIENTED COMPETENCIES				
3. Identified criteria for an appropriate solution to the problem.	NO	YES 0 1 2 3	NO	YES 0 1 2 3
4. Generated solutions or alternatives to the problem.	NO	YES 0 1 2 3	NO	YES 0 1 2 3
5. Evaluated solution(s): Identified positive or negative consequences of the proposed solutions.	NO	YES 0 1 2 3	NO	YES 0 1 2 3
DISCUSSION-MANAGEMENT COMPETENCIES				
6. Maintained task focus: Helped the group stay on or return to the task, issue, or topic the group was discussing.	NO	YES 0 1 2 3	NO	YES 0 1 2 3
7. Managed group interaction: Appropriately initiated and terminated discussion, contributed to the discussion, or invited others to contribute to the discussion.	NO	YES 0 1 2 3	NO	YES 0 1 2 3
RELATIONAL COMPETENCIES				
8. Managed conflict: Appropriately and constructively helped the group stay focused on issues rather than personalities when conflict occured.	NO	YES 0 1 2 3	NO	YES 0 1 2 3
9. Maintained climate: Offered positive verbal comments or nonverbal expressions which helped maintain a positive group climate.	NO	YES 0 1 2 3	NO	YES 0 1 2 3

SCORING: NO = Not observed   YES   0 = Overall inappropriate or inadequate performance of competency   1 = Overall adequate performance of competency

Problem-Oriented Competencies (0–6)		
Solution-Oriented Competencies (0–9)		
Discussion-Mangement Competencies (0–6)		
Relational Competencies (0–6)		

GROUP MEMBER	GROUP MEMBER	GROUP MEMBER	GROUP MEMBER	GROUP ASSESSMENT
NO YES 0 1 2 3	NO YES 0 1 2 3	NO YES 0 1 2 3	NO YES 0 1 2 3	NO YES 0 1 2 3
NO YES 0 1 2 3	NO YES 0 1 2 3	NO YES 0 1 2 3	NO YES 0 1 2 3	NO YES 0 1 2 3
NO YES 0 1 2 3	NO YES 0 1 2 3	NO YES 0 1 2 3	NO YES 0 1 2 3	NO YES 0 1 2 3
NO YES 0 1 2 3	NO YES 0 1 2 3	NO YES 0 1 2 3	NO YES 0 1 2 3	NO YES 0 1 2 3
NO YES 0 1 2 3	NO YES 0 1 2 3	NO YES 0 1 2 3	NO YES 0 1 2 3	NO YES 0 1 2 3
NO YES 0 1 2 3	NO YES 0 1 2 3	NO YES 0 1 2 3	NO YES 0 1 2 3	NO YES 0 1 2 3
NO YES 0 1 2 3	NO YES 0 1 2 3	NO YES 0 1 2 3	NO YES 0 1 2 3	NO YES 0 1 2 3
NO YES 0 1 2 3	NO YES 0 1 2 3	NO YES 0 1 2 3	NO YES 0 1 2 3	NO YES 0 1 2 3
NO YES 0 1 2 3	NO YES 0 1 2 3	NO YES 0 1 2 3	NO YES 0 1 2 3	NO YES 0 1 2 3

2 = Overall good
performance of
competency

3 = Overall excellent
performance of
competency

Relational-Management Competencies are behaviors that focus on dealing with conflict and developing a positive, supportive group climate. Items 8 and 9 reflect this competency; points range from 0 to 6.

5. You can also assess the overall group's or team's ability to perform these competencies. The column marked "Group Assessment" can be used to record your overall impression of how effectively the group or team behaved. Circle "NO" if no one in the group performed this competency. Circle "YES" if at least one person in the group or team performed this competency. Then evaluate how well the entire group performed this competency, using the 0 to 3 scale (0=the competency was observed but was not performed appropriately or effectively.)

Sometimes it is difficult to make so many judgment about group competencies by just viewing a group discussion once. Many people find that it's easier to videotape the group discussion so that you can observe the group discussion more than once.

 Your companion Website has more practice activities, questionnaires, and checklists!
www.ablongman.com/beebe

Notes

1. John K. Brilhart and Lurene M. Jochem, "Effects of Different Patterns on Outcomes of Problem-Solving Discussion," *Journal of Applied Psychology* 48 (1964): 174–79; William E. Jurma, "Effects of Leader Structuring Style and Task Orientation Characteristics of Group Members," *Communication Monographs* 49 (1979): 282–95; Susan Jarboe, "A Comparison of Input-Output, Process-Output, and Input-Process-Output Models of Small Group Problem-Solving Effectiveness," *Communication Monographs* 55 (June 1988): 121–42; Arthur B. VanGundy, *Techniques of Structured Problem Solving* (New York: Van Nostrand Reinhold, 1981).

2. John K. Brilhart and Gloria J. Galanes, *Effective Group Discussion* (Dubuque, IA: Brown, 1992); John F. Cragan and David W. Wright, *Communication in Small Group Discussions* (St. Paul: West, 1986); Brilhart and Jochem, "Effects of Different Patterns on Outcomes of Problem-Solving Discussion"; John Dewey, *How We Think* (Boston: Heath, 1910); R. C. Huseman, "The Role of the Nominal-Group in Small Group-communication," in R. C. Huseman, C. M. Logue, and D. L. Freshley, eds., *Readings in Interpersonal and Organizational Communication*, 3rd ed. (Boston: Holbrook, 1977), 493–507; Carl E. Larson, "Forms of Analysis and Small Group Problem Solving," *Speech Monographs* 36 (1969): 452–55; Norman R. F. Maier, *Problem Solving and Creativity in Individuals and Groups* (Belmont, CA: Brooks/Cole, 1970); James H. McBuirney and Kenneth G. Hance, *The Principles and Methods of Discussion* (New York: Harper, 1939); Raymond S. Ross, *Speech Communication: Fundamentals and Practice* (New York: McGraw-Hill, 1974); David W. Wright, *Small Group-Communication: An Introduction* (Dubuque, IA: Kendall/Hunt, 1975); Charles H. Kepner and Benjamin B. Tregoe, *The Rational Manager* (New York: McGraw-Hill, 1965); Philip B. Crosby, *The Quality Is Free: The Art of Making Quality Certain* (New York: New American Library, 1979); Sud Ingle, *Quality Circles Master Guide: Increasing Productivity with People Power* (Englewood Cliffs, NJ: Prentice-Hall, 1982); Kenneth J. Albert, *How to Solve Business Problems* (New York: McGraw-Hill, 1978); Donald L. Dewar, *Quality Circle Leader Manual and Instructional Guide* (Red Bluff, CA: Quality Circle Institute, 1980);

Dennis S. Gouran, *Discussion: The Process of Group Decision-Making* (New York: Harper & Row, 1974); Arthur B. VanGundy, *Techniques of Structured Problem Solving* (New York: Van Nostrand Reinhold, 1981); Frank LaFasto and Carl Larson, *When Teams Work Best* (Thousand Oaks, CA: Sage, 2001).

3. Dewey, *How We Think;* see also R. Victor Harnack, "John Dewey and Discussion," *Western Speech* 32 (Spring 1969): 137–149.

4. For a complete discussion of the history of teaching group discussion, see Herman Cohen, *The History of Speech Communication: The Emergence of a Discipline, 1914–1945* (Annandale, VA: Speech Communication Association, 1994) 274–322.

5. For an excellent discussion of the history of teaching group discussion, see D. S. Gouran, "Communication in Groups: The Emergence and Evolution of a Field of Study," in L. R. Frey, ed., *The Handbook of Group Communication Theory and Research* (Thousand Oaks, CA: Sage, 1999) 3–36.

6. Robert F. Bales, *Interaction Process Analysis* (Chicago, IL: University of Chicago Press, 1976).

7. For an excellent summary of the literature documenting these problems, see Sunwolf and D. R. Seibold, "The Impact of Formal Procedures on Group Processes, Members, and Task Outcomes," in L. Frey, ed., *The Handbook of Group Communication Theory and Research*, (Thousand Oaks, CA:Sage, 1999) 395–431.

8.. Dennis S. Gouran, Candace Brown, and David R. Henry, "Behavioral Correlates of Perceptions of Quality in Decision-Making Discussion," *Communication Monographs* 45 (1978): 60–65; Linda L. Putnam, "Preference for Procedural Order in Task-Oriented Small Groups," *Communication Monographs* 46 (1979): 193–218; see also VanGundy, *Techniques of Structured Problem Solving*; B. J. Broome and L. Fulbright "A Multistage Influence Model of Barriers to Group Problem Solving: Participant-Generated Agenda for Small Group Research," *Small Group Research* 26 (1995): 25–55; J. P. Klubuilt and P. F. Green, *The Team-Based Problem Solver* (Burr Ridge, IL: Irwin, 1994).

9. David M. Berg, "A Descriptive Analysis of the Distribution and Duration of Themes Discussed by Task-Oriented Small Groups," *Speech Monographs* 34 (1967): 172–75; see also Ernest G. Bormann and Nancy C. Bormann, *Effective Small Group Communication*, 2nd ed. (Minneapolis: Burgess, 1976) 132; Marshall Scott Poole, "Decision Development in Small Groups III: A Multiple Sequence Model of Group Decision Development," *Communication Monographs* 50 (1983): 321–41.

10. R. Y. Hirokawa, R. Ice, and J. Cook, "Preference for Procedural Order, Discussion Structure and Group Decision Performance," *Communication Quarterly* 36 (Summer 1988): 217–26.

11. J. G. Oetzel, "Explaining Individual Communication Processes in Homogeneous and Heterogeneous Groups Through Individualism Collectivism and Self-Construal," *Human Communication Research*, 25 (1998): 202–224.

12. S. R. Hiltz, K. Johnson, and M. Turoff, "Experiments in Group Decision Making: Communication Process and Outcome in Face-to-Face Versus Computerized Conferences, *Human Communication Research* 13 (Winter 1986): 225–52.

13. C. A. Van Lear and E. A. Mabry, "Testing Contrasting Interaction Models for Discriminating Between Consensual and Dissent Decision-Making Groups," *Small Group Research* 30 (1999), 29–58; R. Y. Hirokawa, "Group Communication and Decision-Making Performance: A continued Test of the Functional Perspective," *Human Communication Research* 14 (1985): 487–515.

14. For an excellent review of the literature about various rational and nonrational problem-solving methods, see S. Jarboe, "Procedures for Enhancing Group Decision Making," in R.

Y. Hirokawa and M. S. Poole, eds., *Communication and Group Decision Making* (Thousand Oaks, CA: Sage, 1996).

15. See Charles H. Kepner and Benjamin B. Tregoe, *The Rational Manager* (New York: McGraw-Hill, 1965); our application of is / is not analysis is based on Dennis A. Romig and Laurie J. Romig, *Structured Teamwork ® Guide* (Austin, TX: Performance Resources, 1990); See also Dennis A. Romig, *Breakthrough Teamwork: Outstanding Results Using Structured Teamwork ®* (Chicago: Irwin, 1996).

16. This discussion of the journalist's six questions is based on a discussion by Julius E. Eitington, *The Winning Trainer* (Houston, TX: Gulf Publishing, 1989) 157.

17. P. R. Scholtes, B. L. Joiner, and B. J. Streibel, *The Team Handbook* (Madison, WI: Jointer and Associates, 1996) 2–20.

18. Kurt Lewin, "Frontiers in Group Dynamics," *Human Relations* 1 (1947): 5–42.

19. Eitington, *The Winning Trainer*, 158.

20. K. Ishikawa, *Guide to Quality Control* (Tokyo: Asian Productivity Organization, 1982)

21. Scholtes, Joiner, and Streibel, *The Team Handbook*.

22. For evidence to support this modification of the reflective-thinking pattern, see John K. Brilhart, "An Experimental Comparison of Three Techniques for Communicating a Problem-Solving Pattern to Members of a Discussion Group," *Speech Monographs* 33 (1966): 168–77.

23. Randy Y. Hirokawa, "Why Informed Groups Make Faulty Decisions: An Investigation of Possible Interaction-Based Explanations," *Small Group Behavior* 18 (1987): 3–29; Randy Y. Hirokawa, "Group-Communication and Decision-Making Performance: A Continued Test of the Functional Perspective," *Human Communication Research*, 14 (1985): 487–515; Randy Y. Hirokawa and Kathryn Rost, "Effective Group Decision-Making in Organizations: Field Test of the Vigilant Interaction Theory," *Management Communication Quarterly* 5 (1992): 267–88.

24. A. B. Hollingshead, "The Rank-Order Effect in Group Decision Making," *Organizational Behavior and Human Decision Process*, 68 (1996): 181–193.

25, Federal Electric Corporation, *A Programmed Introduction to PERT* (New York: Wiley, 1963).

26. For example, see Robert F. Bales and Fred L. Strodtbeck, "Phases in Group Problem-Solving," *Journal of Abnormal and Social Psychology* 46 (1951): 485–95; Thomas M. Schiedel and Laura Crowell, "Idea Development in Small Groups," *Quarterly Journal of Speech* 50 (1964): 140–45; B. Aubrey Fisher, "Decision Emergence: Phases in Group Decision-Making," *Speech Monographs* 37 (1970): 53–66; and Poole, "Decision Development."

27. Chapter 8 discusses in detail the phases of a group's growth and development.

28. Ernest G. Bormann, *Discussion and Group Methods: Theory and Practice*, 2nd ed. (New York: Harper & Row, 1975), 282.

29. Randy Y. Hirokawa, "Consensus Group Decision-Making, Quality of Decision and Group Satisfaction: An Attempt to Sort 'Fact' from 'Fiction'," *Central States Speech Journal* 33 (1982): 407–15; Randy Y. Hirokawa, "Why Informed Groups Make Faulty Decisions: An Investigation of Possible Interaction-Based Explanations," *Small Group Behavior* 18 (1987): 3–29.

30. Norman R. F. Maier, *Problem-Solving and Discussions and Conferences* (New York: McGraw-Hill, 1963) 123.

31. Beatrice Schultz, Sandra M. Ketrow, and Daphne M. Urban, "Improving Decision Quality in the Small Group: The Role of the Reminder," *Small Group Research* 26 (November 1995): 521–41.

32. Alex F. Osborn, *Applied Imagination* (New York: Scribner's, 1962).

33. Roger L. Firestien, "Effects of Creative Problem Solving Training on Communication Behaviors in Small Groups," *Small Group Research* 21 (November 1990): 507–21.

34. D. A. Leonard and W. C. Swap, *When Sparks Fly: Igniting Creativity in Groups* (Boston: Harvard Business School, 1999)

35. Andre L. Delberg, Andrew H. Van de Ven, and David H. Gustafson, *Group Techniques for Program Planning: A Guide to Nominal-Group and Delphi Processes* (Glenview, IL. Scott, Foresman, 1975) 7–16.

36. Gerry Philipsen, Anthony Mulac, and David Dietrich, "The Effects of Social Interaction on Group Generation of Ideas," *Communication Monographs* 46 (June 1979): 119–25; Fredric M. Jablin, "Cultivating Imagination: Factors That Enhance and Inhibit Creativity in Brainstorming Groups," *Human Communication Research* 7, no. 3 (Spring 1981): 245–58; Susan Jarboe, "A Comparison of Input-Output, Process-Output, and Input-Process-Output Models of Small Group Problem Solving Effectiveness;" Incorporating individual or silent brainstorming into the traditional brainstorming approach emerges from the nominal-group technique suggested by Andre L. Delbecq, Andrew H. Van de Ven, and David H. Gustafson, *Group Techniques for Program Planning: A Guide to Nominal-Group and Delphi Processes* (Glenview, IL: Scott, Foresman, 1975), 7–16; see also Susan Jarboe, "Enhancing Creativity in Groups: Theoretical Boundaries and Pragmatic Limitations." paper presented at the annual meeting of the Speech Communication Association, Atlanta, Georgia, Nov. 1, 1991. See Fred M. Jablin and David R. Seibold, "Implications for Problem-Solving Groups of Empirical Research on 'Brainstorming': A Critical Review of the Literature," *Southern Speech Communication Journal* 43 (1978): 327–56; Gerry Philipsen, Anthony Mulac, and David Dietrich, "The Effects of Social Interaction on Group Generation of Ideas," *Communication Monographs* 46 (June 1979): 119–25. See also VanGundy, *Techniques of Structured Problem Solving*.

37. J. J. Sosik, B. J. Avolio, and S. S. Kahai, "Inspiring Group Creativity: Comparing Anonymous and Identified Electronic Brainstorming," *Small Group Research* 29 (1998): 3–31.

38. D. H. Gustafson, R. K. Shukla, A. Delbecq, and G. W. Walster, "A Comparative Study of Differences in Subjective Likelihood Estimates Made by Individuals, Interacting Groups, Delphi Groups and Nominal-Groups," *Organizational Behavior and Human Performance* 9 (1973): 280–91; VanGundy, *Techniques of Structured Problem Solving*.

39. Jarboe, "A Comparison of Input-Output, Process-Output, and Input-Process-Output Models."

40. Delberg, Van de Ven, and Gustafson, *Group Techniques*.

41. Eileen K. Aranda, Luis Aranda, and Kristi Conlon, *Teams: Structure, Process, Culture, and Politics* (Englewood Cliffs, NJ: Prentice Hall, 1998) 90.

42. M. C. Roy, S. Gauvin, and M. Limayem, "Electronic Group Brainstorming: The Role of Feedback on Productivity," *Small Group Research* 27 (1996): 215–47.

43.. J. J. Sosik, B. J. Avolio, and S. S. Kahai, "Inspiring Group Creativity: Comparing Anonymous and Identified Electronic Brainstorming," *Small Group Research*, 29 (1998): 3–31; W. H. Cooper, R. B. Gallupe, S. Pollard, and J. Cadsby, "Some Liberating Effects of Anonymous Electronic Brainstorming," *Small Group Research* 29 (1998): 147–77.

44. Sosik, Avolio, and Kahai, "Inspiring Group Creativity: Comparing Anonymous and Identified Electronic Brainstorming."

45. A. K. Offner, T. J. Kramer, and J. P. Winter, "The Effects of Facilitation, Recording, and Pauses on Group Brainstorming," *Small Group Research* 27 (1996): 283–98; V. Brown and P. B. Paulus, "A Simple Dynamic Model of Social Factors in Group Brainstorming, *Small Group Research* 27 (1996): 91–114; M. W. Kramer, C. L. Kuo, and J. C. Dailey, "The Impact of Brainstorming Techniques on Subsequent Group Processes," *Small Group Research* 28

(1997): 218–42; V. Brown, M. Tumeo, T. S. Larey, and P. B. Paulus, "Modeling Cognitive Interactions During Group Brainstorming," *Small Group Research* 29 (1997): 495–526.

46. J. R. Kelly and S. J. Karau, "Entrainment of Creativity in Small Groups," *Small Group Research* 24 (May 1993): 179–98.

47. For an excellent review of group communication and creativity, see Jarboe, "Group Communication and Creativity Processes," in L. Frey, ed. *The Handbook of Group Communication Theory and Research* (Thousand Oaks, CA: Sage, 1999) 335–368.

48. Eitington, *Winning Trainer*.

49. Eitington, *Winning Trainer*.

50. Romig and Romig, *Structured Teamwork Guide*.

51. E. deBono, *Sur/petition: Creating Value Monopolies When Everyone Is Merely Competing* (New York: HarperBusiness, 1992).

52. Roger L. Firestien, "Effects of Creative Problem Solving Training on Communication Behaviors in Small Groups," *Small Group Research* 21 (November 1990): 507–521.

53. Alvin A. Goldberg and Carl E. Larson, *Group Communication: Discussion Processes and Applications* (Englewood Cliffs, NJ: Prentice Hall, 1975) 149.

54. Goldberg and Larson, *Group-Communication*, 150.

55. Goldberg and Larson, *Group-Communication*, 150.

56. Goldberg and Larson, *Group-Communication*, 150.

57. Carl E. Larson, "Forms of Analysis and Small Group Problem-Solving," *Speech Monographs* 36 (1969): 452–55.

58. Norman R. F. Maier, "An Experimental Test of the Effect of Training on Discussion Leadership," *Human Relations* 6 (1953): 166–73.

59. Dennis G. Gouran, "Variables Related to Consensus in Group Discussions of Questions of Policy," *Speech Monographs* 36 (1969): 385–391; Thomas J. Knutson, "An Experimental Study of the Effects of Orientation Behavior on Small Group Consensus," *Speech Monographs* 39 (1972): 159–65; John A. Kline, "Orientation and Group Consensus," *Central States Speech Journal* 23 (1972): 44–47; Steven A. Beebe, "Orientation as a Determinant of Group Consensus and Satisfaction," *Resources in Education* 13 (October 1978): 19–25.

60. LaFasto and Larson, *When Teams Work Best*.

61. See R. Y. Hirokawa and A. J. Salazar, "Task Group Communication and Decision-Making Performance," in L. Frey, ed., *The Handbook of Group Communication Theory and Research* (Thousand Oaks, CA: Sage, 1999) 167–191; Sunwolf and Seibold, "The Impact of Formal Procedures on Group Processes, Members, and Task Outcomes," in L. Frey, ed., *The Handbook of Group Communication Theory and Research*, (Thousand Oaks, CA: Sage, 1999) 395–431.

62. This activity was developed by Russ Wittrup, Department of Speech Communication, Southwest Texas State.

63. J. Piven and D. Borgenicht, *The Worst-Case Scenario Survival Handbook* (San Francisco, CA: Chronicle Books, 1999) 120.

64. Steven A. Beebe, J. Kevin Barge, and Colleen McCormick, *The Competent Group Communicator,* presented at the National Communication Association Conference, New York, New York, November, 1998), 120–123.

Objectives:

After studying this chapter, you will be able to:

▶ Explain why conflict occurs in small groups.

▶ Describe the negative impact that conflict has on group communication.

▶ List three myths about conflict.

▶ Identify strategies for managing different types of conflict.

▶ Describe four conflict-management principles.

▶ Define the concept of groupthink.

▶ Identify six symptoms of groupthink.

▶ Apply techniques for reducing groupthink.

▶ Define consensus.

▶ Apply techniques for managing conflict and reaching consensus in small groups.

Managing Conflict

"When we all think alike, then no one is thinking."

— Walter Lippman

C onflict happens. Social psychologists and communication researchers say that people inevitably disagree when they interact.[1] Throughout history, people have been involved in conflicts ranging from family feuds to world wars. Whether groups are involved in negotiating international trade agreements or deciding how to repave a parking lot, their members experience conflict.

This chapter gives you some ideas about the causes of conflict and presents some strategies for managing it in groups and teams. You will learn how not to eliminate group conflict but how to understand it and its importance in your group deliberations.

First, we will define conflict and note why it occurs so often. Second, we will look at three common misconceptions about conflict in small groups. Third, we will examine three types of conflict and offer suggestions for managing each type. Fourth, we will discuss groupthink, a phenomenon that occurs when small groups have too little disagreement or controversy. Finally, we will discuss consensus and offer suggestions for helping groups to reach agreement. Despite the prevalence of conflict in group and team deliberations, communication researchers Steven Farmer and Jonelle Rothe note that much of what we know about group conflict has been applied from research that has investigated interpersonal conflict.[2] The prime objective of this chapter is to help you understand how conflict in groups and teams can be both useful and detrimental to collaborative decision making.

What Is Conflict?

Conflict occurs when members disagree over two or more options that a group can take in trying to make a decision, resolve a problem, or achieve a goal. Conflict also occurs when an individual's goal is incompatible with the goals of others. Joseph Folger and Marshall Scott Poole define conflict as "the interaction of interdependent people who perceive incompatible goals and interference from each other in achieving these goals.[3] As suggested by this definition, conflict occurs when people in a group have the freedom and opportunity to make choices (they are interdependent people) and one or more group members want something different from what others want (they have incompatible goals). In addition, when individuals or groups keep others from achieving a desired goal (interference), conflict is likely.

If a group experienced no conflict, it would have little to discuss. One value of conflict is that it makes a group test and challenge ideas. Conflict can also, however, be detrimental to group interaction and group decision making. Conflict has a negative impact on a group when it (1) keeps the group from completing its task, (2) interferes with the quality of the group's decision or productivity, or (3) threatens the existence of the group.[4]

What causes conflict in groups and teams? Conflict results from differences between group members—*differences* in personality, perception, information, and power or influence. Because people are unique, their different attitudes, beliefs, and values will inevitably surface and cause conflict. No matter how much they try to empathize with others, people still have individual perspectives on the world. People also differ in the amount of knowledge they have on various topics. In groups, they soon realize that some members are more experienced or more widely read than others. This difference in information contributes to different attitudes. People also have different levels of power, status, and influence over others—differences that can increase conflict. People with power often try to use that power to influence others, and most do not like to be told what to do or think.

Conflict does not just "happen." You can often discern phases or stages of conflict development. As we discussed in Chapter 8, communication scholar B. Aubrey Fisher found that group deliberations can be organized around four phases: Orientation, conflict, emergence, and reinforcement.[5] Several researchers have discovered that the conflict phase in groups often emerges in predictable stages.[6]

Conflict in groups can be directed either toward people (interpersonal conflict), ideas (task conflict), or both people and ideas. One research team found that conflict often occurs because of perceived inequity; if we think someone has more resources or is getting more than his or her fair share, conflict often results.[7] When the conflict is directed toward people, we often first try to manage the conflict by avoiding the individual or the topic of conflict. If the conflict is more task-centered, we usually first try more integrative approaches by seeking solutions that are agreeable to all parties. One of the prime effects of conflict and discord that occurs in groups is that the seeming lack of progress toward the group's goals results in a lack of motivation to keep working at a solution to resolve the conflict.[8] It is important for group and team members to recognize that conflict is a natural byproduct of human interaction; when tension occurs, patience, tolerance, and a focus on the goals of the group should be priorities.

Misconceptions about Conflict

People often have misconceptions about the role of conflict in groups because they think that conflict is bad and should be avoided. With higher rates of divorce, crime, and international political tensions, it is understandable that people view conflict negatively. The following myths will examine some of the feelings you may have about conflict and determine whether a different attitude can improve the quality of your group discussions.[9]

Misconception 1: In Group Discussions, Conflict Should Be Avoided at All Costs Do you feel uncomfortable when conflicts occur in a group? You may believe that groups should not experience conflict, that conflict is unnatural, or that if people express conflicting points of view, you should try to squelch disagreement. Conflict, however, is a natural by product of communication; unless participants in your group share the same attitudes, beliefs, and values (an unlikely situation), there will be some conflict. Several researchers have discovered that conflict is an important, indeed useful, part of group communication.[10] Members who believe that conflict is unhealthy become frustrated when conflict erupts in a group. They should realize that conflict probably will occur and that it is a natural and healthy part of group communication.

Research suggests that when conflict occurs, group members are often challenged to research issues in greater detail and learn more about the issues under discussion.[11] In the end, conflict can enhance learning and spur more in-depth analysis.

Misconception 2: All Conflict Occurs Because People Do Not Understand One Another Have you ever been in a heated disagreement with someone and then shouted, "You just don't understand me!"? You easily assume that conflict occurs because another person does not understand your position. Not all conflict occurs because of mis-understandings, however. You may believe that if others really understood you, they would agree with you. As Robert Doolittle observed,

> . . . many conflicts result from more than mere misunderstandings. Indeed, some of the most serious conflicts occur among individuals and groups who understand each other very well but who strongly disagree.[12]

Conflict can result from not understanding another group member's message, but some conflicts intensify when that person clarifies his or her point.

Misconception 3: All Conflict Can Be Resolved Perhaps you consider yourself an optimist. You like to think that problems can be solved. You may also feel that if a conflict arises, a compromise will resolve it. However, you should realize that not all conflicts can be resolved. Realistically, many disagreements are not simple. Fundamental differences between those who oppose abortion and those who support it can obviously not be resolved easily, if at all. Some ideologies are so far apart that resolving conflicts between them is unlikely. This does not mean that whenever a conflict arises in your group, you should despair and say, "Oh, well, no use trying to solve this disagreement." That position also oversimplifies the conflict-management process. Because some conflicts cannot be resolved, group members may have to focus on differences over which they are most like-ly to reach agreement.

If you find yourself arbitrating a conflict in a small group, first decide which issues are most likely to be resolved. If you assume that all conflict can be resolved just by apply-ing the right techniques, you may become frustrated. However, you must also be wary of the self-fulfilling prophecy. If you hastily reach the conclusion that the conflict cannot be resolved, you may behave in a way that fulfills your prediction.

Types of Conflict

Communication scholars Gerald Miller and Mark Steinberg identified three common types of interpersonal conflict: (1) pseudo-conflict, (2) simple conflict, and (3) ego conflict.[13] They suggest that by identifying the type of conflict in a group, you will be better able to manage it. The following sections look at these three types of conflict in the context of a small group.

Pseudo-Conflict: When People Misunderstand One Another

Some conflict occurs because of misunderstandings. **Pseudo-conflict** occurs when individ-uals agree, but, because of poor communication, appear to each other to disagree. *Pseudo* means fake or false. Thus, pseudo-conflict is conflict between people who really agree on issues but who do not understand that their differences are caused by misunderstandings or misinterpretations. "Oh, I see," said Mark after several minutes of heatedly defending a position he had suggested to the group. "I just misunderstood you. I guess we really agree."

To manage pseudo-conflict, consider these strategies:

▶   Ask others what they mean by terms or phrases they use.

Groups must find ways of managing conflict and channeling energy constructively. In what ways might conflict be healthy?

▶ Establish a supportive rather than defensive climate if misunderstandings occur.

▶ Become an active listener by using the skills we discussed in Chapter 5:

Stop: Tune into what your partner is saying rather than your own thoughts.

Look: Pay attention to unspoken messages and monitor the emotional climate.

Listen: Focus on key details and link them to major ideas.

Question: Ask appropriate questions about information or ideas that are unclear to you.

Paraphrase content: To test your understanding, summarize your conception of what someone is saying.

Paraphrase feelings: When appropriate, check your perception of your partner's feelings.

Research clearly supports the importance of good listening skills in small groups and teams.[14]

Simple Conflict: When People Disagree about Issues

Simple conflict occurs when each of two individuals knows what the other wants, but neither can achieve a goal without preventing the other from achieving one. "Simple conflict involves one person saying, 'I want to do X,' and another saying, ' I want to do Y,' when X and Y are incompatible forms of behavior."[15] Although the conflict may seem far from simple, it is called "simple conflict" because the issues are clear and each party understands the problem. For example, in a corporation with only a limited amount of money to invest in new-product expansion, one board member may want to invest in real estate and another wants to make capital improvements. The issue is clear; the individuals simply believe the company should take different courses of action.

When you understand what someone is saying but simply disagree with his or her point, consider using these skills:

▶ Clarify your perception and your partner's perception of the message.

▶ Keep the discussion focused on issues, not personalities.

▶ Use facts that support your point rather than opinions or emotional arguments.

▶ Use a structured problem-solving approach to organize the discussion: Define, analyze, identify several solutions, evaluate the solutions, select the best one.

▶ When appropriate, look for ways to compromise.

▶ Make the conflict a group concern rather than a conflict between just two people; ask others for information and data.

▶ If there are several issues, tackle issues one at a time; decide which issues are the most important.

▶ Find areas of agreement.

▶ If possible, postpone the decision until additional research can be conducted. Such a delay may also lessen tensions.

Ego Conflict: When Personalities Clash

Of the types of conflict under discussion, the third is the most difficult to manage. **Ego conflict** occurs when individuals become defensive about their positions because they think they are being personally attacked. Ego conflicts are charged with emotion, and defensiveness in one individual often causes defensiveness in others. "Just because you're the chair of the group doesn't give *you* the right to railroad decision making," snaps Frank. "Well, you're just jealous. You think you should have been elected chairperson," retorts Ed. Based on his study of small group communication, Dennis Devine suggests that group members locked in a disagreement about issues (simple conflict) can quickly evolve into a more emotionally charged discussion that becomes personal (ego conflict) unless group members consciously monitor how they interact with each other.[16]

If you are trying to mediate an ego conflict, find issues the disagreeing parties can agree on. Identify and emphasize the common ground between them, and encourage them to describe the sequence of events that created the conflict. A key immediate concern when ego conflict flares up in a group is to permit the disagreement to be verbalized without heightening the emotional tension. Just venting anger and irritation won't lessen tensions, nor will simply ignoring the conflict make the tension go away. Research clearly documents that the emotional climate in a group shapes how effectively the conflict will be managed.[17]

Here are additional strategies that may help manage the clash of egos:

▶ Encourage active listening.

▶ Return the discussion to the key issues under discussion.

▶ Try to turn the discussion into a problem to be solved rather than a conflict someone has to win.

- Seek to cool the emotional climate by lowering your voice and speaking more calmly, not in a patronizing way but in a way that signals your interest in dialogue rather than emotional argument.

- Be descriptive rather than evaluative or judgmental when discussing the issues of contention. As we discussed in Chapter 5, a supportive communication climate is more likely to emerge if group members (1) describe the problem rather than evaluate others, (2) focus on issues rather than on trying to control others, (3) communicate in the moment rather than plotting and scheming how to manipulate others, (4) empathize with others rather than ignoring them or remaining aloof, (5) treat others as equals rather than acting superior, (6) avoid making harsh pronouncements, and (7) present their point of view as one option rather than the only one.

"Gentlemen! Gentlemen! May we please start the meeting?"

©The New Yorker Collection 1987 James Stevenson from cartoonbank.com

- Develop rules or procedures that permit differences of opinion.

- Unless the disagreement is central to the nature of the group, agree to disagree and return to areas of agreement.

REVIEW

Summary of Three Conflict Types

	PSEUDO-CONFLICT	SIMPLE CONFLICT	EGO-CONFLICT
Source of conflict	Misunderstanding individuals' perceptions of the problem.	Individual disagreement over which course of action to pursue	Defense of ego: Individual believes he or she is being attacked personally.
Suggestions for managing conflict	1. Ask for clarification of perceptions.	1. Listen and clarify perceptions.	1. Let members express their concerns, but do not permit personal attacks.
	2. Establish a supportive rather than a defensive climate.	2. Make sure issues are clear to all group members.	2. Employ active listening.

3. Employ active listening: • *Stop* • *Look* • *Listen* • *Question* • *Paraphrase content* • *Paraphrase feelings*	3. Use a problem-solving approach to manage differences of opinion.	3. Call for a cooling-off period.
	4. Keep discussion focused on the issues.	4. Try to keep discussion focused on issues (simple conflict).
	5. Use facts rather than opinions for evidence.	5. Encourage parties to be descriptive rather than evaluative and judgmental.
	6. Look for alternatives or compromise positions.	6. Use a problem-solving approach to manage differences of opinion.
	7. Make the conflict a group concern rather than an individual concern.	7. Speak slowly and calmly.
	8. Determine which conflicts are the most important to resolve.	8. Agree to disagree.
	9. If appropriate, postpone the decision while additional research is conducted. This delay also helps relieve tensions.	

Conflict and Diversity in Small Groups

At the root of most conflicts are differences—differences in understanding, perception, attitudes, or preferred action. Yet one of the key advantages of working in groups and teams is the opportunity to capitalize on the different perspectives that group and team members have. As the saying goes, if both of us agree, then one of us is irrelevant. The challenge is to use group diversity without becoming locked in intractable conflict. Although we've emphasized that not all conflict is bad nor should it be avoided, entrenched conflict decreases a group's effectiveness.

Several researchers have examined whether group members' differences in race, culture, age, gender, and other variables enhances or detracts from group performance. Ralph Rodrigues suggests that it's not differences in such demographic characteristics as race, age, or gender that affect group performance, but differences in underlying values or approaches to problems.[18] Leonard Karakowsky and Jacob Siegel offer a different explanation for how issues of diversity impact group discussion; they suggest that it's not the racial or cultural makeup of the group, but the presence of a number or proportion of minorities in a group, that affects group conflict. If only one or two members of a racial minority are present, these minority members may feel isolated and are less likely to contribute. But if there are a sizable number of racial minorities in the group, then there is less likelihood that the minority opinion will be ignored.[19] Although some research suggests that group diversity can decrease team performance[20] other studies that suggest that racial, cultural, gender, and age diversity enhance performance by presenting different viewpoints.[21]

Cultural differences can contribute to disagreement, because of different perceptions and our views of the world. Your **world view** is your fundamental outlook on reality, and your place in the universe, and purpose in life.[22] For example, people from Eastern cultures (Japan, China, Taiwan) tend to view humans as one with nature; people from West-

Collaborating

E T H I C A L L Y

The unethical group communicator makes conflict personal. The hallmark of constructive conflict is its focus on ideas rather than on people. Destructive conflict chips away at a person's sense of worth and self-esteem. You can usually tell when conflict moves from simple conflict (disagreement about ideas) to ego conflict (personal attacks about the other person): The emotional climate of a group goes up a notch; voices become louder, and body posture becomes more tense. The ethical communicator guards against making disagreement a personal battle between people, but rather seeks to focus on the discussion about ideas. But when you and your ideas are under attack, it's hard not to become defensive. Is your only recourse to just sit there and "take it"? No.

The most powerful strategies to help untangle conflict when it gets personal are to first listen and use effective feedback skills, to first make sure you understand the areas of disagreement. Second, be mindful or conscious of how you are framing the conflict. Guard against assuming someone is "out to get you." In reality, sometimes group members *do* make their attacks personal. When that happens, use descriptive language to describe how the personal attacks make you feel. If progress is not being made in addressing the substantive issues underlying the conflict, it may be best for the group to take a break, to let the emotion-charged atmosphere cool a bit.

ern cultures (United States, northern Europe) often see humans as having characteristics that distinguish them from nature. This one generalization is not true, of course, of all Easterners or Westerners, but it illustrates how culture—our learned system of knowledge, behavior, attitudes, beliefs, values, and norms—can have a profound effect on our interactions with others.

In small group interactions, your cultural expectations about how conflict should be managed may clash with those of someone from another culture who has different fundamental assumptions about managing or resolving differences. As we noted, research suggests that group members who are in the cultural or ethnic minority may tend to talk less.[23] Unless group members are sensitive to such diminished contributions, good ideas may be lost because minority-group members are reluctant to speak. Other research suggests that when there are cultural or ethnic differences in a group, a cooperative approach to managing conflict encourages quieter individuals to participate and enhances the quality of the group's discussion.[24] Two frameworks for describing cultural differences shed light on how culture can explain why some conflicts develop and fester.

Individualistic and Collectivistic Cultural Approaches to Conflict

In Chapter 1 we noted that some cultures expect and nurture a team or collective approach to working with others; more individualistic cultures, such as the United States, place greater value on individual achievement. This culturally learned difference can explain why some individuals, who place different values on the role of the individual or the team, manage conflict as they do. Stella Ting-Toomey suggests that people in individualistic cultures are more likely to use direct, confrontational methods of managing disagreements than people who value a collective or team approach to group work.[25] She also suggests that people from collectivistic cultures, especially those who place considerable stock in nonverbal messages, are more comfortable with nonconfrontational and indirect methods of resolving differences. She suspects this difference may be because people from individualistic cultures tend to approach problem solving from a linear perspective, whereas people from collectivistic cultures often use a more intuitive problem-solving process. Ting-Toomey finds that people from individualistic cultures are more likely to use facts or principles as a basis for approaching conflict, negotiation, or persuasion situations.[26] People from collectivistic cultures adopt more relationship-based messages to manage differences. It is important for people from collectivistic cultures to save face by not being portrayed as having lost a confrontation.

High-Context and Low-Context Cultural Approaches to Conflict

In Chapter 6 we noted that a high-context culture is one in which considerable weight is given to the context of unspoken messages. In a low-context culture, such as the United States, more emphasis is placed on words and their explicit meaning than on implicit, nonverbal cues.[27] Researchers have found that people in low-context cultures give greater importance to task or instrumental issues than do people in high-context cultures.[28] In high-context cultures, the expressive or emotional aspects of managing the conflict take on special importance. In expressive conflict the goal is often to express feelings and release tension.[29] Keeping the relationship in balance, maintaining the friendship, and managing the emotional climate often take a higher priority in a high-context culture than achieving the outcome. Here again, saving face and avoiding embarrassment for all parties are more important in high-context cultures than in low-context cultures.

A similar conclusion has been put forward about differences between the way men and women manage disagreements in North America. Women tend to emphasize expressive goals in conflict whereas men emphasize instrumental or task objectives.[30] Such a generalization needs to be tempered by considering each individual as unique, even though some gender patterns in conflict-management styles have been observed.

In your group deliberations, knowing that culture and gender differences exist can help explain why some strategies will be more effective than others. We caution you, however, to avoid stereotyping others by cultural, national, ethnic, or gender differences alone. For example, it would be most inappropriate to draw a stereotyped conclusion that all Asians will emphasize expressive rather than instrumental objectives in conflict. But knowing that cultural differences exist can give you greater insight into why some conflict-management strategies are more or less effective, depending on the preferred approach others may have for managing differences. Taking an egocentric view (assuming your perspective is correct) or ethnocentric view (assuming your cultural methods of managing conflict are superior to others) can be detrimental to effective communication.

Conflict Management Styles

Regardless of our cultural backgrounds or the types of conflict we experience, research suggests that each of us behaves in predictable ways to manage disagreements with others. What is your conflict-management style? Do you tackle conflict head-on or seek ways to remove yourself from the fray? Although these are only two options available for managing conflict, reduced to its essence, conflict-management style often boils down to fight or flight.

R. Kilmann and K. Thomas suggest that your conflict-management style is based on two factors: (1) how concerned you are for other people and (2) how concerned you are for yourself.[31] Linda Putnam and C. Wilson have identified three general styles for managing conflict: (1) nonconfrontational, (2) controlling, and (3) cooperative.[32]

Nonconfrontational

Some people work hard to avoid conflict with others. They do not like to argue and would rather withdraw when someone disagrees with them. Or, if they see a conflict brewing, they take a giant step away from the potential dispute. If a group member disagrees with someone who often avoids or withdraws from conflict, the nonconfrontational person may either have no response at all or readily change his or her opinion and agree.

This style is effective at times. Avoiding an immediate attack from another group member may give you time to think of a more appropriate response rather than blurting out the first thing that comes to your mind. And agreeing with others if you are, in fact, wrong can be the best way to repair a relationship so you can continue to work with another team member.

When conflict occurs because of fundamental differences in values, culture, or other factors of diversity, researchers suggest group members simply need to budget more time for discussion. And although it's always important to have clear group goals, during periods of conflict, especially conflict fueled by diversity, it is vital to have clear goals that are understood by *each* group member to help keep conflict focused on issues rather than personalities.[33]

However, if your only conflict-management style is to withdraw or give in, you may find that your unassertive behavior diminishes your effectiveness in group discussions. Avoiding conflict does not make the source of the problem go away; it still exists. There are times when it is in your best interest, as well as in the best interest of the group, to continue exploring options rather than capitulate quickly. If you always agree with others, you may find your ideas and suggestions being discounted.

Controlling

A person who likes to control is someone who wants to get his or her way. Some group members will just be more dominant than others; dominant members talk more than other group members.[34] The controlling person may seek to win others over by using constructive strategies such as marshaling facts, statistics, and other evidence to persuade others. Or they may use more destructive methods—blaming others or trying to bully or coerce them. As we discussed in Chapter 5, when you attempt to control someone, he or she may become defensive. Someone who uses this approach has adopted a win/lose philosophy. He or she wants to win at the expense of someone else. If you know someone with a controlling style, or if you use this style yourself, then you have experienced both the advantages and disadvantages of competition.

Is it always inappropriate to cling to what you believe and try to convince others to support your position? No. If you have information that you know is accurate and you are sure that you have the correct answer, you may be justified in persuading others to see your point of view. Or you may have ethical reasons for opposing the majority opinion. If some group members are advocating a course of action that is immoral or illegal, or that violates your personal instincts of what is right and wrong, it is appropriate to stick to your position and advocate a more ethical course of action. One of the virtues of teamwork is the likelihood that one group member has information or insight that other group members do not have.

The problem occurs if you try to control others without being sensitive to their needs or rights. It also can be detrimental if your method of controlling others is to outlast or outshout other group members by threatening them or using unethical means of persuasion, such as knowingly using false information to win. When assertiveness crosses the line into aggression, most group members find the controlling style does not wear well over the course of several group meetings.

Cooperative

Group members who take a cooperative approach seek solutions to problems rather than viewing conflict as a game in which one person wins and another loses. A cooperative style balances both expressive and instrumental goals. Several research studies have found that when there are cultural differences among group members, a cooperative approach to conflict-management works best.[35] Essential elements of a cooperative style include leaving personal grievances out of the discussion and describing problems without being judgmental or evaluative. A team member who adopts a cooperative approach asks, "What do we both want?" rather than saying "Here's what I want."

Like the other two approaches we have discussed, this style has advantages and disadvantages. There may be times when initially avoiding a confrontation may help initiate a dialogue with someone. Or there may be some issues about which you may not be able to compromise or modify your method of pursuing your goals. However, many if not most conflicts can benefit from being approached as problems to be solved rather than as victories to be won. As we have already noted, a cooperative approach to managing differences seems to work best if your group is culturally or ethnically diverse.[36] Given the importance of developing group communication competency, we will review cooperative conflict-management principles and skills in more detail.

Cooperative Conflict Management: Principles and Skills

What principles and strategies can help a group cooperatively manage conflict? No simple checklist of techniques will miraculously resolve or manage group differences. Research supporting the principle that focusing on shared interest and developing a collaborative conflict-management style is usually preferred over more-combative conflict-management styles.[37] However, based on several studies of what works and what does not work when managing conflict, Roger Fisher and William Ury identified the following four conflict-management principles,[38] which we will discuss.

Separate the People from the Problem

When conflict becomes personal and egos become involved, it is very difficult to develop a positive climate in which differences can be managed. As we discussed in Chapter 5, if people feel they are being evaluated and strategically manipulated, they will respond with defensiveness. Thus, this principle suggests that it is better to deal with interpersonal issues before tackling the problem causing the conflict. Separating the person from the problem means valuing the other individual as a person, treating her (or him) as an equal, and empathizing with her feelings. A key to valuing others is to use good listening skills. It is also useful to acknowledge the other person's feelings. Emotion is the fuel of conflict. Several scholars agree that efforts to manage our feelings facilitate the conflict-management process.[39]

One strategy for constructively expressing how you feel toward others in conflict is to use the approach John Gottman and his colleagues call the X-Y-Z formula.[40] According to this method, you say "When you do X, in situation Y, I feel Z." Here's an example: "When you are 15 minutes late to our staff meetings, I feel like you don't care about us or our meetings."

When you are the recipient of someone's wrath, you could use the X-Y-Z formula to explain how being yelled at makes it difficult for you to listen effectively. Trying to understand and manage your own and others' feelings helps separate personal issues from issues of substance. Joyce Hocker and William Wilmot suggest that when you are the receiver of someone's emotional outburst, you could consider the following actions.[41]

1. Acknowledge the person's feelings.

2. Determine what specific behavior is causing the intense feelings.

3. Assess the intensity and importance of the issue.

4. Invite the other person to join you in working toward solutions.

5. Make a positive relational statement.

Research also supports the value of using well-crafted arguments rather than emotion-laden opinions to help a group sort through periods of contention.[42] No technique or simple formula exists to help you manage the challenging task of separating personal from substantive issues. Using good listening skills, acknowledging how others feel, and expressing your own feelings (without ranting and raving) make a good start toward mediating challenging conflict situations.

Focusing on Shared Interests

The words to one old song begin with the advice "Accentuate the positive. Eliminate the negative." A cooperative style is characterized by focusing on areas of agreement and what all parties have in common. If, for example, you are in a group debating whether public schools should distribute condoms, group members are more likely to have a productive discussion if they verbalize the goals and values they hold in common. A comment such as "We all agree that we want to reduce the spread of AIDS" might be a good place to start such a discussion.

Conflict is goal-driven. The individuals embroiled in the conflict want something. Unless goals are clear to everyone, it will be difficult to manage the conflict well. If you are involved in conflict, determine what your goals are. Then, identify your partner's goals. Finally, identify where goals overlap and where there are differences.

Do not confuse a goal with the strategy for achieving what you and a feuding group member want. For example, you may ask the group to make fewer copies on the copy machine. Your goal is to save money, because you are in charge of managing the office. Asking that your colleagues make fewer copies is a strategy that you have suggested for achieving your goal. Clarifying the underlying goal rather than only debating the merits of one strategy for achieving it should help unravel clashes over issues or personalities.

Generating Many Options to Solve Problems

During negotiation, group members who adamantly hold to only one solution create a competitive climate. Cooperative conflict managers are more likely to use brainstorming, nominal-group technique, or other strategies such as those discussed in Chapter 9 for identifying a variety of options to manage the disagreement; they seek several solutions to overcome obstacles. Research by Shaila Miranda suggests that using e-mail or other electronic support systems to generate and evaluate ideas can also be a productive way of increasing the number of options a group or team might consider.[43] Sometimes feuding group members become fixated on only one approach to their goal. When conflict-management degenerates into what amounts to a verbal arm-wrestling match, where combatants perceive only one way to win, the conflict is less likely to be managed successfully.

Basing Decisions on Objective Criteria

Criteria are the standards for an acceptable solution to a problem. Typical criteria are such things as a limit to how much the solution can cost or a deadline by which a solution must be implemented. If, for example, group members agree that a solution must decrease the spread of AIDS but also not cost more than $1 million to implement, the group is using criteria to help identify a mutually acceptable solution. If the solution is based on both whether a person subjectively agrees with an idea and whether the solution achieves a specified outcome, conflict is more likely to be cooperatively resolved.

REVIEW

Conflict Management Principles

1. Separate the people from the problem.
2. Focus on shared interests.
3. Generate many options to solve problems.
4. Base decisions on objective criteria.

When People Are Not Cooperative: Dealing with Difficult Group Members

Evidence suggests that managers spend up to 25 percent of their time dealing with conflict.[44] One author boldly claims that 98 percent of the problems we face are "people problems."[45] Scholars call them "group deviants"; you may call them a pain in the neck. Even though we hope that you will not have to deal with difficult or cantankerous group members, we are not naive. Not all group members will separate people from the problem, focus on shared interests, be eager to search for more alternatives, or base decisions on objective criteria. Our individualistic cultural traditions often make it challenging to develop collaborative groups and teams. It sometimes takes special "people skills" to deal with some group members. Drawing on the principles and skills of the cooperative conflict-management style, we offer the following tips for dealing with the more obstreperous group members.

1. *Manage your emotions.* When we are emotionally charged, we may find it difficult to practice rational, logical methods of managing conflict. What happens to our bodies when we become upset? One researcher offers this description:

   > Our adrenaline flows faster and our strength increases by about 20 percent. . . . The veins become enlarged and the cortical centers where thinking takes place do not perform nearly as well. . . . the blood supply to the problem-solving part of the brain is severely decreased because, under stress, a greater portion of blood is diverted to the body's extremities.[46]

   It is normal to feel angry when someone constantly seems to say or do things that make you feel judged or evaluated. In that situation, you may say or do something you later regret. Although some people advocate expressing anger, to "clear the air," expressing uncensored emotions can make matters worse. Communication researchers Barbara Gayle and Raymond Preiss confirmed what most of us intuitively know: Unresolved conflict is a breeding ground for emotional upheaval in groups and organizations.[47] Although it's been said that time heals all wounds, there are instances when ignoring hurt feelings can make the conflict escalate; leaders and team members need to recognize when to be active rather than passive in addressing emotional volatility.[48] If you are emotionally aroused when someone provokes you, you will be less likely to listen well and deal logically with the problem. Thus, engaging your listening skills can help diffuse the conflict. Another strategy for managing emotions involves focusing on your breathing to restore personal calm. Taking a slow, deep breath can help soothe your spirit and give you another focus besides mindlessly lashing out at others. When your emotions are charged you experience physiological changes. Breathing slowly can help restore balance to the body and be a positive, constructive way to regain control. If you are in charge of a group and you see that the emotional intensity is dramatically increasing, you may want to suggest that the group take a short break.

To manage your emotions, also, use such strategies as self-talk. Realize you are upset (become consciously competent) and make an effort to gain control over your feelings. Thoughts are linked to feelings, and your mental messages can affect how you feel. Eleanor Roosevelt said "No one can make you feel inferior without your consent."

Finally, help manage the emotional climate by avoiding personal attacks and name calling; such outbursts may make you feel better initially but will likely lead to a further deteriorating relationship.

2. *Describe what is upsetting you.* Try to avoid lashing back at the offending person. Use a descriptive "I" message to explain to the other person how you are feeling; for example, "I find it difficult to listen to you when you raise your voice at me," or "I notice that is the fourth time you have interrupted me when I was trying to explain my point." The goal is not to increase the conflict. "You shouldn't yell at me" or "You shouldn't interrupt me" are examples of "you" statements. Such statements are evaluative and are likely to increase resentment and anger.

3. *Disclose your feelings.* After describing the behavior that offends or irritates you, disclose how you feel when the behavior occurs: "When I'm interrupted, I feel that my opinion isn't valued" or "I become increasingly frustrated when I try to contribute to our meeting but I don't feel you are listening." When disclosing your feelings, try to avoid emotional overstatement such as "I've never been so upset in all my life." Such hyperbole raises the emotional stakes and can trigger a new volley of retorts.

4. *Return to the issue of contention.* The only way to return to a cooperative style is to get back to the issue that is fueling the disagreement. Sometimes there may be a hidden agenda that makes it difficult to confront the key issues. A wise person once said that often what we fight about is not what we fight about. Although an argument may seem on the surface to be over a substantive issue—such as which solution to adopt or whose research to use—the underlying issue may be about power and control. Only if the underlying issue is exposed and addressed will the conflict be managed.

These general suggestions provide underlying principles for dealing with difficult group members, but you may need more specific strategies for managing such people. Table 10.1 offers several specific ways to deal with group members who perform such self-

Table 10.1 How to Deal with Difficult Group Members

WHAT THE GROUP MEMBER DOES	OPTIONS FOR MANAGING THE PROBLEM
Dominates: Tries to tell people what to do without seeking permission from the group; tells rather than asks; monopolizes the conversation.	1. Use gatekeeping skills to invite other group members to participate; explicitly state that you'd like to hear what others have to say. 2. In private, ask the dominating group member to be less domineering and to give others an opportunity to participate. 3. Channel the energy the dominator has by giving him or her a specific task to accomplish, such as record the minutes of the meeting or periodically summarize the group's progress. 4. The group or team may collectively decide to confront the domineering member; clearly describe the behavior that the group perceives as inappropriate.
Blocks Progress: Has a negative attitude. Is often stubborn and disagreeable without a clear reason. When the group is making progress, the blocker seems to unproductively keep the group from achieving its goal.	1. Ask for specific evidence as to why he or she does not support the group's position. 2. Calmly confront the blocker by explaining how consistently being negative creates a negative group climate. 3. Use humor to help diffuse the tension that the blocker creates. 4. Assign the blocker the role of becoming devil's advocate (to argue against the general sentiment of the group) before the group makes a decision; giving the blocker permission to be negative at certain times can help the group avoid groupthink.
Irresponsible: Does not carry through with assignments, is often absent or late to meetings.	1. Speak to the group member privately to convince the offending group member to pull his/her own weight. Explain how the irresponsible group member is hurting other group members and the overall success of the group. 2. Assign a mentor. Call the person or send e-mail to remind him or her to attend the meeting. Ask for a progress report on the status of assigned work. Work one-on-one trying to help the irresponsible member see how his or her behavior hurts the group. Provide more structure. 3. Ask for help. After trying to confront the offending group member first privately and then collectively without results, ask for help from a supervisor or instructor. 4. Clarify who will get the credit. To minimize social loafing, tell the offending member that when the final product is complete the group will clearly indicate the lack of participation from the irresponsible group member.

Table 10.1 *How to Deal with Difficult Group Members (cont'd)*

Unethically Aggressive: Is verbally abusive toward other group members or purposefully disconfirms others. Tries to take credit for the work of others.	**1.** Unethical behavior should not be endorsed with silence. Immediately describe the offensive behavior to the aggressor, and indicate the negative effect such behavior has on individuals or the entire group. **2.** Several group members may confront the offending group member. Collectively don't let a norm get established that tolerates mean-spirited actions toward others. **3.** If the inappropriate behavior is directed toward someone else in the group, become an advocate for your colleague. Support other group members who are attacked or singled out. **4.** Seek help from an instructor or supervisor. Sometimes a bully only responds to a person of greater power. Seek help from someone in authority outside the group to stop the unethical, offending behavior toward others.

focused roles as dominator and blocker, or who are irresponsible or unethically aggressive. Remember *No one can ultimately change the behavior of another person.* Competent communicators have the knowledge, skill, and motivation to behave appropriately and effectively.

Groupthink: Conflict Avoidance

Sondra Baxter, chair of the board of Eastern Microtech Company, was meeting with the board of directors to decide whether Eastern Microtech would merge with Southern Microtech Company. Baxter called the meeting to order. After the reading and approval of the minutes from the last meeting, Baxter stated that she thought the merger would benefit both companies. As soon as Baxter finished speaking, other board members quickly chimed in, offering their support for the merger. At first, no board members stated any objections to the deal; they fully supported Baxter's decision. Then, one member said that the merger might violate antitrust laws by creating a monopoly in the southeastern United States. He also noted that the government probably would oppose the merger. Other board members quickly tried to gloss over the potential problem, one member confidently stating, "The government should not have any power to affect how we run our corporation. After all, it's our company."

After additional supportive comments from board members, the group voted to approve the merger, with even the reluctant group member joining in. After the meeting, one member commented, "I wish all the group meetings I participated in would go as smoothly as our board meetings. We seem to get along so well together. Sondra does a great job as chairperson." "Yes," observed another member, "She certainly has our respect. We always support what she has to say."

On first analysis of this meeting, you might think it effective. The chairperson appears to have the support of the group, whose members have little uncertainty. Looking at the meeting more closely, however, you see that the group is not functioning as well as it should; it is not taking advantage of the benefits of working together. This board is a victim of groupthink.

Groupthink is the illusion of agreement[49]—a type of thought that occurs when a group strives to minimize conflict, maximize cohesiveness, and reach a consensus without critically testing, analyzing, and evaluating ideas. When a group reaches decisions too quickly, it does not properly consider the implications of its decisions. Groupthink results in an ineffective consensus; too little conflict often lowers the quality of group decisions. When a group does not take time to examine the positive and negative consequences of alternative decisions, the quality of its decision is likely to suffer.

Sociologist Irving Janis believes that many poor decisions and policies are the result of groupthink.[50] In 1999 eleven students at Texas A&M University were tragically killed when the traditional pre-football-game bonfire they were building collapsed; many other students were injured. Investigators found that a structural-engineering professor tried to warn university officials for years the bonfire's design was unsafe; other engineering-faculty members who also thought the bonfire was a disaster waiting to happen finally stopped trying to influence the university; no one would listen.[51] The decision to launch the flawed space shuttle *Challenger* on that unforgettable January morning in 1986 was also tinged by groupthink.[52] Corporate executives and others did not challenge assumptions in the construction and launch procedures; disaster resulted. The pressure for consensus resulted in groupthink.

Groups with highly esteemed leaders are most prone to groupthink. Because these leaders' ideas are often viewed as sacrosanct, few members disagree with them. A group may also suffer from groupthink if its members consider themselves highly cohesive and take pride in getting along so well with one another in providing support and encouragement to members' ideas.

One research study found that groupthink is most likely to occur when (1) the group is apathetic about the task, (2) group members have low expectations about their ability to be successful, (3) there is at least one highly qualified, credible group member, (4) one group member is exceptionally persuasive, and (5) there is a norm that group members should conform rather than express negative opinions.[53]

Although some small group communication scholars question the theoretical soundness of the theory of groupthink, it continues to serve as a useful and practical way of helping groups understand why they make poor decisions.[54]

Symptoms of Groupthink

Can you identify groupthink when it occurs in groups to which you belong? Here are some of the common symptoms of groupthink.[55] See if you can think of some of your own communication experiences that exemplify this phenomenon.

Critical Thinking Is Not Encouraged or Rewarded
If you are working in a group that considers disagreement or controversy counterproductive, chances are that groupthink is alive and well in that group. One advantage of working in groups is having an

opportunity to evaluate ideas so that you can select the best possible solution. If group members seem proud that peace and harmony prevail at their meetings, they may suffer from groupthink.

Members Believe That Their Group Can Do No Wrong   During the 1972 presidential election, members of the committee to reelect President Nixon did not consider that they might fail to obtain information from Democratic headquarters. They thought their group was invulnerable. But the burglary of the Watergate office and the subsequent coverup ultimately led to the resignation of President Nixon. This sense of invulnerability is a classic symptom of groupthink. Another symptom is that members dismiss potential threats to the group as minor problems. If your group is consistently overconfident in dealing with problems that may interfere with its goals, it may suffer from groupthink.[56]

Members Are Too Concerned About Justifying Their Actions   Members of highly cohesive groups like to feel that they are acting in their group's best interests. Therefore, groups that experience groupthink like to rationalize their positions on issues. A group susceptible to groupthink is too concerned about convincing itself that it has made proper decisions in the past and will make good decisions in the future.

Members Apply Pressure to Those Who Do Not Support the Group   Have you ever voiced an opinion contrary to the majority opinion and quickly realized that other members were trying to pressure you into going along with the rest of the group? Groups prone to groupthink have a low tolerance for members who do not "go along." They see controversy and conflict injected by a dissenting member as a threat to esprit de corps. Therefore, a person voicing an idea different from the group's position is often punished. Sometimes pressure is subtle, taking the form of frowns or grimaces. Group members may not socialize with the dissenting member, or they may not listen attentively to the dissident. Usually their first response is to try to convince this member to reconsider his or her position. But if the member still does not agree with the others, he or she may be expelled from the group. Of course, if a group member is just being stubborn, the others should try to reason with the dissenter. Do not, however, be too quick to label someone as a troublemaker simply because he or she has an opinion different from that of other group members.

Members Often Believe That They Have Reached a True Consensus   A significant problem in groups that suffer from groupthink is that members are not aware of the phenomenon. They think they have reached genuine consensus. For example, suppose you and your friends are trying to decide which movie to rent on Friday night. Someone suggests *Gone with the Wind*. Even though you have already seen the movie on television, you do not want to be contentious, so you agree with the suggestion. Other group members also agree.

After your group has seen the movie and you are returning the tape to the video store, you overhear another one of your friends say, "I enjoyed the movie better when I saw it the first time." After a quick poll of the group, you discover that most of your friends had already seen the movie! They agreed to see it only because they did not want to hurt anyone's feelings. They thought everyone else was in agreement. Although the group appeared to reach consensus, only a few people actually agreed with the decision. Therefore, even if you think that the rest of the group agrees and that you are the only dissenter, your group could still be experiencing groupthink. Just because your group seems to have reached a consensus does not necessarily mean that all the members truly agree.

Members Are Too Concerned About Reinforcing the Leader's Beliefs Leaders of small groups often emerge because they suggest some of the best ideas, motivate group members, or devote themselves to group goals more than others do. If group members place too much emphasis on the credibility or infallibility of their leader, groupthink may occur. Leaders who like to be surrounded by yes people (who always agree with their ideas) lose the advantage of having their ideas tested. Most people do not like criticism and do not like to be told that their ideas are inept or inappropriate. Therefore, group leaders are understandably attracted to those who agree with them. Leaders sensitive to the problem of groupthink will solicit and tolerate all group viewpoints, because testing the quality of solutions requires different opinions.

One researcher has found empirical support for the symptoms of groupthink. Rebecca Cline found that groupthink groups do express more agreement without clarification and also use simpler and fewer substantiated agreements than non-groupthink groups.[57] She also found that groups that experience groupthink spend about 10 percent more of their discussion time making statements of agreement or disagreement than non-groupthink groups. Groups that experience groupthink perpetuate the illusion of agreement by sprinkling in frequent comments such as "Yeah, I see what you're saying," "That's right," or "Sure."

REVIEW

Symptoms of Groupthink

▶ Critical thinking is not encouraged or rewarded.

▶ Members think their group can do no wrong.

▶ Members are too concerned about justifying their actions.

▶ Members apply pressure to those who do not support the group.

▶ Members often believe that they have reached a true consensus.

▶ Members are too concerned about reinforcing the leader's beliefs.

Suggestions to Reduce Groupthink

You may think that groupthink, which is characterized by a lack of conflict or controversy, should not occur in an effective task-oriented group, but what you really want to know is "How can I reduce the chances of groupthink occurring in my group?" You expect theory to do more than just describe what happens; it should also suggest ways of improving communication. To help prevent groupthink, consider the following specific suggestions based on Janis's initial observations, as well as on the theories and the research of other small group communication researchers.

1. *The group leader should encourage critical, independent thinking.* The leader should make clear that he or she does not want the group to reach agreement until each member has critically evaluated the issues. Most group leaders want to command the respect

Groupthink results in ineffective consensus because of the drive to minimize conflict. How do you deal with conflict in group activities?

of their groups, but a leader's insistence that the group always agree with him or her does not constitute respect; instead, it may demonstrate a fear of disagreement. Thus, if you find yourself a leader in a small group, you should encourage disagreement not just for the sake of argument but to eliminate groupthink. Even if you are not a leader, you can encourage a healthy discussion by voicing any objections you have to the ideas being discussed. Do not permit instant, uncritical agreement in your group.

2. *Group members should be sensitive to status differences that may affect decision making.* Imagine that you are a young architect assigned to help design a new dinner theater for a large futuristic shopping center. When you first meet with the other architects assigned to the project, the senior member of your firm presents the group with a rough sketch of a theater patterned after a nineteenth-century American opera house. Although the design is practical and attractive, you feel that it does not fit in with the ultramodern design of the rest of the center. Because of the difference in status between the younger architects and the senior architect, you and your contemporaries are tempted to laud the design and keep your reservations to yourselves. Doing so would result in groupthink. Groups should not yield to status differences when evaluating ideas, issues, and solutions to problems. Instead, they should consider the merits of suggestions, weigh evidence, and make decisions about the validity of ideas without being too concerned about the status of those making suggestions. Of course, this is easier to propose than to implement.

Numerous studies suggest that a person with more credibility is going to be more persuasive.[58] Cereal companies know this when they hire famous athletes to sell breakfast food. The message is "Don't worry about the quality of the product. If this Olympic gold-medal winner eats this stuff, you'll like it too." The athlete's fame and status do not necessarily make the cereal good; however, you still might buy the cereal, making a decision based on emotion rather than fact. Group members sometimes make decisions this way, too. Avoid agreeing with a decision just because of the status or credibility of the person making it. Evaluate the quality of the solution on its own merits.

3. *Invite someone from outside the group to evaluate the group's decision-making process.* Sometimes an objective point of view from outside the group can help avoid groupthink. Many large companies hire consultants to evaluate organizational decision making, but you do not have to be part of a multinational corporation to ask someone to analyze your group's decision-making process. Ask someone from outside your group to sit in on one of your meetings. At the end of the meeting, ask the observer to summarize his or her observations and evaluations of the group. An outside observer may make some members uncomfortable, but if you explain why the visitor is there, the group will probably accept the visitor and eagerly await objective observations. Sometimes an outsider can identify unproductive group norms more readily than group members can.

4. *Assign a group member the role of devil's advocate.* If no disagreement develops in a group, members may enjoy getting along and never realize that their group suffers from groupthink. If you find yourself in a group of pacifists, play devil's advocate by trying to raise objections and potential problems. Assign someone to consider the negative aspects of a suggestion before it is implemented. It could save the group from groupthink and enhance the quality of the decision.

5. *Ask group members to subdivide into small groups (or to work individually) and to consider potential problems with the suggested solutions.* In large groups, all members most likely will not be able to voice their objections and reservations. The U.S. Congress does most of its work in small committees. Members of Congress realize that in order to hear and thoroughly evaluate bills and resolutions, small groups of representatives must work together in committees. If you are working in a group too large for everyone to discuss the issues, suggest breaking into groups of two or three, with each group composing a list of objections to the proposals. The lists could be forwarded to the group secretary, who then could weed out duplicate objections and identify common points of contention. Even in a group of seven or eight, two subcommittees could evaluate the recommendations of the group. Group members should be able to participate frequently and evaluate the issues carefully. Individuals could also write down their objections to the proposed recommendations and then present them to the group.

    One technique that may reduce groupthink is to have groups divide into two teams to debate an issue. The principle is simple: Develop a group structure that encourages critical thinking. As we learned in the last chapter, vigilant thinking fosters quality decisions.

6. *Consider using technology to help your group gather and evaluate ideas.* One study found that having group members share and test ideas and evidence through group decision support system (GDSS) technology via a computer network rather than always meeting face-to-face may facilitate more extensive testing of ideas and opin-

ions.[59] It may not be possible for some of the groups you participate in to use such methods to help you generate ideas. Considerable research, however, suggests that the quality of group decisions can be enhanced if group members contribute ideas by using e-mail or other software programs to help gather and evaluate ideas.[60] One advantage to using GDSS methods in reducing groupthink is that ideas can be presented anonymously. Certain software programs let group members share ideas without revealing whether a member is the boss or the new intern. GDSS technology also helps separate the process of generating ideas from evaluating ideas.

Identifying and correcting groupthink should help improve the quality of your group's decisions by capitalizing on opposing viewpoints. A textbook summary of suggestions for dealing with groupthink may lead you to think that this problem can be corrected easily. It cannot. Because many people think that conflict should be avoided, they need specific guidelines for identifying and avoiding groupthink. In essence, be critical of ideas, not people. Remember that some controversy is useful. A decision-making group uses conflict to seek the best decision everyone can agree on—it seeks consensus. The last section of this chapter will discuss managing conflict in the search for consensus.

REVIEW

Suggestions to Reduce Groupthink

▶ As a group leader, encourage critical, independent thinking.

▶ Be sensitive to status differences that may affect decision making.

▶ Invite someone from outside the group to evaluate the group's decision-making process.

▶ Assign a group member the role of devil's advocate.

▶ Ask group members to subdivide into small groups (or to work individually) and to consider potential problems with suggested solutions.

Consensus: Reaching Agreement Through Communication

Some conflict is inevitable in groups, but this does not mean that all group discussions are doomed to end in disagreement and conflict. Conflict can be managed. **Consensus** occurs when all group members support and are committed to a decision. Even if a group does not reach consensus on key issues, it is not necessarily a failure. Good decisions can certainly emerge from groups whose members do not all completely agree on decisions. The U.S. Congress, for example, rarely achieves consensus; that does not mean, however, that its legislative process is ineffective.

Although conflict and controversy can improve the quality of group decision making, it is worthwhile to aim for consensus. A few words about consensus may help you form more realistic expectations about working in small groups. The following sections will also suggest some specific ways to help your group reach agreement.

The Nature of Consensus

Consensus should not come too quickly. If it does, your group is probably a victim of groupthink. Nor does consensus usually come easily. Sometimes group agreement is built on agreements on minor points raised during the discussion. To achieve consensus, group members should try to emphasize these areas of agreement. This can be a time-consuming process, and some members may lose patience before they reach agreement. Regardless of how long a group takes to reach consensus, consensus generally results from careful and thoughtful communication between members of the group.

Is taking the time to reach consensus worth the effort? Groups that reach consensus (not groupthink) and also effectively use good discussion methods, such as testing and challenging evidence and ideas, achieve a better-quality decision.[61] Evidence also suggests that groups that achieve consensus are likely to continue to maintain agreement several weeks later.[62]

To achieve consensus, some personal preferences must be surrendered for the overall well-being of the group. Group members must decide, both individually and collectively, whether they can achieve consensus. If two or three members refuse to change their minds on their positions, the rest of the group may decide that reaching consensus is not worth the extra time. Some group communication theorists suggest that groups might do better to postpone a decision if consensus cannot be reached, particularly if the group making the decision will also implement it. If several group members oppose the solution, they will be less eager to put it into practice. Ultimately, if consensus cannot be reached, a group should abide by the decision of the majority.

Suggestions for Reaching Consensus

Communication researchers agree that group members usually go through considerable effort before reaching consensus. Using specific communication strategies may help members more readily foster consensus in group and team meetings.

We suggest you keep three key pieces of advice in mind when striving for group consensus.

1. Because groups have a tendency to change topics frequently and get off track, help keep the group remain oriented toward its goal. Groups and teams often fail to reach agreement because they engage in discussion that is not relevant to the issue at hand; groups digress.

2. Be other-oriented and sensitive to the ideas of others. Listen without interrupting. Make an honest effort to set aside your own ideas and seek to understand the ideas of others.

3. Promote honest group-member interaction and dialogue. Genuine consensus is more likely to occur if group and team members honestly express their thoughts and feelings; withholding ideas and suggestions may lead to groupthink.

To help you focus on the group goal, be other-oriented, and honestly share information with group and team members, we present several specific research-based strategies that can promote group and team consensus.[63]

Keeping the Group Oriented Toward Its Goal The following strategies can help your group reach consensus by staying focused and on task.

Keep the focus on the group's goal rather than only on specific strategies to achieve the goal: Focusing on shared interests and reminding the group what the goals are can help get groups unstuck from debating only one or two strategies to achieve the goal. Group members sometimes fall in love with an idea or strategy and won't let go of it. One way to move forward is to explicitly and frequently remind the group what the over-arching goal is that you are trying to achieve.

Display known facts for all group members to see: Consider using a chalkboard, flipchart, or overhead projector to display what is really known about the issues confronting the group. When group members cannot agree, they often retreat to restating opinions rather than advocating an idea based on hard evidence. If all group members can be reminded of what is known, consensus may be more easily obtained.

One way to display facts is to use the is/is not technique. Draw a line down the middle of the chalkboard or flip chart. On one side of the line note what is known about the present issue. On the other side, identify what is unknown or is mere speculation. Separating facts from speculation can help group members focus on data rather than unproven inferences.[64]

Use metadiscussional phrases: **Metadiscussion** literally means discussion about discussion. In other words, a metadiscussional statement focuses on the discussion process rather than on the topic under consideration.[65] Metadiscussional statements include "Aren't we getting a little off the subject?" or "John, we haven't heard from you yet. What do you think?" or "Let's summarize our areas of agreement." These statements contain information and advice about the problem-solving process rather than about the issue at hand. Several studies show that groups whose members help orient the group toward its goal by (1) relying on facts rather than opinions, (2) making useful, constructive suggestions, and (3) trying to resolve conflict, are more likely to reach agreement than groups whose members do not try to keep the group focused on its goal.[66]

One of the essential task competencies that we identified in Chapter 1 is to maintain a focus on the group's task. Metadiscussional phrases are ways of helping to keep the group or team focused on the task or meeting agenda. This is an exceptionally powerful skill to learn and use because you can offer metadiscussional statements even if you are not the designated leader of the group.

Do not wait until the very end of the deliberations to suggest solutions: Research suggests that groups that delay identifying specific solutions until the very end of the discussion are less likely to reach consensus than those groups that think about solutions earlier in the deliberations.[67] Of course, before jumping to solutions, groups need to analyze and assess the present situation. But groups that only identify solutions at the tail end of discussions have more difficulty reaching consensus.

Be Other-Oriented: Listen to the Ideas of Others What follows are tips and suggestions to help manage the relational tension that usually occurs when groups can't reach consensus.

Avoid always arguing for your own position: People often defend a solution or suggestion just because it is theirs. Here is a suggestion that may help you develop a more objective point of view: If you find yourself becoming defensive over an idea you suggested, assume that your idea has become the property of the group; it no longer belongs to you. Present your position as clearly as possible, then listen to other members' reactions and consider them carefully before you push for your point. Just because people disagree with your idea does not necessarily mean they respect you less.

Do not assume that someone must win and someone must lose: When discussion becomes deadlocked, try not to view the discussion in terms of "us" versus "them" or "me" versus "the group." Try not to view communication as a game in which someone wins and others lose. Be willing to compromise and modify your original position. Of course, if compromising means finding a solution that is marginally acceptable to everyone but does not really solve a problem, then seek a better solution.

Use group-oriented rather than self-oriented pronouns: Harry liked to talk about the problem as *he* saw it. He often began sentences with phrases such as, "I think this is a good idea," or, "My suggestion is to . . . ." Studies suggest that groups that reach consensus generally use more pronouns like we, us, and our, while groups that do not reach consensus use more pronouns like I, me, my, and mine.[68] Using group-oriented words can foster cohesiveness.

Avoid opinionated statements that indicate a closed mind: Communication scholars consistently find that opinionated statements and low tolerance for dissenting points of view often inhibit agreement. This is especially apparent when the opinionated person is the discussion leader. A group with a less-opinionated leader is more likely to reach agreement. Remember that using facts and relying on information obtained by direct observation are probably the best ways to avoid being too opinionated.

Make an effort to clarify misunderstandings: Although not all disagreements arise because conflicting parties fail to understand one another, misunderstanding another's meaning sometimes does create conflict and adversely affect group consensus. Dealing with misunderstanding is simple. Ask a group member to explain a particular word or statement that you do not understand. Constantly solicit feedback from your listeners. For example, repeat the previous speaker's point and ask if you've got it right before you state your position on an issue. This procedure can become time-consuming and stilted if overused, but it can help when misunderstandings about meanings arise. It may also be helpful for you to remember that meanings are conveyed through people, not words. Stated another way, the meaning of a word comes from a person's unique perspective, perception, and experience.

Emphasize areas of agreement: When the group gets bogged down in conflict and disagreement, it may prove useful to stop and identify the issues and information on which group members do agree. One study found that groups whose members were able to keep refocusing the group on areas of agreement, particularly following episodes of disagreement, were more likely to reach consensus than groups that continued to accentuate the negative.[69]

Promote Honest Interaction and Dialogue

To help groups and teams avoid a false consensus (groupthink) and to share ideas in a climate of openness and honesty consider these suggestions.

Do not change your mind too quickly just to avoid conflict: Although you may have to compromise to reach agreement, beware of changing your mind too quickly just to reach consensus. Groupthink occurs when group members do not test and challenge the ideas of others. When agreement seems to come too fast and too easily, be suspicious. Make certain that you have explored other alternatives and that everyone accepts the solution for basically the same reasons. Beware of the tendency to avoid conflict. Of course, you should not produce conflict just for the sake of conflict, but do not be upset if disagreements arise. Reaching consensus takes time and often requires compromise. Be patient.

Avoid easy techniques that reduce conflict: You may be tempted to flip a coin or to take a simple majority vote when you cannot resolve a disagreement. Resist that temptation, especially early in your deliberation. If possible, avoid making a decision until the entire group can agree. Of course, at times, a majority vote is the only way to resolve a conflict. Just be certain that the group explores other alternatives before it makes a hasty decision to avoid conflict. When time permits, gaining consensus through communication is best.

Seek out differences of opinion: Remember that disagreements may improve the quality of a group's decision. With a variety of opinions and information, a group has a better chance of finding a good solution. Also remember that complex problems seldom have just one solution. Perhaps more than one of the suggestions offered will work. Actively recruit opposing viewpoints if everyone seems to be agreeing without much discussion. You could appoint someone to play the role of devil's advocate if members are reluctant to offer criticism. Of course, do not belabor the point if you think that group members genuinely agree after considerable discussion. Test ideas that a group accepts too eagerly.

Try to involve everyone in the discussion; frequently contribute to the group: Again, the more varied the suggestions, solutions, and information, the greater the chance that a group will reach quality solutions and achieve consensus. Encourage less-talkative members to contribute to the group. Several studies suggest that members will be more satisfied with a solution if they have had an opportunity to express their opinions and to offer suggestions.[70] Remember not to dominate the discussion. Good listening is important, too, and you may need to encourage others to speak out and assert themselves.

Use a variety of methods to reach agreement: One researcher has found that groups are more likely to reach agreement if members try several approaches to resolve a deadlocked situation rather than using just one method of seeking consensus.[71] Consider (1) combining two or more ideas into one solution; (2) building, changing, or extending existing ideas; (3) using effective persuasion skills to convince others to agree; and (4) developing new ideas to move the discussion forward rather than just rehashing old ideas.

Expand the number of ideas and alternatives: One reason a group may not agree is because none of the ideas or solutions being discussed are good ones. Each solution on the table may have flaws. The task should change from trying to reach agreement on the alternatives in front of the group to generating more alternatives.[73] Switching from a debate to brainstorming may help pry group members away from a foolish adherence to existing solutions. Consider using Delphi technique, affinity technique or nominal-group technique as we discussed in Chapter 9 as a structured way to set more ideas on the table when the group seems stuck.

In summary, research suggests that groups that search for areas of agreement while critically testing ideas and reducing ambiguity are more likely to reach consensus than groups that don't do these things. Rather than just saying "No, you're wrong," identify specific issues that need to be clarified. Groups that focus on disagreement about procedures rather than on substantive issues are less likely to reach consensus.[74] Building consensus takes not time and skill and is not necessarily the goal of the group, but if possible, building consensus may result in a better-quality decision.

Suggestions for Reaching Consensus

Keep the Group Oriented Toward Its Goal

EFFECTIVE GROUP MEMBERS	INEFFECTIVE GROUP MEMBERS
• Help keep the group focused on the goal.	• Go off on tangents and do not stay focused on the agenda.
• Display known facts for all members in the group to see.	• Rely only on oral summaries or no summaries of issues or facts about which members agree.
• Talk about the discussion process using metadiscussional phrases that help orient the group toward its goal.	• Do little to help summarize or clarify group discussion.
• Suggest possible solutions throughout the group's deliberation.	• Wait until time is about to run out before suggesting solutions.

Be Other-Oriented: Listen to the Ideas of Others

EFFECTIVE GROUP MEMBERS	INEFFECTIVE GROUP MEMBERS
• Avoid always arguing for their own position.	• Argue for an idea because it is their own.
• Approach conflict as a problem to be solved rather than a win/lose situation.	• Assume that someone will win and someone will lose the argument.
• Use group-oriented pronouns to talk about the group.	• Talk about individual accomplishments rather than group accomplishments.
• Avoid opinionated statements that are not based on facts or evidence.	• Are closed-minded and inflexible.
• Clarify misunderstandings.	• Do not clarify misunderstandings or check to see whether their message is understood.
• Emphasize areas of agreement.	• Ignore areas of agreement.

Promote Honest Interaction and Dialogue

EFFECTIVE GROUP MEMBERS	INEFFECTIVE GROUP MEMBERS
• Do not change their minds quickly just to avoid conflict.	• Give in to the opinion of group members just to avoid conflict.
• Avoid easy conflict-reducing techniques	• Find easy ways to reduce the conflict, such as taking a quick vote without holding a discussion.
• Seek out differences of opinion. Try to involve everyone in the discussion and make frequent, meaningful contributions to the group.	• Do not ferret out a variety of viewpoints. Permit one person to monopolize the discussion or fail to draw out quiet group members.

• Use a variety of methods to reach agreement.	• Use only one or two approaches to reach agreement.
• Expand the number of ideas and alternatives. Use brainstorming, Delphi technique, affinity technique, or nominal-group technique.	• Seek a limited number of options or solutions.

Putting Principles into Practice

Conflict can have both positive and negative effects on a group. Conflict occurs because people are different, because they have their own ways of doing things. These differences affect the way people perceive and approach problem solving.

Cooperative Conflict Management Principles

▶ Separate the people from the problem.

▶ Focus on shared interests.

Collaborating via

TECHNOLOGY

Need some extra help or tips for managing group tension and conflict? The following online resources offer information and strategies for working through disagreement in groups and teams.

www.mapnp.org/library/grp_skill/grp_skll.htm
 This comprehensive list of links to a variety of skills and topics in groups offers resources on conflict management and facilitating face-to-face group discussion.

www.nova.edu/shss/DCAR
 Nova Southwestern University supports a well-maintained Website chock full of conflict-management resources that may be just what you and your group need to manage group tension and disagreement.

www.mapnp.org/library/grp_skll/facltate/facltak.htm
 This site offers numerous links to tip, tools, and suggestions for facilitating group discussion.

- ▶ Generate many options to solve problems.
- ▶ Base decisions on objective criteria.

Groupthink

The absence of conflict or a false sense of agreement is called groupthink. It occurs when group members are reluctant to voice their feelings and objections to issues. To help reduce the likelihood of groupthink, review the following suggestions:

- ▶ If you are the group leader, encourage critical, independent thinking.
- ▶ Be sensitive to status differences that may affect decision making.
- ▶ Invite someone from outside the group to evaluate the group's decision-making.
- ▶ Assign a group member the role of devil's advocate.
- ▶ Ask members to subdivide into small groups to consider potential problems with suggested solutions.

Consensus

Consider applying the following suggestions to help reach consensus and to help manage the conflicts and disagreements that arise in groups.

- ▶ Keep the group oriented toward its goal.

  Keep the focus on the group's goal rather than only on specific strategies to achieve the goal.

  Display known facts for all group members to see.

  Use metadiscussional phrases.

  Do not wait until the very end of the deliberations to suggest solutions.

- ▶ Be other-oriented: Listen to the ideas of others.

  Avoid always arguing for your own position.

  Do not assume that someone must win and someone must lose.

  Use group-oriented rather than self-oriented pronouns.

  Avoid opinionated statements that indicate a closed mind.

  Make an effort to clarify misunderstandings.

  Emphasize areas of agreement.

- ▶ Promote honest interaction and dialogue.

  Do not change your mind too quickly just to avoid conflict.

  Avoid easy techniques that reduce conflict.

  Seek out differences of opinion.

  Try to involve everyone in the discussion; frequently contribute to the group.

  Use a variety of methods to reach agreement.

  Expand the number of ideas and alternatives.

PRACTICE

Agree/Disagree Statements about Conflict

Read each statement once, and mark whether you agree (A) or disagree (D) with it. Take five or six minutes to do this.

1. Most people find an argument interesting and exciting.

2. In most conflicts someone must win and someone must lose. That's the way conflict is.

3. The best way to handle a conflict is simply to let everyone cool off.

4. Most people get upset with a person who disagrees with them.

5. Most hidden agendas are probably best kept hidden to ensure a positive social climate.

6. If people spend enough time together, they will find something to disagree about and will eventually become upset with one another.

7. Conflicts can be solved if people just take the time to listen to one another.

8. Conflict hinders a group's work.

9. If you disagree with someone in a group, it is usually better to keep quiet than to get the group off track with your personal difference of opinion.

10. When a group cannot reach a decision, members should abide by the decision of the group leader if he or she is qualified and competent.

11. To compromise is to take the easy way out of conflict.

12. Some people produce more conflict and tension than others. These people should be restricted from decision-making groups.

After you have marked the preceding statements, break up into small groups and try to agree or disagree unanimously with each statement. Try in particular to find reasons for differences of opinion. If your group cannot reach agreement or disagreement, you may change the wording in any statement to promote consensus. Assign one group member to observe your group interactions. After your group has attempted to reach consensus, the observer should report how effectively the group used the guidelines suggested in this chapter.

Win as Much as You Can

This activity is designed to explore the effects of trust and conflict on communication.[75] Your instructor will explain how this exercise is to be conducted.

4X's: Lose $1 each
3X's: Win $1 each 1Y: Lose $3
2X's: Win $2 each 2Y's: Lose $2 each
1X: Win $3 3Y's: Lose $1 each
4Y's: Win $1

Directions: For ten successive rounds, you and your partner will choose either an X or a Y. Each round's "payoff" depends on the pattern made in your cluster.

Strategy: Confer with your partner on each round to make a joint decision. Before rounds 5, 8, and 10, confer with the other pairs in your cluster. There are three key rules:

1. Do not confer with the other members of your cluster unless you are given specific permission to do so. This applies to nonverbal and verbal communication.

2. Each pair must agree on a single choice for each round.

3. Make sure the other members of your cluster do not know your pair's choice until you are instructed to reveal it.

Round	Time Allowed	Confer with	Choice	$ Won	$ Lost	$ Balance	
1	2 min.	Partner					
2	1 min.	Partner					
3	1 min.	Partner					
4	1 min.	Partner					
5	3 min. 1 min.	Cluster Partner					Bonus round pay is multiplied by 3
6	1 min.	Partner					
7	1 min.	Partner					
8	3 min.	Cluster					Pay is multiplied by 5
9	1 min.	Partner					
10	3 min.	Cluster					Pay is multiplied by 10

Your companion Website has more practice activities, questionnaires, and checklists!
www.ablongman.com/beebe

Notes

1. G. Kraus, "The Psychodynamics of Constructive Aggression in Small Groups," *Small Group Research* 28 (1997): 122–45.

2. S. M. Farmer and J. Roth, "Conflict- Handling Behavior in Work Groups: Effects of Group Structure, Decision Processes, and Time, " *Small Group Research* 29 (1998): 669–713.

4 Joseph P. Folger and Marshall Scott Poole, *Working Through Conflict: A Communication Perspective* (Glenview, IL.: Scott, Foresman, 1984) 4.

3. Michael Burgoon, Judee K. Heston, and James McCroskey, *Small Group Communication: A Functional Approach* (New York: Holt, Rinehart & Winston, 1974) 76.

4. B. Aubrey Fisher, "Decision Emergence: Phases in Group Decision-Making," *Speech Monographs* 37 (1970): 60.

5. Linda L. Putnam, "Conflict in Group Decision-Making," in Randy Y. Hirokawa and Marshall Scott Poole, eds., *Communication and Group Decision-Making* (Beverly Hills, CA: Sage, 1986) 190–91.

6. Victor D. Wall and Lindal L. Nolan, "Small Group Conflict: A Look at Equity, Satisfaction, and Styles of Conflict-Management," *Small Group Behavior* 18, no. 2 (May 1987): 188–211.

8. M. Nussbaum, M. Singer, R. Rosas, M. Castillo, E. Flies, R. Lara, R. Sommers, "Decision Support System for Conflict Diagnosis in Personnel Selection, " *Information & Management* 36 (1999): 55–62.

9. Portions of the following discussion of misconceptions about conflict were adapted from Robert J. Doolittle, *Orientations to Communication and Conflict* (Chicago, IL: Science Research Associates, 1976) 7–9.

10. See Fred E. Jandt, (ed.), *Conflict Resolution Through Communication* (New York: Harper & Row, 1973).

11. C. R. Franz and K. G. Jin, "The Structure of Group Conflict in a Collaborative Work Group During Information Systems Development," *Journal of Applied Communication Research* 23 (1995): 108–27.

12. Doolittle, *Orientations to Communication* 8.

13. Gerald R. Miller and Mark Steinberg, *Between People: New Analysis of Interpersonal Communication* (Chicago: Science Research Associates, 1975), 264.

14. S. D. Johnson and C. Bechler, "Examining the Relationship Between Listening Effectiveness and Leadership Emergence: Perceptions, Behaviors, and Recall," *Small Group Research* 29 (1998): 452–71.

15. Miller and Steinberg, *Between People*.

16. D. J. Devine, "Effects of Cognitive Ability, Task Knowledge, Information Sharing, and Conflict on Group Decision-Making Effectiveness," *Small Group Research* 30 (1999): 608-634.

17. B. M. Gayle and R. W. Preiss, "Assessing Emotionality in Organizational Conflicts," *Management Communication Quarterly*, 12 (1998): 280-302; A. Ostell, "Managing Dysfunctional Emotions in Organizations," *Journal of Management Studies*, 33 (1996): 525-557.

18. R. Rodriquez, "Challenging Demographic Reductionism: A Pilot Study Investigating Diversity in Group Composition," *Small Group research* 26 (1998): 744–759.

19. L. Karakowsky and J. P. Siegel, "The Effects of Proportional Representation on Intragroup Behavior in Mixed-Race Decision-Making Groups," *Small Group Research*, 30 (1999): 259-279.

20. T. A. Timmerman, "Racial Diversity, Age Diversity, Interdependence, and Team Performance," *Small Group Research,* 31 (2000): 592-606.

21. Farmer and Roth, "Conflict-Handling Behavior in Work Groups."

22. See Donald W. Klopf, *Intercultural Encounters: Fundamentals of Intercultural Communication* (Englewood, CA: Morton, 1998).

23. C. Kirchmeyer and A. Cohen, "Multicultural Groups," *Group & Organization Management* 17 (June 1992): 153–70.

24. C. L. Wong, D. Tjosvold, and F. Lee, "Managing Conflict in a Diverse Work Force: A Chinese Perspective in North America," *Small Group Research* 23 (August 1992): 302–21.

25. S. Ting-Toomey, "Toward a Theory of Conflict and Culture," in W. Gudykunst, L. Stewart, and S. Ting-Toomey, eds., *Communication, Culture, and Organizational Processes* (Beverly Hills, CA: Sage, 1985).

26. S. Ting-Toomey, "A Face Negotiation Theory," in Y. Kim and W. Gudykunst eds., *Theories in Intercultural Communication* (Newbury Park, CA: Sage, 1988).

27. Ting-Toomey, "Conflict and Culture."

28. See also an excellent review of conflict and culture research in William B. Gudykunst, *Bridging Difference: Effective Intergroup Communication* (Newbury Park, CA: Sage, 1994).

29. Ting-Toomey, "A Face Negotiation Theory."

30. For an excellent review of conflict and gender, see M. Argyle, *The Psychology of Interpersonal Behavior* (London: Penguin Books, 1994).

31. R. Kilmann and K. Thomas, "Interpersonal Conflict-Handling Behavior as Reflections of Jungian Personality Dimensions," *Psychological Reports* 37 (1975): 971–80.

32. L. L. Putnam and C. E. Wilson, "Communicative Strategies in Organizational Conflicts: Reliability and Validity of a Measurement Scale," in M. Burgoon, ed., *Communication Yearbook* 6 (Beverly Hills CA: Sage, 1982).

33. J. G. Oetzel, "Explaining Individual Communication Processes in Homogeneous and Heterogeneous Groups Through Individualism-Collectivism and Self-Construal," *Human Communication Research*, 25 (1998): 202-224; H. C. Triandis *Individualism and Collectivism* (Boulder, CO: Westview, 1995); W. B. Gudykunst, Y. Matsumoto, S. Ting-Toomey, T. Nishida, K. S. Kim and S. Heyman, "The Influence of Cultural Individualism-Collectivism, Self Construals, and Individual Values on Communication Styles Across Cultures," *Human Communication Research*, 22 (1996): 510.

34. T. M. Brown and C. E. Miller, "Communication Networks in Task-Performing Groups: Effects of Task Complexity, Time Pressure, and Interpersonal Dominance," *Small Group Research* 31 (2000): 131–157.

35. Kirchmeyer and Cohen, "Multicultural Groups;" Wong, Tjosvold, and Lee, "Managing Conflict in a Diverse Work Force."

36. Kirchmeyer and Cohen, "Multicultural Groups;" Wong, Tjosvold, and Lee, "Managing Conflict in a Diverse Work Force."

37. D. Weider-Hatfield and J. D. Hatfield, "Superiors' Conflict Management Strategies and Subordinate Outcomes," *Management Communication Quarterly*, 10 (1996): 189-208; also see P. J. Carnevale and T. M. Probst, "Social Values and Social Conflict in Creative Problem Solving Categorization," *Journal of Personality and Social Psychology*, 74 (1998): 1300-1309.

38. R. Fisher and W. Ury, *Getting to Yes: Negotiating Agreement without Giving In* (Boston: Houghton Mifflin, 1991).

39. See Joyce L. Hocker and William W. Wilmot, *Interpersonal Conflict-management* (Madison, WI: Brown and Benchmark, 1998). Fisher and Ury, *Getting to Yes*; Robert Bolton, *People Skills: How to Assert Yourself, Listen to Others and Resolve Conflict* (New York: Simon & Schuster, 1979), 217; Dennis A. Romig and Laurie J. Romig, *Structured Teamwork*

Guide (Austin, TX.: Performance Resource, 1990); see also Dennis A. Romig, *Breakthrough Teamwork: Outstanding Results Using Structured Teamwork*, (New York: Irwin, 1996).

40. J. Gottman, C. Notarius, J. Gonso, and H. Markman, *A Couple's Guide to Communication* (Champaign, IL: Research Press, 1976).

41. Hocker and Wilmot, *Interpersonal Conflict-Management*.

42. R. A. Meyers and D. E. Brashers, "Argument in Group Decision Making: Explicating a Process Model and Investigating the Argument-Outcome Link," *Communication Monographs*, 65 (1998): 261-281.

43. Shaila M. Miranda, "Avoidance of Groupthink: Meeting Management Using Group Support Systems," *Small Group Communication Research* 25, no. 1 (February 1994): 105–36.

44. K. Thomas and W. Schmidt, "A Survey of Managerial Interests with Respect to Conflict," *Academy of Management Journal* 19 (1976): 315–18.

45. J. M. Juran, *Juran on Planning for Quality* (New York: Free Press, 1988).

46. Boulton, *People Skills,* 217.

47. Gayle and Preiss, "Assessing Emotionality in Organizational Conflicts."

48. A. Ostell, "Managing Dysfunctional Emotionality in Organizations," *Journal of Management Studies* 33 (1996): 523–557.

49. Rebecca J. Welch Cline, "Detecting Groupthink: Methods for Observing the Illusion of Unanimity," *Communication Quarterly* 38, no. 2 (Spring 1990): 112–26.

50. Irving L. Janis, *Victims of Groupthink* (Boston: Houghton Mifflin, 1973).

51. R. K. M. Haurwitz, "Faculty Doubted Bonfire's Stability," *Austin-American Statesman,* (December 10, 1999), p. A1.52. Randy Y. Hirokawa, Dennis S. Gouran, and Amy Martz, "Understanding the Sources of Faulty Group Decision Making: A Lesson from the Challenger Disaster," *Small Group Behavior* 19, no. 4 (November 1988): 411–33.

53. J. F. Veiga, "The Frequency of Self-Limiting Behavior in Groups: A Measure and an Explanation," *Human Relations* 44 (1991): 877–95.

54. M. D. Street. "Groupthink: An Examination of Theoretical Issues, Implications, and Future Research Suggestions," *Small Group Research* 28 (1997): 72–93; M.D. Street and W. P. Anthony, "A Conceptual Framework Establishing the Relationship Between Groupthink and Escalating Commitment Behavior," *Small Group Research* 28 (1997): 267–93; A. A. Mohaned and F. A. Wiebe, "Toward a Process Theory of Groupthink," *Small Group Research* 27 (1996): 416–30; K. Granstrom and D. Stiwne "A Bipolar Model of Groupthink: An Expansion of Janis's Concept," *Small Group Research* 29 (1998): 32–56.

55. Adapted from Irving L. Janis, "Groupthink," *Psychology Today* 5 Nov. 1971): 43–46, 74–76.

56. W. Park, "A Review of Research on Groupthink," *Journal of Behavioral Decision Making*, 3 (1990): 229–245; M. D. Street, "Groupthink: An Examination of Theoretical Issues, Implications and Future Research Suggestions," *Small Group Research*, 28 (1997): 72-93; M. D. Street and W. P. Anthony, "A Conceptual Framework Establishing The Relationship Between Groupthink and Escalating commitment Behavior," *Small Group Research,* 28 (1997): 267–293.

57. Cline, "Detecting Groupthink," 112–26.

58. See Kenneth Andersen and Theodore Clevenger, Jr., "A Summary of Experimental Research in Ethos," *Speech Monographs* 30 (1963): 59–78.

59. S. M. Miranda, "Avoidance of Groupthink."

60. S. M. Miranda, "Avoidance of Groupthink."

61. Randy Y. Hirokawa, "Consensus Group Decision-Making, Quality of Decision and Group Satisfaction: An Attempt to Sort 'Fact' from 'Fiction'," *Central States Speech Journal* 33 (Summer 1982): 407–15.

62. Rolayne S. DeStephen and Randy Y. Hirokawa, "Small Group Consensus: Stability of Group Support of the Decision, Task Process, and Group Relationships," *Small Group Behavior* 19, no. 2 (May 1988): 227–39.

63. Portions of the following section on consensus were adapted from John A. Kline, "Ten Techniques for Reaching Consensus in Small Groups," *Air Force Reserve Officer Training Corps Education Journal* 19 (Spring 1977): 19–21.

64. See Hirokawa, "Consensus Group Decision-Making"; Randy Y. Hirokawa, "Discussion Procedures and Decision-Making Performance: A Test of the Functional Perspective," *Human Communication Research* 12, no. 2 (Winter 1985): 203–24; Randy Y. Hirokawa and Dirk R. Scheerhorn, "Communication in Faulty Group Decision-Making," in Randy Y. Hirokawa and Marshall Scott Poole, eds., *Communication and Group Decision-Making* (Beverly Hills, CA: Sage, 1986).

65. See Dennis S. Gouran, "Variables Related to Consensus in Group Discussions of Questions of Policy," *Speech Monographs* 36 (August 1969): 385–91; Thomas J. Knutson, "An Experimental Study of the Effects of Orientation Behavior on Small Group Consensus," *Speech Monographs* 39 (August 1972): 159–65; John A. Kline, "Orientation and Group Consensus," *Central States Speech Journal* 23 (Spring 1972): 44–47.

66. Gouran, "Variables," 385–91; Knutson, "Experimental Study," Kline, "Orientation," 44–47.

67. Randy Y. Hirokawa, "Consensus Group Decision-Making, Quality of Decision and Group Satisfaction: An Attempt to Sort 'Fact' from 'Fiction'," *Central States Speech Journal* 33 (Summer 1982): 407–15.

68. See John A. Kline and James L. Hullinger, "Redundancy, Self Orientation, and Group Consensus," *Speech Monographs* 40 (March 1973): 72–74.

69. C. A. VanLear and E. A. Mabry, "Testing Contrasting Interaction Models for Discriminating Between Consensual and Dissentient Decision-Making Groups," *Small Group Research*, 30 (1999): 29-58.

70. See Henry W. Riecken, "The Effect of Talkativeness on Ability to Influence Group Solutions of Problems," *Sociometry* 21 (1958): 309–21.

71. Roger C. Pace, "Communication Patterns in High and Low Consensus Discussion: A Descriptive Analysis," *Southern Speech Communication Journal* 53 (Winter 1988): 184–202.

72. Pace, "Communication Patterns in High and Low Consensus Discussion."

73. C. A. VanLear and E. A. Mabry, "Testing Contrasting Interaction Models for Discriminating Between Consensual and Dissentient Decision-Making Groups."

74. J. William Pfeiffer and John E. Jones, eds., *A Handbook of Structured Experiences for Human Relations Training*, vol. 2 (La Jolla, CA: University Associates, 1974), 62–67.

Objectives:

After studying this chapter,
you will be able to:

▶ Discuss three approaches to the study
  of leadership.

▶ Describe three styles of leadership.

▶ Explain the relationship between situational variables and the effectiveness of
  different leadership styles.

▶ Analyze a small group meeting and
  determine which leadership behaviors
  will move the group toward its goal.

▶ Describe your own leadership style.

▶ Determine those situations in which
  you are most likely to be an effective
  leader.

▶ Be a more effective group leader and
  participant.

▶ Explain the purpose of simulation in
  leadership training.

▶ Identify three transformational leadership skills.

Leadership

> "The first responsibility of a leader is to define reality.
> The last is to say thank you. In between, the leader is a servant."
> —Max De Pree

Before beginning this chapter, consider the following statements about leadership:

Leaders are born and not made.

An effective leader is always in control of the group process.

A leader is a person who gets others to do the work.

Leadership is a set of functions distributed throughout the group.

The leader should know more than other group members about the topic of discussion.

An authoritarian leader is better than one who allows the group to function without control.

It is best for a group to have only one leader.

A person who has been appointed leader is the leader.

What do you think about these statements? With which ones do you agree? Disagree? If it has not happened already, be assured that one day you will find yourself in a leadership position—on a committee, in an organization, or perhaps in the military. In fact, whenever you participate in a decision-making group your attitudes about leadership will affect your behavior, the behavior of others, and the effectiveness of the group.

This chapter provides information about the nature of leadership in groups to help you become a more effective group participant and offers some specific suggestions to help you become an effective leader.

What Is Leadership?

When you think about "leadership," what comes to mind? A fearless commanding officer leading troops into battle? The president of the United States addressing the country on national television? The student-body president coordinating and representing student efforts? Perhaps you think of the chairperson of a committee you are on. For our purposes here we shall define **leadership** as communication that influences, guides, directs, or controls a group.

Traditionally, the study of leadership has centered on people who are successful in leadership positions. Researchers argued that by looking at successful leaders they could identify attributes or individual traits that best predict good leadership ability. Identifying such traits would be tremendously valuable to those in business, government, or the military who are responsible for promoting others to positions of leadership.

Trait Perspective: Characteristics of Effective Leaders

Over the last several decades, researchers have conducted scores of trait studies indicating that leaders often have attributes such as intelligence, enthusiasm, dominance, self-confidence, social participation, and egalitarianism.[1] Other researchers found physical traits to be related to leadership ability. Leaders seemed to be larger, more active and energetic, and better looking than others.[2] Still other researchers found that leaders possess tact, cheerfulness, a sense of justice, discipline, versatility, and self-control. One alleged study conducted by a branch of the military determined that leaders love good, red meat and aggressively pursue desserts.

The **trait perspective**—a view of leadership as the personal attributes or qualities that leaders possess—seemed like a good idea at the time but actually yielded very little useful information. Although correlations between traits and leadership generally have been positive, they occasionally have been weak.[3] Traits useful in one situation, such as leading troops into battle, are not necessarily the traits required for other leadership positions, such as conducting a business meeting.

A further problem with the trait approach is that it does not identify which traits are important to *become* a leader and which are important to *maintain* the position. These studies also fail to adequately distinguish between leaders and followers who possess the same traits, and they are not useful to group participants wishing to improve their leadership skills. After all, people cannot make themselves larger, more energetic, or more aggressive pursuers of desserts. Therefore, we will consider the trait approach to be a "historical perspective" and proceed from there.

Functional Perspective: Group Needs and Roles

Rather than focusing on the characteristics of individual leaders, the **functional perspective** examines leadership as behaviors that may be performed by any group member to maximize group effectiveness. Dean Barnlund and Franklyn Haiman identify leadership behaviors as those that guide, influence, direct, or control others in a group.[4] This is a much more fruitful approach for those interested in improving their leadership abilities. Although the trait approach might help identify the sort of person who should be appointed to a leadership position, the functional approach describes the specific communicative behaviors a leader needs in order for a group to function effectively. By understanding these behaviors, people can participate more effectively in group discussions.

According to advocates of the functional approach, the major distinctions in leadership behaviors fall into two categories: (1) **task leadership** and (2) **process leadership** (also called *group building* or *maintenance*). Task-oriented behaviors aim specifically at accomplishing a group goal. Process-oriented behaviors help maintain a satisfactory interpersonal climate within a group. Both types of leadership are essential.

Task Leadership

When groups convene to solve problems, make decisions, plan activities, or determine policy, they are frequently hampered by group members' random behavior. Even when they

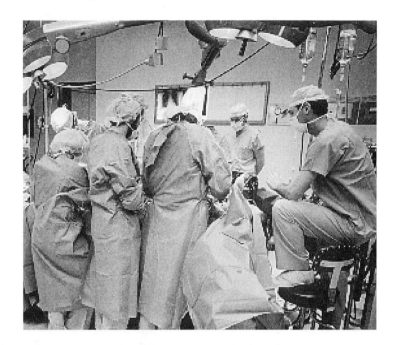

In the operating room, the role of each member of the surgical team is defined by the tasks required. What type of leader is best suited to lead such a team?

get down to business, group process strays. Discussion becomes tangential, and groups lose track of where they are going. Sometimes one person monopolizes the conversation while others remain silent. Sometimes groups just cannot seem to get started. At such times, members may blame their designated leaders for their failure.

A group leader has a responsibility to keep a group moving, but research in group process has shown that anyone can perform the behaviors that keep a group on track. Just because a person has the title "leader" does not necessarily mean that he or she is best equipped to do the job. If leadership is a set of functions that are often distributed, a group is still quite capable of getting its job done regardless of who is designated leader. If you are a member of a disorganized group, you can provide the leadership the group needs even though you are not the leader.

Chapter 4 described the diversity of roles in small groups. The following list summarizes a few task-leadership behaviors and the ways in which they help a group move toward its goal:

▶ *Initiating*: Task-oriented group discussions need to generate ideas. Sometimes ideas are related to procedural matters; at other times a group needs to generate ideas to solve problems. If, for example, you just finished Chapter 8 on problem solving and can see that your group has not adequately defined its problem before suggesting solutions, you might say "Listen. I'm afraid that we're all proposing solutions before we've really agreed on the nature of the problem itself. Let's take a few minutes and talk some more about the problem so that we know we're all discussing the same thing."

By proposing a change in the group's deliberations, you are initiating a procedural change—in this case, one that will probably benefit the group. To "initiate" means to "begin." If you say "Let's get this meeting under way," you have begun a change (assuming the group follows your suggestion). If, later in the meeting, you say, "Let's consider an alternate plan" or "Let's generate some more ideas before evaluating what we have here," again you will probably alter the course of the group's action. You are initiating. Without someone who initiates discussion, a group has no direction. The ability to initiate is an important group behavior and one that anyone can contribute.

▶ *Coordinating*: Different people bring different expectations, beliefs, attitudes, values, and experiences to a group. The contributions of each member are unique, yet all are directed toward a common group goal. Given the diversity in small groups, coordinating is often an important leadership function. Communicative behavior that helps a group explore the contributions of all members is valuable. If, for example, you see a connection between the ideas that two members bring to the group, you should point it out to help focus the group. Coordinating members' efforts can help them see the "groupness" of their activities and reduce their uncertainty about the group, its problem, and its solutions.

▶ *Summarizing*: Groups can get long-winded. Often, in the middle of a discussion members cannot tell just where the discussion began and where it is going. It does not take many tangential remarks to get the group off track. Even when the group is on track, it is sometimes useful to stop and assess its progress. Summarizing reduces group uncertainty by showing how far the discussion has progressed and what it still needs to accomplish. By understanding when a group needs a summary—and then providing it—you can help move the group toward its goal. Even if the group does not accept your summary, you will still reveal discrepancies among group members' perceptions, thus opening the door to more clarification and less uncertainty.

▶ *Elaborating*: Sometimes good ideas are ignored until they are elaborated on enough to be visualized. Suppose you are at a meeting of your fraternity or sorority, which is trying to determine ways of increasing next year's pledge class. Someone in the group suggests that redecorating the recreation room might help. Several things might happen in the discussion: (1) Members might begin to evaluate the idea, some being in favor and some not, (2) another idea might be suggested and recorded, or (3) you (or someone else) might elaborate on the idea by describing how the room might look with new carpeting, a pool table, soft lighting, and a new sofa. Whereas redecoration might have fallen flat by itself, your elaboration gives it a fighting chance. Good ideas are often left unexplored because people fail to elaborate on them.

Initiating, coordinating, summarizing, and elaborating are types of communicative behaviors. Although these are some of the more important types of contributions you can make, the list is by no means complete. Task leadership is any behavior that influences group process and helps accomplish the group's task. Making suggestions, offering new ideas, giving information or opinions, asking for more information, and making procedural observations or recommendations are all task-oriented leadership behaviors that can contribute to a group's effort. Viewing leadership from the functional approach, leadership skill is associated with the ability to analyze a group's process and to choose appropriate behaviors.

Process Leadership

For a group to accomplish its task, members must address themselves to it. For a group to function effectively, it needs to concern *itself with itself!* Groups are composed of people, and people have needs. (In fact, the family is a small group specifically adapted to meeting individual needs.) People do not leave their needs at home when they come to a meeting; they bring them along. Effective group communication must be addressed to the external task of the group and to the needs of its members. Failing to maintain a satisfying group climate can lead to a breakdown in a group's performance. In this respect, small groups resemble automobiles. Cars are great for getting you where you want to go, but they require regular tuning and maintenance in order to run reliably and efficiently. In fact, if an owner does not maintain a car, eventually it will break down. So it is with groups: They, too, need tuning and maintaining.

Leadership research consistently indicates that groups have both task and process needs. The process dimension is often called "group building and maintenance." Process-leadership behaviors maintain interpersonal relations in a group and facilitate a climate satisfying to members and conducive to accomplishing the group's task. Group process-leaders are really communication facilitators.

Chapter 5 discussed group climate from the perspective of individual and interpersonal needs. The following list presents some specific process-leadership behaviors that enhance climate from the perspective of leadership and group needs.

▶ *Tension Release*: Think of times you have studied for exams. You cram more and more information into your head until you reach a point where it all seems futile. Everything runs together; ideas blur. You know it is time for a break. After a cup of coffee and some relaxing conversation, you return to your books with renewed energy.

  Sometimes the most effective leadership you can provide for a group is suggesting a coffee break. When a group is tired, when its task is difficult, when the hour is late, when tension and stress are high, a group needs relief. A joke, a bit of humor, a break, or even a move for adjournment can often provide just what a group needs—tension release. An occasional break or a good laugh can renew a group's energy and improve member satisfaction.

  Some people seem to be naturally sensitive to a group's need for tension release. Knowing that tension release is a necessary leadership function can alert anyone—even the most task-oriented individual—to that need.

▶ *Gatekeeping*: As we noted in Chapter 1, an advantage of working in small groups is that several heads are better than one. The very diversity that makes group communication so complex also gives it strength. A group possesses more experience and intelligence than does any individual, but experience and individual insight are only useful to a group if they are shared.

  Some people like to talk more than others, and in some groups two or three people monopolize the conversation while others remain relatively silent. This fairly common occurrence poses a problem for a group in two ways: First, quiet members are just as likely to possess useful information and ideas as are more vocal group members, and their ideas may never surface unless they say something. Second, people who talk more tend to be more satisfied with a group. Members who do

Coaching is an activity that requires both task and process leadership skills. What might happen if this coach had poor leadership skills?

not talk much can have a negative effect on a group in both the task and process dimensions.

Gatekeeping is aimed at coordinating discussion so that members can air their views. It may take the form of eliciting input ("Harvey, you must have given this a lot of thought. What are your views of the problem?") or even of limiting the contributions of more verbal group members ("Can we perhaps limit our comments to two or three minutes so that we can get everyone's ideas before we have to adjourn?"). Gatekeeping is an important leadership function because it ensures more input along the task dimension and higher member satisfaction along the process dimension.

▶ *Encouraging*: People like praise. They feel good when someone recognizes them for their contributions. Offering encouragement is a leadership behavior aimed at increasing the esteem of group members and raising their hopes, confidence, and aspirations. Improving the morale of a group can increase cohesiveness, member satisfaction, and productivity.

▶ *Mediating*: Conflict is a normal, healthy part of group interaction. However, mismanaged conflict can lead to hurt feelings, physical or mental withdrawal from a group, reduced cohesiveness, and general disruption. Mediating is aimed at resolving conflict between group members and releasing any tension associated with the conflict. Whenever conflict becomes person-oriented rather than issue-oriented, it is a particularly appropriate time for mediation.

WANDA: I think that the plan I'm proposing has considerable merit and meets our needs.

HAROLD: That's ridiculous. It'll never work.

WANDA: Get off my case! I don't see you proposing any better solutions.

This potentially volatile situation could easily disrupt the group. You often have to work in groups with people you do not especially like. Obviously, Harold and Wanda do not get along well, but groups can function effectively in spite of personality clashes. They need to focus discussion on issues rather than on personalities. At times, interpersonal difficulties become so severe that they cannot be resolved by simply focusing on a group's task. Such difficulties can be a serious encumbrance to a group and need to be dealt with either within or outside the group; ignoring problems will not make them go away.

The preceding list of behaviors that contribute to a group's process or maintenance needs is not complete. More complete lists appear in Chapters 4 and 12. The behaviors just described are some of those that are more essential to task and process leadership. They are included here to illustrate their importance and to help you examine your own leadership behavior in groups.

Both task and process leadership are essential to the success of a small group. If a group does not make progress on its task, members probably will feel frustrated and unsatisfied. In addition, if a group does not maintain a comfortable environment, members tend to focus their attention and energy on their own dissatisfaction with the group rather than on their assigned task.

Situational Perspective: Adapting Style to Context

So far this chapter has discussed the trait and functional approaches to leadership study and has explored some task and process leadership roles. The **situational perspective** to group leadership accommodates all these factors—leadership behaviors, task needs, and process needs—but also takes into account leadership style and situation. When you complete the task-process-leadership questionnaire at the end of this chapter you may have some new insights about your own leadership behavior in groups. In interpreting the results of that questionnaire, you will find that the degree of your concern for task and for people is related to leadership style, an essential concept in the situational perspective.

Leadership Style

Your beliefs and attitudes about leadership will affect your behavior in small groups. **Leadership style** is a relatively consistent pattern of behavior reflecting a leader's beliefs and attitudes. Although no two people act as leaders in precisely the same way, people do lead with three basic styles: (1) authoritarian (or autocratic), (2) democratic, and (3) laissez-faire.

Authoritarian leaders assume positions of intellectual and behavioral superiority in groups. They make the decisions, give the orders, and generally control all activities. Democratic leaders have more faith in the group than authoritarian leaders do and consequently try to involve members in making decisions. Laissez-faire leaders see themselves as no better or no worse than other group members. They assume the group will direct itself. Laissez-faire leaders avoid dominating groups. In one of the earliest studies of the effects of leadership style, researchers compared groups of school children led by graduate

Table 11.1 Leader Behavior in Three "Social Climates"

AUTHORITARIAN	DEMOCRATIC	LAISSEZ-FAIRE
1. Leader makes all determination of policy.	**1.** All policies are a matter of group discussion and decision, encouraged and assigned by leader.	**1.** Complete freedom for group or individual decision; minimum of leader participation.
2. The leader dictates techniques and activity steps one at a time, so that future steps are always largely uncertain.	**2.** Activity perspective gained during discussion period; general steps to group goal sketched, and when technical advice needed, leader suggests alternative procedures.	**2.** Leader supplies various materials, making it clear he or she will supply information when asked, but taking no other part in discussion.
3. Leader usually dictates particular work task and work companion of each member.	**3.** Members free to work with anyone; division of tasks left up to the group.	**3.** Complete nonparticipation of leader.
4. Leader tends to be "personal" in praise and criticism of each member's work; remains aloof from active group participation except when demonstrating.	**4.** Leader "objective" or "fact-minded" in praise and criticism, trying to be regular group member in spirit without doing too much of the work.	**4.** Leader makes infrequent, spontaneous comments on member activities unless questioned; makes no attempt to appraise or regulate course of events.

students who had been specifically trained in one of the three leadership styles. The researchers defined the styles as shown in Table 11.1.[5]

Briefly, here are the results of the study:

1. Groups with democratic leaders generally were better satisfied and functioned in a more orderly and positive way.

2. Groups with authoritarian leaders were more aggressive or more apathetic (depending on the group).

3. Members of democratic groups were better satisfied than members of laissez-faire groups; a majority of group members preferred democratic to authoritarian, although some members were better satisfied in authoritarian groups.

4. Authoritarian groups spent more time engaged in productive work, but only when the leader was present.

It is tempting to conclude that humanistic, participatory, democratic leadership will invariably lead to greater satisfaction and higher productivity. Unfortunately, the evidence

*"And now at this point in the meeting I'd like to shift
the blame away from me and onto someone else."*

does not warrant such a generalization. Several studies have shown that no one leadership style is effective in all situations. What works at General Motors may not work in a family business. An effective student body president may be a poor camp counselor. The expectations of one group differ from those of other groups.[6]

Recent research on the effectiveness of different leadership styles has suggested that effective leadership is contingent on a variety of interrelated factors, such as culture, time constraints, group compatibility, and the nature of a group's task. Although the functional approach reveals the importance of fulfilling various leadership roles in a group, it does not explain which roles are most appropriate in which situation. It is clear that you need to consider the setting in which leadership behavior occurs.

The situational approach views leadership as an interaction between style and various situational factors. Consider the following case study.

A CASE STUDY

Having been offered some very attractive extra retirement benefits by top management, Arthur agreed to take early retirement at age 62. Once an ambitious and young junior executive for the company, Arthur had, in recent years, taken a rather relaxed, anything-goes attitude as director of his division. As a result, his team had been showing the lowest productivity record in the company, and his subordinates were not receiving attractive salary increments and other rewards from top management. Morale was very low, and employees were discontented.

Hoping to rejuvenate the group, management replaced Arthur with an extremely bright, dynamic, and aggressive young manager named Marilyn. Marilyn's instructions were these: "Get your team's productivity up by 20 percent over the next twelve months, or we'll fire the whole group and start from scratch with a new manager and new employees."

Marilyn began by studying the records of employees in her group to determine the strengths and weaknesses of each. She then drew up a set of goals and objectives for each employee and made assignments accordingly. She set a rigid timetable for each employee and made all employees directly accountable to her.

Employee response was overwhelmingly positive. Out of chaos came order. Each person knew what was expected and had tangible goals to achieve. Employees felt united behind their new leader as they all strove to achieve their objective of a one-year, 20 percent increase in productivity.

At the end of the year, productivity was up not 20 percent but 35 percent! Management was thrilled and awarded Marilyn a large raise and the company's certificate of achievement.

Feeling that she had a viable formula for success, Marilyn moved into the second year as she had into the first—setting goals for each employee, holding them accountable, and so forth. However, things went less smoothly the second year. Employees who had been quick to respond the first year were less responsive. Although the work she assigned was usually completed on time, its quality was declining. Employees had a morale problem: Those who had once looked up to Marilyn as "Boss" were now sarcastically calling her "Queen Bee" and reminiscing about "the good old days" when Arthur was their manager.

Marilyn's behavior as a manager had not changed, yet her leadership was no longer effective. Something needed to be done, but what?

David Korten has proposed that under certain conditions groups are pressured to have centralized, authoritarian leadership but that as these conditions change, groups often develop a more democratic, participative form of leadership. Korten's work may give us an answer to Marilyn's problem.

Korten says that groups with highly structured goals and high stress move toward authoritarian leadership. The preceding study is an example of this. When Marilyn took over as manager, the group was given a very specific goal—to raise productivity by 20 percent. At the same time, employees had a good deal of stress; if they failed, they would lose their jobs. In such situations, groups appreciate an authoritarian style, and it is effective.

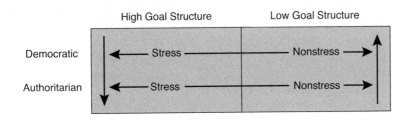

Figure 11.1 Relation of Stress, Goal Structuring, and Leadership Patterns

Source: David C. Korten, "Situational Determinants of Leadership Structure," *Journal of Conflict Resolution 6* (1962) 222–35.

Think of times when you were in a group with clear goals but with members uncertain of how to achieve them. Remember when a group felt a good deal of stress because of an impending deadline or a group grade. At such times group members will gladly follow any leader who can give direction and show them the means to that goal. When the situation changes—that is, when the group feels less uncertain, has less stress, and has less structured goals—the group has less of a need for authoritarian leadership and instead needs more participative democratic leadership. Figure 11.1 represents Korten's situational leadership model. To clarify this point, return to the case study.

Although Marilyn's style of leadership in the first year was appropriate, the situation changed at the end of that year. Employees had reached their goal and replaced it with a much more loosely structured goal—that of continuing what they had been doing. Simultaneously, employees felt less external stress. They no longer operated under the "20 percent ultimatum." Having learned what they had to do as a group to succeed, employees were now ready to attend to their individual needs. They needed a more democratic, people-oriented style of leadership.

Korten's model is applicable even on an international scale. Consider the differences between leadership and goal structure in the developing world and in the United States. Citizens of developing countries are seeking a new way of life that they as yet have not attained; therefore, their goals are structured, concrete, and operational. By contrast, Americans focus more on maintaining processes than on changing them. The relationship of these goals to leadership styles in the two regions is obvious.

In the preceding case study, if Marilyn is to lead effectively she has two basic options. She can either change her leadership style and encourage more participation from her employees (more process, less task); or she can continue her authoritarian style by creating new stress or the illusion of stress. The latter solution may seem unethical, but it is commonly used.

Hersey and Blanchard's Situational Model

Like other situational leadership theories, Paul Hersey and Kenneth Blanchard's model uses various combinations of task- and relationship-oriented leadership behavior to describe leadership style as it relates to different situations.[7] In this case, the maturity of the group is the situational variable.

Take a few minutes to examine their model in Figure 11.2. Note that the two axes of the model represent the now-familiar task and relationship (process) dimensions of leadership behavior, reflecting different leaders' orientations. Quadrant S1 represents a leader whose orientation is high task and low relationship; quadrant S2, high task and high relationship, and so on. To these various combinations, Hersey and Blanchard gave the terms *telling*, *selling*, *participating*, and *delegating*. A telling style is extremely directive. A selling style is also directive, but a leader is concerned that the group accept and internalize orders given. A participating style is driven primarily by concern for relationships and a need for all group members to share in decision making. In a delegating style, a leader takes a hands-off attitude and allows the group to direct itself.

According to Hersey and Blanchard, these four leadership styles are more or less appropriate depending on a group's maturity. Note across the bottom of the Hersey and Blanchard model a scale labeled M4 (high maturity) to M1 (low maturity). Here, *maturity* refers not to chronological age or emotional maturity, but to the degree of experience group members have with one another in that group. When you view maturity in combination with the rest of the model, you can see that a "telling" style is most appropriate with groups that are just starting out, perhaps in their orientation stage of development. As groups mature, effective leadership allows for more autonomy. "Just as parents should relinquish control as a function of the increasing maturity of their children, so too should leaders share more decision-making power as their subordinates acquire greater experience with and commitment to their tasks."[8]

Communication scholar Sarah Trenholm offers the following example of how the theory might apply to a classroom:

Consider teaching style as a form of leadership. Hersey and Blanchard would suggest that at the beginning of a course of study, with inexperienced students, a highly direc-

Figure 11.2 Hershey and Blanchard's Situational-Leadership Model

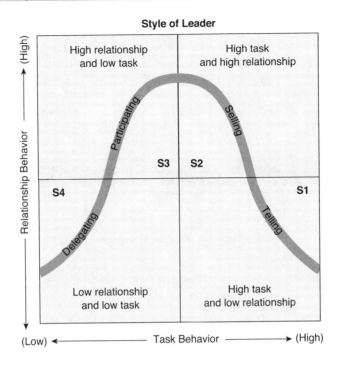

Style of Leader

High relationship and low task

High task and high relationship

S3 S2

S4 S1

Low relationship and low task

High task and low relationship

Relationship Behavior (High)

Participating

Selling

Delegating

Telling

(Low) ◄——— Task Behavior ———► (High)

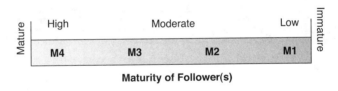

Mature			Immature
High	Moderate		Low
M4	M3	M2	M1

Maturity of Follower(s)

Source: Paul Hersey and Ken Blanchard, *Management of Organizational Behavior: Utilizing Human Resources,* 6th ed. (Upper Saddle River, NJ: Prentice Hall, 1982) 248. Reprinted by permission.

tive telling style is best. The teacher who tells a freshman class, "You decide what and how you want to learn. It's entirely up to you," is using a delegating style, which will fail, because at this point, students are not yet ready to take full responsibility for their own learning. As the course progresses, however, and as the students feel more comfortable with the course and each other, the teacher might use selling and participating styles, and perhaps end up with a delegating approach. More mature students may be ready for autonomy and may even resent being told what to do.[9]

The Hersey and Blanchard model is widely used in training managers and executives, probably because it shows how managers can change styles according to their subordinates' maturity level. A delegating style can be used with one employee or group and a telling style with another.[10]

Some Observations on the Situational Approach to Leadership

At first glance, the situational approach seems to cover all bases. It looks at the style, task needs, process needs, and situational variables that influence groups. Unfortunately, most research using this approach has focused on the behavior of leaders rather than on leadership as a process of realizing group goals.[11] Thus, while the situational approach is useful, it is, perhaps, not as helpful to the student of small group communication as is the functional approach. Achieving a group goal involves everyone in the group, not just the leader. Consequently, students and scholars continue to be concerned over the influence that group members' verbal and nonverbal statements have on group goals.

REVIEW

Perspectives on Leadership

Trait approach:	Attempts to identify characteristics common to successful leaders
Functional approach:	Views leadership as a set of behaviors that may be shared by all group members
Situational approach:	Relates effective leadership to interaction between leadership style and the group situation

Transformational Leadership

A relatively new theory of leadership, which describes leadership in organizations, is **transformational leadership**. As described in management and public-administration literature, transformational leadership has four defining characteristics, called the Four I's: (1) Idealized leadership, (2) Inspirational motivation, (3) Intellectual stimulation, and (4) Individual consideration.

Contrasted with transactional leaders, who manage within the existing norms of their organizations, the transformational leader changes the organization by realigning its culture with a new vision and a restructuring of its shared assumptions and norms. Transformational leaders have a sense of vision and purpose. In contrast with the Four I's, author Peter Senge proposes three critical skills of transformational leadership: (1) building shared vision, (2) surfacing and challenging mental models, and (3) engaging in systems thinking.[12] *Building shared vision* is similar to establishing mutuality of concern (see Chapter 3). It involves encouraging individuals to express their visions of group or organizational goals while encouraging the development of a common, positive view. *Surfacing and testing mental models* is a process of identifying and challenging assumptions while avoiding defensiveness—a daunting task requiring supportive communication skills (see Chapter 5). *Systems thinking* is a process we have argued for throughout this book. Understanding groups and organizations and the great complexity that characterizes them requires that leaders look beyond day-to-day operations to find underlying themes, forces of change, and interrelationships.[13]

In the film *The Empire Strikes Back*, Luke Skywalker watches as Yoda levitates his spaceship out of the swamp.

LUKE: "I don't believe it!"

YODA: "That is why you fail."

Often, the secret to *reaching* a goal (or vision) lies in the *belief* that it *can* be reached. Belief in the *vision* becomes more powerful than the followers' belief in lack, limitation, and doubt. This *belief-system shift* empowers followers to a higher level of commitment and achievement. Its effect may even be so powerful as to convert followers into leaders and leaders into moral agents.[14]

In innovative transformational organizational cultures, we are likely to see assumptions and norms such as these: People can be trusted; everyone has a contribution to make; complex problems should be handled at the lowest possible level. In a transformational culture, norms are flexible enough to adapt to changing external environments. Superiors serve as mentors, coaches, role models, and leaders.[15]

Transformational leadership is not so much a set of behaviors that one can observe or emulate as it is a philosophy of leadership and change.[16] Small groups everywhere operate within the cultures of larger organizations and thus are affected by and a part of those cultures. Teams in organizations will be the topic of our next chapter.

Emergent Leadership in Small Groups

The Minnesota Studies

A fascinating series of leadership studies begun at the University of Minnesota (called the Minnesota Studies) sought the answer to the question "Who is most likely to emerge as the perceived leader of a leaderless discussion group?" Led by Professor Ernest Bormann, the Minnesota Studies formed and observed "test-tube groups" that engaged in leaderless group discussions.

Most people think of a leader as someone who takes charge and organizes a discussion. Predictably, group members often perceive as leaders those who actively participate in the group and who direct communication toward procedural matters. Although studies show a clear correlation between perceived leadership and talkativeness, especially task-oriented talkativeness,[17] those who talk most are not the only ones who become leaders in leaderless groups. In fact, most groups do not select leaders at all. The Minnesota Studies show that leaders emerge through a method of residues in which group members are rejected until only one remains. The first members to go are the quiet ones who do not actively participate in the early stages of a group's discussion. The next to go are the talkative but overaggressive or dogmatic group members who are perceived to be too inflexible for leadership positions.

After this initial phase of elimination, a group enters a second phase, in which roughly half the group members remain in contention for the leadership role. This phase moves much more slowly than the first phase, and it is a good deal more painful and frustrating. One by one, the group rejects contenders until only one or two remain. Often, members reject would-be leaders because their style is perceived as disturbing. In the Minnesota Studies' classroom discussion groups, members often rejected an authoritarian style on the grounds that the person was "too bossy" or "dictatorial." (Of course, some people may consider the authoritarian style inappropriate in a classroom discussion group, but they may consider it highly appropriate in other situations, especially those that involve extreme stress.) In another study, Deborah Baker found that specific communication behaviors increase the likelihood of rejection as leader.[18] Group members who seem unable to contribute to either the group's tasks or organization because they are quiet, vague, tentative, self-effacing, or always asking others for direction are usually rejected. In this second phase of role emergence, the Minnesota Studies also found that, to some extent, groups with two or more men rejected female contenders. Groups containing only one man often selected a female leader and isolated the man—a pattern that may be changing.

Task-motivated group members often rejected a contender who was perceived as too process-oriented—that is, too concerned about everyone's feelings and moods to be decisive. Likewise, process-oriented members tended to reject those they saw as too concerned with the task.

According to Bormann,

> In the final analysis groups accepted the contender who provided the optimum blend of task efficiency and personal consideration. The leader who emerged was the one that others thought would be of most value to the entire group and whose orders and directions they trusted and could follow.[19]

The Minnesota Studies give fascinating insight into the process through which group leaders emerge. Although this information does not tell you how to behave in order to rise to leadership positions, it does alert you to the process through which leadership emerges. These studies also highlight the complexity of small groups and explain, to an extent, why a person who assumes a leadership role in one group may not do so in another and why a person who is perceived to be a leader in two groups may not assume the same role in each.

Recent research has added to our knowledge of emergent leadership in groups. New evidence has revealed that emergent leaders typically display more effective listening skills and may be more extroverted.[20] There is also new evidence that individual task ability contributes to emergent leadership, as does commitment to the group's assigned goals.[21] In this regard, group goals are often strongly influenced by the emergent leader's personal goals for the group.[22]

Leadership and Gender

A review of research literature on the subject of gender and leadership reveals that times, indeed, are changing.[23] Research in the 1960s and 1970s found that women were reluctant to assume leadership roles:[24] That group members perceived males as more independent, rational, confident, and influential than females and viewed males as leaders more often than females.[25] In 1979 researchers noted that females exceeded males in being receptive

ETHICALLY

*E*ducational leaders Alexander and Helen Astin observe that effective leadership in groups and organizations encompasses the following values:

▶ To create a supportive environment where people can grow, thrive, and live in peace with one another,

▶ To promote harmony with nature and thereby provide sustainability for future generations; and

▶ To create communities of reciprocal care and shared responsibility where every person matters and each person's welfare and dignity is respected and supported.[26]

The Astins were talking not only about group and team leadership, but leadership in large organizations. Do these lofty goals also relate to our discussion of effective leadership in groups and teams?

to ideas, fostering interpersonal relations, showing concern, and being attentive to others. Males in the same study in actual organizational settings exceeded females in dominance, being quick to challenge others and controlling the course of conversation. The researchers noted that female leadership styles were more compatible with human-resource theories of how managers should behave.[27]

In 1981, research reported that the influence of gender on leadership emergence was most evident early in the process and dissipated over time.[28] By the late 1980s some studies were reporting no difference in the way males and females are perceived in leadership roles.[29] Also in the 1980s there was a substantial body of research distinguishing *psychological* gender (introduced in Chapter 4) from *biological* gender. This research supported the argument that the most effective leader was that androgynous individual who could draw from a repertoire of both traditionally male and female behaviors.[30] Research in the 1990s continues to support this view.[31]

Researcher Katherine Hawkins identified task-relevant communication as being the sole significant predictor in her study of emergent leadership, regardless of the gender of the candidate for leadership. Her study also noted no significant gender differences in the production of task-relevant communication.[32] Such communication, it seems, is the key to emergent leadership in task-oriented group interaction, for either gender. Other recent research has found that female managers are rated higher at putting people at ease but that gender makes no difference in perceptions of leadership ability once a manager has gained organizational experience.[33] Gender composition, too, may have an effect on team outcomes. Some research has suggested that having more females as informal leaders within a team enhances the team's performance.[34]

Research consistently indicates that the productivity of a group improves if its members are trained. In one study, team-building intervention among a group of department leaders resulted in a measurable increase in the ability to raise issues and manage conflict; an increase in mutual praise, support, and cooperation; clarification of roles and responsibilities; and long-term commitment to teamwork and innovation. The author concluded that a communication-focused team-building intervention can have positive, lasting results.[35] **Training** involves instruction to develop skills. Most of the instruction you receive in university classrooms involves what and how you *think*; training emphasizes what you can *do*.

The simplest form of leadership training provides members with feedback on their performance.[36] Evidence suggests that when members receive such feedback, they tend to work harder, particularly when they are being evaluated by an expert.[37] This technique of observation and feedback is the mainstay of most leadership training programs. Whether other group members provide feedback, or an observer or a video monitor does, people need a more objective eye than their own to see what they are doing and how they can do it better. Beyond the basics, leadership training ranges from the simple and inexpensive to the elaborate and expensive. Given the various definitions of leadership outlined in this chapter, training may justifiably encompass any or all of the principles and skills outlined in this book. Often, training will include a simulation exercise.

A **simulation** is a structured exercise that creates conditions that participants might confront outside the training environment. It provides a context in which participants can experiment with new behaviors without any risks. The war games that are a part of military training are one example of simulation; the conditions of war are recreated so that trainees can try out new behaviors in a situation that is not life threatening. Likewise, many leadership and management training programs recreate conditions of the work environment with hypothetical written reports, financial documents, and background information—in which trainees can experiment. Thus simulations are important to leadership training because they add a context that approximates the actual circumstances for which participants are trained.

Although most training focuses more on behavior than it does on cognition, good training is multidimensional; that is, it incorporates more than one level of learning. Training effectiveness depends on many factors, including team and individual competencies, task requirements, and features of the work environment.[38]

Good training should provide you an expanded repertoire of behaviors and the understanding and awareness to make judgments about why, how, and when to use those behaviors. To learn effectively, you need to be aware of both principles and practice.

We conclude this chapter as it began, with a translated quotation, this time from Lao Tsu, who wrote these words 2,500 years ago. They remain as true today as ever.

> *The wicked leader is he whom the people despise,*
> *The good leader is he whom the people revere.*
> *The great leader is he whom the people say,*
> *"We did it ourselves."*

The most effective leadership behavior is that which best meets the needs of the group. Groups have both task and process needs; these and other situational variables determine the most appropriate type of leadership behavior for groups. Here are some suggestions on how to apply what you have learned.

If you are the designated leader or chairperson of a group:

▶ The rest of the group will have certain expectations of you as leader. For example, they probably will expect you to be particularly influential on matters of procedure. You should meet such expectations.

▶ Prepare a realistic agenda well in advance and distribute it to all group members. At the meeting, help the group stick to its agenda.

▶ Analyze the group's situation—its time constraints, goal structure, stress, leader–member relations, and so on.

▶ Consider your own orientation toward group work. Are you motivated primarily by task concerns or by people concerns? Some situations call for decisive, authoritarian action. Is this what you are good at? If not, you may want to delegate authority to someone who is more task-oriented, at least until the crisis has passed. Does your concern for task outweigh your concern for group-member relations? At times you may want to follow a laissez-faire leadership style and let person-oriented group members take over for a while. Adapt your style to the situation, and use the resources of the group to everyone's advantage.

▶ In an ad hoc group that meets only once or twice, the leadership style you choose is not nearly as important as in a committee that meets regularly over a long period of time. In most long-term situations, a democratic style of leadership is preferable. Provide procedural structure for the group, but encourage as much participation as possible. Increased member participation can breed a better solution.

▶ Remember that groups have task and process needs. Members need to get the job done, but they also need encouragement, praise, and thanks.

If you are not the designated leader or chairperson of the group:

▶ Although you have less control in this situation because of the different expectations the group has of you, you are still influential. You can still demonstrate leadership behavior.

▶ Use your knowledge about small group communication—leadership, problem solving, growth, and development—to analyze what is going on in the group. Consider your own strengths as a group member. What roles do you fulfill best in the group? Use your strengths to provide what the group needs and to support those who have other needed skills.

▶ Occasionally a group suffers a leadership void. This often occurs when leaders are appointed by an outside source or when leaders are elected at the first meeting before group members have had a chance to evaluate one another as potential leaders. In these cases, rely on the functional approach, because any member of the group (including you) can provide leadership. But watch out for delicate egos. When leaders do not live up to expectations, group members will disapprove of them. In a small group this can result in an attempt to overthrow a leader or in a resentful and ineffectual group climate. Members set aside the group's task while they hassle over who is in charge. Almost invariably, such groups produce unsatisfactory results and bruised egos. For a more effective strategy, work around an ineffectual leader (every rule, of course, has exceptions). Any group member can provide leadership while leaving a leader's self-esteem intact.

▶ Sometimes a small group contains a wealth of leadership talent. Leadership is not (or *should* not be) a contest for status and power. Individual goals must be placed behind group goals. Good leaders need good followers and supporters.

Usually, the most effective leaders are those who put the group ahead of their own ego needs. In every group the effectiveness of leadership depends on the situation, sensitivity to the group's needs, and the ability to adapt your communicative behavior to meet those needs. Effective leaders bring out the leadership in others.

PRACTICE

1. Chapters 4 and 11 introduced you to functional leadership roles that help groups move toward their goals by addressing task as well as process (group building and maintenance) concerns. Begin this exercise by writing these roles on index cards, one role per card.

   Distribute the cards randomly, and anonymously, throughout your group. Take a few minutes to review the sections in Chapters 4 and 11 that describe these roles.

   Spend 15 to 20 minutes discussing an ongoing project or a topic assigned by your instructor during which you assume the role written on your index card. After 20 minutes, reshuffle and redistribute the role cards. Assume your new roles and continue the discussion for another 15 to 20 minutes.

   Now discuss the following questions in your groups:

   ▶ Can you identify who was enacting each role?

   ▶ Whose roles were most consistent with their natural behavior?

   ▶ Whose roles were the most "out of character"?

   ▶ As a result of these assigned roles, did the group seem to function better or worse than usual? Why?

▶ Were some roles difficult or impossible to enact in this situation? Why?

▶ Who in your group is naturally most task oriented? Most process oriented?

2. Consider the stages in problem solving that are described in Chapter 9. Identify which leadership functions might be the most appropriate at each stage of development.

3. Consider the dialogue between Harold and Wanda presented early in this chapter. List five responses that would help the group, and especially Harold and Wanda, resolve the conflict.

 Your companion Website has more practice activities, questionnaires, and checklists! **www.ablongman.com/beebe**

Notes

1. A. Paul Hare, *Handbook of Small Group Research*, 2nd ed. (New York: Free Press, 1976).

2. Dane Archer, "The Face of Power: Physical Attractiveness as a Non-Verbal Predictor of Small Group Stratification," *Proceedings of the 81st Annual Convention of the American Psychological Association* 8 (1973), Part 1: 177–78.

3. Hare, *Handbook* 278.

4. Dean Barnlund and Franklyn Haiman, *The Dynamics of Discussion* (Boston: Houghton Mifflin, 1960) 275–79.

5. Ralph White and Ronald Lippitt, "Leader Behavior and Member Reaction in Three 'Social Climates'," in Dorwin Cartwright and Alvin Zander, eds., *Group Dynamics*, 3rd ed. (New York: Harper & Row, 1968) 319.

6. John Gastil, "A Meta-Analtytic Review of the Productivity and Satisfaction of Democratic and Autocratic Leadership," *Small Group Research* 25 (1994): 384–410.

7. Paul Hersey and Kenneth Blanchard, *Management of Organizational Behavior: Utilizing Human Resources*, 6th ed. (Englewood Cliffs, NJ: Prentice Hall, 1992).

8. Victor H. Vroom and Arthur G. Jago, *The New Leadership: Managing Participation in Organizations* (Englewood Cliffs, NJ: Prentice Hall, 1988) 52.

9. Sarah Trenholm, *Human Communication Theory* (Englewood Cliffs, NJ: Prentice Hall, 1990).

10. Vroom and Jago, *New Leadership* 52.

11. Dennis Gorman, "Conceptual and Methodological Approaches to the Study of Leadership," *Central States Speech Journal* 21 (Winter 1970): 217–23.

12. Peter M. Senge, "Leading Learning Organizations," in Richard Beckhard et al., eds., *The Leader of the Future* (San Francisco: Jossey-Bass, 1996).

13. Peter M. Senge, "The Leader's New Work: Building Learning Organizations," *Sloan Management Review* 32, no. 1, (whole issue) (Fall 1990).

14. Lynn Little, "Transformational Leadership, " *Academic Leadership* 15 (Nov. 1999): 4–5.

15. Bernard M. Bass and M. J. Avolio, "Transformational Leadership and Organizational Culture," *International Journal of Public Administration* 17 (1994): 541–54.

16. Francis J. Yammarino and Alan J. Dubinsky, "Transformational Leadership Theory: Using Levels of Analysis to Determine Boundary Conditions," *Personnel Psychology* 47 (1994): 787–809.

17. J. Kevin Barge et al., "Relational Competence and Leadership Emergence: An Exploratory Study," paper presented at the annual meeting of the Central States Speech Association, Schaumberg, Illinois, 14–16 April, 1988.

18. Deborah C. Baker, "A Qualitative and Quantitative Analysis of Verbal Style and the Elimination of Potential Leaders in small groups," *Communication Quarterly* 38 (1990): 13–26.

19. Ernest Bormann, *Discussion and Group Methods*, 2nd ed. (New York: Harper & Row, 1975) 256.

20. Scott D. Johnson and Curt Bechler, "Examining the Relationship Between Listening Effectiveness and Leadership Emergence," *Small Group Research* 29 (1998): 452–71.

21. Bryan L. Bonner, "The Effects of Extroversion on Influence in Ambiguous Group Tasks," *Small Group Research* 31 (2000): 225–244.

22. Gita De Souza and Howard J. Klein, "Emergent Leadership in the Group Goal-Setting Process," *Small Group Research* 26 (1995): 475–96.

23. For example, see the review of literature in Patricia Hayes Andrews, "Sex and Gender Differences in Group Communication: Impact on the Facilitation Process," *Small Group Research* 23 (1992): 74–94.

24. E. I. Megargee, "Influence of Sex Roles on the Manifestation of Leadership," *Journal of Applied Psychology* 53(1969): 377–82.

25. C. Nemeth, J. Endicott, and J. Wachtler, "From the 50's to the 70's: Women in Jury Deliberations," *Sociometry* 39(1976): 293–304.

26. Alexander Astin and Helen Astin, "Principles of Transformative Leadership." *American Association for Higher Education Bulletin* 53 (Nov. 2001): 3–6.

27. J. E. Baird and P. H. Bradley, "Styles of Management and Communication: A Comparative Study of Men and Women," *Communication Monographs* 46 (1979): 101–11.

28. B. Spillman, R. Spillman, and K. Reinking, "Leader Emergence: Dynamic Analysis of the Effects of Sex and Androgyny," *Small Group Behavior* 12 (1981): 139–57.

29. J. R. Goktepe and C. E. Schneier, "Sex and Gender Effects in Evaluating Emergent Leaders in Small Groups," *Sex Roles* 19 (1988): 29–36. See also E. Kushell and R. Newton, "Gender, Leadership Style, and Subordinate Satisfaction: An Experiment," *Sex Roles* 14 (1986): 203–9.

30. See V. P. Hans and N. Eisenberg, "The Effects of Sex Role Attitudes and Group Composition on Men and Women in Groups," *Sex Roles* 12 (1985): 477–90.

31. Judith A. Kolb, "Are We Still Stereotyping Leadership? A Look at Gender and Other Predictors of Leader Emergence," *Small Group Research* 28 (1997): 370–93.

32. Katherine W. Hawkins, "Effects of Gender and Communication Content on Leadership Emergence in Small, Task-Oriented Groups," *Small Group Research* 26 (1995): 234–49.

33. Katherine B. Knott and Elizabeth J. Natalle, "Sex Differences, Organizational Level, and Superiors' Evaluation of Managerial Leadership," *Management Communication Quarterly* 10 (1997): 523–40.

34. Mitchell J. Neubert, "Too Much of a Good Thing or the More the Merrier?" *Small Group Research* 30 (1999): 635–646.

35. Susan B. Glaser, "Teamwork and Communication," *Management Communication Quarterly* 7 (1994): 282–96.

36. Rita Spoelde-Claes, "The Effect of Varying Feedback on the Effectiveness of a Small Group on a Physical Task," *Psychologica Belgica* 13, no. 1 (1973): 61–68.

37. Murray Webster, Jr., "Source of Evaluations and Expectations for Performance," *Sociometry* 32, no. 3 (1969): 243–58.

38. Andrea B. Hollingshead, "Group and Individual Training: The Impact of Practice on Performance," *Small Group Research* 29 (1998): 254–80.

Chapter Outline:

Objectives:

After studying this chapter, you will be able to:

▶ Identify four group approaches to improving quality in an organization.

▶ Give a meeting structure by preparing an agenda.

▶ Help facilitate interaction during a meeting.

▶ Identify what participants and leaders should do during a meeting.

▶ List and describe how groups and teams can effectively use technology to enhance work productivity and quality.

Improving Productivity in Groups and Teams

> *"Never doubt that a thoughtful group of concerned citizens can change the world. Indeed, it's the only thing that ever has."*
> — Margaret Mead

"Do more with less." "Work smarter, not harder." "Do it right the first time." These slogans crystallize the constant quest to increase productivity and get more quality work accomplished. Leaders in today's organization want both increased productivity (more work produced) as well as improved quality (fewer errors and mistakes). Many businesses and other organizations turn to small groups, teams, and task forces to improve both efficiency and quality. Evidence indicates that to achieve these two goals of productivity and quality leaders will continue, if not increase, their reliance on groups and teams. Roger Mosvick and Robert Nelson report:

▶ Most business in the United States is accomplished in group or team meetings.

▶ The average manager or professional spends almost one-fourth of every work week in group or team meetings.

▶ Top-level managers spend up to two-thirds of their time in meetings or preparing for meetings.

▶ People plan to spend more time in meetings and teamwork in the future. Business organizations expect a 5 to 9 percent increase in the number of meetings held.[1]

Chances are you will earn your living working with others in an organization. Whether you work in a business or for an educational, medical, or governmental institution, your job success will likely depend on your ability to produce a high volume of quality work. Even if you will earn your living working at home in front of your computer, you will undoubtedly be part of a larger organization networked to other people or involved in a team enterprise. The point is, most likely you will find yourself in an organization working with others in small groups.

In this chapter we focus on skills and principles that can help you improve both your work productivity and quality. Although every chapter in this book includes information and skills that can be applied to improving productivity and quality, we will present here specific formats and ideas that are related to enhancing your effectiveness as you work with others.

Principles and Practices of Improving Work Quality

Total quality management (TQM)—a management emphasis that began in the 1990s—continues to drive management philosophy in the twenty-first century.[2] Products of high standards from international markets have placed a new emphasis on the importance of quality. Many organizations have found that employees are the best source of ideas and innovations for improving work quality.

One of the principal leaders of the quality movement was the late W. Edwards Deming. He was a professor of statistics who realized that meaningful application of data coupled with empowering team collaboration can enhance work quality. He is often credited with helping Japanese organizations to increase their work quality dramatically. He identified fourteen points that, if implemented, he believed would transform an organization into an effective community producing quality goods and services. Many of his ideas emphasize the importance of collaboration and coordinated group effort. His often-quoted fourteen points are summarized in Table 12.1.

Managers have used a variety of group formats to tap employee expertise to achieve the goal of work quality. Quality circles, *Kaizen*, focus groups, and self-directed teams, are four team approaches that have been used to improve the quality of goods and services produced.

Quality Circles

A **quality circle** is a group of five to fifteen employees who meet on a regular basis for the purpose of improving work productivity, morale, and overall work quality.[3] Typical tasks of quality circles include the following:

- ▶ Improving the quality of services or products
- ▶ Reducing the number of work-related errors
- ▶ Promoting cost reduction
- ▶ Developing improved teamwork
- ▶ Developing better work methods
- ▶ Improving efficiency in the organization
- ▶ Improving relations between management and employees
- ▶ Promoting participants' leadership skills
- ▶ Enhancing employees' career and personal development
- ▶ Improving communication throughout the organization
- ▶ Increasing everyone's awareness of safety

The concept of quality circles was an extension of Deming's quality principles. Quality circles were first embraced by Japanese management. After their success in Japan, quality circles were eventually implemented in the United States and were especially popular during the 1980s and 1990s; they remain in use in some organizations today. Quality circles appear to be most successful when members have had training in how to work together as a team and have a clear understanding of the overarching group goal. In an individualist culture, it remains a challenge for workers to work toward collectivist goals.

Employees trained in quality circles receive basic information about group communication principles and practices. Many of the concepts presented in this text—such as group relationships, cohesiveness, roles, consensus, decision making, problem solving, and conflict management—are part of the training of quality circle-members. Quality-circle group members are also given training in statistics to help them analyze production output and quality.

Leaders of quality circles are given additional training in leading groups and facilitating group interaction. Quality-circle facilitators are primarily procedural leaders responsible for developing agendas, scheduling meetings, and ensuring equal participation by all group members.

Table 12.1 How to Improve Quality: Dr. Deming's Fourteen Points

1. Create constancy of purpose toward improvement of product and service, with the aim to become competitive and stay in business, and to provide jobs.

2. Adopt the new philosophy. We are in a new economic age. Western management must awaken to the challenge, learn their responsibilities, and take on leadership for change.

3. Cease dependence on inspection to achieve quality. Eliminate the need for inspection on a mass basis by building quality into the product in the first place.

4. End the practice of awarding business on the basis of price tag. Instead, minimize total cost.

5. Improve constantly and forever the system of production and service, to improve quality and productivity, and thus constantly decrease costs.

6. Institute training on the job.

7. Institute leadership. The aim of leadership should be to help people and machines and gadgets to do a better job. Leadership of management is in need of overhaul, as well as leadership of production workers.

8. Drive out fear, so that everyone may work effectively for the company.

9. Break down barriers between departments. People in research, design, sales, and production must work as a team, to foresee problems of production and in use that may be encountered with the product or service.

10. Eliminate slogans, exhortations, and targets for the workforce asking for zero defects and new levels of productivity. Such exhortations only create adversarial relationships, as the bulk of the causes of low quality and low productivity belong to the system and thus lie beyond the power of the workforce.

11. (a) Eliminate work standards (quotas) on the factory floor; substitute leadership. (b) Eliminate management by objective. Eliminate management by numbers, numerical goals; substitute leadership.

12. (a) Remove barriers that rob the hourly worker of his right to pride of workmanship. The responsibility of supervisors must be changed from sheer numbers to quality. (b) Remove barriers that rob people in management and in engineering of their right to pride of workmanship. This means, *inter alia*, abolishment of the annual or merit rating and of management by objective.

13. Institute a vigorous program of education and self-improvement.

14. Put everybody in the company to work to accomplish the transformation. The transformation is everybody's job.

Source: Peter R. Scholtes, *The Team Handbook* (Madison, WI: Joiner Associates, 1996).

Participative decision making is one of the most valuable approaches to analyzing, managing, and solving problems in business and industry. Quality circles can be effective if employees have the skills to make quality decisions.

Kaizen

Kaizen is a Japanese word that means "continual improvement."[4] Every product, process, and management decision can be improved, according to *kaizen* principles, which can apply not only to groups but to an entire organization. Several large and small companies in the United States use *kaizen* methods when they seek to complete their task more effectively and efficiently. Perhaps you have heard the adage "If it ain't broke, don't fix it." *Kaizen* operates on the assumption "If it ain't broke, fix it anyway." According to *kaizen* principles, everything can be improved.

Kaizen groups can be either permanent or temporary. The first task of a *kaizen* group is to identify the areas where work performance can be improved. The group needs to gather statistics that indicate the quality (or lack of quality) of the products or services being produced. Armed with information about how effectively the group is completing its mission, the *kaizen* team can begin suggesting methods for improving the process. *Kaizen* groups usually organize their work around the steps of the decision-making process that we discussed in Chapter 8.

Step 1: Assess the present situation.

Step 2: Creatively expand alternatives to determine how the group can improve quality.

Step 3: Select the best alternatives by narrowing the list of suggestions to those that will have the most impact.

Finally, the group selects action steps and then either recommends that specific action be taken or implements the changes themselves.

Kaizen groups operate on many of the same assumptions as quality circles. The goal, however, is focused on continually assessing how the group can improve. The *kaizen* assumption is that no product or process is ever perfect.

Focus Groups

One group format used to gather information from others is the **focus group**—a small group of individuals selected to discuss particular topics so that group leaders can better understand how individuals view these topics. Advertisers often use focus groups for market research. The objective of most focus groups is to gather information and help analyze products or issues. The information gleaned from focus groups helps later on when decisions need to be made about problems related to the topics under discussion.

If a soap company wants to understand how consumers like the soap it sells, it could form a focus group to tap individual attitudes and reactions to the product. Seven to ten people could be invited to discuss what they like and dislike about the soap. The focus-group leader, who is trained in group communication skills, engages the group in discussion and listens carefully to members talk about the product. Whereas written questionnaires are used to assess consumer attitudes about the soap, a focus group lets the group leader probe for more detail. The group session can help the company better understand how to sell its product.

A focus-group discussion is like a group interview. Universities, large corporations, and political candidates also use focus groups to understand how others perceive their strengths and weaknesses.

Self-Directed Work Teams

As we noted in Chapter 1, a team is a coordinated group of individuals organized to work together to achieve a common goal. Effective teams typically have well-defined team-member roles and responsibilities, explicit expectations about how the work should be organized, clear and elevating goals, and collaborative methods that tap the resources of the team. A **self-directed work team** is a group that is given responsibility to achieve results without being micro-managed from the outside.

Three elements are vital to creating an effective self-directed work team. First, the team must feel true **empowerment**—the sense of having both the responsibility and the authority to chart their course to achieve the team goal. Empowerment does not mean the team is cut off from the organization to do as it wishes. To be empowered means that the team has the authority to make decisions and achieve results while still being accountable to the organization. Research clearly supports the conclusion that empowered teams get results.[5]

A second element of an effective self-directed work team is **autonomy**. To be autonomous means that the group is able to make decisions and implement its decisions without always asking for permission from somebody else. During the past two decades, with increased emphasis on teams in the workplace there has been a steady rise in the number of autonomous groups in business and industry. Researchers have found convincing evidence that autonomous groups get results—although not all the time.[6] Autonomy is especially important when the team members' tasks are highly interdependent. Interdependence means that team coordination and collaboration are important; what team members do is dependent on what other team members do. The greater the interdependence of a team, the more important it is for the team to be autonomous.

A third element of developing a successfully functioning self-directed work team is team training. Competence requires more than knowledge of what makes a team effective. It also requires skill and motivation to use one's knowledge and skills. Thus, effective team training should present more than principles of how teams work. Team training should instill a sense of commitment and motivation; unless team members want to achieve a high-performing team it will be difficult for the team to succeed. Finally, team training should develop team members' skills.

Besides having excellent communication skills, team members should be skilled in using statistics to evaluate the quality of their work. For example, team members should learn how to use data and plot them on charts and graphs to determine whether the team is achieving its goal. Effective teams have learned how to establish norms and ground rules to design clearly understood team operating procedures.

Typical team-building workshops also focus on many of the same communication skills you have learned in your group communication course. Those skills include problem-solving, decision-making, listening, paraphrasing, conflict-management, goal-setting, and presentation skills.

Does team training work? Does training really result in improved team performance? The answer is yes.[7] The key, however, is to ensure that the training team members receive meets their needs and focuses on the development of skills—specific behaviors that result in improved performance.

REVIEW

Elements of Effective Self-Directed Team Success

Empowerment	The team has the responsibility and authority to achieve the team goal.
Autonomy	The team can make its own decisions without interference from others.
Training in Team Skills	Team members learn how to solve problems, make decisions, listen, paraphrase, manage conflict, set goals and ground rules, and clearly present information to others.

To be effective, employees who work in quality circles and organizational groups and teams also need support from the structure of the organization in which they function. Susan Wheelan and her colleagues have identified the factors that predict enhanced group and team productivity in and organization.[8]

1. Group and team members have the resources (both people and technical tools) to achieve the goal.

2. There is a defined "work territory"; group and team members know their role within the larger organization in which they work.

3. The success and accomplishments of the group are recognized by the organization; the organization values and rewards innovation and quality.

4. The team's mission and objectives are clearly understood by other people in the organization.

5. The group has appropriate autonomy; they are free to make their own decisions without interference from others outside the group.

6. The group members have positive relationships with members of other groups and teams in the organization.

In conducting their research, Wheelan and her colleagues reached a remarkable conclusion: *If group and team members in an organization perceive that they are a well-functioning team, they usually are highly productive.*[9] Although one could argue that this is nothing more than a self-fulfilling prophecy, group members do seem to have the ability to evaluate their group's internal dynamics. Viewed from a different perspective, these results suggest that if you're working in a group and you can detect problems in how the group does its work (such as no clear goals, fuzzy roles, an unfocused agenda), then the group will in all probability be less productive. Group members often know when they are not part of a winning team.

A committee meeting is a collection of the unfit chosen from the unwilling by the incompetent to do the unnecessary.

"At Electronic Data Systems," said Ross Perot, "when we saw a snake, we'd kill it. At General Motors, when they saw a snake, they'd form a committee."

If you want to get a job done, give it to an individual; if you want to have it studied, give it to a committee.

Sign on conference wall: "A meeting is no substitute for progress."

Business meetings are important. They demonstrate how many people the company can do without.

Frankly, most people do not like meetings. Although this generalization has exceptions, it is safe to venture that few individuals relish the thought of a weekly appointment calendar peppered with frequent meetings. MCI Worldcom Conferencing research found that most professionals spend nearly three hours a day in business meetings with more than one-third of participants reporting that the meetings are a waste of time. Many of today's techno-savvy meeting goers have learned the art of paging themselves to have an excuse to duck out of a meetings.[10] President John Kennedy said, "Most committee meetings consist of twelve people to do the work of one." Humorist Dave Barry compared business meetings with funerals, in the sense that "you have a gathering of people who are wearing uncomfortable clothing and would rather be somewhere else. The major difference is that most funerals have a definite purpose. Also, nothing is ever really buried in a meeting."[11] Why are meetings held in such low esteem? Probably because many meetings are not well managed either by the meeting leader or the meeting participants. What bothers meeting attendees the most? The list below reports the results of recent studies that ranked meeting "sins."[12]

1. Getting off the subject
2. No goals or agenda
3. Too lengthy
4. Poor or inadequate preparation
5. Inconclusive
6. Disorganized
7. Ineffective leadership/lack of control
8. Irrelevance of information discussed
9. Time wasted during meetings
10. Starting late
11. Not effective for making decisions
12. Interruptions from within and without

13. Individuals dominate/aggrandize discussion

14. Rambling, redundant, or digressive discussion

15. No published results or follow-up actions

16. No premeeting orientation/canceled or postponed meetings

To be effective, a meeting needs to balance two things: **Structure** and **interaction**. Throughout the book we talk about the importance of helping a group stay on task by structuring the interaction; following the steps of reflective thinking when solving a problem (as discussed in chapter 9) is one way of helping a group stay on task. As you examine the preceding list, note how many of the problems associated with meetings stem from a lack of clear structure or agenda. But while structure is important, group members need to have the freedom to express ideas and react to the comments of others. If there is too much structure, the meeting is not really a meeting; it is a speech where one person talks and others listen. In contrast, with too much unstructured interaction, a group meeting bounces along with no clear focus. In unstructured meetings, minimal attention is given to the time it takes to get the job done.[13] In the sections ahead, we offer suggestions for providing both structure and interaction in group meetings. An agenda is the prime tool of structuring a group meeting. Facilitation skills and ways of planning interaction can ensure that meeting participants will be free to interact, yet that their contributions will be relevant and on target.

Giving Meetings Structure

Getting off the subject and having no goals or agenda are the two most often mentioned complaints about meetings. As we just noted, the principal tool to ensure that meetings are appropriately structured and the deliberation achieves the intended goal is a meeting **agenda**—a list of key issues, ideas, and information that will be presented in the order in which they will be discussed. Uncertainty and lack of an agenda can serve as major barriers to accomplishing a task as a group. Consider the following steps in drafting your meeting agenda.

Determine the Meeting Goal(s) One cardinal rule of meetings is this: Meet only when there is a specific purpose and when it is advantageous or desirable to discuss issues, solve problems, or make decisions as a group. Before beginning to draft an agenda, you need to know the meeting goal. Meeting goals usually fall into one of three categories: (1) information needs to be shared, (2) issues need to be discussed, or (3) action needs to be taken.

As you prepare for a meeting, identify what you would like to have happen as a result of the meeting.[14] A typical goal might be "At the end of this meeting we will have selected the firm that will produce our new advertising campaign," or, "At the end of this meeting we will have reviewed the applicants for the management position and identified our top three choices." Without a specific goal that is known to both leader and participants, little is accomplished.

Identify Items That Need to Be Discussed to Achieve the Goal With the goal in mind, you next need to determine how to structure the meeting to achieve the goal. Consider generating a list of topics that are essential to accomplishing the goal: What information needs to be shared, what issues need to be discussed, what action needs to be taken? In the brainstorming phase, do not worry about the order of the items; you can rearrange the items later.

Organize the Agenda Items to Achieve the Goal After you have a list of items to be addressed, organize them in some logical way. A key constraint in organizing items and determining what to include on a meeting agenda is the amount of time budgeted for the meeting. Many meeting planners underestimate the amount of time discussion will take.

When you have identified potential agenda items, review your meeting goal(s) and eliminate any items that do not help you achieve your goal. Armed with your meeting goal and your list of agenda items, begin drafting your meeting agenda.[15] Consider organizing it around the three meeting goals: Information items, discussion items, and action items.

Most meeting experts suggest that your first agenda item should be to ask the group to approve or modify the agenda you have prepared. If meeting participants make no modifications, you then know that your agenda was on target. Before making final decisions about which items you should cover and the order in which you should cover them, estimate how long you think it might take to deal with each item. You may want to address several small issues first before tackling major ones. Or, you may decide to arrange your agenda items in terms of priority: Discuss the most-important items first and less-important ones later.

REVIEW

How to Prepare a Goal–Centered Meeting Agenda

1. Determine your meeting goals.

2. Identify what needs to be discussed to achieve the goals.

3. Organize the agenda items to achieve the goals.

John Tropman and Gershom Morningstar recommend using the "bell-curve agenda."[16] As indicated in Figure 12.1, the middle of the meeting is reserved for the most challenging or controversial issues. The opening and closing of the meeting include more routine or less vital issues.

Figure 12.1 Bell-Curve Agenda

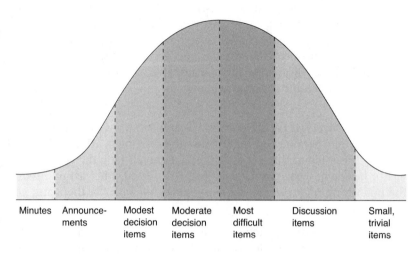

Minutes   Announce-   Modest   Moderate   Most   Discussion   Small,
          ments   decision decision   difficult   items   trivial
                      items   items   items   items

Source: John E. Tropman and Gershom Clark Morningstar, *Meetings: How to Make Them Work for You* (New York: Van Nostrand Reinhold, 1996) 56. Reprinted by permission.

In contrast to Tropman and Morningstar's recommendations, others suggest that you avoid putting routine announcements and reports at the beginning of a meeting. This is because meeting members are less sensitive to the time constraints of a meeting at its beginning and thus may spend too much time and energy on routine matters. To take advantage of the early energy in a group, they recommend starting with a discussion or action item that will involve all meeting participants.

Often issues are discussed during meetings but nothing happens afterward. As the following sample meeting agenda shows, one of your last agenda items should be to summarize the action that needs to be taken following the meeting.

SAMPLE AGENDA

Meeting goal: To review updates from committees and make a decision about donating to the school-volunteer program.

I.   Finalize meeting agenda

II.   Discussion items

    A. What are the problems with our new work-report system?

    B. What are the advantages and disadvantages of the new product-team proposal (distributed by e-mail).

III. Action items

    A. Approve new personnel policy (distributed by e-mail).

    B. Make a decision about the following issue: Should we donate $5,000 to school-volunteer program?

IV.   Information items

       A.   New employee-orientation report

       B.   Planning-committee report

       C.   Finance-committee report

       D.   Announcements

V.   Summarize action that needs to be taken after today's meeting.

Distribute your agenda to the meeting participants well in advance of the meeting. Meeting participants should come prepared to discuss the issues on the agenda. Obviously, if they do not have an agenda before the meeting, they cannot come prepared for a meaningful discussion.

REVIEW

Meeting Agenda Pitfalls and Strategies

POTENTIAL PITFALL	SUGGESTED STRATEGY
Participants will tend to spend time on early agenda items.	Make the first agenda item something worthy of discussion rather than beginning with a trivial report or announcement.
Participants will find a way to talk even if you don't want them to talk.	Invite input and discussion early in the meeting rather than having participants trying to interrupt.
Participants aren't prepared to have a meeting; they have not read what they were supposed to read.	Take a few minutes to have participants read information or have them prepare by writing ideas or suggestions using the silent-brainstorming technique.
Participants won't stick to the agenda.	Remind the group what the goals are or, with input from the group, change the agenda item.
A meeting is scheduled late in the day or participants are tired.	Schedule an early agenda item that involves all meeting participants rather than having participants sitting silently; use early-meeting energy.
There is a controversial agenda item that will create conflict and disagreement.	Put one or more items on the agenda ahead of the conflict-producing item about which you are certain that there will be agreement. You can establish a feeling of accomplishment and agreement before tackling the more conflict-producing items.

Becoming a Meeting Facilitator: Managing Group and Team Interaction

The essential task of a meeting facilitator is to manage the interaction in order to achieve the goals of the group. Without interaction—the give-and-take dialogue and contributions that participants make during meetings—meetings become monologues. But with too much interaction, meetings can become disorganized with rambling, redundant, or digressive discussions that waste time and are inconclusive. Meeting leaders and participants can help ensure a balance of structure and interaction by using the facilitation skills of gatekeeping, reminding the group of meeting goals, helping the group be sensitive to the time that elapses during discussion, and using strategies that structure group interaction.

Be a Gatekeeper   As we learned earlier in the book, a gatekeeper encourages less-talkative members to participate and tries to limit lengthy contributions by other group members. Meetings should not consist of a monologue from the meeting leader or be dominated by just a few participants. As a meeting leader, it is your job to make sure that you involve all meeting participants in the discussion.

Focus on the Goal   As also stressed throughout this book, members need to understand a group's goals. When this is accomplished, the group's agenda for each meeting should provide a road map for moving toward those goals. A leader often has to keep the group on course, and one of the most effective tools for doing so is summarizing. Periodically, use the metadiscussion skill (discussion about discussion) that we talked about in Chapter 10 and review your understanding of the group's progress with brief comments such as "Okay. Dennis agrees with John that we need to determine how much our project will cost. Are we ready for the next issue?" Such summaries help a group take stock of what it has done and what it has yet to accomplish. Communication researchers Fred Niederman and Roger Volkema, in studying the effects of meeting facilitators on group productivity, found that the most experienced facilitators helped orient the group toward the goal, help them adapt to what was happening in the group, and involved the group in developing the agenda for the meeting.[17]

Monitor Time   Another job of a meeting leader is to keep track of how much time has been spent on the planned agenda items and how much time remains. Think of your agenda as a map, helping you plan where you want to go. Think of the clock as your gas gauge, telling you the amount of fuel you have to get where you want to go. In a meeting, just as on any car trip, you need to know where you are going and how much fuel you need to get you to your destination. If you are running out of fuel (time), you will either need to fill up the tank (budget more time) or recognize that you will not get where you want to go. Begin each meeting by asking how long members can meet. If you face two or three crucial agenda items, and one-third of your group has to leave in an hour, you will want to make certain to schedule important items early in the meeting.

Structure Interaction   To ensure that all members participate in the discussion you may need to use some of the prescriptive decision-making and problem-solving tools and techniques mentioned in Chapter 9. For example, if your meeting goal is to identify new ideas to solve a particular problem, consider using brain storming or nominal-group technique as a way to generate ideas. The *is/is not*, journalist's six questions, and the Pareto chart are other tools you can use to invite people to contribute ideas yet structure the interaction so that meeting members do not lose sight of their goals. A key task of the meeting facilitator is to orchestrate meaningful interaction during the meeting so that all participants have the opportunity to give input. Structured methods of inviting involvement (often having group members write individually and then share their ideas with the group) are effective in garnering contributions from all group members.

Another strategy that can help encourage interaction is to phrase each discussion item on the printed agenda as a question. Questions give the discussion focus. As we discussed in Chapter 7, discussion questions are a useful tool to help encourage focused and productive discussion.

Leading Meetings

As mentioned, a meeting leader needs to be especially sensitive to balancing meeting structure with interaction. An effective meeting leader should facilitate rather than dictate how the group will conduct the meeting. One study found that team leaders who simply listened and waited for team members to contribute ideas before stating their own ideas resulted in more and better ideas than when the leader spoke first.[18] Different groups accept (or tolerate) different levels of direction from their designated leaders. One simple rule of thumb is this: *When the leader emerges naturally from the group or leads a one-time-only ad hoc group, then the group will allow him or her to be more directive.* Beyond this simple rule, certain tasks are generally expected of leaders. One of the most important leader tasks is to keep the group focused on its agenda during the meeting. Of course, that means the leader needs to have an agenda. We strongly urge that agendas be distributed well in advance of a meeting. As we have stressed, give participants a chance to shape the agenda both before the meeting and as the meeting opens. In general, meeting leaders are expected to do the following:

▶ Call the group together, which may involve finding out when participants can meet.

▶ Call the meeting to order.

▶ If it is a formal meeting, determine if there is a **quorum**—the minimum number of people who must be present to conduct business.

▶ Keep the meeting moving; go on to the next agenda item when a point is saturated. Use effective gatekeeping skills.

▶ Use a flipchart, chalkboard, or dry erase board to summarize meeting progress; the written notes of a meeting become the "group mind" and help keep the group on track. Give the meeting structure.

▶ If it is a formal meeting, decide when to take a vote. Make sure the issues are clear before a vote is taken.

▶ Prepare a committee report (or delegate someone to prepare a report) after one or many meetings. Groups need a record of their progress. Many meetings designate someone to be a secretary and prepare the minutes or summary of what occurred at the meeting.

How to Facilitate Meeting Interaction

FACILITATION SKILL	SKILL DESCRIPTION	EXAMPLES
Use gatekeeping skills.	Listen to the discussion to encourage less-talkative members to participate and limit the contributions of ververbalizers.	"Dale, we've not heard from you. Do you have some thoughts on this idea? or, "Heather, I know you have some strong opinions about this project but I'd like to hear from others who have not spoken on the issue."
Focus the group's attention on the agenda or goal of the discussion.	Especially when discussion seems to be off target, remind the group what the purpose of the meeting is or state the goal of the group.	"Although we seem to be interested in talking about some of the recent hassles we've had at the university, I'd like to bring us back to our purpose of today's meeting. Let's return to our second agenda item, to help us solve the problem we're addressing."
Monitor the group's use of time.	Remind the group how much time is left for discussion if the group gets unnecessarily bogged down on one issue; suggest a strategy to help the group move on to another issue.	"I note that we've been talking about this issue for over 20 minutes, and we only have 15 minutes left in our discussion. Would you like to continue talking about this issue or appoint a subcommittee to tackle this problem and get back to us with a recommendation?"
Provide appropriate structure to channel discussion, and keep it focused on the issues at hand.	Consider inviting all group members to write their ideas on paper before verbalizing; consider using silent brainstorming, nominal-group technique, affinity technique, *is/is not*, T-chart, or force-field analysis. Also, phrase issues for discussion as a question on the printed agenda rather than just listing a topic to talk about.	"We have a couple of options to consider. Why don't we first each write down advantages and disadvantages of each option and then share our ideas with the entire group."

T E C H N O L O G Y

Parliamentary Procedure

All groups need structure—a way of helping a group stay focused on its task. The larger the group the greater the need for structure. In effect, parliamentary procedures provide the needed structure to help large groups stay focused on the business at hand. Recent research suggests that parliamentary procedure is an effective method of helping larger groups get tasks done. The most comprehensive guide to parliamentary procedure is *Roberts' Rules of Order*. The following Websites offer an excellent review of the essential elements of parliamentary procedure.

www.robertsrules.com

www.constitution.org/rror/rror_01.htm

One of the time-tested strategies for leading a large group is **parliamentary procedure**—a comprehensive set of rules that prescribes how to take action on specific issues that come before the group; it provides an orderly way for large groups (of twenty or more people) to conduct business, although it is less useful for small groups (in which it leads to win/lose patterns of decision making rather than consensus).

All groups need structure. The larger the group the greater the need for structure. In effect, parliamentary procedure provides the needed structure to help large groups stay focused on the business at hand. Recent research suggests that parliamentary procedure can be an effective method of adding structure and rules to coordinate quality discussion in a large group.[19] For a complete guide to parliamentary procedure, consult *Roberts' Rules of Order* or the *Sturgis Standard Code of Parliamentary Procedure*.

Participating in Meetings

So far we have stressed the responsibilities of the meeting leader to give the meeting structure and ensure interaction, but meeting participants have similar obligations. In many respects, each meeting participant has leadership responsibilities. Leadership, as noted in Chapter 11, means "to influence." As a meeting participant, you will have many opportunities to influence the group process. Be sensitive to both the level of structure and the interaction in the meeting. Use such skills as metadiscussion (discussion about discussion), which we presented in Chapter 10 to help keep the group on track.

Your key obligation as a meeting participant is to come to the meeting prepared to work. If the leader has distributed an agenda before the meeting (as leaders should), then you have a clear sense of how to prepare and what information you should bring to the meeting. Even if no agenda has been provided, try to anticipate what will be discussed. If you have no clue as to what will be on the agenda, contact the meeting leader and ask him or her how to prepare.

Mosvick and Nelson, in their book, *We've Got to Start Meeting Like This!* identify six guidelines of competent meeting participants.[20]

1. *Organize your contributions.* Just as a well-organized speech makes a better presentation, well-organized contributions make better meetings. Rambling, disorganized, disjointed ideas increase the likelihood that the meeting will become sidetracked.

2. *Speak when your contribution is relevant.* Before you make a comment, listen to the person who is speaking. Is your comment useful and helpful? Groups are easily distracted by irrelevant contributions.

3. *Make one point at a time.* Even though you may be bursting with good ideas and suggestions, your colleagues will be more likely to listen to your ideas if you present them one at a time rather than as a string of unrelated points.

4. *Speak clearly and forcefully.* No, we are not advocating that you aggressively try to dominate the conversation. Unassertive mumbling, however, will probably get lost in the verbal shuffle of most meetings.

5. *Support your ideas with evidence.* One of the key determinants of good decisions and effective solutions that we discussed in Chapter 7 is the use of evidence to support your ideas and opinions. Opinions are ubiquitous: Everyone has one. Facts, statistics, and well-selected examples help keep the group focused on the task.

6. *Listen actively to all aspects of the discussion.* Group meetings provide one of the most challenging listening contexts. When several people are attempting to make points and counterarguments, you will have to gear up your powers of concentration and listening. Checking your understanding by summarizing or paraphrasing can dramatically improve communication and decrease misunderstanding.[21]

REVIEW

HOW TO GIVE A MEETING STRUCTURE	HOW TO ENSURE MANAGED INTERACTION
▶ Prepare an effective agenda by determining your meeting goals	▶ Use effective gatekeeping skills.
	▶ Use metadiscussion to help the group focus on the goals
▶ Identify what needs to be discussed to achieve the goals	▶ Help the group be sensitive to time that has elapsed and that remains for deliberation
▶ Organize the agenda to achieve the goals	▶ Use strategies to structure interaction (e.g., write before speaking, nominal-group technique, or silent brainstorming).

Principles and Practices of Using Technology in Groups and Teams

Instead of filing into a room and sitting around a table for a meeting, imagine sitting down at your desk, switching on your computer, keying in your password, and tapping out your contributions to a meeting on the screen. Increasingly, organizations are having their members use electronic mail, fax machines, video conferences, and other technologies to interact with one another. With today's technological advances employees can work on team tasks while in different locations. It seems oxymoronic to have a team meeting without meeting in person, but with today's technology, we have the opportunity to hold "virtual meetings" at which no one sits face-to-face. Throughout the book we have discussed the rapidly growing application of computer and Internet technology to group and team collaboration. We conclude this chapter and the book with a review of the principles and practices of collaborating with technology.

Managers today have many choices about how to communicate with workers. Technologies such as e-mail, for example, make it possible to connect people for collaborative decision making without meeting face-to-face. One interesting theory, called **media richness**, seeks to explain and predict why certain types of technologies are effective and others are not.[22] The media or method of communication is said to be rich if it has the following four characteristics: (1) potential for instant feedback, (2) several verbal and nonverbal cues that can be processed by senders and receivers, (3) natural rather than formal or stilted language, and (4) a focus on individuals rather than on a mass of people. Face-to-face meetings and personal conferences are highly media-rich; a memo or an announcement posted on a bulletin board is media-lean.[23]

REVIEW

The Necessary Steps to an Effective Meeting

LEADER

PARTICIPANTS

Before the Meeting

1. Define objective.
2. Select participants.
3. Make preliminary contact with participants to confirm availability.
4. Schedule meeting room and arrange for equipment and refreshments.
5. Prepare agenda.
6. Invite participants and distribute agenda.
7. Make final check of meeting room.

1. Block time on schedule.
2. Confirm attendance.
3. Define your role.
4. Determine what the leader needs from you.
5. Suggest other participants.
6. Know the objective.
7. Know when and where to meet.
8. Do any required homework.

During the Meeting

1. Start promptly.
2. Follow the agenda.
3. Manage the use of time.
4. Limit/control the discussion.
5. Elicit participation.
6. Help resolve conflicts.
7. Clarify action to be taken.
8. Summarize results.

1. Listen and participate.
2. Be open-minded/receptive.
3. Stay on the agenda and subject.
4. Limit or avoid side conversations and distractions.
5. Ask questions to ensure understanding.
6. Take notes on your action items.

After the Meeting

1. Restore room and return equipment.
2. Evaluate effectiveness as meeting leader.
3. Send out meeting evaluations.
4. Distribute memorandum of discussion.
5. Take any action you agreed to.
6. Follow up on action items.

1. Evaluate meeting.
2. Review memorandum summarizing the discussion.
3. Brief others as appropriate.
4. Take any action agreed to.
5. Follow up on action items.

Table 12.2 **A Continuum of Media–Rich and Media–Lean Methods of Communication**

Face-to-face, one-on-one discussions	Media rich
Face-to-face group meetings	
Video conference	
Telephone	
Computer conference (interactive e-mail)	
Voice mail	
Noninteractive e-mail	
Fax	
Personal letter	
Impersonal memo	
Posted flyer or announcement	Media lean

Source: Adapted from L. K. Trevino, R. L. Draft, and R. H. Lengel, "Understanding Managers' Media Choices: A Symbolic Interactionist Perspective,: in *Organizations and Communication Technology* eds., J. Fulk and C. Steinfield (Newbury Park, CA: Sage 1990) 71–94.

The developers of media richness theory suggest that managers should choose media-rich methods of communicating with employees if the message is ambiguous or potentially ambiguous. With less likelihood of misunderstanding, a less media-rich method will be fine. Group meetings, then, are necessary to discuss issues and ideas where the potential for misunderstanding is high. If the information to be communicated is not ambiguous (people are likely to understand clearly what the message is about), then a memo will suffice. Table 12.2 shows a continuum of rich and lean communication media, some of which we discuss in more detail on the following pages.

Telephone Conferences

The telephone conference call—one of the first uses of technology to support group and team meetings—involves a group of people agreeing to "meet" at a certain time by phone. To hold a conference call you need a special telephone service, available from most telephone companies, so that several people in different locations can be connected at the same time. Without this special service, if you call more than one person at the same time you'll obviously get a busy signal.

A conference call allows several people who cannot meet face to face to provide input. It saves both time and money when people are separated by a long distance. Even if they are in the same city, it can expedite decision making without the time needed to travel to another office for a meeting. Sometimes the biggest challenge in holding a meeting is finding a time when all meeting participants are available. A telephone conference makes it easier for people to connect but it does have disadvantages.

One of the obvious ones is that you miss many nonverbal cues. Yes, you still can detect emotions from vocal cues, but without facial expressions, posture, and gestures, you may sometimes not accurately understand the meaning of messages. As we discussed in Chapter 6, nonverbal cues help regulate communication interaction. Have you ever had the experience of talking over someone else's words on the phone? Without the nonverbal regulatory cues, it's trickier to know when to start and stop talking. This problem of regulating communication becomes worse if you have several people on a conference call.

When you participate in a conference phone call, you should introduce yourself and announce your name before you speak at the beginning of the call. "Hello, this is Steve...." may be all you need to say if people already know you. If you're speaking to people who don't know you, then you'll want to provide more information about yourself. Remember, groups have a period of orientation, especially with a telephone conference, so you'll need to help orient the group to who you are. And just as in other meetings, you will need a balance of structure and interaction. A written agenda (perhaps sent prior to the call by fax or e-mail) would be a good way to keep the meeting on track.

Electronic Mail

Electronic mail, usually called **e-mail,** is one of the most prevalent technological methods used to send and receive messages in organizations. Many people use e-mail to send and receive messages about personal and work-related topics. To send an e-mail message, the sender simply types a message and then electronically "mails" it to one or more people. Through the Internet and the World Wide Web, a network of many computer-communication systems, people can communicate with one another from anywhere on the globe. All you need is a telephone, a computer, a modem (which permits your computer to send messages over the phone), and the appropriate software. With the advent of wireless and satellite technology, it is becoming increasingly easier to be in touch with friends and colleagues.

Communicating via e-mail can be effective for the discussion of routine business. There is some evidence, however, that groups that make decisions by e-mail are less likely to reach consensus.[24] Other research, in pointing to the value of e-mail meetings, suggests that electronic correspondence minimizes status differences that may be present if people meet face-to-face.[25] Another study found that language style has a significant impact on the impression you make when communicating via e-mail. In general, someone who uses a more powerful language style is perceived as more powerful, credible, even physically attractive, than someone whose language style is weak or timid. Yet another research team found that groups who use e-mail while solving problems are more likely to do a better job of analyzing the problem than groups that interact face-to-face.[26] The research on using e-mail groups, however, is still in its early stages.[27]

E-mail users can participate in what is called **synchronous communication**—communication interaction that is taking place in real time. This is what happens when you talk to someone on the telephone—you talk and another person responds immediately to what you've said. A real-time e-mail "conversation" is clearly not as immediate as holding a face-to-face discussion. (It takes time for you and your partner to exchange messages, so there is some time delay in expressing ideas.)

A **chat room** is an Internet site where participants can synchronously post and receive messages. If you are "talking" to someone in a chat room, your messages are synchronized in response to each other, somewhat like having a big meeting in cyberspace. Synchronous communication has the advantage of getting immediate feedback to your messages, making it more like a real conversation. The disadvantage is that you and your partner or partners have to both be using a computer at the same time, and you also can't see the people you are talking with.

Asynchronous communication is e-mail interaction in which messages are sent and responded to with a delay in time—somewhat like posting a message on a bulletin board and waiting for someone to read and respond to it later. Asynchronous communication has the advantage of not having to be logged on to a chat room at the same time as your communication partners. You can post a message and then check back later to see how others have responded, much like sending a memo to someone and then waiting for a response. Of course, you lose the value of getting immediate feedback, and it takes more time to get work accomplished because you don't get instant responses from others.

As with telephone conferencing, one disadvantage of e-mail and other forms of electronic communication is the loss of emotional information communicated by facial expression, vocal inflection, gestures, and body posture.[28] Some people use emoticons—keyboard symbols that are typed in certain visual arrangements expressing emotions—or just put their feelings into words: "I have a big grin on my face as I read what you sent me." Putting your e-mail message in all capital letters is another way to add emotional richness: IT'S LIKE SHOUTING AT SOMEONE. But be careful using all capital letters. Your readers may think you are rude if your message seems to scream at them.

Video Conferences

The **video conference**—a relatively media-rich use of technology—occurs when two or more individuals are linked by closed-circuit or satellite-linked TV. The participants meet in specially equipped media rooms where TV cameras broadcast (or in this case "narrow" cast) the

Managers should choose media-rich methods of communicating with employees if the message is potentially ambiguous. What sorts of messages might you not want to communicate via email?

meeting to the other participants. The video conference has the obvious advantage of permitting groups to interact over long distances when it may be very expensive to have all members travel to one destination. And the video conference has an advantage over a conference phone call because nonverbal messages—such as facial expressions, eye contact, and posture—which provide more accurate sending and receiving of relational messages, can be seen. Video conferences are expensive, however, and when sensitive decisions and challenging problems need to be solved, individuals prefer a more media-rich method of managing the uncertainty and ambiguity. A software program called *One Touch* is a multimedia system that incorporates electronic voting keypads as well as audio and video systems to structure interaction. This system is especially designed for large corporations in multiple locations. One research team concluded that a video meeting is more likely to be successful if group members have met one another prior to the video meeting.[29] Another study found that video conferences are better than face-to-face meetings at handling more structured discussion.[30] Group members also seem to prepare better for a video conference than for a face-to-face meeting; perhaps because of its expense and novelty, group members view a video conference as more important.

Adapting Your Message Delivery for Video Conferences   Satellite video teleconferences and the video software that permits you to see and be seen via the Internet are becoming increasingly common. Should your speech delivery be different when talking to meeting participants via a video camera? The basic principles of effective delivery—for example, having eye contact with the camera when speaking to someone not present, having an audible and varied vocal quality, and avoiding distracting gestures and mannerisms—should serve you well. But you may want to consider some additional guidelines if your message is telecast to others.

1.   *Monitor your gestures and facial expressions*. The television camera has the effect of amplifying gestures and facial expressions. We usually don't see newscasters or other

TV communicators use excessive gestures. Keep your hands quiet and avoid fidgeting with pens, hair, or clothing. Also, try to keep your hands away from you face.

2. *Don't interrupt others*. This is good advice in any meeting or conference situation, but it is especially important if the meeting is televised. If the camera is not on you when you are speaking, others may not know who is talking. Also, talking over others adds to confusion, and key points may be lost—both yours and those of the person who had the floor.

3. *Dress for TV success*. White clothing may create a glare on TV. Men may want to wear a light blue rather than a white shirt and women should also consider nonwhite clothing. Solid colors look best. Also avoid large patterns, shiny jewelry, and other jangling fashion accents.

4. *Become familiar with the technology*. Arrive for a teleconference in plenty of time to become acquainted with the equipment, use of microphones, and camera placement.

With the increased use of relatively inexpensive cameras that can be connected to a personal computer, it is easier and less expensive than in the past to hold a video conference meeting. But to have more than two people participate in the meeting will still take special equipment.

When participating in a video conference, just like in other meetings, you will need an agenda to provide appropriate meeting structure. Also, because people can see you, you'll want to monitor your appearance just as you would in a face-to-face meeting. It's usually best to have a technician help coordinate the logistics of setting up the meeting, making sure both the cameras and microphones are working well and that all goes smoothly.

Group Decision Support Systems

A new line of software has emerged to help make face-to-face meetings more efficient. As we noted in Chapter 2, group decision support systems (GDSSs) consist of computer hardware and software that add structure to meetings. This technology is usually used with live interaction. For example, a group may be discussing a particular problem and the facilitator may stop discussion and suggest that each group member do silent brainstorming at a computer terminal. A large screen then projects the results of the brainstorming for all group members to see and evaluate.[31] Increasingly, groups and teams can have the benefits of using a group decision support system without meeting in rooms with special hardware and software; the advent of many computer software programs now permit electronic collaboration with greater ease. Although research on the use and value of these technologies is relatively new, some conclusions are emerging.[32]

Generating Ideas

▶ GDSSs can help generate more ideas than unstructured, face-to-face brainstorming sessions because status differences are diminished and people can contribute anonymously.

Problem Solving

▶ Electronically mediated communication (such as e-mail and video conferences) seems to work best for more structured, linear tasks.

▶ Computer technology and its rapid transfer of information does not inherently lead to better solutions and decisions. Problems are solved by people. Technology may simply allow greater access to accurate information, help structure the process, and keep a group focused on facts, but decisions will still be made by people skilled in the art and science of decision making and problem solving.

▶ The increased speed of information transfer allows less time for reflection. Thus, technology may help us make mistakes faster.

▶ Participating in computer-mediated meetings appears to be less satisfying for many people than participating in face-to-face meetings even though the patterns of communication are similar.

▶ In computer-mediated meetings, ideas can be captured and recorded with speed and accuracy.

▶ Some group members using computer-mediated technology do a poorer job of evaluating the pros and cons of alternatives.

▶ GDSS groups perform better if there are rewards and incentives for the entire group than if there are no rewards.

Managing Relationships

▶ Some (but not all) group members find it more difficult to negotiate relationship issues when messages are mediated by technology; it may take more time for relationships to develop in GDSS groups than in face-to-face collaborations.

▶ Researchers have found that cliques and coalitions are more prevalent in computer-mediated meetings than in face-to-face discussions.

▶ Conflict seems to be more skillfully managed during face-to-face interaction rather than electronic means when group and team participants are using collaborative conflict-management approaches.

▶ People who develop skills in using technology and managing information will become more powerful and important in organizations than people who do not use technology effectively.

Collaborating

E T H I C A L L Y

Be True to Your Ethical Principles

You're probably familiar with the old saying "Go along to get along." Throughout this book we've championed the value of reaching consensus and developing a supportive communication climate when you work in groups and teams. But don't get the idea that lack of conflict is to be valued above a violation of your own ethical principles. Sometimes during an especially boring or tedious meeting, the group will make a decision just to move on to the next agenda item. If you know that your group is about ready to make a decision or to take some action that is against your own ethical standards, don't remain silent. Although you do have an obligation to be interpersonally supportive of others, this support should not be offered at the expense of your own fundamental values. Remember, groups and teams sometimes make decisions that affect the lives of people not in the group. Don't just go along with the group if you know an action is wrong or illegal.

▶ Female-only groups reported greater satisfaction, sent more words per message, and reported higher levels of group development than male-only or mixed-sex groups.

Critical Thinking

▶ Use of technology and media increases the amount of information people have to process. People will need to develop critical thinking and information analysis skills to sort out useful from less useful information; people need information-triage skills (see Chapter 7).

▶ Using e-mail to send and receive messages may contribute to greater polarization of opinions; group members may take more extreme positions when putting information in writing than when communicating orally.

▶ Computer-mediated meetings are less effective when the task is complex, although some research suggests richer media (face-to-face) are not always preferable.

▶ Groups that collaborate electronically appear to have a greater level of understanding of the issues involved than face-to-face collaborations.

Technical Support

▶ Experts note that electronic and mediated messages will be more effective if participants have a "techno-partner" or media expert to help handle the hardware and software glitches.

What accounts for the differences in the way people collaborate electronically, compared to face-to-face discussion? Researchers have concluded that the major factors to explain the differences are (1)During electronic collaboration most of the time the contributions are anonymous; group members don't know who is saying what, so all ideas are evaluated without regard to status differences in the group. (2) There is more equal participation in groups that collaborate electronically than during face-to-face meetings. And (3) group members have more equal influence over the group and one another when interacting electronically rather than in face-to-face discussions; people are more likely to dominate the discussion in face-to-face meetings than during electronic collaboration.[33]

Putting Principles into Practice

Most of the work in organizations is accomplished in group and teams. This chapter has identified some of the principles and skills that can enhance your effectiveness when working with others on the job. Consider the following methods of improving quality and productivity:

▶ When you want to gather information from others, consider using a focus group.

▶ When you want to improve work quality, consider two group approaches: Quality circles and *kaizen*.

▶ When your group does not meet together face-to-face, use technology to share information.

▶ Self-directed work teams function best when team members feel empowered and have adequate training in team skills.

We also reviewed several principles and skills to help make group meetings efficient and effective.

▶ Meetings need a balance of structure and information.

▶ When you lead a group, always prepare an agenda by (1) determining your meeting goal, (2) identifying items to achieve the goal, and (3) organizing the agenda items.

▶ Find ways to involve all members in the meeting. Draw out quiet members; avoid letting a verbose member dominate a meeting.

▶ When conducting a formal meeting, use parliamentary procedure to help give the meeting structure and order.

▶ When you participate in a meeting, make sure your comments are organized, relevant, clear, and supported with evidence. Also make sure you listen to others and monitor your nonverbal messages.

PRACTICE

Meeting Assessment

Attend a meeting on your campus or in your community. Evaluate the meeting by determining which violations of procedures listed on page 335 and 336 are evident. Write a report suggesting what changes you would make if you were leading the meeting.

Analyzing Group Skills in Organizations

Visit an organization in your community—perhaps a school, factory, or hospital. Interview the individual responsible for training workers to determine what kind of training in small group skills the workers receive. If they have a quality-circle program or other participative team format, find out what kind of training group members receive. If the organization has no training program in group communication skills, ask what kinds of skills the organization most values.

The Computer–Networking Case [34]

John Hager, vice president for operations of Southwest Technical Insurance Company (SWT Insurance), called Bob Morgan, director of human resource development, into his office. Starting the conversation, Hager said, "I know you've been busy grappling with a disability complaint, Bob, but I have another problem that I'd like you to help me with."

"As you know, Bob," Hager continued, "our firm has invested substantial sums of money in computers in our local offices. Right now, I'm not concerned about the larger word-processing centers that have replaced the steno pools in the home office. I'm primarily concerned with SWT's 265 local offices and think we may need to link our computers into a more-sophisticated network. Each workstation, complete with computers and software, costs about $5,000. We took this step to improve our productivity in our branches. But lately, we're wondering what we've bought for our money."

"What are some of your specific reservations?" asked Bob.

"Well, the word-processing centers look impressive, but what are they really accomplishing for SWT? We really don't know whether employees are better satisfied or more productive using the new equipment. Do we need to invest in linking the computer centers together? What kind of network do we need? We also suspect that younger employees may be more favorably inclined toward word processing than the older employees. Other members of the executive committee and I would like your human-resources management team to provide us with some answers to these questions. Our overall goal is to do the work as efficiently as possible, with happy workers."

After thinking for a moment, Morgan replied, "John, those are excellent questions. This is just the kind of problem-solving task the folks in personnel research should be tackling. I'll work with them to develop a preliminary report and share our suggested approach with you in a couple of weeks."

Questions

1. What is the problem that needs to be solved?

2. What decisions need to be made?

3. How would you recommend that Bob Morgan approach his assignment? Draft a plan that outlines how Morgan's personnel-research team should proceed. What should they do first, second, third, and so on?

4. How could Morgan's personnel-research group use a teamwork approach to complete its task?

 Your companion Website has more practice activities, questionnaires, and checklists!
www.ablongman.com/beebe

Notes

1. Roger K. Mosvick and Robert B. Nelson, *We've Got to Start Meeting Like This!* (Glenview, IL: Scott, Foresman, 1987).

2. For a comprehensive discussion of using groups and teams to enhance organizational quality, see Peter R. Scholtes, *The Team Handbook* (Madison, WI: Joiner Associates, 1996); see also Michael Argyle, *Cooperation: The Basis of Sociability* (London: Routledge, 1991) 115–31; Dennis A. Romig, *Breakthrough Teamwork: Outstanding Results Using Structured Teamwork* (Chicago: Irwin, 1996).

3. *Positive Personnel Practices: Quality Circles' Participant's Manual* (Prospect Heights, IL: Waveland Press, 1982).

4. Masaaki Imai, *Kaizen: The Key to Japan's Competitive Success* (New York: McGraw-Hill, 1986).

5. W. J. Burpitt and William J. Bigoness, "Leadership and Innovation Among Teams: The Impact of Empowerment," *Small Group Research* 28 (1998): 414–423.

6. R. A. Guzzo and M.W. Dickson, "Teams in Organization: Recent Research on Performance and Effectiveness," *Annual Review of Psychology* 47 (1996): 307–338: C. W. Langred, "Work-Group

Design and Autonomy: A Field Study of the Interaction Between Task Interdependence and Group Autonomy" *Small Group Research* 31 (2000): 54–70; R. C. Liden, S. J. Wayne and L. K. Bradway, "Task Interdependence as a Moderator of the Relation Between Group Control and Performance," *Human Relations* 50 (1997): 169–181.

7. C. C. Morrow, M. Q. Jarrett, and M. T. Rupinski, "An Investigation of the Effect and Economic Utility of Corporate-Wide Training," *Personnel Psychology* 50 (1997): 91–119.

8. S. A. Wheelan, D. Murphy, E. Tsumura, and S. F. Kline, "Member Perceptions of Internal Group Dynamics and Productivity, *Small Group Research* 29 (1998): 371–393.

9. Wheelan, Murphy, Tsumura, and Kline, "Member Perceptions of Internal Group Dynamics and Productivity."

10. "Survive Meetings with High-Tech Tools," *USA Today Online* (22 Jan. 1999) (www.usatoday.com).

11. Dave Barry, *Dave Barry's Guide to Life* (New York: Wings Books, 1991) 311.

12. Mosvick and Nelson, *We've Got to Start Meeting Like This!*

13. Steven A. Beebe and John T. Masterson, "Toward a Model of Small Group Communication: Application for Teaching and Research," *Florida Speech Communication Journal* 8, no. 2 (1980): 9–15.

14. See Dennis A. Romig and Laurie J. Romig, *Breakthrough Teamwork* (Chicago: Irwin, 1996); Thomas A. Kayser, *Mining Group Gold* (El Segundo, CA: Serif Publishing, 1990).

15. Henry L. Ewbank, Jr., *Meeting Management* (Dubuque, IA: Brown, 1968).

16. Suggestions about organizing meeting agendas are based on Michael Doyle and David Straus, *How to Make Meetings Work* (New York: Playboy Press, 1976); Mosvick and Nelson, *We've Got to Start Meeting Like This!;* Gay Lumsden and Donald Lumsden, *Communicating in Groups and Teams: Sharing Leadership* (Belmont, CA: Wadsworth, 1993); Dan B. Curtis, James J. Floyd, and Jerry L. Winsor, *Business and Professional Communication* (New York: Harper-Collins, 1992); Romig and Romig, *Structured Teamwork Guide*; Thomas A. Kayser, *Mining Group Gold*; John E. Tropman and Gershom Clark Morningstar, *Meetings: How to Make Them Work for You* (New York: Van Nostrand Reinhold, 1985) 56; John E. Tropman, *Making Meetings Work* (Thousand Oaks, CA: Sage 1996).

17. F. Niederman and R. J. Volkema, "The Effects of Facilitator Characteristics on Meeting Preparation, Set Up, and Implementation," *Small Group Research* 30 (1999): 330–360.

18. Timothy Ludwig and E. S. Geller, "Assigned Versus Participatory Goal Setting and Response Generalization: Managing Injury Control Among Professional Pizza Deliveries," *Journal of Applied Psychology* 82 (1997): 253–261; For an excellent review of facilitation and collaborative leadership in teams and organizations, see Dennis A. Romig, *Side by Side Leadership*, (Austin, TX: Bard, 2001) 9, 103–110.

19. Al Weitzel and Patricia Geist, "Parliamentary Procedure in a Community Group: Communication and Vigilant Decision Making," *Communication Monographs* 65 (1998): 244–59.

20. Mosvick and Nelson, *We've Got to Start Meeting Like This!*

21. Marion E. Haynes, *Effective Meeting Skills* (Los Altos, CA: Crisp Publications, 1988).

22. R. H. Lengel and R. L. Daft, "The Selection of Communication Media as an Executive Skill," *Academy of Management Executive* 2 (1988): 225–32.

23. Lengel and Daft, "The Selection of Communication Media as an Executive Skill."

24. See the excellent review of the effect of technology on group decision making in M. S. Poole and G. DeSanctis, "Microlevel Structuration in Computer-Supported Group Decision Making," *Human Communication Research* 19 (1992): 5–49.

25. V. J. Dubrovsky, S. Kiesler, and B. N. Sethna, "The Equalization Phenomenon: Status Effects in Computer-Mediated and Face-to-Face Decision-Making Groups," *Human Computer Interaction* 6 (1991): 119–46.

26. A. I. Shirani, M. H. A. Tafti, J. F. Affisco, "Task and Technology Fit: A Comparison of Two Technologies for Synchronous and Asynchronous Group Communication," *Information & Management* 36 (1999): 139–150.

27. M. Adkins and D. E. Brashers, "The Power of Language in Computer-Mediated Groups," *Management Communication Quarterly* 8 (1995): 289–322.

28. Ronald E. Rice and Gail Love, "Electronic Emotion: Socioemotional Context in a Computer-Mediated Communication Network," *Communication Research*, 014 (February 1987): 85–108.

29. See R. Johansen, J. Vallee, and K. Spangler, *Electronic Meetings: Technical Alternatives and Social Choices* (Reading, MA: Addison-Wesley, 1979).

30. P. L. McLeod and J. K. Liker, "Electronic Meeting Systems: Evidence from a Low Structure Environment," *Information Systems Research* 3 (1992): 195–223.

31. Michael Finley, "Welcome to the Electronic Meeting," *Training* (July 1991): 29–32. See also Marshall Scott Poole and G. Desanctis, "Microlevel Structuration in Computer-Supported Group Decision Making," *Human Communication Research* 19 (1992): 5–49.

32. For an excellent review of communication technology and group communication, see C. R. Scott, "Communication Technology and Group Communication, " in L. Frey, ed., *The Handbook of Group Communication Theory and Research* (Thousand Oaks, CA: Sage, 1999) 432–472; also see N. N. Kamel and R. M. Davison, "Applying CSCW Technology to Overcome Traditional Barriers in Group Interactions," *Information & Management* 34 (1998): 209–219; R. C. W. Kwok and M. Khalifa, "Effects of GSS on Knowledge Acquisition" *Information & Management* 34 (1998): 307–315; B. P. Robichaux and R. B. Cooper, "GSS Participation: A Cultural Examination," *Information & Management* 33 (1998): 287–300; A. Shirani, M. Aiken, and J. G. P. Paolillo, "Group Decision Support Systems and Incentive Structures." *Information & Management* 33 (1998): 231–240; B. A. Jain and J. S. Solomon, "The Effect of Task Complexity and Conflict Handling Styles on Computer-Supported Negotiations," *Information & Management* 37 (2000): 161–168; D. P. Brandon and A. B. Hollingshead, "Collaborative Learning and Computer-Supported Groups," *Communication Education* 48 (1999): 109–126.

33. C. R. Scott, L. Quinn, C. E. Timmerman, and D. M. Garrett, "Ironic Uses of Group Communication Technology: Evidence from Meeting Transcripts and Interviews with Group Decision Support Systems Users," *Communication Quarterly* 46 (1998):353–374; K. J. Chun, H. K. Park, "Examining the Conflicting Results of GDSS Research," *Information & Management* 33 (1998): 313–325.

34. This case study is adapted from Raymond S. Ross, *Small Groups in Organizational Settings* (Englewood Cliffs, NJ: Prentice Hall, 1989).

A

Appendix:
Communicating
to an
Audience

Throughout this book we have featured principles and skills that can help you communicate with others in groups, meetings, and teams. Most of the groups in which you communicate will be private discussions among members of your group. Some groups, however, are designed so that others can listen to the discussion. **Public-communication formats** help an audience understand all sides of an issue, particularly if individuals with diverse viewpoints are involved in the discussion. Three public-communication formats will be considered in the following sections: (1) panel discussions, (2) symposium presentations, and (3) forum presentations. We will also offer some general guidelines for speaking to an audience.

Panel Discussions

A **panel discussion**—the most frequently used public group discussion format—is usually intended to inform an audience about a specific issue or problem. It is defined as a group discussion that takes place before an audience with the purpose of: (1) informing the audience about issues of interest, (2) solving a problem, or (3) encouraging the audience to evaluate the pros and cons of a controversial issue.

An appointed moderator or chairperson usually organizes a panel discussion. The moderator's job is to keep the discussion on track. The moderator opens the discussion by announcing the discussion question. Most panel discussions include at least three panelists; if they include more than eight or nine, the panelists have difficulty participating equally. Because the panel is presented for the benefit of an audience, organizers should take care that the audience can see and hear the discussion clearly. Panelists usually sit in a semicircle or behind a table. Although they should be informed about the subject they will discuss, they should not rehearse their discussion; the conversation should be extemporaneous. Panelists may use notes to help them remember facts and statistics, but they should not use a prepared text.

After announcing the discussion question or topic, the moderator briefly introduces the panel members, perhaps noting each one's qualifications for being on the panel. To begin the discussion, the moderator may then direct a specific question to one or more panelists. An effective moderator encourages all panelists to participate. If one panelist seems reluctant, the moderator may direct a specific question to that person. If one panelist tends to dominate the discussion, the moderator may suggest politely that other panel members be given an opportunity to participate. Rather than let the discussion continue until the group has nothing more to say on the issue, a specific time limit should be set on the discussion. Most panel discussions last about an hour, but the time limit can be tailored to the needs of the audience and the topic. At the conclusion of the discussion, the moderator may either summarize comments made by the group members or ask another group member to do so. Often the summary is followed by an invitation to the audience to ask the panel questions.

Symposium Presentations

A **symposium presentation** is another public discussion format, consisting of a series of short speeches usually unified by a central theme or issue. Unlike participants in a panel discussion, participants in a symposium either come with prepared speeches or speak extemporaneously from an outline. The speakers are usually experts who represent contrasting points of view. For example, imagine that your physics instructor has invited four experts in the field of nuclear energy to speak to your class. Each expert has selected a specific aspect of nuclear energy to present. Your instructor probably will briefly introduce the speakers, announce the central topic of discussion, and ask the speakers to address themselves to a discussion question. Then each will speak from eight to ten minutes. The speakers probably will not talk informally between speeches; they most likely will know in advance what general areas the other speakers will discuss. After the speeches, your instructor may summarize the major ideas presented and allow the audience to participate in an open forum.

Technically, a symposium is not really a form of group discussion, because there is little or no interaction among the participants. But a symposium often concludes with a more informal panel discussion or forum. A major advantage of the symposium is that it is easy to organize: Just line up three or four speakers to discuss a designated topic. In addition, when speakers with contrasting viewpoints present their ideas, a lively discussion often follows. Make sure that the speakers know their time limits and address their assigned topics. An able moderator can prevent a symposium from digressing into irrelevant issues. Also announce a time limit for the audience forum following a symposium.

Forum Presentations

Group discussion encourages more interaction and participation than other forms of communication (such as public speaking). A **forum presentation** takes maximum advantage of the principle that when many people participate improved decisions can result. The word forum originated with the Romans. The *forum* was the public marketplace where Roman citizens could assemble and voice their opinions about the issues of the day. A forum discussion generally follows a panel discussion or symposium, but can also come after a single speaker's presentation. A forum permits an audience to get involved in the discussion. Rather than playing a passive role, as in a panel discussion, the audience directs questions and responses to a chairperson or to a group of individuals. When holding a news conference, the president of the United States presents a prepared statement, followed by questions and responses from reporters—a forum. Some talk radio stations have forum discussions on issues of the day. Many communities conduct town meetings or public hearings in which citizens can voice their opinions about issues affecting the community. The audience in a forum has an opportunity to provide feedback. Comments from audience members sometimes can be used to determine how successfully a speaker or panel has enlightened the audience. The questions and responses also give the featured speakers an opportunity to clarify and elaborate their viewpoints.

Public–Communication Group Formats

FORMAT	DESCRIPTION
Panel	An unrehearsed discussion that takes place before an audience to inform, solve a problem, or make a decision
Symposium	A series of short speeches unified by a central theme or issue
Forum	A discussion that frequently follows a panel or symposium presentation and allows audience members to respond

Planning What to Say to an Audience

Speaking to an audience involves skills in planning what you are going to say and presenting your information to your listeners. Your school probably offers a course in public speaking. The discussion that follows highlights some of the essential skills public presenters should master when speaking to an audience whether in a panel, symposium, or forum-group presentation.[1] The more formal the presentation (a symposium presentation, for example), the more planning it requires. We will offer some general tips for both planning a presentation and presenting your ideas to others.

Speakers need a plan. Speakers who are part of a group effort to communicate with an audience need a plan that is coordinated with other group members. Central to all these planning elements is a consideration of your audience. Your first and foremost priority when speaking to an audience is to make sure you consider their needs and backgrounds. A speaking plan also typically involves clarifying and coordinating your topic with other group members, deciding on your specific purpose or objective, identifying your central ideas, and supporting and organizing your ideas.

Analyze Your Audience

Analyzing your audience means finding out as much as you can about your listeners. Why will they be listening to you? What are their expectations? What are their attitudes toward you, your group, and your topic? Answers to these questions can help you make choices throughout the planning process. If you are speaking to a captive audience—people who have little choice as to whether to attend or not, such as your classmates in small-group-communication class—you need to be especially sensitive to their needs. Class members may have to show up. If that is the case, your group needs to work extra hard to immediately make the information interesting and relevant to the listeners.

Have a Clear Objective

Keep your specific presentation objective clearly in mind as you prepare for your public presentation. Is your goal primarily to inform the audience about decisions your group has already made? Or is your goal to persuade your listeners to adopt a solution you are proposing? You might give a public presentation to let the audience eavesdrop on your conversation as you debate issues and share information. If an audience is present, though, you should be keenly aware of the audience's needs and not be lost in conversation that ignores those who came to hear what you have to say. It is a good idea for all group members involved in the presentation to talk explicitly about the overall goal of the group in sharing information and ideas with the audience.

Identify Your Major Ideas

What are the key points you will make? When you speak in public, do not just start sharing unrelated pieces of information; think about major ideas you want to share. If you were to boil your information down to one, two, or three ideas, what would they be? The major points you want to address flow from the information you have gathered and the discussion that may have taken place in your group.

Support Your Major Ideas

A presentation to an audience does not consist of just asserting points or drawing a conclusion and sharing the conclusion with your listeners. Support your major points with evidence or examples. We discussed the types and tests of evidence in Chapter 7. In addition to using facts, examples, opinions, and statistics, you could also support a point you are making with a hypothetical example or a personal story. Realize, however, that although hypothetical examples and personal experiences can add great interest to your presentation, they are not sufficient to prove a point. Their value lies in illustrating ideas and issues. Again, we urge you to keep your audience in mind as you make choices about how you will support your major points. It is also a good idea to check with other group members to make sure that you are not duplicating information your colleagues plan to share.

Organize Your Ideas

The last step in developing a presentation plan is to arrange your major ideas and supporting material in a logical way. If you are relating a sequence of steps or discussing the history of an issue, you probably will use *chronological order*, which means arranging your ideas by telling your listeners what happened first, second, third, and so forth.

Another classic method of organizing ideas is called *topical*. In this approach, you simply organize your presentation by topics or natural divisions in your presentation. If you are informing an audience about the functions of your local government, you could arrange your presentation topically by saying: "Our government provides for our safety through the police and fire departments, our education through schools and libraries, and our transportation through funding public transportation and maintaining our roads."

Spatial arrangement, in which you organize information according to location or position, is another approach. In describing your campus to your listeners, you could first talk about the west campus, the central campus, and finally the east campus, rather than hopscotching around a map depicting the layout of your school.

Other ways to organize information include:

Problem solution: First talk about the problem and then the solution

Pro versus con: Compare advantages and disadvantages

Complexity: Move from simple ideas to more complex ones

Regardless of the specific method you select, make sure your overall organizational strategy makes sense both to you and to your listeners. Most public-speaking teachers strongly urge speakers to develop an outline of their presentation. The introduction to the presentation should, at a minimum, provide an overview of the key ideas and catch and hold the listeners' attention. The body of the presentation presents the key ideas and supporting material. The conclusion's prime function is to summarize and, if appropriate, call for listeners to take specific action.

Presenting Information to an Audience

With your objective in mind, key ideas, thoughtfully prepared, and a logical organization of your points at hand, you are ready to consider how to deliver your information to your listeners. As we discussed in Chapter 6, your unspoken messages play a major role in communicating your ideas and feelings to your listeners.

Select Your Method of Delivery

There are four primary delivery methods from which to select: (1) manuscript (reading), (2) memorized, (3) impromptu, and (4) extemporaneous style. Most speech teachers have definite biases about which methods are most and least effective. We do not recommend that you read from a manuscript. Such an approach is stilted and does not permit you to adapt to your listeners. Giving a presentation totally from memory also has its pitfalls, especially if you have many statistics or other forms of evidence that you want to share. You run the risk of forgetting key points. Speaking impromptu means that you speak with minimal or no preparation—you just try to wing it. This has some obvious disadvantages as well. Impromptu speaking negates all the suggestions we made for planning your presentation. The style of delivery that seems to work best is extemporaneous delivery. You know the major ideas you want to present, you also may have an outline, yet the exact wording of your presentation has not been memorized. This has the advantage of encouraging you to plan your message but gives you the flexibility to adapt to the specific audience to which you are speaking. Your delivery also sounds more natural and interesting when you speak extemporaneously than when you read or memorize your remarks.

Use Effective Delivery Skills

When speaking to an audience, there are several fundamental principles to keep in mind. First and foremost, have eye contact with your audience. Research suggests this is the single most important nonverbal delivery variable.[2]

When speaking in a group presentation, it is not unusual to deliver your message while remaining seated around a table. If your group remains seated, you can still use gestures to emphasize key points and add interest and animation to your talk. Effective gestures should be natural, not overly dramatic, and be coordinated with your verbal message. Usually speakers use fewer gestures when seated than when standing to give a speech. If you are participating in a symposium presentation, more than likely you will be expected to stand when you speak. When standing, ensure that your posture communicates your interest in your listeners.

Besides having eye contact and monitoring your physical delivery, you have a fundamental obligation to speak so others can hear you and to convey interest and enthusiasm in your voice. Speaking with adequate volume and using variations in pitch, rate, and quality are essential to effective speech delivery.

Consider Using Visual Aids

Many groups find that using visual aids helps communicate statistical information and survey results, and can help dramatize the problem the group is attempting to solve. One group, wanting to illustrate the parking problem on campus, made a video to show exactly how overcrowded the parking lots were. Audio and video interviews can also play a role in adding interest and credibility to a group's effort to document problems and solutions. However, we caution you against overusing visual aids. The purpose of most group presentations is to present information, not to entertain. Resist the temptation to spend so much time and energy on visuals, video, and audio material that your overall objective takes a backseat to your method of presentation.

The types of visual aids you can use include objects, models, people, drawings, photographs, slides, maps, and graphs. Bar, pie, and line graphs are especially effective in presenting statistical information to an audience. Other types of visual aids include charts that you make yourself or design on your computer, and videos or audiotapes.

Among the most effective types of visual aids are overhead transparencies. These are usually inexpensive, yet can be made ahead of time to clearly present information in an effective way. When using an overhead projector and transparency, consider the following suggestions:

▶ Turn the projector off when you are not showing your visual.

▶ Do not put too much information on one visual. Many experts recommend no more than seven lines of type, using at least an 18-point type font.

▶ Consider revealing a transparency one line at a time rather than showing the entire transparency; you are better able to control your listeners' attention.

▶ Consider using color to add interest.

When using any type of visual aid consider the following guidelines:

▶ Make sure all audience members can see it easily.

▶ Give yourself plenty of time to prepare your visual aid before you speak.

▶ Rehearse with your visual aid.

▶ Have eye contact with your audience, not your visual aid.

▶ Talk about your visual aid, do not just show it.

▶ Do not pass objects among your audience while you are speaking; it distracts from your oral presentation.

▶ Use handouts during the presentation only if your listeners need to have the information in front of them while you speak.

▶ Keep your visual aids simple.

The last suggestion we offer when using visual aids is to have a back-up plan if your visual aid is crucial to your presentation. Taking an extra extension cord, making another copy of your homemade video, or making sure the overhead projector has a spare bulb are examples of making back-up plans to ensure that your presentation goes smoothly.

Use other group members to help you manage the visual aids. Consider asking someone to help change the transparencies on the overhead projector or ask for help in displaying charts or graphs. Since you are part of a team, involve other group members to help you present information clearly and effectively.

Using Computer–Generated Graphics

It is becoming increasingly common for individuals, groups, and teams to illustrate a public presentation using computer-generated graphics. A computer-generated visual aid can add credibility and interest to your presentation if the technology is used effectively. Such widely used software programs as PowerPoint make it very easy to produce professional-looking visual aids.

You will need to develop your visuals using a computer and special software that permits you to add color, pictures, sound, photographs, and even video footage. Many college and university computer labs can give you access to both hardware and software to prepare computer-generated graphics. To present your visuals, you will need a computer and a video projection system. If you are inexperienced at using computer-generated graphics, find someone to teach you the basics of designing visuals.

When using a computer to develop your visuals, keep the following suggestions in mind.

▶ Allow plenty of time to design the graphics. If you are familiar with the software, it may not take you long to draft quality visuals but you should still not wait until the last minute to develop them.

▶ Don't get carried away with the technology. Your goal is to communicate ideas, not to dazzle your listeners with glitzy graphics. Computer-graphics software programs such as PowerPoint let you select a background for your messages. Use a common background or template for your presentation to give your information a unified look. As with other types of visual aids, simple ideas are best.

▶ Consider the effects of room lighting on your presentation. Although video projectors and LCD panels are improving, many projection systems require that you turn the lights off or have a very dimly lit room. Fluorescent light, especially, washes out the image projected by video projectors. Make sure your have the proper equipment to project a clear image to your audience.

Notes

1. Our suggestions for helping you plan and present your speech are adapted from Steven A. Beebe and Susan J. Beebe, *Public Speaking: An Audience-Centered Approach,* 5th ed. (Boston: Allyn and Bacon, 2003).

2. See Steven A. Beebe, "Eye Contact: A Nonverbal Determinant of Speaker Credibility," *Speech Teacher* 23 (January 1971): 21–25; Steven A. Beebe, "Effects of Eye Contact, Posture, and Vocal Inflection upon Credibility and Comprehension," *Australian Scan Journal of Nonverbal Communication* 7–8 (1979–80): 57–80.

G

Glossary

Action chart. A grid that lists the tasks that need to be done and identifies who will be responsible for each task.

Activity tracks. Phases of problem solving that do not follow linear, step-by-step patterns.

Adaptor. A nonverbal behavior that helps people respond to their immediate environment.

Ad hoc committee. A committee that disbands when it completes its task.

Affect display. A nonverbal behavior that communicates emotion.

Affection. The human need to express and receive warmth and closeness.

Affinity technique. A method of generating and organizing ideas by using Post-it notes; group members write each idea on a note and then sort the ideas into common categories.

Agenda. The listing of topics or tasks to be discussed or completed in a meeting.

Allness statement. A simple but untrue generalization.

Asynchronous communication. E-mail interaction in which messages are sent and responded to with a delay in time; the communication thus does not occur in real time.

Attitude. A learned predisposition to respond to something in a favorable, neutral, or unfavorable way.

Autonomous work group. A group charged with achieving specific tasks without outside interference.

Autonomy. The ability to make independent decisions or take action without asking for permission from someone else.

Belief. The way in which you structure what you believe to be true and false—your reality.

Brainstorming. A problem-solving technique that helps a group generate creative solutions to a problem.

Breakpoint. A point in a group discussion when members shift to a different activity.

Bypassing. A barrier to communication that occurs when two people interpret the same word differently.

Category system. A list of terms assigned to determine the frequency of related behaviors.

Causal reasoning. The process of relating two or more events in such a way as to conclude that one event caused the other.

Cause-and-effect diagram. An analysis tool (also called *fishbone diagram*) that charts the causes and effects of a problem or outcome.

Chat room. An Internet site in cyberspace where participants can synchronously post and receive messages.

Charge. The purpose of the team, group, or committee.

Closed-ended question. A question that asks a person to choose from among several supplied responses.

Coercive power. The ability to punish people for acting or not acting in a certain way.

Cohesiveness. The degree of attraction members feel toward one another and their group.

Collectivistic culture. A culture that favors group or team achievement over individual achievement.

Committee. A small group given a specific task by a larger group or individual.

Communication. The process that allows a group to move toward its goals. The process of acting on information.

Communication competence. Communicative behavior that is both effective and appropriate in a given context.

Communication network. A pattern of interaction within a group; who talks to whom.

Competent group communicator. A person who is able to interact appropriately and effectively with others in small groups.

Complementarity. The tendency individuals have to be attracted to others who have knowledge, skills, or other attributes that they themselves do not have but that they admire.

Conclusion. The logical outcome of an argument that stems from the major premise and the minor premise.

Confirming response. A communication response that causes a person to value himself or herself more.

Conflict. Disagreement over available options caused by seemingly incompatible goals among group members and their thinking that others can keep them from achieving those goals.

Conflict phase. Fisher's second phase of group interaction, in which disagreement and individual differences arise.

Confrontation. The second phase of group conflict, when group members express disagreement openly. Group members may choose sides and form subgroups in opposition to other subgroups.

Consensus. The support and commitment of all group members to a decision.

Control. The human need for status and power.

Cooperation requirement. The degree to which a group's success depends on its using member resources.

Criteria. Standards for an acceptable solution to a problem.

Cross-functional team role training. Training members of a team to perform several roles or duties of other team members.

Culture. A learned system of knowledge, behavior, attitudes, beliefs, values, and norms that is shared by a group of people.

Data splitting. Analyzing information effectively.

Decision making. Making a choice from among several alternatives.

Decision-making group. A group whose purpose is to make a choice from among several alternatives.

Deductive reasoning. The process of going from a general statement or principle to a specific conclusion.

Defensive communication. Communicative behavior that arouses in another person the need to protect his or her self-concept.

Delphi technique. Absentee brainstorming. Individuals not meeting face to face share ideas about how to solve a problem or generate ideas by using written messages.

Descriptive problem-solving approach. A method of helping people understand how a group solves a problem.

Disconfirming response. A response that causes another person to value himself or herself less.

Discussion-management competencies. Small-group communication competencies that help a group maintain a focus on the task and manage interaction.

Dyad. Two people.

Ego conflict. Conflict that occurs when individuals become defensive because they feel they are being attacked.

Electronic brainstorming. A method of generating creative ideas using computers; group members write ideas on a computer where all other members can see the ideas generated.

E-mail. Electronic mail. A system using computer terminals to send and receive written messages, and using the computer screen to view messages and the keyboard to encode messages.

Emblem. A nonverbal cue with a specific verbal counterpart—word, letter, or number.

Emergence phase. Fisher's third phase of group interaction, in which a group begins to manage disagreement and conflict.

Empowerment. The sense of having both the responsibility and the authority to make decisions and achieve work results.

Entropy. The measure of randomness and chaos in a system.

Equifinality. A systems-theory principle that a final state may be reached by multiple paths and from different initial states.

Expert power. The influence someone has over others because of greater knowledge and information.

Explanatory function. The power theories have to explain things.

Fact–inference confusion. Mistaking a conclusion you have drawn for an observation.

Fallacy. False reasoning that occurs when someone attempts to persuade without adequate evidence or with arguments that are irrelevant or inappropriate.

Fantasy. In symbolic-convergence theory, the creative and imaginative shared interpretation of events which fulfills a group psychological or rhetorical need.

Fantasy chain. A string of connected stories that revolve around a common theme that occurs when a group is sharing a group fantasy.

Fantasy theme. The common or related content of the stories that the group is sharing during a group fantasy.

Fishbone diagram. An analysis tool (also called cause-and-effect diagram) that charts the causes and effects of a problem or outcome; it is called a fishbone diagram because the chart resembles the skeleton of a fish.

Flowchart. A step-by-step diagram of a multistep process.

Focus group. A group of individuals selected to discuss a particular topic so that the group's leaders can better understand how the individuals view that topic.

Force-field analysis. A method of structuring the analysis of a problem to assess the driving and restraining forces that contribute to the goal one wishes to achieve.

Forum presentation. A discussion that directly follows a panel discussion or symposium and allows audience members to respond to ideas.

Function. The effect or consequence of a given behavior within a group system.

Functional perspective. A view of leadership that assumes all group members can initiate leadership behaviors.

Functional problem-solving approach. A method that identifies key communicative processes that contribute to effective problem solving.

Ground rules. Explicit, agreed-on prescriptions of what is acceptable and appropriate behavior in a group or team.

Group climate. The emotional environment of a group that affects and is affected by interaction among members.

Group cohesiveness. The degree of attraction members feel toward one another and their group.

Group decision making. The process by which a group arrives at the best decision from among available alternatives.

Group decision support systems (GDSS). Computer hardware and software used to link computer terminals together for purposes of holding an "electronic meeting" without individuals meeting face-to-face.

Grouphate. The dread and repulsion people sometimes feel about working in groups and teams, participating in meetings.

Group maintenance role. A behavior that helps a group maintain its social dimension.

Group support system (GSS). Any computer-based information system used to support intellectual collaborative work.

Group task role. A behavior that helps a group achieve its purpose.

Groupthink. A type of thought exhibited by group members who try to minimize conflict and reach consensus without critically testing, analyzing, and evaluating ideas.

Hidden agenda. A private goal toward which an individual works while appearing to work toward the group's goal.

High-context culture. A culture that emphasizes nonverbal communication.

High-contact culture. Cultures in which people tend to touch others and to require less personal space.

Ideal-solution format. A problem-solving method that helps a group define a problem, speculate about an ideal solution, and identify the obstacles that keep it from achieving its goal.

Illustrator. A nonverbal behavior that accompanies and embellishes verbal communication.

Immediacy. A quality of nonverbal communication that refers to whether an individual likes or dislikes another person.

Inclusion. The human need for affiliation with others.

Individual role. A behavior that calls attention to individual contributions of group members.

Individualism. A tendency to focus on individual accomplishment.

Inductive reasoning. The method of arriving at a general conclusion through the use of specific instances or examples.

Information triage. The process of sorting through information you receive to assess the importance, value, or relevance of the information.

Interaction. The dialogue that reflects the give-and-take contributions that participants make while participating in a group. Talk or group discussion.

Interaction diagram. A means of identifying and recording the frequency and direction of communication networks in groups.

Interdependence. A relationship among components in a system wherein a change in one component affects all other components.

Interpersonal need. A human need that can be fulfilled by others.

Is/is not analysis. A method of separating the causes from the symptoms of a problem by assessing such issues as what is/is not the problem, what are/are not symptoms of the problem, when and where did the problem occur/not occur.

Journalist's six questions. The six questions— *who? what? when? where? why? how?*—that news reporters use to analyze an event.

Kaizen. A team approach to improving the quality of goods and services; from the Japanese term meaning "continual improvement."

Knowledge. Appropriate cognitive understanding or accurate information about a subject— one of the elements necessary for an individual to possess in order to be competent.

Leadership. Behavior that influences, guides, directs, or controls a group.

Leadership style. A leader's relatively consistent behavior pattern that reflects his or her beliefs and attitudes; classified as authoritarian, laissez-faire, or democratic.

Legitimate power. Power derived from being elected or appointed to control a group.

Listening. An active, complex process of selecting, attending, understanding, and remembering.

Low-contact culture. A culture in which people are uncomfortable being touched and require more personal space.

Low-context culture. A culture that emphasizes verbal expression.

Major premise. A general statement that is the first element of a syllogism.

Maintenance roles. Roles that define a group's social atmosphere.

Media-richness. The quality of a communication method that has (1) potential for instant feedback, (2) verbal and nonverbal cues that can be processed by senders and receivers, (3) natural language, and (4) a focus on individuals.

Mediated setting. A context for communication that is not face-to-face but instead occurs through a phone line, fiber-optic cable, TV signal, or other means.

Metacommunication. An aspect of a message that provides information about how the whole message should be interpreted; communication about communication.

Metadiscussion. A statement about the discussion itself rather than about the discussion's topic.

Method theories. Special theories that offer prescriptions for behavior.

Minor premise. A specific statement about an example that is linked to the major premise; it is the second element of a syllogism.

Mission statement. A concise description of the goals or desired outcomes of the team.

Monochronic time. A typically Western view of time as linear and segmented. Contrast: polychronic.

Motivation. An internal drive to achieve a goal.

Mutuality of concern. The degree to which members share the same level of commitment to a group.

Nominal-group technique. A problem-solving brainstorming method in which members work individually on ideas, rank suggested solutions, and then report their findings for group discussion.

Nonverbal communication. Communication behavior that does not rely on written or spoken words.

Norm. A standard that separates appropriate from inappropriate behavior.

Open-ended question. A question that allows a person to respond freely, because it does not provide suggested answers.

Orientation phase. Fisher's first phase of small-group interaction, in which members try to understand one another and the task before their group.

Panel discussion. A group discussion intended to inform an audience about a problem.

Paralanguage. Vocal cues, such as pitch, rate, volume, and quality, which provide information to other people.

Pareto principle. The source of 80 percent of the problems comes from 20 percent of the incidents.

Parliamentary procedure. A comprehensive set of rules that prescribes how to take action on specific issues that come before a group and how to organize all aspects of group governance. For a complete guide to parliamentary procedure see *Roberts' Rules of Order*.

Perception checking. The skill of asking someone whether your interpretation of his or her message is accurate. There are three steps: Observe the behavior, think about what the behavior may mean, ask whether your interpretation is accurate.

Plagiarism. The act of presenting the words or ideas of someone else as though they were your own.

Polychronic time. A view of time in which many things happen simultaneously and there is little emphasis on precision in time. Contrast: monochronic.

Potency. A dimension of nonverbal communication that conveys status and power.

Power. The resources an individual has with which to exert control over others.

Predictive function. The ability theories have to predict events.

Prescriptive problem-solving approach. A method that suggests specific agendas or techniques for improving group problem solving.

Primary group. A group that fulfills people's needs to associate with others (such as the family).

Primary tension. Anxiety and tension that occur when a group first meets.

Problem solving. A process that attempts to overcome or manage an obstacle in order to reach a goal.

Problem-solving competencies. Small group communication competencies, defining the problem and analyzing the problem, that help a group focus on the problem under discussion.

Problem solving group. A group that exists to resolve an issue or overcome an obstacle.

Process leadership. Communication directed toward maintaining interpersonal relations and a positive group climate; also called *group building* and *maintenance*.

Process theories. General theories that explain human behaviors across a variety of contexts.

Pseudo-conflict. Conflict that occurs when individuals disagree because of inaccurate communication.

Public-communication format. An organized group discussion presented to an audience.

Quality circle. A group of five to fifteen employees who meet on a regular basis to help with corporate decision making (to improve work productivity, company morale, or work quality).

Question of fact. A question that asks whether something is true or false.

Question of policy. A question that asks whether a group should change a procedure or behavior.

Question of value. A question that asks the worth or desirability of something.

Quorum. The minimum number of people who must be present to conduct business.

Random-word technique. While a group is brainstorming, one person is assigned the task of saying a random word; the word is supposed to act as a trigger for new or creative ideas.

Reasoning. The process of drawing conclusions from information.

Referent power. The power of interpersonal attraction.

Reflective thinking. John Dewey's problem-solving method, which identifies and defines a problem, analyzes it, suggests possible solutions for it, selects the best solution for it, and tests and implements that solution.

Regulator. A nonverbal behavior that helps a group control the flow of communication.

Reinforcement phase. Fisher's fourth phase of group interaction, in which members express positive feelings toward a group and its decision.

Relational activity. An activity dealing with behaviors that sustain or damage relationships among group members.

Relational communication. Verbal and nonverbal messages that create the social fabric of a group by promoting relationships between and among group members.

Relational competencies. Small group communication competencies that help a group manage conflict and maintain a positive group climate.

Responsiveness. A dimension of nonverbal communication that communicates activity, energy, and interest.

Reverse brainstorming. Asking group members to brainstorm ideas or solutions that would make the problem worse. After generating such a list, the group then considers the implications of doing the opposite of what was identified.

Reward power. The power to provide rewards for desired behavior.

RISK technique. A discussion technique designed to assess how group members will respond to and manage a change in policy or procedure.

Role. A consistent behavior pattern resulting from your expectations of yourself, your actual behavior, and the expectations others have of you.

Rolestorming. Asking group members to assume the role of someone other than themselves to help spur creative solutions to a problem during the brainstorming process.

Rule. A followable prescription for acceptable behavior. Rules identify the appropriate or expected behavior of group members.

Secondary group. A group that exists to accomplish a task or achieve a goal in contrast with a primary group—a group whose main purpose is to fulfill the basic need to associate with others.

Secondary tension. Conflict over group norms, roles, and differences among member opinions.

Self-concept. The characteristics and attributes an individual believes himself or herself to have.

Self-directed work team. A team that is given responsibility to achieve results without being micro-managed from outside the team.

Self-disclosure. The deliberate communication of information about yourself to others.

Silent brainstorming. Holding a period of individual brainstorming before group members share their ideas with the group. Integral to nominal group technique, or may be used as part of brainstorming.

Similarity. The tendency of individuals with like experiences, beliefs, attitudes, and values to be attracted to one another.

Simple conflict. Conflict that occurs when each of two people knows what the other wants but neither can achieve his or her goal without keeping the other from doing so.

Simulation. A structured exercise that creates conditions that participants might encounter outside the training session.

Single-question format. A problem-solving agenda that helps a group identify key issues and subissues of a problem.

Situational perspective. A perspective that views leadership as the interrelationships among group needs and goals, leadership style, and situation.

Small group. At least three people interacting with one another.

Small group communication. Interaction among a small group of people who share a common purpose or goal, who feel a sense of belonging to a group, and who exert influence on one another.

Small group ecology. The consistent way in which people arrange themselves in small groups.

Social exchange theory. A description of human relationships in terms of their costs and rewards.

Social facilitation. The tendency for the presence of others to affect human behavior; others present may result in people working harder.

Social loafing. The tendency for people to hold back on their contributions (loaf) in a group because they assume someone else will do the work.

Solution multiplicity. The number of available choices that will solve a problem.

Speech communication. The process by which people make sense of their world and share that sense with others; what people say and how they say it.

Standing committee. A committee that remains active for an extended period of time.

Status. An individual's position of importance.

Structure. Procedures that help organize a group to achieve its goal. The use of agendas, techniques (e.g., nominal-group technique), step-by-step problem-solving formats or other strategies that help keep group discussion focused and on task.

Structuration theory. A general framework that explains how people use rules and resources to interact in a social system.

Study group. A group whose primary purpose is to gather information and learn new ideas.

Survey research. A method of sampling several people's attitudes, beliefs, values, behavior, or knowledge.

Syllogism. A way of structuring an argument in three parts: (1) a major premise, (2) a minor premise, and (3) a conclusion.

Symbolic convergence theory. The development of a group consciousness and identity through the sharing of fantasies or stories which are often chained together and have a common theme.

Symposium presentation. A series of short speeches unified by a central issue or theme.

Synchronous communication. E-mail interaction that takes place in real time.

Synergy. A condition in which the whole is greater than the sum of its parts.

System. An organic whole composed of interdependent elements.

Systems theory. An orderly strategy for understanding the complexity of groups in terms of input, processes, and output.

Task difficulty. The amount of mental effort required to solve a problem or complete a task.

Task leadership. Communication directed toward accomplishing a group's task or goal.

Task-process activity. An activity a group undergoes to manage its task or its reason for convening.

Task role. A role a member assumes to help accomplish the group's task.

Task-contingency theory. The relationship between communication and the type of task before a group.

Task-oriented small group. A group with a specific objective to achieve, problem to solve, or decision to make.

T-chart. A diagram that looks like a large "T" drawn on a board or flipchart, where the "pros" of a particular proposition are listed on one side of the middle line and the "cons" are listed on the other side.

Team. A group of individuals organized to work together to achieve a common goal.

Territoriality. Use of space to claim or defend a given area.

Therapy group. A group led by a trained professional whose purpose is to help individuals with personal problems.

Topical focus. An activity at any given time that deals with the issues under discussion by a group.

Total quality management (TQM). A management emphasis that seeks to minimize errors and produce quality work.

Training. Instruction emphasizing skill development.

Trait perspective. A view of leadership as the personal attributes or qualities that leaders possess.

Transformational leadership. Leadership that aims toward an organization's change by realigning its culture around a new vision.

Transactive process. A process in which messages are sent and received simultaneously.

Value. A person's perception of what is right or wrong, good or bad.

Video conference. The use of video technology to link two or more individuals by closed-circuit or satellite-linked TV.

Vigilant thinkers. People who use logic, reasoning, evidence, and data to analyze issues and problems; they also establish clear decision criteria and evaluate the positive and negative consequences of a decision.

World view. One's fundamental outlook on reality and one's place in the universe and purpose in life.

X-Y-Z formula. A way to describe feelings by saying: when you do X, in situation Y, I feel Z.

CREDITS

Photo Credits

Page 10: © Carrie Boretz/The Image Works; 14: Reprinted with special permission of King Features Syndicate; 18: © Susan Lapides/Design Conceptions; 22: © Jose Carillo/PhotoEdit; 38: © The New Yorker Collection 2000 Nick Downes from cartoonbank.com; 40: © Kathy Sloane/Photo Researchers; 42: © Eastcott/The Image Works; 56: Fredrik D. Bodin/Stock Boston; 57: © Robert Brenner/PhotoEdit; 61: © The New Yorker Collection 2000 Leo Cullum from cartoonbank.com; 77: © Bill Bachman/PhotoEdit; 80: NON SEQUITUR © 1995 Wiley Miller. Dist. By UNIVERSAL PRESS SYNDICATE. Reprinted with permission. All rights reserved; 85: © Collins/Monkmeyer; 108: © Mark Litzler; 109: © Mike Mazzaschi/Stock Boston; 113: © David Wells/The Image Bank; 135: © Cindy Charles/PhotoEdit; 139: © Doug Plummer/Photo Researchers; 144: DILBERT © United Features Syndicate; 149: © Robert A. Issacs/Photo Researchers; 168: FOR BETTER OR FOR WORSE © United Features Syndicate; 170: © SuperStock; 183: © Robert Brenner/PhotoEdit; 194: © Bruce Ayres/Stone/GettyImages; 197: © The New Yorker Collection 1997 Charles Barsotti from cartoonbank.com; 205: © B. Daemmrich/The Image Works; 233: © Gale Zucker/Stock Boston; 236: By permission of Jerry Van Amerongen and Creators Syndicate, Inc.; 244: J. Pickerell/The Image Works; 261: © Jeff Greenberg/PhotoEdit; 263, © The New Yorker Collection 1987 James Stevenson from cartoonbank.com; 278: © Jack Spratt/The Image Works; 297: © David E. Kennedy/TexasStock; 300: © Gale Zucker/Stock Boston; 303: © The New Yorker Collection 1985 Michael Maslin from cartoonbank.com; 326: DILBERT © United Features Syndicate; 339: © Amy Etra/PhotoEdit

Text Credits

Page 20: Table 1.1 "Individualism and Collectivism in Small Groups" adapted from *Mind Your Manners: Managing Business Cultures in Europe* by John Mole. Published 1995 by Nicholas Brealey Publishing, Ltd., London; 23: "Important Skills for Group and Team Members" adapted from K. W. Hawkins and B. P. Fillon, "Perceived Communication Skill Needs for Work Groups," *Communication Research Reports* 16 (1999): 167-74; 39: Table 2.1 "Increase in Potential Relationships with an Increase in Group Size" from "A Quantitative Analysis of Intergroup Relationships" by William M. Klephart in *American Journal of Sociology,* 60. Copyright © 1950 University of Chicago Press. Reprinted with permission; 143: Table 6.1 from *Intercultural Encounters: The Fundamentals of Intercultural Communication* by Donald W. Klopf. Copyright © 1998 Morton Publishing Company, Englewood, Colorado and Understanding Cultural Differences by Edward T. Hall and Mildred R. Hall. Copyright © 1989 Intercultural Press, Yarmouth, Maine; 148: Figure 6.1 "High/Low Contexts" adapted from *Intercultural Encounters: The Fundamentals of Intercultural Communication* by Donald W. Klopf (page 33). Copyright © 1995 Morton Publishing Company, Englewood, CO and Meeting News, June 1993; 162: Table 6.2 "Comparing High- and Low-Contact Cultures" from *Beyond Culture* by Edward T. Hall. Copyright © 1976 Doubleday, Garden City, New York; 208: Table 8.2 "North America and Japanese Decision-Making Assumptions Compared" from "Managerial Attitudes Toward Decision-Making: North America and Japan" by Teruyuki Kume in *Communication, Cul-*

ture and Organizational Processes edited by William B. Gudykunst, Lea P. Stewart, and Stella Ting-Tooney. Copyright © 1985 Sage Publication, Inc. Reprinted by permission; **212:** Excerpts from *Joining Together: Group-Therapy and Group Skills,* Seventh Edition by David W. Johnson and Frank P. Johnson. Copyright © 2000 Allyn & Bacon, Needham Heights, MA.; **225:** Figure 9.3 "Force Field Analysis" from *The Winning Trainer,* Third Edition by Julius E. Eitington. Copyright © 1996 Gulf Publishing Company. Used with permission. All rights reserved; **238:** Excerpts from *Teams: Structure, Process, Culture, and Politics* by Eileen K. Aranda, Luis Aranda, and Kristi Conlon, Copyright © 1998 Prentice Hall, Upper Saddle River, NJ. Reprinted with Permission; **305:** Figure 11.1 "Relation of Stress, Goal Structuring, and Leadership Patterns" from "Situational Determinants of Leadership Structure" by David C. Korten in *Journal of Conflict Resolution,* Volume 6, Number 3, September 1962, pp. 222-235. Reprinted by permission; **307:** Figure 11.2 Figure 11.3 "Hersey and Blanchard's Situational Leadership Model" from *Management of Organizational Behavior: Utilizing Human Resources,* Sixth Edition by Paul Hersey and Ken Blanchard (page 248). Copyright © 1982, Prentice-Hall, Upper Saddle River, NJ. Reprinted by permission; **321:** Table 12.1 "How to Improve Quality: Dr. Deming's 14 Points" a summary of Dr. Deming's 14 points from *The Team Handbook* by Peter R. Scholtes. Copyright © 1988 Oriel Incoporated. Reprinted with permission; **328:** Figure 12.1 "Bell Curve Agenda" from *Meetings: How to Make Them Work for You* by John E. Tropman and Gershom Clark Morningstar. Copyright © 1985 Van Nostrand Reinhold. Reprinted with permission; **335:** Review Box "The Necessary Steps to an Effective Meeting" from *Effective Meeting Skill* by Marion Haynes (page 391). Published by Crisp Publications; **336:** Table 12.2 "A Continuum of Media-Rich and Media-Lean Methods of Communication" from *Organizational Communication: Approaches and Processes* by Katherine Miller. Copyright © 1995 Wadsworth, Belmont, CA. Adapted with permission.

Index

A

ABI/Inform, 173
Absentee brainstorming, 236–237
Accountability for Website information, 174–175
Accuracy of Website, 175
Acquaintance with group members, 164–165
Action charts, 229–230
Action-oriented team members, 10
Action plans, 11
Active listening, 116–117
  ego conflict and, 262
Activities of group, 63
Activity tracks, 200–201
Adams, Herbert, 113–115
Adaptation to needs of group, 245
Adaptors, 135–136
  lying and, 146
Ad hominem fallacy, 183
Advantages of teamwork, 11–13
Affect displays, 135
Affection need, 54
Affinity technique, 237–238
Agenda, 327–329
  bell-curve agenda, 327–328
  benefits of, 219
  pitfalls, list of, 329
  preparation for meeting with, 333
  sample agenda, 328–329
  for structuring discussion, 218
Aggressive members, dealing with, 274
Aggressor role, 76
  power and, 90
Agreement about content, 112
Alcoholics Anonymous, 18
All I Really Need to Know I Learned in Kindergarten (Fulghum), 25
Allness statements, 118
Altavista, 174
Ambiguity
  cultural assumptions and, 209
  of norms, 80
Analysis function, 203–204
Analyzing problem
  cause-and-effect (fishbone) diagram, 225–226
  force field analysis, 224–225
  is/is not analysis, 221–222
  listening and, 114
  plans for, 165–166
  rankings and ratings, 227–228
  reflective thinking and, 222–226
  solutions, analyzing, 227–228
Anger
  conflict and, 262
  with difficult group members, 271–272
  facial expression for, 138
Apollo XIII, 132
Appearance
  attractive people, 62–63, 141
  of leaders, 296
  as nonverbal communication, 141
  for video conferences, 340
Aranda, Eileen K., 238–239

Aranda, Luis, 238–239
Astin, Alexander, 311
Astin, Helen, 311
Asynchronous communication, 338
Attacking the person fallacy, 183
Attendance at meetings, 14
Attitudes
  conflict and, 259
  disclosure of, 94
  questions of value and, 169
Attraction to group
  activities of group as, 63
  goals of group, 64
  interpersonal attraction, 60–62
  membership and, 64
  physical attractiveness and, 62–63
Attractive people, 62–63, 141
Audience
  analyzing, 350
  effective delivery skills, 352–353
  for forum presentations, 349
  goals in speaking to, 350–351
  identifying ideas for, 351
  method of delivery, 352
  organizing ideas for, 351–352
  for panel discussions, 348
  supporting ideas for, 351
  for symposium presentations, 348
  visual aids for, 353
Augustine, Saint, 89
Authoritarian leaders, 301–302
  case study, 304–305
Autocratic decision-making, 91
Autonomy of self-directed work teams, 323

B

Backlund, Phil, 149–150
Baird, John, 144
Baker, Deborah, 310
Ballard, Dawna, 142
Bandwagon fallacy, 182
Barge, J. Kevin, 60, 203
Barman, Ernest, 201
Barnlund, Dean, 37, 296
Barriers, identifying, 11
Barry, Dave, 325
Becker, S. W., 139–140
Behaviors, norms and, 79
Being needs, 53
Beliefs
  conflict and, 259
  goals, reaching, 309
  questions of value and, 169–170
Belief-system shift, 309
Bell-curve agenda, 327–328
Belonging
  need for, 53
  sense of, 5
Benne, Kenneth D., 75
Berger, Charles, 91
Bias
  in prejudging communications, 115–116
  problem-solving and, 195
Bierstedt, Robert, 89

Biographical information disclosures, 94
Biological gender, 311
Bishop, Marilyn E., 85–86
Blanchard, Kenneth, 305–307
Blind persons, 85
Blockers, 76
  management of, 273
  power and, 90
Bormann, Ernest G., 42, 77, 87, 95, 125, 231, 309–311
Bowers, John W., 175
Brainstorming, 232–242
  affinity technique, 237–238
  application to group, 239–241
  cooperative conflict management and, 270
  Delphi Technique, 236–237
  electronic brainstorming, 237
  in meetings, 330
  nominal-group technique (NGT), 234–236
  piggybacking, 234
  random-word technique, 240
  reverse brainstorming, 240
  rolestorming, 240
  silent brainstorming, 234–236
  time for, 239, 240
  traditional steps, 233–234
Braithwaite, Dawn, 85
Breakpoints, 201
Briggs, Nancy, 147
Broome, Benjamin, 195
Brown, Vincent, 133
Building shared vision, 308
Burgoon, Judee, 145
Bypassing, 118

C

Captive audiences, 350
Carnegie, Andrew, 132
Causal fallacy, 182
Causal reasoning, 179
Cause-and-effect (fishbone) diagram, 225–226
Census Bureau Website, 176
Center for the Study of Work Teams Website, 200
Certainty. *See* Ambiguity; Uncertainty
Chalkboards
  affinity technique using, 238
  facts, displaying, 282
Challenger space shuttle, 275
Charts
  facts, displaying, 282
  for implementing solutions, 229–230
  Pareto charts, 222
  for speeches, 353–354
  T-charts, 227, 228
Chat rooms, 338
Chronological organization of speech, 351
Clarifying expectations, 11
Clarifying responses, 112
Cliché communication, 94